the first

readings
on teaching
reading

the first R

readings on teaching reading

SAM LEATON SEBESTA
CARL J. WALLEN

SRA

SCIENCE RESEARCH ASSOCIATES, INC.
Chicago, Palo Alto, Toronto, Henley-on-Thames, Sydney
A Subsidiary of IBM

4888

acknowledgments

From p. 148 (Hardbound edition) "For quite a while . . . as she lived" in A TREE GROWS IN BROOKLYN by Betty Smith (Harper & Row, 1943). Reprinted by permission of the publishers. Permission covering British rights William Heinemann Ltd.

THE BRIGHT KEY: Thoughts on the Relation of Business to Research and Education. Monroe E. Spaght. Copyright © 1965 by Meredith Press. Reprinted by permission of Appleton-Century-Crofts, Educational Division, Meredith Corporation.

"The Right to Read: Education's New National Priority" James E. Allen, Jr. From *The American School Board Journal* 157 (October 1969):25–27. Reprinted with permission of The American School Board Journal.

"The Concept of Maturity in Reading" by William S. Gray and Bernice Rogers. From *Maturity, Its Nature and Appraisal,* chapter 3. © 1956 by *The University of Chicago. Published* 1956. *Composed and printed by* The University of Chicago Press, Chicago, Illinois, U.S.A. Reprinted with permission of the publisher.

Clark W. Heath, *What People Are: A Study of Normal Young Men.* Copyright 1946, Harvard University Press. Reprinted with permission of the publisher.

Karl A. Menninger, *The Human Mind.* Copyright 1937, Alfred A. Knopf, Inc. Reprinted with permission of the publisher.

Ethel Kawin, *Parenthood in a Free Nation.* © 1954 by The University of Chicago Press. Reprinted with permission of the publisher.

H. A. Overstreet, *The Mature Mind.* Copyright 1949, 1959, W. W. Norton & Co. Inc. Reprinted with permission of the publisher.

H. R. Huse, *The Illiteracy of the Literate.* New York: D. Appleton-Century Co., 1933. Reprinted with permission of the publisher.

How to Read a Book: The Art of Getting a Liberal Education. © 1940, 1966 by Mortimer J. Adler. Reprinted by permission of Simon and Schuster, Inc.

The Art of Book Reading by Stella S. Center. © 1952, Charles Scribner's Sons. Reprinted with permission of the publisher.

"Reading: A View from the Child" by Jerry L. Johns. From *The Reading Teacher* 23 (April 1970):647–48. Reprinted with permission of Jerry L. Johns and the International Reading Association.

In view of the physical impossibility of putting all the necessary credits on the copyright page, the acknowledgments for use of the permissionable material are continued on pages 485–490.

contents

ONE

purposes and positions 1

TWO

language and the factors in reading 63

THREE

organizing for instruction: procedures   151

FOUR

organizing for instruction: materials   203

FIVE

organizing for instruction: personnel   259

SIX

guiding responses to reading   297

SEVEN

EIGHT

authors' preface

There has been a kind of desperation about the schools. It is an urgency born of allegedly wasted time and thwarted purpose. The topic of reading is central to this mood and mode. Several of the selections we have chosen for this book contain statements that underlie these feelings: gleanings from a darkling plain, warnings and threats, and little condolence.

Nevertheless, hope and excitement are to be found. It is unlikely that any decade prior to the seventies has shown such active concern harnessed to the intensive search for goals, and ways to achieve them. And there is the ultimate promise of fulfilled expectations. A decade ago attention often centered on closed issues: how to choose the best of known approaches to the subject, how to do a better job of what we were already doing. Present concerns probe open issues: Why learn to read? What have we overlooked in reading factors and their interaction with related areas? A decade ago we would ask, "What is the best system of grouping?" Today we ask, "*Why* group? *When,* if ever? And if so, *how?*" Debate on reading, once consigned by general agreement to modest measures of procedure, is now more daringly directed at its roots.

Startling new programs and suggestions emerge. The single basal-reader series with accompanying manuals (sometimes dictatorial) are replaced with far-ranging systems. Everything, it seems, gets into the act: film, television, the computer, video cassettes — all sorts of other-than-book media are used to carry other-than-print messages in order to teach the reading of books. But children's books are changing too. Rebecca of Sunnybrook Farm,

Nancy Drew, even Holden Caulfield would be unlikely to claim kin with some taboo-smashing heroes and antiheroes found in recent juvenile literature.

Personnel? Once we may have acted as if the certified teacher ought to suffice: reading instruction belonged to the schools and the schools belonged to the generalist teacher. But today's reading-specialist and paraprofessional programs include all ranges and stages of ability.

Some of the innovations are, to be sure, no more than freshly gilded relics. Fifteen or twenty years ago Mrs. Push might have taught individualized reading laced with a carefully sequenced, self-assembled, automatic-revising set of skill materials with built-in indestructibility. She is understandably chagrined today to be told: *You* must be revamped or discarded. You must use this new system — individualized materials, and a carefully sequenced set of skills materials. The test of maturity in a new age is whether one can view the past in honest perspective.

Each of the above paragraphs reflects concerns that underlie the selection and assembling of readings for this book. We attempted a synthesis to bring together items that reveal reading in all of its current complexity. We recognized both the despair and the hope, some signs of startling innovation, and some voices of the past that speak more distinctly for the future than our transitional state of affairs may permit us to realize. The situation goes beyond current debate over approaches and the marketplace of materials and devices. It calls for rethinking the basic strategies and tenets of the skill and the art of reading. With this in mind we attempted, by means of chapter introductions and summary questions, to help our readers synthesize their thinking too.

At times we argued as we made the selections and wrote the introductions. We even argued a little about the contents of this preface. The argument clarified our thinking. We hope that you, too, will argue and that the arguments will bring clarity and a desire to take positive action. Such results are not so unlikely as they may seem for, beneath the controversy over exactly what we are after in reading and exactly how to go about achieving it, there is really a shared concern and a shared goal. We want, for everyone, the right to read. Perhaps basically there are two purposes for this desire. He who reads is able to negotiate his world with firmer understanding — to control some of the strands of his destiny: the long step from ignorance to wisdom. And he who reads is enabled to find surcease from the pressures inherent in our patterns of living. They are the age-old purposes given new hope: the purposes of knowledge and sanctuary.

> For quite a while, Francie had been spelling out letters, sounding them and then putting the sounds together to mean a word. But one day, she looked at a page and the word "mouse" had instantaneous meaning. She looked at the word and the picture of a gray mouse scampered through her mind. She looked further and when she saw "horse," she heard him pawing the ground and saw the sun glint on his glossy coat. The word "running" hit her suddenly and she breathed hard as though running herself. The barrier between the individual sound of each letter and the whole meaning of the word was removed and the printed word meant a thing at one quick glance. She read a few pages rapidly and almost became ill with excitement. She wanted to shout it out. She could read! She could read!
> From that time on, the world was hers for the reading. She would never be lonely again, never miss the lack of intimate friends. Books became her friends and there was one for every mood. There was poetry for quiet companionship. There was adventure when she tired of quiet hours. There would be love stories when she came into adolescence, and when she wanted to feel a closeness to someone she could read a biography. On that day when she first knew she could read, she made a vow to read one book a day as long as she lived.*

Sam Leaton Sebesta

Carl J. Wallen

*Betty Smith. *A Tree Grows in Brooklyn.* New York: Harper & Row, 1943.

ONE

purposes
and
positions

objectives

As a result of reading these articles and answering the questions at the end of the chapter you should be better able to:

▦ explain and justify your point of view about the purpose of reading instruction

▦ explain and justify your position on how your purpose of reading instruction might be attained

rationale

A quotation from Lincoln summarizes well the theme of this chapter: "If we could first know where we are and whither we are tending, we could better judge what to do and how to do it." To paraphrase, until we have a purpose for reading instruction, we will have difficulty in figuring out how to accomplish that purpose. Hopefully, by the time you finish chapter 1 you will have begun to formulate your own purpose and position about reading instruction.

introduction

Purposes. Examining purposes is unnatural for most Americans, holding as they do the pragmatic view that discussions about means are more important, and certainly more interesting, than discussions about ends. In writing about the aims of education Martin Mayer *(The Schools)* commented that discussions about the aims of education are among the dullest and most fruitless of human pursuits. More attention is given to the comparative virtues of the phonics method and the look-say method than to the question of what either method ought to accomplish. But if we agree with Charles Silberman *(Crisis in the Classroom)* that "mindlessness" is the central problem of education, then we must address ourselves to the dull and fruitless subject of purpose. A quick historical review may provide a perspective for this examination.

Immediately after the invention of movable type printing was a novelty and reading was viewed as being a distinguishing characteristic of the cultivated man. The purpose of reading was to show that you were sufficiently wealthy to afford the time and tutoring required to learn, and the refinement needed to care. The only people for whom reading served a more utilitarian purpose were the growing number of merchants.

The dominant purpose of American education in the eighteenth and nineteenth centuries was the maintenance of the yet infant democracy, especially with the continuing waves of immigrants sweeping across from Europe. Education and democracy were considered inseparable, as Thomas Jefferson noted: "If a nation expects to be ignorant and free, in a state of civilization, it expects what never was and never will be." The maintenance of democracy demanded that individuals understand and think about what they read. Some have suggested that understanding was purposely kept at a level that enabled people to read just well enough to obey the laws and buy the products: education produced law-abiding consumers. George Macaulay Trevelyan *(English Social History)*, among others, has lamented that while education has made it possible for large numbers of the population to read they are not able to distinguish what is worth reading.

Corollary to the purpose of maintenance, or controlling individuals, was an emphasis on individual achievement. Americans take much pride in the fact that Abraham Lincoln was born in a log cabin, and that Andrew Carnegie was the son of a poor Scottish weaver. The commitment to individual achievement remains high. President Kennedy stated, "First, and most important, is that every American girl and boy have the opportunity to develop whatever talents he has." Individual achievement is related to the maintenance of democracy because the fortunes of a democratic society depend upon the opportunity for all the children of all the people to develop themselves to their fullest capacity regardless of any unfortunate circumstances they may have inherited.

A currently evolving purpose for reading is the education of men who can feel and act as well as think, as stressed by John Gardner:[1]

> The modern world needs men who can work with complex organizations and yet retain their individuality, who can master technology yet retain their humanity, who can move easily between reflection and action.

The relation of thinking and feeling is exemplified by Sylvia Ashton-Warner in her work with children in New Zealand. She had them select words that *they wanted* to learn. Eventually they wrote their own stories from the words. Ashton-Warner saw her purpose as helping each child express his own unique ideas and feelings.

Positions. Plato noted that "the directions in which education starts a man will determine his future life." Teachers all too often start their students in undesirable and unintended directions because they fail to realize that education is not only a preparation for life, it is life itself. Students see the entire context in which instructional exercises are presented, and often the con-

---

1. Monroe E. Spaght. THE BRIGHT KEY: Thoughts on the Relation of Business to Research and Education, New York: Appleton-Century-Crofts, 1965. Introductory chapter by John Gardner.

text has a greater effect on learning than the exercises. Jerry Johns, in an article reprinted here, points out that many elementary children regard reading as doing workbook pages and saying "a bunch of words." The children apparently do not separate the context of the workbook from the instructional exercises.

Two examples may illustrate the importance of the context in which instruction occurs. Silberman *(Crisis in the Classroom)* describes an incident where a teacher encouraged a child to abandon such literary works as those by E. B. White *(Stuart Little, Charlotte's Web)* and start reading much shorter and easier books. The students were to submit book reports on 4 × 6 cards. The longer books required more space to report and more time to read. Although the literary works were not considered appropriate for school because the reports were too long to fit on the cards, the teacher did encourage the child to continue reading them at home. What do you imagine this child is learning about "school reading"?

Harper Lee, in *To Kill a Mockingbird,* satirizes the routine-oriented teacher by describing a girl's first day in the first grade. The teacher, fresh out of teacher's college and loaded with knowledge about the latest reading methods, is horrified when she learns that the child can already read the newspaper. She sternly warns the little girl that she should receive no more instruction at home; the teacher would try to undo the harm already done. The final blow comes when the girl is discovered writing a letter to a friend during the time she is supposed to be watching the teacher flash cards at the class containing words such as *the* and *cat.* The teacher immediately informs her that children don't write in the first grade, they print. They don't write until they get into the third grade.

As you feel yourself settling on an appropriate approach to teaching reading, you should raise the question, "Will this really lead me to the purposes I have established?" A close examination might reveal some clues as to whether it is really leading to purposes you consider important.

The articles in chapter 1 have been selected to provide a source of ideas to help you define your own purpose and position. The first three articles give three perspectives on the purpose for reading. Allen *(The Right to Read: Education's New National Priority)* sees reading from the viewpoint of the society. Gray and Rogers *(The Concept of Maturity in Reading)* see reading from the viewpoint of the adult. And to balance it all, Johns *(Reading: A View from the Child)* does just what the title indicates. You will probably find that in defining your purpose you will borrow something from all three.

You may possibly find the Postman and Staats' articles rather disturbing, for quite opposite reasons. They have been selected to provide two contrary views about positions. Probably you will not find yourself eagerly embracing either position, but you will find them helpful in defining a place somewhere between the two extremes.

Individuals who are unable to read
have been denied a right as fundamental as the right to life, liberty,
and the pursuit of happiness, Allen
maintains. Too many Americans are
being denied their right to read.
Allen proposes Right to Read Program as a major national effort to
eradicate illiteracy, once and for all.

The Right to Read: Education's New National Priority

JAMES E. ALLEN JR.

Imagine, if you can, what your life would be like if you could not read, or if your reading skill were so meager as to limit you to the simplest of writings, and if for you the door to the whole world of knowledge and inspiration available through the printed word had never opened.

For more than a quarter of our population this is true. For them, education, in a very important way, has been a failure, and they stand as a reproach to all of us who hold in our hands the shaping of the opportunity for education.

These individuals have been denied a right — a right as fundamental as the right to life, liberty, and the pursuit of happiness — the right to read.

The suppression of the individual which for so long characterized the governance of nations rested on the ignorance of the many and the learning of the few. With the invention of movable type there was created a source of widespread learning that held hope for the eventual abolishment of ignorance and for removal of the barrier to the participation of the common man in the determination of his destiny.

The education for all, necessary as a foundation of a democratic society, became a possibility, making feasible the quest for the realization of this concept which honors the dignity and worth of the individual.

Thus, from the beginning of our nation, the importance of education has been recognized. Education has come to mean many things and to encompass a wide range of information and experiences, but certainly it must still include, as it did in the beginning, the ability to read.

Those who do not gain this ability in the course of their early education lack a skill necessary to all other areas of learning and are being denied a fundamental educational right — the right to read.

It is true, of course, that the inability to read effectively is only one of the many vexing problems facing American education, just as heart disease and cancer represent only limited dimensions of our national health problems. Yet, we have seen the value of concentrating attention on such medical concerns.

The inability to read effectively, contaminating as it does every other dimension of education, is clearly one challenge deserving of our concentrated efforts. As we learn how to attack this deficiency cooperatively we will not only be getting at this foundation of learning, but will be gaining the strength and the skills to meet together many other educational problems.

From a variety of statistical information accumulated by the U.S. Office of Education regarding reading deficiencies throughout the country these shocking facts stand out:

One out of every four students nationwide has significant reading deficiencies.

In large city school systems up to half of the students read below expectation.

There are more than three million illiterates in our adult population.

About half of the unemployed youth, ages 16 to 21, are functionally illiterate.

Three-quarters of the juvenile offenders in New York City are two or more years retarded in reading.

In a recent U.S. Armed Forces program called Project 100,000, 68.2 percent of the young men fell below grade 7 in reading and academic ability.

The tragedy of these statistics is that they represent a barrier to success that for many young adults produces the misery of a life marked by poverty, unemployment, alienation and, in many cases, crime.

It must be recognized also, however, that for the majority who do acquire the basic reading skills, there can also be a barrier which limits the fulfillment of their right to read. This barrier exists when the skill of reading is not accompanied by the *desire* to read. We fail, therefore, just as much in assuring the right to read when the desire is absent as when the skills are missing.

It is inexcusable that, in this day when man has achieved such giant steps in the development of his potential, when many of his accomplishments approach the miraculous, there still should be those who cannot read.

While still commissioner in New York State, I had begun to develop plans for launching a statewide, concentrated attack on reading deficiencies. Now I have national responsibilities and my view of the educational scene from this level convinces me that there is no higher nationwide priority in the field of education than the provision of the right to read for all, and that the Office of Education and the Department of Health, Education, and Welfare can do no greater service for the cause of education than to spearhead a nationwide attack to eliminate this failure of our education efforts.

Therefore, as U.S. Commissioner of Education, I am herewith proclaiming my belief that *we should immediately set for ourselves the goal of assuring that by the end of the 1970s the right to read shall be a reality for all—that no one shall be leaving our schools without the skill and the desire necessary to read to the full limits of his capability.*

This is education's "moon"—the target for the decade ahead. With the same zeal, dedication, perseverance, and concentration that made possible man's giant step of last July 20, this moon too can be reached.

While it is obviously impossible to expect that our target could encompass the complete elimination of the reading deficiencies of the out-of-school population also, this decade devoted to the improvement of reading should include a new and intensive attack in this area of need, bringing to bear the kind of widespread concentration of effort and resources that will be given to in-school youth.

To hit the target by the end of the 70s, to achieve a goal of such enormous dimensions, involvement will have to reach far beyond the forces of education.

Necessary will be committed participation and support of the Congress; state and local political leaders and legislative bodies; business, industry, and labor; civic and community groups; publishers; advertising organizations; television, radio, and the press; research and scientific organizations; foundations; the entertainment industry; the sports world; and, perhaps most essential of all, the understanding and support of an enlightened and enthusiastic public. In other words, *I am calling for a total national commitment to and involvement in the achievement of the "right to read" goal.*

This is a proper goal for our society because it will not only correct the injustice done to individuals by the denial of their right to read, but it will also, because of its widespread social and cultural effect, benefit and strengthen the entire fabric of our society.

I can already hear the excuses, the expressions of fear and reservation, the "yes, buts" with which many will greet this challenge. To accept these is to continue the rationalization, the justifications for failure that for too long have persisted, demoralizing our will and generating a defeatist attitude.

Of course, this goal cannot be easily attained. It will be far more difficult than the landing on the moon. But the time is right, I believe, to try, for so much is at stake and there are so many favorable auguries for success.

This is a time when we have accumulated an enormous amount of research and expertise in the field of reading. Few other areas of learning have been so thoroughly and widely studied. May I add here parenthetically, however, that we must avoid the danger of allowing education's reading "moonshot" to become bogged down in debate over *methods* of the teaching of reading. It is the *goal* that must concern us.

This is a time when science and technology have given us a whole new array of resources to apply to the solution of the reading problem.

This is a time when school boards and school administrators are less preoccupied than at any time since World War II with the pressing problems which have been created by ever-increasing student enrollment.

This is a time of growing understanding of the effects of environment and other factors on the ability to learn.

This is a time when preschool educational opportunities are being more generally incorporated into the public education system.

This is a time when new federal legislation has provided increased funds for attacking problems such as that of the improvement of reading.

This is a time when there is a great latent readiness to support a program that holds promise for the improvement of reading. The concern of parents, public officials, and the general citizenry about the effectiveness of the schools seems to find a focus in the problem of reading failures. The failure to teach everyone to read is a strong factor in the loss of full confidence in our schools that is finding expression in large numbers of defeated budgets and bond issues, in student and community unrest, and in the growing tendency to seek new instrumentalities for educational reform outside of the traditional system. This is in a sense a negative situation that needs only a believable expectation of success in solving the problem to transform it into a tremendous positive force. The relatively simple, universally understood objective, implicit in the "right to read" goal, standing out clearly amidst the confusions of the complexity of the educational endeavor of these days, can be the rallying point for the renewed confidence in our schools that will gather to them a new surge of enthusiastic public support.

The cumulative effect of the conjunction of so many positive factors at this particular time can but serve to reduce doubts and to support that reasonable degree of assurance of success that mandates the attempt.

While the main task of carrying out the activities necessary to achieve the goal of the right to read for all by the end of the 70s will fall upon the states and local school boards, the federal government has a vital supportive role to play. It is not the role of the federal government to make specific plans, nor to prescribe the programs and methods to be used. The diverse needs and conditions of the various states and their communities require the flexibility of approach that our decentralized system makes possible. The main contribution that can be made at the federal level will be the coordination of the effort, the marshalling of forces and resources on a nationwide basis, and the provision of the technical, administrative, and financial assistance required, all done in a spirit of total commitment.

It *is* possible for the 70s to be the decade in which the right to read becomes a reality for all, with no one leaving our schools lacking the skill and the desire necessary to read to the full limits of his capability — and it is our duty to set for ourselves this target.

The months immediately ahead should be a time of preparation in the hope that next summer will see the beginning of the count-down, with the launch scheduled for the opening of the 1970–71 school year.

I therefore call upon you to take upon yourselves the obligation of assuring that every child in your district and in your state will learn to read, and I request that you begin immediately in your own district and state to consider how this goal can be achieved, to assemble resources, to plan, and to determine what actions you will take under state leadership so that the school year 1969–70 can be recorded as the year when together we set in motion the nationwide effort that will erase this intolerable deficit in American education.

The U.S. Office of Education has already begun this kind of activity, and we shall be consulting with school boards and all other educational forces, as well as with representatives of the total national community, as to procedures.

The decade of the 70s will see the two-hundredth anniversary of our nation. A most appropriate celebration of that event — a celebration that would honor the true spirit of the democratic concept, and recognize the fundamental importance ascribed to education from the beginning of our nation—would be to secure for all of our citizens that right to read which so long ago made possible the feasibility of a democratic society and continues to undergird its strength.

Continuing toleration of the failure to give everyone the ability to read breaks faith with the commitment to equality of opportunity which is the foundation of our public education system. Having arrived at a time which holds forth the possibility of eliminating this failure we must, in all justice, seize the opportunity with the utmost vigor and determination.

Remarkable success has been achieved by our educational system, but so long as there is one boy or girl who leaves school unable to read to the full extent of his capability, we cannot escape the charge of failure in carrying out the responsibility entrusted to us.

The purpose of reading instruction ought to be to prepare mature readers, say Gray and Rogers. Among other abilities, the mature reader has the ability to "translate words into meanings, to secure a clear grasp and understanding of the ideas presented, and to sense the mood and feelings intended."

The Concept of Maturity in Reading

WILLIAM S. GRAY
BERNICE ROGERS

At the beginning of this study it seemed advisable to select a term to be used in designating the level of the competence in reading required to meet current needs. After considering various possibilities, the phrase "maturity in reading" was selected. It was chosen because it connotes, better than any other term considered, a broad range of reading interests and behavior and a high level of competence in reading.

In order to use the term *maturity* as a helpful guide in planning this study, its meaning must be defined explicitly. A survey of the literature of various fields showed that the use of the word *maturity* usually implies some basic hypothesis concerning the behavior or activity involved. In such fields, for example, as psychiatry, psychology, and education, it suggests certain basic notions about human growth and development. Similarly, its use in the field of reading implies certain assumptions concerning the attitudes, interests, and skills involved. These varying concepts can be examined to advantage under two headings: "Concepts of General Maturity" and "Assumptions Concerning Reading Maturity." The conclusions reached will form an ideological basis for the explorations reported in the chapters that follow.

Concepts of General Maturity

Specialists in the field of human development have discussed at length the nature of general maturity. The meanings attached to the term vary widely with their orientation or special interest in the field. Whereas these differing points of view are by no means mutually exclusive, they do tend to place emphasis on different personal characteristics or aspects of behavior.

The psychoanalyst, for example, focuses attention on the growth of the individual toward capacity to handle his own feelings and emotions. This goal is to be achieved by channeling emotions into constructive and pleasurable activity rather than into infantile, sadistic, or self-destructive behavior. This view is well stated by Saul[1] and is characteristic also of the viewpoint of most specialists who adopt the dynamic or depth psychology orientation.

Other psychologists, such as Allport[2] in the United States and Pear[3] in England, have stressed the autonomous quality of the mature individual. This implies that he possesses a unifying philosophy of life which includes a vital concern for other people and for the broader social issues faced today. Such interests are not due to a dependent attitude or a driving sense of need to adjust to other people. They result rather from a self-directed, voluntary desire to be a vital part of the social scene. This view of maturity emphasizes constructive adjustments with the external world which are freely and insightfully determined by the individual. It assumes also that he can and does, to some extent, control his environment instead of being the victim of it.

Some effort has been devoted to the empirical study of normal, well-adjusted persons. It is very limited, however, as compared to the amount of time and energy which has been spent in studying the diseased personality. Heath,[4] for example, studied the traits of young men who were normal in the sense that they had made a good adjustment with their environment. He concluded that they were "well integrated, pragmatic, practical, organizing, [possessing] vital affect, friendly, humanistic." They were found frequently to be slower in maturing than their less sensitized, less complex, less distinguished age mates.

Another empirical study[5] focused on the personality variables most closely related to problem-solving ability. The variables considered were rigidity and anxiety. It was found that in situations requiring recall through recognition, the rigid and anxious person was apparently able to function efficiently. In new situations, however, in which improvising and the reorganization of previous experiences were essential, as contrasted merely with stereotyped behavior, flexibility and capacity to adjust were essential characteristics.

The finding just presented harmonizes closely with the clinically derived view of Menninger.[6] He concluded that the healthy mind is characterized by "an even temper, an alert intelligence, socially considerate behavior, and a happy disposition." He affirmed also that mature individuals are able to adjust to the world and to one another "with a maximum of effectiveness and happiness." During recent years eclectic points of view have been reported which give emphasis to both the emotional-adjustment aspects of maturity and the goals of autonomy, social responsibility, and capacity to engage in problem-solving effectively. One such statement was prepared by the Advisory Committee for the Parent Education Project at the University of Chicago.[7] The six characteristics considered by the committee to be indicative of a "mature responsible citizen of a democracy" are: (1) feelings of security and adequacy; (2) understanding of self and others; (3) recognition of democratic values and goals; (4) problem-solving attitudes and methods; (5) self-discipline, responsibility, and freedom; (6) constructive attitudes toward change. These items direct attention to goals to be reached and changes to which one must adjust.

Of special importance is the view of Overstreet,[8] as reported in *The Mature Mind*. He sought to bring together the discoveries of the various scientific disciplines—psychology, psychiatry, sociology, anthropology—and to fuse them into a unified picture of what makes for maturity in human behavior. His concept of the mature person is "not one who has come to a certain level of achievement and stopped there." It is rather that of a person "whose *linkages with life* are constantly becoming stronger and richer because his attitudes are such as to encourage their growth rather than their stoppage."[9] The areas in which he views this maturation process include attitudes toward knowledge, social responsibility, vocational adjustment, communication skill, social maturity, empathic relationships, and grasp of meaning wholes. He emphasizes, furthermore, the inter-relatedness of these various areas and the effect of growth in any one area on growth or lack of growth in other areas. He rejects the notion of social adjustment alone as a criterion of maturity, stressing, instead, the full and creative development of each individual's unique powers for constructive participation in the business of living.

A third eclectic point of view is that of Havighurst[10] and his co-workers in the field of human development. They have identified a series of successive maturational tasks, each of which depends to a great extent on the successful achievement of previous tasks. Within this framework the tasks appropriate to each age group are discussed in their psychological, biological, and cultural contexts. In such analyses cultural levels are further broken down into social-class groupings.

The tasks considered are based on needs of various types. Some of them spring from within the individual, such as the need for acceptance, recognition, affiliation, and the like. Others are determined by the demands which society makes upon individuals, such as economic independence, ability to communicate and to compete, and capacity to acquire concepts and understandings. Still others spring from both individual and cultural needs, such as that of building values which will help to promote peace throughout the world. Pervading the notion of continuous growth in all these areas are the concepts of autonomy, social responsibility, and adjustment.

Each of the broader, more inclusive concepts of maturity discussed includes a common basic characteristic. It is the belief that growth and change occur after maturity is attained. It follows, therefore, that maturity is recognized as a process rather than a level of achievement or a specific pattern of behavior. For example, Overstreet suggests that it is not the extent of a man's knowledge that determines his level of maturity but rather his attitudes toward knowledge and his effort to acquire it. In addition, general maturity implies capacity for self-direction, a keen sense of social responsibility, and capacity to adjust to different groups and times. Because of its vitality, this general view was accepted as basic to the more specialized characteristics of reading maturity explored in this study.

Assumptions Concerning Reading Maturity

Attention is directed, next, to prevailing concepts of efficient, or mature, readers. We are concerned particularly with the basic characteristics involved, their relationship to maturity in general, and the extent to which they provide a framework within which to organize the current study.

The survey of pertinent literature proved to be very illuminating. It showed, first, that whereas the need is widely recognized for a high level of competence in reading among young people and adults, very few detailed analyses have been made of what is involved. Equally true is the fact that writers who discuss such matters approach the problem from different viewpoints, as is true of those who write on general maturity. Furthermore, most writers limit their discussions, either explicitly or implicitly, to certain kinds of material. Some indicate clearly the types of reading material to which their discussions apply; others do not. Again, the views presented overlap to such an extent that they defy classification. It seems advisable, therefore, to present separately a series of selected concepts that are fairly representative of current thinking.

More than two decades ago Huse,[11] in discussing the reading needs of citizens of a democracy, gave vigorous emphasis to the importance of a clear grasp of the meaning of what is read. In his judgment, reading for understanding is to be contrasted with mechanical reading. It involves the translation of the meanings represented by the symbols into understandings that can be expressed in the reader's own words. Equally important is their translation "into terms of purpose, authority, and validity."[12] Unless this is done, "the public is the inevitable victim of fraud both commercial and literary," and "the mental life of the people may be corrupted,"[13] or indeed dissipated. In Huse's judgment a high level of "capacity to translate is an indispensable requisite of a literate citizen."

Philbrick,[14] who approached the problem from the semantic point of view, stressed the importance of both penetrating and critical reading. He maintains that the effective reader should habitually look for the following items in a piece of writing: (1) the sense (the facts, the statements that the author makes); (2) the author's attitude toward the facts; (3) the author's attitude toward his reader; and (4) the mood (the feeling or emotions induced by the author). As the reader seeks to identify these items, he should study carefully the meanings of the particular words used. Likewise he should be alert to the use of propaganda devices and emotive language and guard against false interpretations. In addition, he should think critically about the soundness, value, and implications of the ideas and draw valid conclusions concerning them.

As a guide in securing a liberal education, Adler[15] focused attention on the steps involved in reading books effectively. He describes maturity in reading as the ability to use reading to discover ways of living the good life and of participating effectively as a member of society in discharging well the responsibilities of free men. He specifies clearly the type of material which, in his judgment, merits careful study. It presents serious ideas written by great thinkers, past and present.

The art of reading well is, in his judgment, "intimately related to the art of thinking well, clearly, critically, fully." It involves a penetrating understanding of a book's contents. This is secured through an interpretation of the basic words used, a grasp of the author's leading propositions, a knowledge of his arguments, and a recognition of the extent to which he solved the problems posed. In addition, the mature reader reacts critically to the ideas and conclusions presented, in order to know how safely and fully he may be guided by them.

Of major importance also are the purposes to be achieved through reading at the mature level. They include, according to Adler,[16] its use as a tool for the realization of one's own potentials, for knowing and understanding others and the society of which one is a part, and for achieving the good society as the reader develops for himself, through reading, his own concept of a good society. This view appears to coincide closely with the concept of maturity in general discussed earlier.

From a widely different point of view Center[17] discusses the essential characteristics of a mature reader. In her judgment, a mature reader reads many kinds of material for many purposes — pleasure, information, understanding, guidance, inspiration. Of primary importance are a genuine enthusiasm for reading, an "irresistible compulsion to read," and the habit of reading for "intelligent delight." Equally important is ability to read critically any kind of material from which may be derived either pleasure or profit. The mature reader should be able to adjust his pace "according to the implications of the composition"; have a high capacity for recall over a long period of time, if necessary; read in many subject areas; sample many types of literature; and read widely and critically in some particular area. Center considers that the mature, critical reader comprehends not only surface meanings but also implied and "periphery" meanings. He also brings wide experience to his interpretation of the materials read and, in turn, greatly enriches his background of understanding through vicarious experience.

The foregoing analysis differs from the three that precede it in that it emphasizes keen enjoyment of reading and breadth of reading interests. It agrees with them in its recognition of the importance of a penetrating grasp of meaning and critical reaction to the ideas presented. It also recognizes that growth both in and through reading is an ongoing process.

Further insight concerning the characteristics of the mature reader has been secured through objective studies. Using the case-study technique, Strang[18] secured a broad range of information about given individuals. It enabled her to identify underlying personality and behavior patterns and therefore to interpret the constellation of forces operating to determine the individual's reading pattern. On the basis of the results of a series of case studies, Strang concluded that the following characteristics are associated with maturity in reading: a wide reading vocabulary;

superior comprehension of what is read, including facility to express the ideas apprehended; broad interest in world events and social problems; above-average rate of reading; and, in general, a high abstract verbal ability. In addition, she found that the materials read by a mature reader usually have a central core or radix[19] which determines to a greater or less extent the individual's reading pattern.

A reexamination of the foregoing statements indicates that the following characteristics help to distinguish a mature reader:

1. A genuine enthusiasm for reading.
2. Tendency to read (a) a wide variety of materials that contribute pleasure, widen horizons, and stimulate creative thinking; (b) serious materials which promote a growing understanding of one's self, of others, and of problems of a social, moral, and ethical nature; and (c) intensively in a particular field or materials relating to a central core or radix.
3. Ability to translate words into meanings, to secure a clear grasp and understanding of the ideas presented, and to sense clearly the mood and feelings intended.
4. Capacity for and habit of making use of all that one knows or can find out in interpreting or construing the meaning of the ideas read.
5. Ability to perceive strengths and weaknesses in what is read, to detect bias and propaganda, and to think critically concerning the validity and values of the ideas presented and the adequacy and soundness of the author's presentation, views, and conclusions. This involves an emotional apprehension, either favorable or unfavorable, as well as a penetrating intellectual grasp of what is read.
6. Tendency to fuse the new ideas acquired through reading with previous experience, thus acquiring new or clearer understandings, broadened interests, rational attitudes, improved patterns of thinking and behaving, and richer and more stable personalities.
7. Capacity to adjust one's reading pace to the needs of the occasion and to the demands of adequate interpretation.

In order to give appropriate meaning to some of these characteristics, they must be interpreted in terms of the characteristics of general maturity. If, for example, the reader is no longer childishly ego centered and has acquired interest in the larger world outside himself, his selection of reading materials will be influenced by that fact. If he has also acquired a set of social values or standards, his interpretations of materials read will be determined to a considerable extent by them. In such cases there may be time and some inclination for sheer pleasure reading, but it will be peripheral to his central reading focus.

As implied by the foregoing summary, there is a possible conflict between the tendency to read intensively and that to read extensively. Even the mature person may have difficulty in resolving this conflict because of limited time and varied interests. But the acquisition of the type of mature perspective that Overstreet talks about—the ability and insistence on seeing things as wholes, squarely, and in their full social context—will help to maintain balance between excessive probing of too few areas and extreme superficiality in many areas.

A conflict arises also between free emotional reactions to what is read and rational reactions which assume the suspension of judgment until all the evidence is at hand. If a mature reader possesses what Overstreet calls "the ability to grow in the use of knowledge," he will understand the difference between the two types of reaction. He will also be aware of the conditions or situations which justify the one or the other. Obviously, the ability to react rationally to what is read is determined to a large extent by the reader's maturity in other areas of his life.

Concluding Statement

The foregoing analysis has been more or less detailed in an effort to make explicit the kinds of assumptions about maturity in reading that are basic to this study. In the light of the evidence presented, reading maturity must be conceived in close relationship to general maturity. Briefly stated, the latter is distinguished by an adequate development of each individual's attitudes, understandings, and abilities to enable him to participate fully and creatively in the all-round business of living. According to this view, a mature person is not one who has merely come to a certain level of achievement. He is rather one whose contacts with life are constantly becoming broader and richer because his interests and attitudes are such as to encourage their development.

Maturity in reading as one aspect of total development is distinguished by the attainment of those interests, attitudes, and skills which enable young people and adults to participate eagerly, independently, and effectively in all the reading activities essential to a full, rich, and productive life. It is assumed that, in the satisfaction of interests and needs through reading, a mature reader will continue to grow in capacity to interpret broadly and deeply.

The dear people do not know how long it takes to learn to read. I have been at it all my life and I cannot yet say I have reached the goal. — GOETHE

Notes

1. Leon J. Saul. *Emotional Maturity.* Philadelphia: J. B. Lippincott, 1947.

2. Gordon Allport. *Personality: A Psychological Interpretation.* New York: Henry Holt & Co., 1939, 1946.

3. T. H. Pear. *The Maturing Mind.* London: Thomas Nelson & Sons, 1938.

4. Clark W. Heath. *What People Are: A Study of Normal Young Men.* Cambridge, Mass.: Harvard University Press, 1946, p. 30.

5. Eugene L. Gaier. "Selected Personality Variables and the Learning Process." *Psychological Monographs, General and Applied* vol. 66, no. 17. Washington, D. C.: American Psychological Association, 1952.

6. Karl A. Menninger. *The Human Mind.* New York: Alfred A. Knopf, 1937, introduction to chap. 1.

7. Ethel Kawin. *Parenthood in a Free Nation.* Chicago: University of Chicago, 1954. Parent Education Project in cooperation with the Fund for Adult Education. Members of the panel of scholars who validated this list of characteristics were: Robert J. Havighurst, Helen L. Koch, William C. Menninger, Esther Middlewood, Ralph J. Ojemann, Sybil Richardson, Benjamin Spock, and Ruth Strang.

8. H. A. Overstreet. *The Mature Mind.* New York: W. W. Norton & Co., 1949.

9. Ibid., p. 43.

10. Robert J. Havighurst. *Developmental Tasks and Education.* New York: Longmans, Green & Co., 1950.

11. H. R. Huse. *The Illiteracy of the Literate.* New York: D. Appleton-Century Co., 1933.

12. Ibid., p. 8.

13. Ibid., p. 9.

14. F. A. Philbrick. *Understanding English: An Introduction to Semantics.* New York: Macmillan, 1942.

15. Mortimer J. Adler. *How To Read a Book: The Art of Getting a Liberal Education.* New York: Simon & Schuster, 1940.

16. Ibid.

17. Stella S. Center. *The Art of Book Reading.* New York: Charles Scribner's Sons, 1952.

18. Ruth Strang. *Explorations in Reading Patterns.* Chicago: University of Chicago Press, 1942.

19. Ibid., p. 4.

> Many elementary school children
> view the purpose of reading as "say-
> ing a bunch of words" or "doing
> workbook pages." The children, and
> possibly even their teachers, seem to
> be confusing ends and means, pur-
> poses and procedures.

Reading: A View from the Child

Russell Stauffer (1969) reports in a recent text on reading instruction the results of asking teachers the question, "What is reading?" After providing the reader with some representative definitions given by teachers, Stauffer concluded that if such definitions were typical of the way most classroom teachers defined reading, ". . . it is urgent that a better understanding of the concept *reading* be acquired by teachers." It is not difficult to see why reading authorities want classroom teachers to acquire an understanding of all that reading involves. A better understanding of the concept *reading* would likely result in teachers' providing better learning experiences for the children in their classrooms. Fortunately, graduate courses in reading as well as in-service programs provide classroom teachers with an opportunity to acquire a better concept of reading.

Recent classroom experiences by this author suggest that a better understanding of reading should also be acquired by elementary children who engage in the reading process. Over the past three years, the author has asked children in grades four through six to answer the question, "What is reading?" Following are some definitions that are representative of those that have been given by elementary children in these grades:

1. Reading is a book. If you don't know the words, sound them out.
2. Reading is when you see a group of words in a sentence.
3. When we read stories and do workbook pages.
4. Reading is something you do to learn from books.
5. Reading is something you do when you look at the words and you say them aloud or silently.
6. Reading is when you read a word and it tells you something.
7. You see, words have names and they have certain letters. You look at the letters and you put them together and you read a whole bunch of words together.
8. Reading is when you say a bunch of words.

If these responses can be assumed to represent the "typical" child's concept of reading, it is readily apparent that children, like teachers, need to acquire a better understanding of reading. As crude as some of the above responses may seem, recent attempts by severely disabled readers to answer the same question revealed little or no understanding of the reading process. The typical response of ten of the twelve children was "I don't know." Perhaps one of the contributing factors to children's reading problems is a failure of some children to understand what is involved in the reading process.

The plea of the article is simple. College and university professors have knowledge about the reading process that would enable them to communicate a better understanding of the concept of reading to teachers. Hopefully, professors will be able to communicate this knowledge to teachers. Unless classroom teachers, however, communicate similar information to their pupils, the fullest benefits of such information will not be utilized. Some evidence has been offered to suggest that many children need to acquire a better understanding of reading. Would it not be beneficial, then, to tell children what reading is all about? After all, they are the ones who are being taught.

Reference

Stauffer, R. G. *Directing Reading Maturity as a Cognitive Process.* New York: Harper and Row, 1969, p. 5.

Postman views the school as a political institution, and so rather naturally looks for the political purposes of reading instruction. Reading is not considered as a neutral skill. He takes the position that reading methods are the means by which those in power maintain control over the individual. The child is taught minimal reading skills so that he will be an obedient citizen, an enthusiastic consumer, and a believer in the myths and superstitions of the society. Because teachers use reading methods, Postman considers them a "most sinister political group, whose continued presence and strength are more a cause for alarm than celebration."

The Politics of Reading *

NEIL POSTMAN

Dr. Postman challenges the common assumptions that the literacy process is politically neutral and is the only, or even the best, avenue to jobs and aesthetic riches. He sees a predominantly literacy-based curriculum as obsolete and reactionary in the context of recent advances in electronic communications technology, and recommends broadening the base of school curricula to include "multi-media literacy."

Teachers of reading comprise a most sinister political group, whose continued presence and strength are more a cause for alarm than celebration. I offer this thought as a defensible proposition, all the more worthy of consideration because so few people will take it seriously.

My argument rests on a fundamental and, I think, unassailable assumption about education: namely, that all educational practices are profoundly political in the sense that they are designed to produce one sort of human being rather than another — which is to say, an educational system always proceeds from some model of what a human being *ought* to be like. In the broadest sense, a political ideology is a conglomerate of systems for promoting certain modes of thinking and behavior. And there is no

*An earlier version of this article was presented as the keynote address at the Lehigh University Reading Conference, January 24, 1970.

system I can think of that more directly tries to do this than the schools. There is not one thing that is done to, for, with, or against a student in school that is not rooted in a political bias, ideology, or notion. This includes everything from the arrangement of seats in a classroom, to the rituals practiced in the auditorium, to the textbooks used in lessons, to the dress required of both teachers and students, to the tests given, to the subjects that are taught, and most emphatically, to the intellectual skills that are promoted. And what is called reading, it seems to me, just about heads the list. For to teach reading, or even to promote vigorously the teaching of reading, is to take a definite political position on how people should behave and on what they ought to value. Now, teachers, I have found, respond in one of three ways to such an assertion. Some of them deny it. Some of them concede it but without guilt or defensiveness of any kind. And some of them don't know what it means. I want to address myself to the latter, because in responding to them I can include all the arguments I would use in dealing with the others.

In asserting that the teaching of reading is essentially a political enterprise, the most obvious question I am asking is, "What is reading good for?" When I ask this question of reading teachers, I am supplied with a wide range of answers. Those who take the low ground will usually say that skill in reading is necessary in order for a youngster to do well in school. The elementary teacher is preparing the youngster for the junior high teacher, who prepares him for the senior high teacher, who, in turn, prepares him for the college teacher, and so on. Now, this answer is true but hardly satisfactory. In fact, it amounts to a description of the *rules* of the school game but says nothing about the purpose of these rules. So, when teachers are pushed a little further, they sometimes answer that the school system, at all levels, makes reading skill a precondition to success because unless one can read well, he is denied access to gainful and interesting employment as an adult. This answer raises at least a half-dozen political questions, the most interesting of which is whether or not one's childhood education ought to be concerned with one's future employment. I am aware that most people take it as axiomatic that the schooling process should prepare youth for a tranquil entry into our economy, but this is a political view that I think deserves some challenge. For instance, when one considers that the second most common cause of death among adolescents in the U.S. is suicide, or that more people are hospitalized for mental illness than all other illnesses combined, or that one out of every twenty-two murders in the United States is committed by a parent against his own child, or that more than half of all high school students have already taken habit-forming, hallucinogenic, or potentially addictive narcotics, or that by the end of this year, there will be more than one million school dropouts around, one can easily prepare a case which insists that the schooling process be designed for purposes other than vocational training. If it is legitimate at all for schools to claim a concern for the adult life of students, then why not pervasive and compulsory programs in mental health, sex, or marriage and the family? Besides, the number of jobs that require reading skill much beyond what teachers call a "fifth-grade level" is probably quite small and scarcely justifies the massive, compulsory, unrelenting reading programs that characterize most schools.

But most reading teachers would probably deny that their major purpose is to prepare students to satisfy far-off vocational requirements. Instead, they would take the high ground and insist that the basic purpose of reading instruction is to open the student's mind to the wonders and riches of the written word, to give him access to great fiction and poetry, to permit him to function as an informed citizen, to have him experience the sheer pleasure of reading. Now, this is a satisfactory answer indeed but, in my opinion, it is almost totally untrue.

And to the extent that it is true, it is true in a way quite different from anything one might expect. For instance, it is probably true that in a highly complex society, one cannot be governed unless he can read forms, regulations, notices, catalogues, road signs, and the like. Thus, some minimal reading skill is necessary if you are to be a "good citizen," but "good citizen" here means one who can follow the instructions of those who govern him. If you cannot read, you cannot be an obedient citizen. You are also a good citizen if you are an enthusiastic consumer. And so, some minimal reading competence is required if you are going to develop a keen interest in all the products that it is necessary for you to buy. If you do not read, you will be a relatively poor market. In order to be a good and loyal citizen, it is also necessary for you to believe in the myths and superstitions of your society. Therefore, a certain minimal reading skill is needed so that you can learn what these are, or have them reinforced. Imagine what would happen in a school if a Social Studies text were introduced that described the growth of American civilization as being characterized by four major developments: 1) insurrection against a legally constituted government, in order to achieve a political identity; 2) genocide against the indigenous population, in order to get land; 3) keeping human beings as slaves, in order to achieve an economic base; and 4) the importation of "coolie" labor, in order to build the railroads. Whether this view of American history is true or not is beside the point. It is at least as true or false as the conventional view *and* it would scarcely be allowed to appear unchallenged in a school-book intended for youth. What I am saying here is that an important function of the teaching of reading is to make students accessible to political and historical myth. It is entirely possible that the main reason middle-class whites are so concerned to get lower-class blacks to read is that blacks will remain relatively inaccessible to standard-brand beliefs unless and until they are minimally literate. It just may be too dangerous, politically, for any substantial minority of our population *not* to believe that our flags are sacred, our history is noble, our government is representative, our laws are just, and our institutions are viable. A reading public is a responsible public, by which is meant that it believes most or all of these superstitions, and which is probably why we still have literacy tests for voting.

One of the standard beliefs about the reading process is that it is more or less neutral. Reading, the argument goes, is just a skill. What people read is their own business, and the reading teacher merely helps to increase a student's options. If one wants to read about America, one may read DeToqueville or *The Daily News;* if one wants to read literature, one may go to Melville or Jacqueline Susann. In theory, this argument is compelling. In practice, it is pure romantic nonsense. *The New York Daily News* is the most widely read newspaper in America. Most of our students will go to the grave not having read, of their own choosing, a paragraph of DeToqueville or Thoreau or John Stuart Mill or, if you exclude the Gettysburg Address, even Abraham Lincoln. As between Jacqueline Susann and Herman Melville — well, the less said, the better. To put it bluntly, among every one-hundred students who learn to read, my guess is that no more than one will employ the process toward any of the lofty goals which are customarily held before us. The rest will use the process to increase their knowledge of trivia, to maintain themselves at a relatively low level of emotional maturity, and to keep themselves simplistically uninformed about the social and political turmoil around them.

Now, there are teachers who feel that, even if what I say is true, the point is nonetheless irrelevant. After all, they say, the world is not perfect. If people do not have enough time to read deeply, if people do not have sensibilities refined enough to read great literature, if people do not have interests broad enough to be stimulated by the unfamiliar, the fault is not in our symbols, but in ourselves. But there is a point of view that proposes that the "fault," in fact, *does* lie in our symbols. Marshall McLuhan is saying that each medium of communication contains a unique metaphysic — that each medium makes special kinds of claims on our senses, and, therefore, on our behavior. McLuhan himself tells us that he is by no means the first person to have noticed this. Socrates took a very dim view of the written word, on the grounds that it diminishes man's capacity to memorize, and that it forces one to follow an argument rather than to participate in it. He also objected to the fact that once something has been written down, it may easily come to the attention of persons for whom it was not intended. One can well imagine what Socrates would think about wire-tapping and other electronic bugging devices. St. Ambrose, a prolific book writer and reader, once complained to St. Jerome, another prolific writer and reader, that whatever else its virtues, reading was the most antisocial behavior yet devised by man. Other people have made observations about the effects of communications media on the psychology of a culture, but it is quite remarkable how little has been said about this subject. Most criticism of print, or any other medium, has dealt with the content of the medium; and it is only in recent years that we have begun to understand that each medium, *by its very structure,* makes us do things with our bodies, our senses, and our minds that in the long run are probably more important than any other messages communicated by the medium.

Now that it is coming to an end, we are just beginning to wonder about the powerful biases forced upon us by the Age of the Printed Word. McLuhan is telling us that print is a "hot" medium, by which he means that it induces passivity and anesthetizes almost all our senses except the visual. He is also telling us that electronic media, like the LP record and television, are reordering our entire sensorium, restoring some of our sleeping senses, and, in the process, making all of us seek more active participation in life. I think McLuhan is wrong in connecting the *causes* of passivity and activity so directly to the structure of media. I find it sufficient to say that whenever a new medium — a new communications technology — enters a culture, *no matter what its structure,* it gives us a new way of experiencing the world, and consequently, releases tremendous energies and causes people to seek new ways of organizing their institutions. When Gutenberg announced that he could manufacture books, as he put it, "without the help of reed, stylus, or pen but by wondrous agreement, proportion, and harmony of punches and types," he could scarcely imagine that he was about to become the most important political and social revolutionary of the Second Millenium. And yet, that is what happened. Four hundred and fifty years ago, the printed word, far from being a medium that induced passivity, generated cataclysmic change. From the time Martin Luther posted his theses in 1517, the printing press disseminated the most controversial, inflammatory, and wrenching ideas imaginable. The Protestant Reformation would probably not have occurred if not for the printing press. The development of both capitalism and nationalism were obviously linked to the printing press. So were new literary forms, such as the novel and the essay. So were new conceptions of education, such as written examinations. And, of course, so was the concept of scientific methodology, whose ground rules were established by Descartes in his *Discourse on Reason.* Even today in recently illiterate cultures, such as Cuba, print is a medium capable of generating intense involvement, radicalism, artistic innovation, and institutional upheaval. But in those countries where the printed word has been preeminent for over four-hundred years, print retains very few of these capabilities. Print is not dead, it's just old — and old technologies do not generate new patterns of behavior. For us, print is the technology of convention. We have accommodated our senses to it. We have routinized and even ritualized our responses to it. We have devoted our institutions, which are now venerable, to its service. By maintaining the printed word as the keystone of education, we are therefore opting for political and social stasis.

It is 126 years since Professor Morse transmitted a message electronically for the first time in the history of the planet. Surely it is not too soon for educators to give serious thought to the message he sent: "What hath God wrought?" We are very far from knowing the answers to that question, but we do know that electronic media have released unprecedented energies. It's worth saying that the gurus of the peace movement—Bob Dylan, Pete Seeger, Joan Baez, Phil Ochs, for instance—were known to their constituency mostly as voices on LP records. It's worth saying that Vietnam, being our first television war, is also the most unpopular war in our history. It's worth saying that Lyndon Johnson was the first president ever to have resigned because of a "credibility gap." It's worth saying that it is now commonplace for post-TV college sophomores to usurp the authority of college presidents and for young parish priests to instruct their bishops in the ways of *both* man and God. And it's also worth saying that black people, after 350 years of bondage, want their freedom— now. Post-television blacks are, indeed, our true *now* generation.

Electronic media are predictably working to unloose disruptive social and political ideas, along with new forms of sensibility and expression. Whether this is being achieved by the structure of the media, or by their content, or by some combination of both, we cannot be sure. But like Gutenberg's infernal machine of 450 years ago, the electric plug is causing all hell to break loose. Meanwhile, the schools are still pushing the old technology; and, in fact, pushing it with almost hysterical vigor. Everyone's going to learn to read, even if we have to kill them to do it. It is as if the schools were the last bastion of the old culture, and if it has to go, why let's take as many down with us as we can.

For instance, the schools are still the principal source of the idea that literacy is equated with intelligence. Why, the schools even promote the idea that *spelling* is related to intelligence! Of course, if any of this were true, reading teachers would be the smartest people around. One doesn't mean to be unkind, but if that indeed is the case, no one has noticed it. In any event, it is an outrage that children who do not read well, or at all, are treated as if they are stupid. It is also masochistic, since the number of nonreaders will obviously continue to increase and, thereby, the schools will condemn themselves, by their own definition of intelligence, to an increasing number of stupid children. In this way, we will soon have remedial reading-readi- ness classes, along with remedial classes for those not yet ready for their remedial reading-readiness class.

The schools are also still promoting the idea that literacy is the richest source of aesthetic experience. This, in the face of the fact that kids are spending a billion dollars a year to buy LP records and see films. The schools are still promoting the idea that the main source of wisdom is to be found in libraries, from which most schools, incidentally, carefully exclude the most interesting books. The schools are still promoting the idea that the nonliterate person is somehow not fully human, an idea that will surely endear us to the nonliterate peoples of the world. (It is similar to the idea that salvation is obtainable only through Christianity — which is to say, it is untrue, bigoted, reactionary, and based on untenable premises, to boot.)

Worst of all, the schools are using these ideas to keep nonconforming youth — blacks, the politically disaffected, and the economically disadvantaged, among others — in their place. By taking this tack, the schools have become a major force for political conservatism at a time when everything else in the culture screams for rapid reorientation and change.

What would happen if our schools took the drastic political step of trying to make the new technology the keystone of education? The thought will seem less romantic if you remember that the start of the Third Millenium is only thirty-one years away. No one knows, of course, what would happen, but I'd like to make a few guesses. In the first place, the physical environment would be entirely different from what it is now. The school would look something like an electric circus — arranged to accommodate TV cameras and monitors, film projectors, computers, audio and video tape machines, radio, and photographic and stereophonic equipment. As he is now provided with textbooks, each student would be provided with his own still camera, 8 mm. camera, and tape casette. The school library would contain books, of course, but at least as many films, records, video tapes, audio tapes, and computer programs. The major effort of the school would be to assist students in achieving what has been called "multimedia literacy." Therefore, speaking, filmmaking, picture taking, televising, computer programming, listening, perhaps even music playing, drawing, and dancing would be completely acceptable means of expressing intellectual interest and competence. They would certainly be given weight at least equal to reading and writing.

Since intelligence would be defined in a new way, a student's ability to create an idea would be at least as important as his ability to classify and remember the ideas of others. New evaluation procedures would come into being, and standardized tests — the final, desperate refuge of the print-bound bureaucrat — would disappear. Entirely new methods of instruction would evolve. In fact, schools might abandon the notion of teacher instruction altogether. Whatever disciplines lent themselves to packaged, lineal, and segmented presentation would be offered through a computerized and individualized program. And students could choose from a wide variety of such programs whatever they wished to learn about. This means, among other things, that teachers would have to stop acting like teachers and find something useful to do, like, for instance, helping young people to resolve some of their more wrenching emotional problems.

In fact, a school that put electric circuitry at its center would have to be prepared for some serious damage to all of its bureaucratic and hierarchical arrangements. Keep in mind that hierarchies derive their authority from the notion of unequal access to information. Those at the top have access to more information than those at the bottom. That is in fact why they are at the top and the others at the bottom. But today those who are at the bottom of the school hierarchy, namely, the students, have access to at least as much information about most subjects as those at the top. At present, the only way those at the top can maintain control over them is by carefully discriminating against what the students know — that is, by labelling what the students know as unimportant. But suppose cinematography was made a "major" subject instead of English literature? Suppose chemotherapy was made a "major" subject? or space technology? or ecology? or mass communication? or popular music? or photography? or race relations? or urban life? Even an elementary school might then find itself in a situation where the faculty were at the bottom and its students at the top. Certainly, it would be hard to know who are the teachers and who the learners.

And then perhaps a school would become a place where *everybody,* including the adults, is trying to learn something. Such a school would obviously be problem centered, *and* future centered, *and* change centered; and, as such, would be an instrument of cultural and political radicalism. In the process we might find that our youth would also learn to read without pain and with a degree of success and economy not presently known.

I want to close on this thought: teachers of reading represent an important political pressure group. They may not agree with me that they are a sinister political group. But I should think that they would want to ask at least a few questions *before* turning to consider the *techniques* of teaching reading. These questions would be: What is reading good for? What is it better or worse than? What are my motives in promoting it? And the ultimate political question of all, "Whose side am I on?"

Staats and Butterfield take the position that children should receive tangible rewards when they satisfactorily perform reading exercises for which the objectives have been explicitly stated. While the article describes the teaching of only one child, and a seriously disabled one at that, some authorities maintain that the same method is equally effective with all children. Clark and Walberg, in "The Secondary Reinforcement in Teaching Inner-City School Children," *The Journal of Special Education* 3 (1970):177–85, take the position that all teachers in all school systems should be expected to use an explicit system of reward applications with all types of children. Staats and Butterfield describe the operation of a program of explicit reward applications.

Treatment of Nonreading in a Culturally Deprived Juvenile Delinquent: An Application of Reinforcement Principles

ARTHUR W. STAATS, *University of Hawaii*

WILLIAM H. BUTTERFIELD, *University of Michigan*

Staats has previously discussed behavior problems and their treatment in terms of learning principles (1964c, 1963). In doing so it was indicated that problem behaviors can arise in part (1) because behavior that is necessary for adjustment in our society is absent from the individual's repertoire, (2) because behaviors considered undesirable by the society are present in the individual's repertoire, or (3) because the individual's motivational (reinforcement) system was inappropriate in some respects.

Although a complete account is not relevant here, several points pertinent to the above conceptions will be made in introducing the present study. The notion that many behavior problems consist of deficits in behavior is important in the study of child development. Behaviorally speaking, a child is considered to be a problem when he does not acquire behaviors as other children do. It is conceivable that a deficit in behavior could arise because the child simply cannot acquire the behavior involved, even though the conditions of learning have been entirely adequate.

It would be expected, however, that behavioral deficits would also arise in cases where the conditions of learning have been defective. Learning conditions can be defective in different ways. For example, the child may never have received training in the behavior he must later exhibit. Or the training may be poor, even though the "trainers," parents or teachers, and so on, have the best intentions.

In addition, however, a child may be exposed to learning conditions that are appropriate for most children but, due to the particular child's past history of learning, are not appropriate for him. It is especially in these cases that people are most likely to conclude erroneously that since other children learn in the same circumstances, the child's deficit must be because of some personal defect. For example, in cases where the training is long term, adequate reinforcement must be available to maintain the attentional and work behaviors necessary for learning. As Staats has indicated (1964c, 1963, 1962), the reinforcers present in the traditional schoolroom are inadequate for many children. Their attentional behaviors are not maintained, and they do not learn. Thus, a deficit in an individual's behavioral repertoire may arise although he has been presented with the "same" training circumstances from which other children profit. Learning does not take place because the child's previous experience has not provided, in this example, the necessary reinforcer (motivational) system to maintain good learning behaviors. It would seem that in such a circumstance the assumption that the child has a personal defect would be unwarranted and ineffective.

However, after a few years of school attendance where the conditions of learning are not appropriate for the child, he will not have acquired the behavioral repertoires acquired by more fortunate members of the class—whose previous experiences have established an adequate motivational system. Then, lack of skilled behavior is likely to be treated aversively. That is, in the present case, the child with a reading deficit (or other evidence of underachievement) is likely to be gibed at and teased when he is still young, and ignored, avoided, and looked down upon when he is older. Although the individuals doing this may not intend to be aversive, such actions constitute the presentation of aversive stimuli. Furthermore, this presentation of aversive stimuli by other "successful" children, and perhaps by a teacher, would be expected to result in further learning, but learning of an undesirable nature. These successful children, teachers, academic materials, and the total school situation can in this way become learned negative reinforcers, which may be translated to say the child acquires negative attitudes toward school (see Staats, 1964b).

At this point, the child is likely to begin to escape the school situation in various ways (daydreaming, poor attendance, and so on) and to behave aversively in turn to the school and its inhabitants (vandalism, fighting, baiting teachers and students, and the like). Thus, a deficit in behavior, resulting from an inappropriate motivational system, can lead to the further development of inappropriate reinforcers and inappropriate behaviors.

The foregoing is by no means intended as a complete analysis of delinquency, dropouts, and the like. However, it does indicate some of the problems of learning that may occur in school. In addition, it does suggest that an analysis in terms of laboratory-established learning principles, when applied to problems such as in classroom learning of the above type, can yield new research and applied hypotheses. It was with this general strategy that the study of reading acquisition employing learning principles and reinforcement procedures were commenced (Staats, 1964a, 1964d, 1964c, 1962). The present study is a replication and an extension of these various findings to the development of a program for training nonreaders to read. The program, which adapts standard reading materials, is based upon the principle of the reinforcer system employed in the previous studies with the younger children, thus testing the principles of reinforcement in the context of remedial reading training, as well as the feasibility of using the type of reinforcement system with a new type of subject. As such, the study has implications for the study of nonreading children of pre-adolescent, adolescent, and young adult ages. In the present case, the subject was also a culturally deprived delinquent child—and the study thus involves additional information and implications for the special problems associated with education in this population of children.

Methods

Subject

The subject was fourteen years and three months old. He was the fifth child in a Mexican-American family of eleven children and the mother and father. The parental techniques for controlling their children's behavior consisted of physical and verbal abuse. Both parents described their own childhood conditions as primitive. The father was taken out of school after completing the fifth grade to help with his father's work. Each of the subject's four older brothers had been referred to the juvenile court for misbehavior. The parents appeared to be at loss as to how to provide effective control for family members.

The subject had a history of various miscreant behaviors, having been referred to the juvenile department nine times for such things as running away, burglary, incorrigibility, and truancy. During the course of the study the subject was again referred (with three other boys) on a complaint of malicious mischief for shooting light bulbs and windows in a school building with a *bb* gun. He associated with a group of boys who had been in marked difficulty with the law. The subject smoked and on occasion he drank excessively.

The study commenced when the subject was residing with his family. However, after the complaint on malicious mischief he was sent to a juvenile detention home. During his stay there he was allowed to attend school in the daytime. The study was finally concluded when he was committed to an industrial school for juvenile delinquent boys. This occurred because he baited the attendants at the detention home and caused disturbances which, although not serious, were very unpleasant and disruptive.

On the Wechsler Bellevue Form I, given when the subject was 13-10, he received Verbal and Performance IQ's of 77 and 106, respectively, for a Full Scale IQ of 90. The examiner concluded that the subject was probably within the normal range for this test. On the basis of this test and HTP Projective Drawings, the subject was characterized as having a poor attention span and poorly integrated thought processes and as lacking intellectual ambitiousness. He was also described as seeking satisfaction in fantasy and as having good conventional judgment.

The subject had continually received failing grades in all subjects in school. He was described as having "been incorrigible since he came here in the second grade. He has no respect for teachers, steals and lies habitually and uses extremely foul language." The subject had been promoted throughout his school career simply to move him on or to "get rid of him." He was disliked by the teachers and administrators in grade school because of his troublesome behavior and was described by the principal as mentally retarded even though one of the tests taken there indicated a score within the normal range. Another test taken there gave him an IQ of 75. During the study the subject was attending a local high school and taking classes for low-level students.

Reinforcer System

In previous studies (Staats, 1966, 1964d, 1964e), a reinforcer system was demonstrated that was capable of maintaining attention and work behaviors for long term experimental studies. This system worked well with preschool children of ages 2 to 6 and with educable and trainable retardates of ages 8 to 11. The principle of the system was based upon token reinforcers. The tokens were presented contingent upon correct responses and could be exchanged for items the child could keep. In the previous studies toys of various values could be obtained when a sufficient number of tokens had been accrued in visible containers.

This system was adapted for use with the adolescent of the present study. In the adaptation there were three types of token, distinguished by color. The tokens were of different value in terms of the items for which the tokens could be exchanged. A blue token was valued at $1/10$ of one cent. A white token was valued at $1/5$ of a cent. A red token was worth $1/2$ of a cent.

The child's acquisition of tokens was plotted so that visual evidence of the reinforcers was available. The tokens could be used to purchase a variety of items. These items, chosen by the subject, could range in value from pennies to whatever the subject wished to work for. Records were kept of the tokens earned by the subject and of the manner in which the tokens were used.

Reading Materials

The reading material used was taken from Science Research Associates' reading-kit materials. The SRA kits consist of stories developed for, and grouped into, grade levels. Each story includes a series of questions which can be used to assess the reader's comprehension of the story. The reading training program was adapted from the materials as follows:

Vocabulary words. A running list was made of the new words that appeared in the series of stories. The list finally included each different word that appeared in the stories that were presented. From this list, the new vocabulary for each story was selected, and each word was typed on a separate 3×5 card.

Oral reading materials. Each paragraph in the stories was typed on a 5×8 card. Each story could thus be presented to the subject paragraph by paragraph.

Silent reading and comprehensive-question materials. Each story, with its comprehensive questions, was typed on an $8\frac{1}{2} \times 13$ sheet of white paper.

Procedure

Vocabulary presentation. The procedure for each story in the series commenced with the presentation of the new words introduced in that story. The words were presented individually on the cards, and the subject was asked to pronounce them. A correct response to a word-stimulus card was reinforced with a mid-value token. After a correct response to a word, the card was dropped from the group of cards yet to be presented. The subject was instructed to indicate words that he did not know the meaning of, and this information was provided in such cases.

When an incorrect response to a word stimulus occurred, or when the subject gave no response, the instructional technician gave the correct response. The subject then repeated the word while looking at the stimulus word. However, the word card involved was returned to the group of cards still to be presented. A card was not dropped from the group until it was read correctly without prompting. After an error on a word stimulus, only a low-value token was given on the next trial when the word was read correctly without prompting. The vocabulary-presentation phase of the training was continued until each word was read correctly without prompting.

Oral reading. Upon completion of the vocabulary materials, each paragraph was individually presented to the subject in the order in which the paragraph occurred in the story. When correct reading responses were made to each word in the paragraph, a high-value token was given upon completion of the paragraph. When a paragraph contained errors, the subject was corrected, and he repeated the word correctly while looking at the word. The paragraph was put aside, and when the other paragraphs had been completed, the paragraph containing errors was again presented. The paragraph was repeated until it was done correctly in its entirety — at which time a mid-value token was presented. When all paragraphs in a story had been completed correctly, the next phase of the training was begun.

Silent reading and comprehensive questions. Following the oral reading the subject was given the sheet containing the story and questions. He was instructed to read the story silently and to answer the questions beneath the story. He was also instructed that it was important to read to understand the story so that he could answer the questions.

Reinforcement was given on a variable interval schedule for attentive behavior during the silent-reading phase. That is, as long as he appropriately scanned the material he was given a low-value reinforcer an average of every fifteen seconds. The exact time for reinforcement was determined by a table of random numbers varying from one to thirty seconds. Whenever he did anything else than peruse the material, no reinforcement was given. The next interval was then timed from the moment he returned to the silent reading, with the stipulation that no reinforcement be given sooner than five seconds after he returned to the reading. If the interval was less than five seconds, a token was not given until the next interval had also occurred. Timing was done by a continuously running stop-watch. The subject was also given an extra mid-value token at the end of the silently read story on those occasions where he read without moving his lips.

Upon completion of the story, the subject wrote his answers to the questions typed below the story and gave his answers to the technician. For each correct answer, the subject received a high-value token. For an answer with a spelling error, he was reinforced with a mid-value token when he had corrected the answer. For incorrect answers the subject had to reread the appropriate paragraph, correct his answer, and he then received a mid-value token.

Vocabulary review. Some of the vocabulary words presented to the subject in the first phase of training were words he already could read. Many others, however, were words that the procedure was set up to teach. The oral reading phase performance indicated the level of the subject's retention of the words he had learned — and also provided further training trials on the words not already learned. A further assessment of the subject's retention of the words that he did not know in the vocabulary training was made after each twenty stories of the SRA materials had been read. This test of individually presented words for each story was started about three days after completion of the twenty stories and constituted fairly long-term retention.

This test was also used as a review for the subject, and further training on the words was given. This was first done by reinforcing with a low-value token for every word he read correctly. However, the subject's attention was not well maintained by this reinforcement, and the procedure was changed to provide a mid-value token for correctly read words. When he could not read a word, or missed one, he was prompted and had to correctly repeat the name of the word while looking at it. This word card was then put aside and presented later, at which time the subject was reinforced with a low-value token if he read it correctly. If not, the procedure was repeated until a correct unprompted trial occurred.

Achievement tests.   Prior to the commencement of the training, the subject was tested to assess his reading performance, and during the period of experimental training he was given two additional reading-achievement tests. The first one given was the Developmental Reading Test. (At this time his vision and hearing were also tested and found to be normal.) After forty-five training sessions another reading test was given, this time the California Reading Test, Form BB, for grades 1, 2, 3, and L-4. Twenty-five sessions later, just before the termination of the study, the subject was given the California Reading Test, Form BB, for grades 4, 5, and 6. His performance on the three reading tests constituted one of the measures of his progress. The tests were given at the Arizona State University Reading Center.

Training sessions.   The training sessions would ordinarily last for one hour or less, although a few sessions were as short as thirty minutes or as long as two hours. Not all of this time was spent in reading, however. A good deal of time was spent in arranging the materials, recording performance, keeping count of the reinforcers, plotting the reinforcers accrued, and so on. The time spent actually reading was tabulated. During the 4½-month experimental period seventy training sessions were conducted, with an average of about thirty-five minutes spent per session, or a total of forty hours of reading training.

During the period of training the subject made many reading responses. Figure 1 shows the number of single-word reading responses the subject made as a function of the hours of time spent in training. An estimate of the number of single-word reading responses was obtained from tabulating each presentation of a word card, the number of words in the stories, and the reading comprehension questions at the end of each story, as well as the words presented in the later single-word retention

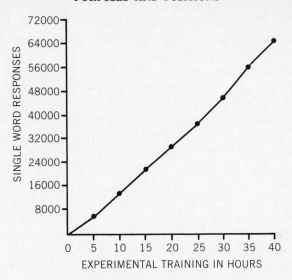

Fig. 1. Number of single-word reading responses as a function of the time in experimental reading training

test. Actually, the number of words in the stories is an estimate obtained from the mean number of words in two out of each five stories. Thus, rather than giving the true absolute number of reading responses made, the figure gives an estimate. However, the most important aspect of the figure is to indicate the rate of this single-word reading-response measure as a function of time in experimental training. As can be seen, as the training progressed the subject covered the reading material at a slightly more rapid rate, as is shown by the slight positive acceleration in the curve. The importance of this result is to indicate that the child's behavior of attending to the task and making the appropriate reading responses did not diminish throughout the period of training. Thus, the reinforcement system employed was capable of maintaining the behavior for a long period of time. During this time the attentional and cooperative behaviors instigated resulted in many, many learning trials—*sine qua non* for the acquisition of achievement in any skill.

Before reading each story the subject was presented with individual cards for all the words included in that story which had not been presented in a previous story. When these words were presented, the subject would read a certain proportion correctly on first presentation, the other words being missed on the first presentation. The ones missed were considered to be new words, words that he had not previously learned. These words were tabulated separately. The cumulative number of these new words as a function of every five stories read is shown by the top curve of figure 2. (The data for the first ten stories are not presented since they were not available for all three curves.) As this curve indicates, 761 new words were presented during the training.

Thus, the subject missed 761 words when they were first presented to him. However, he was given training trials on these words, and then he read them again in the oral reading of the paragraph. The number of these words that he missed in this oral reading phase is plotted in the bottom curve of figure 2. This curve then indicates the number of errors made on the second reading test of the words that had been previously learned. Thus, only 176 words out of 761 (about 23 percent) were missed in the oral reading phase—showing retention for 585 words. The results indicate that the criterion of one correct unprompted reading trial in the original vocabulary-learning phase produced considerable learning when the words were read in context.

The middle curve in figure 2 involves a measure of long-term retention of the words that had been learned. This measure was obtained by testing the subject on the words, presented singly, that had been learned in the preceding twenty stories. This test was given 10 to 15 days after the training occurred. The training thus included the previous single-word presentations of the words, as well as those same words read orally and silently. In addition, however, the subject had also learned a considerable number of other words by the time of this test. As the middle curve shows, when tested 10 to 15 days later, he read 430 of the 761 words correctly, or, conversely, 331 words (about 43 percent) were missed. Thus, the procedures produced retention when the words were later presented out of context after a considerable intervening period.

The results appearing in figure 2 indicate that the child covered a considerable amount of reading material, that he learned to read a number of new words when presented individually or in context, and that he retained a good proportion of what he had learned. The results also indicate that the child improved during the training in his retention. That is, his rate of getting new words in the first-presentation phase continued at a high rate throughout the study. (This supports the results shown in figure 1 indicating that the child's behavior did not weaken during the training.) However, his "rate" of missing the new words on the second and third presentations decreased; that is, he retained more of the words he had learned. Thus, tabulation indicated that

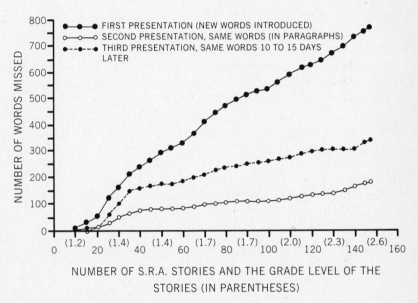

Fig. 2. Number of words missed on first, second, and third presentations for the 150 stories

for the first thirty-five stories only about 33 percent of the words learned were retained 10 to 15 days later, whereas the subject's subsequent retention increased to about 55 percent. It should be noted that this improvement occurred even though the difficulty of the words (as shown in figure 2 by the numbers in parentheses) became progressively greater during the training, moving from the 1.2 grade level of difficulty to the 2.6 grade level.

These results receive support from the data presented in figure 3. As already indicated, on the first presentation of the vocabulary

of a story, some words were missed out of the total presented —
and the subject was then presented with training on these words.
Figure 3 shows the number of the words presented and missed
in ratio to the total number presented as this ratio is related to
the number and difficulty of the stories presented. A smaller ratio
indicates that the subject missed fewer of the total vocabulary
words when they were presented for the first time. As can be
seen in figure 3, as the child read more stories in his training
(even though they became more difficult), he missed fewer and
fewer words that were presented to him. It should be stressed
that he was thus improving in the extent to which he correctly
responded to new words on *first* presentation. This improvement
appeared to be correlated with other observations that indicated
the subject was also beginning to learn to sound out words as a
function of the training. For example, he remarked that when in

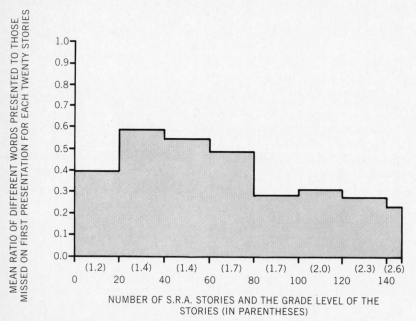

Fig. 3. Ratio of words presented to those missed on first presentation
for the 150 stories

the judge's office he thought a sign said "information" because he
could read the "in" and the "for" and the "mation." In addition,
he reported a number of times that the training was helping him

in school, that reading was getting easier for him in school, that he liked the reading training better as he went along, and so on. It would be expected (as will be supported by other data) that as the reading training improved his reading in school, the things he learned in school would also improve his performance in the reading training. It is this effect that may also be reflected in his increasing ability to read the new words presented to him.

In addition to this direct evidence of the child's progress in reading training, and the foregoing indirect evidence that the reading training was having general effects upon the child's behavior, the study was formulated to obtain other sources of information concerning the child's progress. One means of doing this was to give the child reading achievement tests before beginning the reading training as well as during the training. The results of these tests are shown in figure 4. The first point on the curve is a measurement obtained by use of the Developmental Reading Test giving a total score of reading achievement showing that the subject was performing at the grade 2 level. After forty-

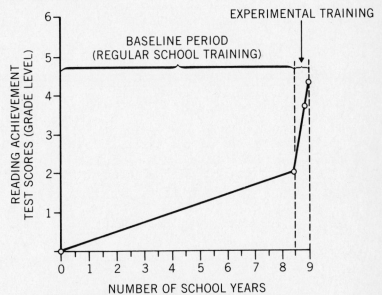

Fig. 4. Reading-achievement test scores as a function of 8½ years of school training and 4½ months of experimental training

five reading-training sessions, the subject's performance on the California Reading Test shows a gain to the 3.8 grade level. By the end of the training, after twenty-five more training sessions, he had advanced to the 4.3 grade level on the California Reading Test.

Another indication of the general effect of the reading training came from the child's performance in school, both in school achievement and deportment. The period of reading training coincided with a school term. The boy received passing grades in all subjects: C in Physical Education, D in General Shop, D in English, and D in Mathematics. It should be emphasized that these grades represent the first courses that this child had ever passed, and thus his finest academic performance.

Furthermore, the subject began to behave better while in school. The boy had always been a behavior problem in school, and this continued into the period during which he received reading training. As figure 5 shows, during the first month of the

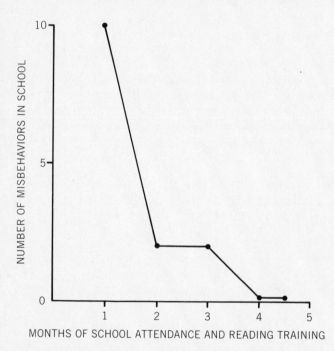

Fig. 5. Number of official misbehaviors in school as a function of time in the experimental training

training he committed ten misbehaviors that resulted in the
receipt of demerits. The behaviors were as follows: disturbance
in class (two times), disobedience in class (five times), loitering
(two times), and tardiness. In the second month he was given
demerits for scuffling on the school grounds and also for creating
a disturbance. In the third month he was given demerits for
cutting a math class and for profanity in class. As the figure
shows, however, no misbehaviors occurred in the fourth month
or in the half month before the conclusion of the school term.

The subject requested that the tokens be exchanged for items
that he wanted in sessions 12, 17, 25, 31, 35, 43, 49, 55, and in
the last session he was given the value of the remaining tokens
in cash. Items included were a pair of "Beatle" shoes, hair
pomade, a phonograph record, an ice cream sundae, a ticket to
a school function, money for his brother who was going to reform
school, and so on. Further information regarding the reinforcement system is given in figure 6. The vertical axis of the graph
represents the ratio of the number of tokens obtained by the
subject relative to the number of single-word reading responses
which he emitted. Lesser ratios thus indicate more reading

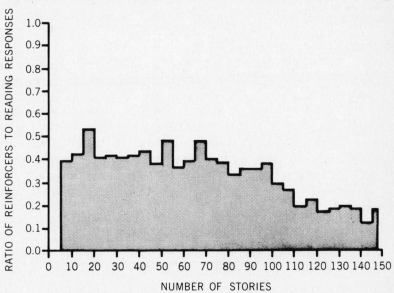

Fig. 6. Ratio of the number of tokens received divided by
the number of reading responses made as a function of
the number of stories read

responses per reinforcer. This ratio was plotted as a function of the progress made in the training program, as given by the number of SRA stories he had completed. As the training progressed the subject gradually made an increasingly greater number of reading responses per reinforcer. This effect was not accomplished by changing the rules by which the reinforcers were administered. The effect, which was planned in the training program, resulted from the fact that the stories became longer as the grade level was raised. Since, for example, paragraph reading was reinforced by the paragraph, the longer the paragraph, the greater the number of reading responses that had to be emitted before reinforcement was obtained. Thus, at the end of training the subject was getting about half as much reinforcement per response as at the beginning of training. It should also be indicated that the stories were more difficult as the training progressed, so the effort involved in reading was increasing — although reinforcement for the reading was decreasing.

During the 4½ months of training, which involved forty hours of reading training and the emission of an estimated 64,307 single-word reading responses, the subject received $20.31.

Discussion

In this section the various aspects of the reading training procedures will first be discussed. Then the implications of the results and analysis will be outlined both for further studies of remedial reading training as well as for a learning conception of certain aspects of cultural deprivation and delinquency.

The method of reading training used in the present study was derived from previous studies (Staats, 1964a; 1962) with preschool children in which words were first presented singly, then in sentences, and finally in short stories. The present study indicated that SRA materials can be adapted for a similar type of presentation in conjunction with the type of reinforcer system previously developed. From the SRA materials it was possible to present single-word training trials and oral-reading training and to develop a silent reading training procedure, all involving reinforcement.

When the training of reading, at least in part, is considered as instrumental (operant) discrimination learning, the learning task consists of having the subject emit the correct speech response while looking at the verbal stimulus—this process being followed by reinforcement. This basic procedure was elaborated in the present study to include two levels of reinforcement. An unprompted reading response on the first trial was reinforced more heavily than one that had been previously missed. This procedure appeared to produce learning that was retained very well when the child later read the words orally in a paragraph, with considerable retention also occurring when the child was tested on the individual words 10 to 15 days later.

It may seem incongruous at first to attempt to reinforce silent reading since this behavior is not observable. However, it should be remembered that the subject actually has two types of behavior in the silent reading act. He looks at the verbal stimuli —that is, attends—and he makes "reading" verbal responses to the verbal stimuli. While the reading responses cannot be monitored when they are covert, the attending behavior can be. Of course, there is a danger involved in reinforcing the behavior of just looking at something. Perhaps the child will do nothing else. If he is heavily reinforced for sitting and looking at a page, and the actual reading responses are effortful, he may not emit the reading responses. The present procedure was set up to eliminate this possibility by using a double contingency. The child was reinforced for simple attention, but the reinforcement was low in value. The opportunity for a greater amount of reinforcement came during the answering of the questions. Thus, although simple attention was reinforced lightly, attention and reading responses were reinforced much more heavily. In this way it was possible to use reinforcement in a procedure designed to maintain reading for understanding, in addition to simple "word-naming." (These results could be generalized to other types of learning.) Furthermore, this procedure provided an opportunity to train the subject to read silently. Although he had a tendency to make vocal or lip responses while reading, it was possible to strengthen reading without these other responses through differentially reinforcing the correct silent reading.

Thus, it may be concluded that the reading program increased the child's reading vocabulary as shown by the various measures of retention used in the study, the tests of reading achievement, as well as the child's improved school performance and his verbal description of improved attitude toward and performance in reading in school. There were also suggestions that the child was acquiring a "unit reading repertoire," that is, the general ability to sound out words through making the correct response to single letters and syllables. Thus, for example, the child made errors on fewer and fewer of the new words presented as the training progressed, even though the words were of greater difficulty. In addition, he retained a greater proportion of the words he learned as he went on. Further research of the present type must be conducted to test the possibilities for using a more phonic system of remedial reading training with the present type of subject.

A final point should be made concerning the training procedures used in the present study. The procedures are very specific and relatively simple. Thus it was not necessary to have a person highly trained in education to administer the training. In the present case the instructional technician was a probation officer. It might also be suggested that anyone with a high school education and the ability to read could have administered the training. This has implications for the practical application of the present methods, since one of the questions that arises in this context concerns the economy of the procedures. The procedures as described involved a ratio of one trainer to one student as many remedial teaching procedures do. But the simplicity of the procedures used in this case suggests the possibility that savings may be effected because the instructional technician need not be so highly trained. Thus, the procedures could be widely applied or adapted by various professionals; for example, social workers, prison officials, remedial teachers, tutors, and so on. In an even more economical application, helpers of professionals could be used to actually administer the procedures; for example, selected delinquents (or prisoners) could administer the procedures to other delinquents. Thus, the procedures could be utilized in various situations, such as settlement houses, homes for juvenile delinquents, prison training programs, parts of adult education, and so on. All that is needed is a suitable system of reinforcers to back up the tokens.

It is relevant to add here that the type of token-reinforcer system employed in the present study was first developed by Staats in 1959 in the context of an exploratory study of remedial reading. Communication of the efficacy of the token-reinforcer system to Jack Michael at the University of Houston began its use there in work with retarded. Further communication with Ayllon led to adoption of the token-reinforcer system in the psychiatric ward (Ayllon and Azrin, 1968). The token-reinforcer system has since been widely employed in various forms in educational and clinical behavior modification studies (for example, see Wolf, Giles, and Hall, 1968; and Ullmann and Krasner, 1969). After the initial development of the token-reinforcement system, Staats also adapted it for work with preschool children in a series of basic and behavior modification studies of various types of complex learning (see Staats, 1968; Staats, Finley, Minke, Wolf, and Brooks, 1964; Staats, Minke, Finley, and Wolf, 1964; Staats, Staats, Schutz, and Wolf, 1962).

Furthermore, additional studies have been conducted in the present project to further substantiate the general efficacy of the reinforcer system and the reading procedures, with various types of subjects. Thus, the present training procedures have been employed successfully in a study involving eighteen additional children (including seven educable retardates as well as several emotionally disturbed children) of junior high school age in Madison, Wisconsin. The instructional technicians were nine average high school students and nine adult volunteers (Staats, et al., 1967).

In a later study (Staats, Minke, and Butts, 1970) thirty-two Negro ghetto children with behavior problems were given the treatment in Milwaukee. The instructional technicians were literate Negro high school children from ghetto schools and two formerly unemployed Negro adults employed on the project in full-time positions. The treatment was conducted for a semester, and the results were again successful. Increases were shown in achievement tests, grades, attendance, and deportment, in comparison to a control group of thirty-two children. In addition, Staats (1968) has conducted a long term project with young children in the study and treatment of cognitive deficits in such areas as first reading acquisition, number skill learning, and writing acquisition. The present methods and principles receive strong support as being generally applicable from these various studies.

In the present study, it may be worth pointing out that the results indicated that the child advanced as many years in reading achievement, as measured by the tests, during the experimental training as he had in his previous school history. A comparison of the relative costs — in the present case about forty hours of time of a person not necessarily trained in teaching and

$20.31 for the reinforcers versus 8½ years of trained teachers' time, albeit in a group situation — suggests that the procedure introduced in the present study may not be uneconomical, even without improvements in the method. And, as will be further described, the child's failure in school may in many cases be considered as a contributor to the child's delinquency — which also carries a high cost to society. The present results, in suggesting that the training procedures may also effect general improvements in behavior, including misbehaviors in school, thus have further implications concerning the economy of the procedures.

The present study, among other things, tests the feasibility of using the type of reinforcing system previously applied successfully to younger children to the study of learning in older children — in this case a fourteen-year-old juvenile delinquent. The reinforcer system worked very well with the present subject, maintaining his attention and working behaviors in good strength for a long period of time. And there was every reason to expect that the study could have been continued for a much longer period, probably as long as it would have taken to train the child to read normally.

It should be noted that although the amount of reinforcement given decreases during the training, as shown in figure 6, the reading behavior is maintained in good strength throughout the study, as shown in figures 1 and 2; thus, less and less reinforcement is needed to maintain the behavior even though the material increases in difficulty. As already described, this occurred because a progressively greater number of reading responses was necessary per reinforcer. This is analogous to gradually raising the ratio of responses to the reinforcers as considered in terms of ratio schedules of reinforcement. Staats has suggested that this type of gradual increase must occur to produce good work behaviors in humans (Staats, 1963).

This result in the present study is in part an answer to the question of whether the use of extrinsic reinforcers in training will produce a child who is dependent upon these reinforcers. It is not possible to discuss this topic fully now. However, it may be said that the extrinsic reinforcement can be gradually decreased until, as was happening with the present child, reading becomes reinforcing itself, or other sources of reinforcement maintain the behavior.

A word should be said concerning the relevance of reinforcement variables in the treatment of non-learning in culturally
deprived children. Typically, as in the present case, such children
do not, as a result of their home experiences, acquire "reinforcer
systems" appropriate for maintaining learning in the traditional
classroom. Rosen (1956) has shown that, in the present terminology, lower class children do not have experiences that make
school involvement and learning itself positively reinforcing.
This deficit, among others that affect the reinforcer system, can
be expected to lead to poor school learning and other behavioral
deficits. In such cases, there are increased opportunities for other
poor social attitudes and undesirable behaviors to develop, as
suggested in the introduction and exemplified in the present case.

The present study suggests that these conditions can be
reversed through the application of learning principles and
reinforcement variables to the task of repairing the child's
behavioral-achievement deficit. There were indications that this
treatment resulted in improvement in the reinforcement value
of (attitudes toward) school for this child and consequently in
the decrease in incidence of misbehaviors in school. The results
thus suggest that under appropriate conditions the deficit in
behavior stemming from the child's inadequate reinforcing system may be, at least in part, repaired by a properly administered,
effective reinforcement system, resulting in a decrease in undesirable behaviors.

A comment should be made about the possibility of a Hawthorne effect; that is, that the social reinforcement provided by
the instructional technician and possible extraexperimental
reinforcement contributed to the results in the present study. It
would be expected that such reinforcers could contribute to the
overall effect—and in the present case the expenditure for the
material reinforcers was small. In general, it can be expected
that individuals will vary in the extent to which social reinforcers
will be effective. For example, in preschool children social reinforcement is ineffective for long term training (Staats, 1964c,
1962), and the same would be expected for many individuals with
behavior problems. Ordinarily, it might be expected that the
weaker other sources of reinforcement are for the individual, the
stronger must be the reinforcer system of the treatment
procedure.

In conclusion, the present study helps support and replicate the previous findings and extends the general procedures and principles to the study of an adolescent child who is culturally deprived and is also a juvenile delinquent. The various sources of data used suggest that the present procedures and principles are applicable to this population also. Based upon these suggestions, further studies will be conducted on culturally deprived children, delinquent and nondelinquent, as well as studies of other types of nonachieving or underachieving readers.

It should also be indicated that the present study indicates the possibility for developing procedures for the objective application and testing of laboratory-derived learning principles within the context of an actual problem of behavior. As previously indicated (Staats, 1968, 1964a), verification of learning principles in the context of a problem of human behavior constitutes one way to further the generality of the principles themselves. It may thus be suggested that such studies have two types of implication: they have implications for people interested in dealing with the problems of human behavior, as well as for those interested in the extension and verification of the basic science.

References

Ayllon, T., and Azrin, N. H. *The Token Economy.* New York: Appleton-Century-Crofts, 1968.

Ellson, D. G., Barber, L., Engle, T. L., and Kampaerth, L. "Programmed Tutoring: A Teaching Aid and a Research Tool," *Reading Research Quarterly* 1 (1965).

Rosen, B. C. "The Achievement Syndrome: A Psychocultural Dimension of Social Stratification," *American Sociological Review* 21 (1956): 203–211.

Staats, A. W. "A Case in and a Strategy for the Extension of Learning Principles to Problems of Human Behavior," in A. W. Staats (ed.), *Human Learning.* New York: Holt, Rinehart & Winston, 1964.(a)

Staats, A. W. "Conditioned Stimuli, Conditioned Reinforcers, and Word Meaning," in A. W. Staats (ed.), *Human Learning.* New York: Holt, Rinehart & Winston, 1964.(b)

Staats, A. W. (ed.) *Human Learning.* New York: Holt, Rinehart & Winston, 1964.(c)

Staats, A. W. "An Integrated-functional Learning Approach to Complex Human Behavior," in B. Kleinmuntz (ed.), *Problem Solving: Research, Method and Theory.* New York: Wiley, 1966.

Staats, A. W. *Learning, Language, and Cognition.* New York: Holt, Rinehart & Winston, 1968.

Staats, A. W., Finley, J. R., Minke, K. A., and Wolf, M. "Reinforcement Variables in the Control of Unit Reading Responses," *Journal of the Experimental Analysis of Behavior* 7 (1964): 139–149.(d)

Staats, A. W., Minke, K. A., and Butts, P. "A Token-Reinforcement Remedial Reading Program Administered by Black Therapy-Technicians to Problem Black Children," *Behavior Therapy* 1 (1970):331–353.

Staats, A. W., Minke, K. A., Finley, J. R., Wolf, M., and Brooks, L. O. "A Reinforcer System and Experimental Procedure for the Laboratory Study of Reading Acquisition," *Child Development* 35 (1964):209–231.

Staats, A. W., Minke, K. A., Goodwin, W., and Landeen, J. "Cognitive Behavior Modification: 'Motivated Learning' Reading Treatment with Subprofessional Therapy-Technicians," *Behavior Research and Therapy* 5 (1967):283–299.

Staats, A. W. with contributions by Staats, C. K. *Complex Human Behavior.* New York: Holt, Rinehart & Winston, 1963.

Staats, A. W., Staats, C. K., Schutz, R. E., and Wolf, M. "The Conditioning of Textual Responses Utilizing 'Extrinsic' Reinforcers," *Journal of the Experimental Analysis of Behavior* 5 (1962):33–40.

Ullmann, L. P., and Krasner, L. *A Psychological Approach to Abnormal Behavior.* New York: Prentice-Hall, 1969.

Wolf, M. M., Giles, E. K., and Hall, R. V. "Experiment with Token-Reinforcement in a Remedial Classroom," *Behavior Research and Therapy* 6 (1968):51–64.

From *Child Development* 36 (1965):925–42.

The present methods of reading training were formulated, and the present paper written by the first author as part of a long-term project applying learning principles and procedures to the experimental study of language-learning and reading. The methods were applied by the second author in his position as an officer of the Maricopa County Juvenile Probation Department. The second author also collected and tabulated the data and aided in its graphic presentation. Appreciation is expressed to Chief Probation Officer John H. Walker for lending cooperation in the conduct of the study. In addition, Mary J. Butterfield made important contributions in the preparation of the reading materials used in the study, Brenda Shields typed the materials, and Janet Munir typed the present manuscript.

study questions

1. What major purpose for reading do you think Allen might consider most important?

2. What might be the major purpose for reading that Gray and Rogers would accept?

3. How about yourself? If you were asked at a P.T.A. meeting to state in nontechnical language, and in fewer than thirty words, what you consider to be the major purpose for reading, what would you say?

4. Do you consider yourself to be a fully literate person, one who has attained the major purpose for reading? By whose standards?

5. If you believe you have not yet attained the goal of full literacy, where does the fault lie? Your teachers? Your schools? Yourself? What can be done about it?

6. What are the major points of disagreement between Postman and Staats, particularly with reference to the context in which instruction occurs?

7. Suppose you were asked to defend the proposition that actually Postman and Staats accept the same major purpose for reading. What would you say?

8. What are some elements of the positions proposed by Postman and by Staats that you find acceptable?

9. Let's go back to the P.T.A. meeting. In another fifty words, explain your position and show how a reading program organized according to your position would attain the purpose you previously identified.

TWO

language and the factors in reading

objectives

As a result of reading these articles and answering the questions at the end of this chapter you should be able to:

- specify factors that are relevant to reading instruction
- list ways of controlling factors in order to improve reading instruction
- explain the use of conceptual models to show interaction of factors

rationale

The preceding chapter directed attention toward motives and goals in reading. Now, for an inside-out look at the reading process itself, we turn to the study of selected elements involved. Because reading is basically a language activity, major concern is directed at language factors. But physical, perceptual, and emotional elements are involved too — and these are included. Perhaps most needed of all is the concept of parts interaction, of how different factors relate to a conceptual model for the reading process — and for this reason we begin with an important exploration of the relation of parts to total theory.

introduction

What goes on when a person reads? What does he do? Why does he do it? What does he gain? So many factors must be examined to answer these questions that we are confronted with a paradox: On one hand, we want to *delimit* the factors we know into some manageable form for study; on the other, we constantly discover new factors.

Early scientific studies of reading factors often centered on eye movement, the "ballet of the eyeballs" as one observer described it. Less formally, however, reading theorists of the nineteenth century also considered methodological factors, including forerunners of the present so-called phonics versus look-say controversy. Throughout the early study of reading, selection or delineation of elements depended predominantly on the definition of reading held by researchers and practitioners. An early nineteenth century definition was, "reading is talking from a book." A hundred years later Thorndike postulated "reading as thinking." The gradual shift in definition influenced the shifting choice of factors deemed important for study. In our opinion the influence of a priori definition and practice has lessened somewhat in recent decades.

A major change has been brought about by increased communication between the reading specialty and related disciplines. For example, linguistic science had little to say about reading instruction (and vice versa) until Leonard Bloomfield crossed the line to publish linguist-looks-at-reading articles in *The Elementary English Review* in 1942. Nearly twenty years passed before the linguist began to appear with dependable frequency in reading instruction periodicals, as consultant or coauthor on basal reading texts and as author of books dealing with the theory and practice of teaching reading. Here is an instance in which a related field disclosed reading factors that resulted in changing the way we perceive the teaching of reading.

More recently the comparatively new field of psycholinguistics has contributed information pertinent to what reading is, how the skill is acquired, and how it operates. Originated in 1952, psycholinguistics is the study of interaction between the language system and the strategies of the user of language. It is noteworthy that the most widely attended meeting of the International Reading Association Convention of 1971 was that devoted to psycholinguistics. Again, this field illustrates the delineation of reading factors through a related discipline rather than from within the reading field itself.

Other disciplines not centrally concerned with language per se have brought awareness of additional important elements to reading—sociology, anthropology, and various other fields mentioned in this chapter. All this points to a need to continually redefine and reconceptualize the factors involved in reading.

As we examine this need, three fundamental ideas should be kept in mind. First, the tendency to embrace one factor as all important in reading development must be avoided; there is simply too much evidence that reading skill depends on a complexity of factors. Thus a language-factor proponent may insist that reading success is completely dependent on grapheme-phoneme (letter-sound) relationship or on morphophonemics or on syntactical control. A sociology-factor enthusiast may proffer that reading success depends on the manipulation of sociologic variables or on adjusting reading instruction to social status. Attention to any single factor as being totally determinant of the general factor of reading itself can be termed *reductionism*. It is unlikely that reductionist theories for teaching reading or defining reading can be of ultimate value.

Second is the realization that factors often have been given arbitrary boundaries. Suppose that we are accustomed to looking for cause-effect relations between home conditions, community environment, and peer influence on the one hand and reading attainment on the other. Now suppose that in each of these factors we begin to see that television plays a large part. Further study may convince us that a new array of factors, a recombining of observations, will tell us more about what we want to know. We might, for example, denote a television factor as a matter for specific study. There is nothing sacred—and nothing permanent—about a list of factors.

Third is the comparatively recent emphasis on factor interaction, the realization that the influence of factors may best be understood not as a "sum of parts" but through a weighing of interrelationships. Older studies of reading difficulty attempted to identify from a list those factors that seemed to be *weak* or *strong*. It quickly became apparent that only limited validity lay in assessing them one by one. Presence or absence of any single factor did not lead to accurate prediction or remediation. But study, say, the interaction between self-concept and socioeconomic level as they affect reading performance — or the interaction of oral syntactical ability, auding, and reading method — and relationships begin to surface. The model building suggested by Jenkinson in the following article gives particular insight into one manner in which the factor interrelationship idea can be expressed for the purpose of clarity and experimentation.

As you read the selections that follow, keep these three ideas in mind: (1) What other factors need to be considered along with the one under scrutiny? (2) Would a new alignment of phenomena, a new way of looking at the findings, result in a more potent set of factors? (3) What evidence does each selection offer regarding interaction of factors, or does the writer appear to ignore influences other than those he is dealing with?

A valid, comprehensive theory of reading would increase our power to study factors and the relation of factors to the total process. Thus far, no such theory has evolved. In a brilliant and sweeping article Jenkinson suggests why—and what might be done to rectify the situation.

Sources of Knowledge for Theories of Reading

MARION D. JENKINSON

I am perhaps being bold, not to say foolish, to undertake to speak to the topic of this paper. My reasons for consenting to do so spring from my own need to explore why, after seventy-five years of research and investigation, there has not emerged a coherent construct within which we can examine reading. Two aphorisms point up my dilemma. "Experience keeps a dear school but fools will learn in no other" (Benjamin Franklin). Yet, on the other hand, as an old Welsh proverb states, "Experience is the fool's best teacher; the wise do not need it".

This paper, then, will attempt first to suggest why this failure has occurred, and then will indicate some points of departure which may be productive for the gradual evolution of theories. More questions will be posed than answers given, but it was Einstein who reminded us that the asking of the right questions may lead to greater knowledge than the discovery of scientific facts. Yet again, I must counteract this with another adage: "The greater fool may ask more than the wisest man can answer".

The following topics will be discussed briefly in the remainder of this paper: the reasons for the failure to evolve theories, model making in reading, some questions concerning the assimilation of meaning, and a triad of sources for a reading model.

Reasons for Failure to Evolve Theories

The first reason is not peculiar to the reading field, but has great pertinence for it. I have been concerned recently with educational epistemology (Jenkinson, 1967). My own concern has been supported in the United States by Cooper (1967). What *are* the sources of our knowledge in education? It seems to me that the traditional six ways of knowing identified by philosophers — appeal to authority, intuition, formal logic, empiricism, pragmatism, and scepticism — should all be applied to our endeavours to know more about what is happening in education. Of course, some of these methods are superior to others for certain purposes, and their effectiveness will depend upon the nature of the thing to be known. My quarrel is that because the empirical method has proved so effective in scientific enquiry, we in education have allowed this to influence us too exclusively. Educational evidence which is not labelled "research", or does not present evidence in what is often a pseudoscientific manner, is usually suspect.

More recently the term "development" or "experiment" has become the magic lamp, by rubbing which we hope to solve our educational problems. On the surface this new dogma appears to espouse pragmatism, the method of evaluating things on the basis of their palpable effects. Yet the variety of conclusions, and the conflicting and partial nature of the evidence from the myriad of reading programs and innovations of the past decade, not only leads to scepticism but also calls for prudence in application of any of the findings. We are still far from codifying the experiential proof of these efforts since we are still at such a primitive stage of collecting significant data. It has been demonstrated frequently that the teacher is the one single important variable contributing to reading success. Yet we are only just beginning to realize that we must examine, in depth, the teacher's behavior and, particularly, language performance in terms both of linguistic mastery and the ways in which language is used to elicit learning.

Another common error which has crept into our educational thought arises from a mistaken notion even of scientific truth. As Wiseman (1966) has suggested:

> Development in the history of science which has led to a clearer and more widespread realization that the distinguishing marks of a scientific hypothesis, as compared, for example, with an affirmation, or belief, is the fact that it must be intrinsically *susceptible to disproof,* rather than that it can be proved to be true. The most that can ever be said about the truth of a hypothesis, even in the more highly developed of the physical sciences, is that all the results obtained so far are in line with what we would have predicted from it.

In reading, we frequently fall into the trap of attempting to "prove or produce" evidence that one method or set of materials is superior to another. Sometimes the burden of truth should lie rather with the established mode. The efficacy of innovation might well be subject to disproof rather than proof.

When one examines the epistemology of reading, it appears that superficially we cover the range of sources suggested above. Yet, I would argue that we need to acquire a true appreciation for a balance of all six methods and develop the skills of knowing when to select the most appropriate one or combination of them for the specific reading area we are examining.

This is not just another plea for an eclectic approach to reading. We should rather recognize those specific and peculiar contributions that differing sources of knowledge, as well as different disciplines, can make. Too often the "eclectic approach" has served to camouflage rather than elucidate our concepts.

Model Making in Reading

Model making in many aspects of education, including reading, is playing a new role. Hopefully, this desire to create models will not decline into a mere mystique, but will enable us through their construction to show interrelationships between concepts and to suggest areas of ignorance. The Maccias (1966) have suggested that educational theorizing might profit much through the use of models, though it is acknowledged that model making in education, as in all the social sciences, is of a special kind and perhaps of a greater complexity than that encountered in the sciences. However, as Eastwood (1966) suggests, though there are many ways of using the term *model,* a systematic enquiry model, the end product of which is explanation rather than a solution of various problems, is most appropriate for people in education to consider. Eastwood further suggests that this may be conceived as a system of four dimensions — the referential, the theoretical, the experimental, and the validational. Such systems should provide a general model which encompasses the framework for the derivation of specific models from which testable hypotheses can be deduced.

One of the most common misunderstandings is that the word *model* is seen as synonymous for theory. It is not appropriate to discourse at length on the distinctions and variety of definitions of the two words. There is a consensus, however, that the two terms are not identical. George (1966) compares a model to a skeleton, whereas the relevant theory can be compared to the complete organism.

My reference to this current work of enquiry into models and theories is really to suggest that in reading we must become more sophisticated in our model making. Several models have been used in reading. The earliest ones were by Gray (1960) with later additions by Robinson (1966). Holmes (1965) used factor analysis to produce his substrata-factor theory of reading, while Smith (1963) has adapted Guilford's model of the intellect to the reading process, and more recently McCullough (1968), Kingston (1961), and Cleland (1965) have suggested other models.

All these models, it is true, attempt to clarify and explicate the relationships between one facet of reading and another. Unfortunately, however, until comparatively recently, they have attempted to cover too many facets in reading. The intellectual, dynamic activity of the reading process has been confused by linking this with the techniques and skills which need to be acquired in the "learning to read" process. In addition, the learning and teaching activity are rarely examined independently.

As I have suggested elsewhere, it would seem that future models should not attempt, at least in the beginning, to be all inclusive (Jenkinson, 1968). We need a series of models of various aspects of reading which may ultimately be capable of being integrated. But a model which deals with the reading process as such, which includes the cognitive interactions, the impact of language and linguistic considerations in the affective as well as in the cognitive domain, and will then attempt to relate these reading operations to other aspects of thinking, is perhaps the most urgently needed. Part of this process may be the differentiation of the reading-thinking action from every other human activity, including ordinary thinking. I feel that this may be a productive point of departure.

A quite separate model is needed to show the interrelationship between the skills, techniques, materials, and media involved in the decoding process. This will then lead to the way in which the child gradually assimilates the understanding of the word which is decoded. Yet the assimilation of understanding at this period will not be identical with the very different aptitudes of the mature reader. It would seem that the acquisition of encoding and decoding in children as they progress through school is entirely dependent on their developing perceptual activities and the acquisition of the appropriate, systematic cognitive abilities. The extent to which the developing abilities influence the amount that the child can assimilate from his reading is still largely a mystery. We do know, however, that as he matures he can apparently understand increasingly complex material. It would seem to me that we shall make greater progress if we do not attempt to account, at least in the same model, for both the developing reader and the mature reader.

One of the problems that continues to plague us is that we lack accurate definitions in reading. It has become imperative that we somehow attempt to agree on some terms within the field. Several of the contributors to the N.S.S.E. volume *Innovation and Change in Reading Instruction* (Robinson, 1968) commented on the problems attendant on trying to simplify ideas from research and experimentation because of the lack of agreement on definitions. Spache (1968) also suggested that the confusion has been further confounded because many of the disciplines which have contributed to our knowledge of the field of reading have their own distinctive terminology for the basic components of reading.

The varied uses of terms to describe conditions or concepts which are often quite similar not only interfere with our exchange of information but retard our ultimate progress toward greater knowledge.

Many sciences have experienced this problem but the time has come, as it did in the other sciences, when a general acceptance of some definitions is essential. It is true that the way to good definitions is paved with difficulties. As Dewey has reminded us, the twin demons of vagueness and ambiguity frequently impinge upon salient definitions. It is ironical, too, that language itself is a major deterrent in accurate defining. Dewey (1933) wrote with cogency on this point.

> A constant source of misunderstanding and mistake is indefiniteness of meaning. Because of vagueness of meaning, we misunderstand things ourselves. Because of ambiguity, we distort and pervert. Conscious distortion of meaning may be enjoyed as nonsense; erroneous meanings may be followed up and got rid of. Vague meanings are too indefinite to allow for analysis and too bulky to support other beliefs. Vagueness prevents testing and responsibility and disguises the unconscious mixing together of half-understood concepts. It is aboriginal, logical sin, the source from which most bad intellectual consequences flow. To totally eliminate indefiniteness is impossible. To reduce it in extent and force requires sincerity and vigor.

The nature of definitions has plagued us from the time of the Greeks, but recently philosophers such as Robinson (1965) have come to some general conclusions about the attributes of functional definitions, and of these we must become aware. Our definitions at one and the same time must be inclusive but never so restrictive that they cannot function. Definitions in reading as in all other sciences must be relative. They must be capable of changing in both basic concepts and in content as new ideas appear. Thus it would seem that the only definitions we can use would be tentative or stipulative definitions, for should rigid definitions be used, these would belie the dynamic character of language and further restrict investigation. Wittgenstein has aptly stated that definitions should not be permitted to give us mental cramp and rigidly limit exploration. Reading as an act and a process may in the end be the most difficult of all to define. Perhaps reading, like mystery, can only be described and evoked.

Moreover, we are often faced in the field of reading with the sceptics, who often exist among the practitioners, who deny the use or validity of theories. Perhaps the concept that "it is all right in theory but it won't do in practice" is merely a way of rejecting something which is difficult to understand. Black (1946) has indicated that Schopenhauer (1932) said all that needs to be said about this type of sophistry.

> The assertion is based upon an impossibility: what is right in theory must work in practice. And if it does not, there is a mistake in the theory; something has been overlooked and not allowed for and consequently what is wrong in practice is wrong in theory too.

And now having examined several problems which seem to have been major deterrents to the formulation and evolution of useful theories about reading, some questions will be posed concerning the assimilation of meaning, since this is basic to the mature reading process. Then some of the sources of knowledge from which we might seek further enlightenment will be examined briefly.

Some Questions Concerning the Assimilation of Meaning

It is a truism that part of our problem in developing a theory has been the complexity of the process involved. Reading must engage the total organism. The recent distinction made by Wiener and Cromber (1967) between acquisition and assimilation of meaning I think is one we have needed to examine for some time.

However, there are innumerable questions to which we still need answers. I can only pose a very few of these at the present time.

1. Is reading comprehension synonymous with thinking? The converse obviously is not true, but if reading is considered to be a type of thinking which is triggered by the printed rather than by the spoken word, what are the controlling variables of the thinking thus aroused?
2. How does this thinking differ from all other types of thinking? It obviously must be controlled to an extent by the thought indigenous to the writer, but though the reader's thought is controlled by the

content, he frequently has to interpolate and extrapolate in order to get the full impact of the author's meaning.

3. What are the differences between spoken and written language? This could apply to the ways in which the thoughts are engendered but is also very important in our understanding of the problems that will face the reader but which may or may not be apparent if the ideas are expressed orally.

4. What are the respective functions of the lexical and structural elements within written material? Again, beginning has been made on this but we need more information.

5. What are the variables residing within the reader which enable him to become receptive to the message of the author? What is the influence of past experience, of prejudice, of bias, of attitudes, of personality variables? What is the effect of general and immediate motivation, of interests, of attitudes of rigidity, of personality structure, of the cognitive style of the reader and his ability to initially submerge his concepts for those of the author? And these constitute but a few of the variables inherent in the reader.

6. What problems arise because of the level of abstraction of the material that is being presented? This is apposite for the mature reader as well as for the child learning to read. Moreover, undoubtedly the reader will be more or less successful according to his familiarity with the content of the matter he is reading and the type of "language game"* which is being undertaken by the author.

7. How do the separate and disparate experiences of individuals lead to a common acceptance of general meaning but which also permit differences of interpretation? What is going to be the future of literacy as compared with "oracy"? [Cf., McLuhan (1964).]

8. Perhaps we need to examine the axiology of reading, the values gained from reading, particularly in the light of current contentions that "oracy" rather than literacy has become the pervasive means of the immediate conveying of meaning. It appears that written material, however, will continue to play an active part in conveying and relating meaning from one area to another and from one generation to another. Since reading permits more effective thinking, the written word will continue to be the most efficacious influence in knowledge extension and exchange in every sphere. [Cf., McLuhan (1964), p. 168.]

The answers to these questions will be complex, but by examining some recent development in "basic" fields, we may obtain productive insights.

*Cf., Wittgenstein, (1958).

A Triad of Sources for a Reading Theory

Although psychology and linguistics were once studied as part of the philosophy of mind, the three subjects are now pursued separately. Chomsky (1966) has himself suggested that this resulting speculation without rational attempts at synthesis has been detrimental to our knowledge of language and its functioning. A very cursory examination follows of each of these three areas of philosophy, psychology, and linguistics as they might contribute to some of the questions posed above.

Philosophy

Philosophers have been concerned for the past thirty years with the problems involved in how meaning is obtained through language. If any current journal of philosophy, either British or American, is selected it will be noticed that much of its content is concerned with language and the strategies involved in language functioning.

Wittgenstein, some thirty years ago, by his insistence that most philosophical questions turned upon the meaning of the language in which the questions were posed, inaugurated this movement for clarity. He emphasized the problems which words impose upon thought and also the problems which thought imposes upon words and the ideas these words attempt to convey. He insisted that meaning was the "meaning of the word *in use*" and that all communication was dependent upon both parties being aware of the "language game" in which they were engaged. Language of science will necessitate an entirely different set of rules and strategies than the language of poetry. It is a different language game.*

Austin (1962) distinguished between statements and the "performative" utterances, and finally replaced this with a more inclusive general theory of "illocutionary" forms which have "perlocutionary" effects. In attempting to analyze the impact of language he termed a "performative" utterance, one in which we purpose to be doing something in saying something: e.g. "I *judge* this to be the best dog in the show" or "I promise . . .", or "I appoint you . . .". These sentences are neither true nor false, but in

*Cf., Wittgenstein, (1958).

the event that there is failure to do what is purported, the utterance becomes null and void. An "illocutionary" utterance is one which contains some sort of action. It contains the performance of an act *in* saying something as opposed to the performance of an act *of* saying something. Illocutionary acts are those of informing, ordering, warning, undertaking, and so on. "Perlocutionary" effects are those which are brought about when words such as "convince," "persuade," "deter," and so on, produce the desired results, e.g. "I persuaded him to stop teasing the cat." These differing yet interlinked utterances producing acts are differing senses or dimensions of the "use of a sentence," or of "the use of language." There are, of course, many more differing types of utterances than the three illustrated. However, discussion of the purpose of utterance has obvious impact upon assimilation of meaning.

The noted American philosopher Quine (1960) has been exploring the relationship of the notion of meaning and the linguistic mechanisms of objective references, as expounded in his book *Word and Object*. He insists that the meaning of a sentence is not an external entity, but is embodied in the words used. The problems of translation, explanation, and explication in terms of language are explored. He examined the anomalies, ambiguities, and conflicts implicit in the referential implications of language. In his most recent series of lectures—the Dewey lectures 1968—Quine (1968) is exploring "ontological relativity" as it pertains to language. Quine recognized the complexity of the problems facing us in language learning:

> The semantic part of learning a word is more complex than the phonetic part, therefore, even in simple cases, we have to see what is stimulating the other speaker. In the case of words not directly ascribing observable traits to things, the learning process is increasingly complex and obscure; and obscurity is the breeding place of mentalistic semantics. What the naturalist insists on is that, even in the complex and obscure parts of language learning, the learner has no data to work with but the overt behavior of other speakers (P. 186.)

He includes, however, the problem of extension reference and the attendant difficulties upon our knowledge of these references.

Langer, on the other hand, found the ordinary language of words so complex for explaining exact meaning that she continued the work of Whitehead and emphasized the value of symbolic forms to convey logical ideas. In her most recent work (Langer, 1967) she is beginning to throw some light on cognitive functioning and its relation to language. Her new attack on the problem of mind and its functioning involves biology, bio-chemistry, and psychology as well as philosophy. She attempts to contribute to a concept of mind adequate and acceptable to both the sciences and the humanities.

"The enormous power of language, whereby we are enabled to form abstract concepts, concatenate them in propositions, apply these to the world of perception and action, making it into a world of "facts," and then manipulate its facts by a process of reasoning, springs from the simpleness of discursive projection." (P. 102.)

These are but a few of the many philosophers who have turned their attention to the elucidation and illumination of the way ideas are conveyed through language, and these studies and many others are of obvious relevance to our study of reading and its comprehension.

Another philosopher, Findlay (1968), has heartened me considerably. He writes:

Modern philosophy is distinguished by the emergence of a new question: how to give meaning to the expressions used in ordinary and philosophical discourse. Early philosophers simply inquired into the truth of this or that assertion, without troubling to raise the prior question as to what precisely such an assertion meant, or whether it really meant anything at all. When the question of sense has been raised, it led to yet another inquiry: in what way or ways a sense had been *given* to some assertion, or in what way or ways a sense *could* be given to it. The question led to yet another question: In what way or ways the sense of an expression could be *taught* or imparted, so that many men could use the expression in an identical way, and give it the same sense. This obviously is a truly fundamental question. For it is plain that most expressions acquire sense for use through a process of teaching. (P. 72.)

At least this indicates that the vital knowledge of language functioning is capable of being learned and, therefore, presumably of being taught.

Linguistics and Psycholinguistics

Again, I can only suggest it is presumptuous of me to attempt in a short period of time to indicate what further contributions might be obtained from the linguists and particularly now because of their closer relation to psycholinguists.

Part of our problem has been in the past that there have been so many differing schools of thought about language structure and functions that it has been almost impossible for anyone outside the field to make any appropriate synthesis of its findings. Perhaps it was unfortunate, too, that in the fifties the interest of most linguists in reading was concentrated almost exclusively upon the grapheme-phoneme relationship. It is only more recently that several of the branches of linguistics and psycholinguistics have begun to explore the effect of structure and lexical meaning on the understanding of language.

Some descriptive linguists, interested primarily in analyzing non-Western languages in order to provide viable writing systems for them, produced grammars and alphabets adequate for their purposes. Applied English linguists relate some of these descriptive methods to the English language and writing system. Abercrombie (1965) has begun to sharpen our awareness of the great differences between actual everyday speech on the one hand, and the "texts" of spoken English analyzed by linguists and English deliberately organized for visual presentation (prose), on the other. And although Abercrombie's book is quite revealing, it does not indicate the more subtle differences the reader must perceive to obtain a meaning closely approximating what he might obtain from the primary source of speech.

Lefevre (1964) was one of the first to point out the implications for reading of the complex interplay of spoken and written English language patterns—above the level of phonemes and graphemes. He emphasized that in reading instruction we must recognize and teach the essential grammatical and syntactical clues in printed English, particularly those that suggest intonation: stress, tune, and junctures or terminals. Insensitivity to some of these signals, I suspect, may underlie problems of differing interpretations that are accorded to much written material. As Lefevre (1968) said in a recently published paper, intonation and sentence patterns are critically important subsystems of the English structural system and are essential to meaning in both speech and writing; moreover, in addition to their lexical meanings, the syntactical functions of words, signaled by grammatical inflections and derivational affixes, must be perceived as important clues to meaning in reading printed English just as they are in hearing English spoken.

At this point, apparently some linguists are beginning to explore analyses of structures at higher levels than that of the single sentence. This discourse analysis, it seems to me, will have an important impact on our understanding of meaning as will be the tagmemicists' analysis. Both of these suggest the possibilities of useful new insights into larger structures of the exposition of all types of prose. The work in this field has primarily been directed towards writing but it seems that it should have pertinence to reading, too.

Undoubtedly the work of Chomsky and the transformational grammarians in revealing that sentences, and thus discourse as a whole, had both a surface and a deep meaning, has had much to offer in expanding our knowledge of how meaning is conveyed. The embeddedness of meaning in deep structures is apparently learned comparatively easily by a child, but although he may use the structures adequately in performance, he may face a very difficult task when he receives these from others. Goodman (1964), in his insistence on the types of miscues which can lead to major errors in understanding, has indicated one of the most productive ways of furthering our understanding, since it is often by examination of errors made, rather than by competence revealed, that our knowledge in any field is enhanced. The distinction which linguists have made between linguistic performance and linguistic competence, as Wardhaugh (1968) has suggested, may be a very important one for our assessing the ability of students to obtain meaning from what they need. This competence at the spoken level may vary quite considerably from the linguistic performance in reading. It may be that the reader will only catch the superficial interpretation and will fail to take into account the more deeply embedded structural elements which occur in the printed word. The printed word tends to be more complex and thus contains more latent embeddedness. Incidentally, the discrepancy between linguistic competence and performance is very evident in children as some recent research by Lyons and Wales (1966) in Britain has shown.

Again, in a sense, I have only dabbled in this vast field of linguistics. My plea is, however, that we continue to use the emerging findings of the linguists and incorporate these into our theories and ultimately into our teaching of reading as efficiently and effectively as possible.

Psychology

It is perhaps most difficult to summarize the contributions of psychology to our knowledge of the reading *process* because they are so diverse. A great many of the findings of behavioral analysis, of child development, including child cognition, of general learning theory, of theories of perception, and of problem solving have been applied to the *teaching* of reading, but few have examined these findings in the light of the mature reader obtaining meaning. In addition, there are so few studies which have focused in depth upon any one area which extend our knowledge of the reading process per se.

The work on cognition is so far the most fruitful field. Undoubtedly Guilford's (1959) model of the intellect has stimulated many workers to explain the relationships between the parameters suggested. When this model, however, was applied to reading there were obvious gaps, inconsistencies, and invalidities. Ausubel's (1967) concept of the pervasiveness of receptive learning as opposed to the less frequent opportunities for discovery learning is also pertinent. The reading process is obviously one of the main vehicles for such receptive learning. The need to know, the "epistemic curiosity" described by Berlyne (1965), has also obvious implications, since books are still a prime source of knowledge. Skinner's concept of verbal behavior is also pertinent. Perhaps we are in more need of workers such as Carroll, who synthesized both in 1959 and 1964, the relationships between psychology and language, than we are of direct researchers.

The concept of the impact of a distinctive cognitive style on all aspects of personality variables, including those of attitudes, flexibility, and ability to tolerate ambivalence, is receiving attention from a variety of psychologists, but as yet there is little to be applied to reading.

The psychology of motivation, including that of interest, is moving forward too, but again the results are scattered and still appear to apply to experimental rather than to real life situations. We need to know more than the superficial interest of what and why people read, but also how they read. The attempt by Gray and Rogers (1956) remains the only thorough study which tries to assess the differing levels of adult reading competence linked with their interests.

There have been a few attempts, mostly by people within the field of reading, to analyze the reading process, but again few of these have dealt with mature readers. The majority of these studies have examined errors made in comprehension in an effort to determine what caused differing interpretive responses. Strang (1965) has given an admirable summary of these to 1965.

Thus, from a psychological point of view, the reading process is dependent upon a reader's prerequisites for learning, his language competence (including reading), and his attitudes and goals. Yet, all these may be vitiated by chemical or neurological factors, of which our knowledge is still minimal.

Conclusion

I have merely explored some of the fringes of those areas of knowledge which seem to impinge upon the eternal conundrum of the meaning of meaning in reading. To develop an appropriate theory, it is evident that we need to bring together related disciplines in coordinated research efforts. The most productive insights frequently emerge from the interplay and friction between the differences of disparate disciplines, from the interfaces where the knowledge of one area borders on another. Regretfully, too, frequently one discipline disparages another, and I can only deplore that too often people in the reading field have reacted negatively to some of the attempts of other disciplines to explain the reading process. But other scholars must also share some of the blame. I think all partners in this future voyage of discovery into the nature of the reading process must move forward in humility, each recognizing the limitations of his own discipline honestly, but also ensuring that the wide avenues of educational epistemology are continually kept open.

In this discussion I have probably revealed my own ignorance more than enlightened yours and undoubtedly as Gray once wrote of the Eton College boys:

> Thought would destroy their paradise
> No more: where ignorance is bliss
> 'Tis folly to be wise.

No doubt it has been foolish wisdom to dally in this, the various sources of knowledge which might illumine the reading process.

Yet again, I am reminded of an appropriate section of Lewis Carroll's *Through the Looking Glass,* a section favored by philosophers.

"When I use a word," Humpty Dumpty said, in a rather scornful tone, "it means just what I choose it to mean, neither more nor less."
"The question is," said Alice, "whether you *can* make words mean so many different things."
"The question is," said Humpty Dumpty, "which is to be the master, that's all."

This passage is usually used to emphasize the intractableness of language. In reading, the meanings of words, lexical, syntactical, and structural, determine to a large extent what the reader *can* comprehend of the writer's ideas. Unless this is so, then the other Humpty Dumpty fable must ensue, and "we shall never put him together again."

References

Abercrombie, D. O. *Studies in Phonetics and Linguistics.* Oxford: Oxford University Press, 1965.

Austin, J. L. *How to Do Things with Words.* Edited by J. O. Urmson. The William James Lectures at Harvard University in 1955. Oxford: Clarendon Press, 1962.

Ausubel, D. P. *Learning Theory and Classroom Practice.* Toronto: Ontario Institute for Studies in Education, 1967, Bulletin no. 1.

Berylne, D. E. *Structure and Direction in Thinking.* New York: Wiley, 1965.

Black, N. *Critical Thinking.* Englewood Cliffs, N.J.: Prentice-Hall, 1946.

Carroll, J. B. "An Operational Model for Language Behaviour." *Anthropological Linguistics* 1(1959):37–54.

Carroll, J. B. "Linguistics and the Psychology of Language." *Review of Educational Research* 34(April 1964):119–26.

Carroll, Lewis. *Through the Looking Glass.* Oxford: Clarendon Press.

Chomsky, N. *Cartesian Linguistics: A Chapter in the History of Rationalist Thought.* New York: Harper and Row, 1966.

Cleland, D. L. "A Construct of Comprehension." *Reading and Inquiry.* (Edited by J. A. Figurel) Conference Proceedings vol 10. Newark, Delaware: International Reading Association., 1965. pp. 59–64.

Cooper, J. A. "Why the Monopoly in Epistemology?" *Phi Delta Kappan* 48(April 1967):406.

Dewey, J. *How We Think.* Boston: Heath, 1933.

Eastwood, G. R. "Uses of Models: Another Dimension." *Alberta Journal of Educational Research* 12(September 1966):230.

Findlay. "The Teaching of Meaning." *Thinking and Meaning.* Entretiens d'Oxford, Organisés par l'Institute Internationale de Philosophie, Editions Nauwelaerts, Louvain, 1963.

George, F. H. Quoted in "Models in Education." *Alberta Journal of Educational Research* 12(September 1966):168.

Goodman, K. "A Linguistic Study of Cues and Miscues in Reading." Paper delivered at the American Educational Research Association, Chicago, February 21, 1964.

Gray, W. S., and Rogers, B. *Maturity in Reading: Its Nature and Appraisal.* Chicago: University of Chicago Press, 1956.

Gray, W. S. "The Major Aspects of Reading." *Sequential Development of Reading Abilities,* edited by H. M. Robinson. Supplementary Education Monographs, no. 90. Chicago: University of Chicago Press, 1960. pp. 8–24.

Guilford, J. P. "Three Faces of Intellect." *American Psychologist* 14(August 1959): 469–79.

Holmes, J. S. "Basic Assumptions Underlying the Sub-Strata Factor." *Reading Research Quarterly* 1(Fall 1965):4–28.

Jenkinson, M. D. "Dispersed Meditations on Curriculum Evaluation." Paper presented at the Third International Curriculum Conference. Oxford, England, September 1967.

Jenkinson, M. D. "Reading: An Eternal Dynamic." Paper given at the presentation of the N.S.S.E. Yearbook, *Innovation and Change in Reading Instructions,* April 1968.

Kingston, A. J. "A Conceptual Model of Reading Comprehension." *Phases of College and Other Reading Programs,* edited by E. P. Bliesmer and A. J. Kingston. Milwaukee: National Reading Conference, 1961. pp. 100–107.

Langer, S. K. *Mind: An Essay on Human Feeling,* Vol. 1. Baltimore: Johns Hopkins Press, 1967.

Lefevre, C. A. "A Multidisciplinary Approach to Language and to Reading: Some Projections." Detroit: Wayne State University Press, 1968. pp. 289–312; 333–36.

Lefevre, C. A. *Linguistics and the Teaching of Reading.* New York: McGraw-Hill, 1964.

Lyons, J., and Wales, R. J. *Psycho-Linguistic Papers.* Edinburgh: The University Press, 1966.

McCullough, C. M. "Balanced Reading Development." *Innovation and Change in Reading Instruction,* N. S. S. E. Yearbook, Part II, 1968. Chicago: University of Chicago Press, 1968.

McLuhan, H. M. *Understanding Media: The Extensions of Man.* New York: McGraw-Hill, 1964. p. 168.

Quine, W. V. "Ontological Relativity." The Dewey Lectures, 1968. *The Journal of Philosophy* 65(April 1968):185–212.

Quine, W. V. *Word and Object.* New York: John Wiley, 1960.

Robinson, R. *Definition.* Oxford: University Press, 1965.

Robinson, H. M. "The Major Aspects of Reading." *Reading: Seventy-Five Years of Progress,* edited by H. Alan Robinson. Supplementary Educational Monographs, no. 96. Chicago: University of Chicago Press, 1966, pp. 22–32.

Robinson, H. M., ed. *Innovation and Change in Reading Instruction, Sixty-Seventh Yearbook of the National Society for the Study of Education.* Chicago: National Society for the Study of Education, 1968.

Schopenhauer, G. *The Art of Controversy.* Oxford University Press, 1932.

Skinner, B. F. *Verbal Behavior.* New York: Appleton-Century-Crofts, 1957.

Smith, D. E. *Toward Better Reading* by G. D. Spache. Champaign, Ill.: Garrard, 1963, pp. 67–72.

Spache, G. D. "Contributions of Allied Fields to the Teaching of Reading." *Innovation and Change in Reading Instruction, Sixty-Seventh Yearbook of the National Society for the Study of Education,* edited by Helen M. Robinson. Chicago: N.S.S.E., 1968. pp. 237–90.

Strang, R. *The Reading Process and Its Ramifications.* Invitational Address, International Reading Association, 1965. pp. 49–74.

Wardhaugh, R. "Recent Research in Linguistics." Paper delivered at the 12th Annual Convention of the International Reading Association, 1968.

Wiener, M., and Cromer, J. "Reading and Reading Difficulty: A Conceptual Analysis." *Harvard Education Review* Fall 1967. pp. 620–43.

Wiseman, S. *Curriculum Evaluation.* Mimeograph, 1966. p. 21.

Wittgenstein, L. *Philosophical Investigations.* Oxford: Basil Blackwell, 1958.

The operational suggestions presented by Betts emerge from his
study of complementary fields: psychology and linguistics. Note that he
correctly forecasts the rise of a "new
discipline" — psycholinguistics.

Reading: Psychological and Linguistic Bases

EMMETT ALBERT BETTS

Efficient reading is a process — basically a thinking process —
which requires the *automatic* use of word-perception skills.
Reading is a process of decoding writing which symbolizes speech
sounds that are used to encode messages. Hence, reading is two
steps removed from the message — a fact that appears to be un-
recognized by some reading specialists, some linguists, and some
psychologists.

Equally important, reading is done by organisms with frontal
lobes — by individuals who vary considerably in motivations,
perceptual skills, and thinking abilities. These individuals *learn*

to listen, talk, read, and write. Because they *learn* to encode and decode spoken and written language signals, their verbal behavior is studied by psychologists. Reading instruction has a psychological as well as a linguistic basis.

Furthermore, there is substantial progress being made today on the sociological as well as on the psychological basis of differentiated reading instruction. Differences among pupils in levels of achievements, language facility, learning rates, and the like have been recognized by the vanguard of reading instruction. But, today, more emphasis is being given to the needs of superior learners. And, today, culturally deprived pupils are being discovered—their motivations, their control over the phonological and grammatical levels of language, their cognitive structures, and so on.

Facets of Reading Instruction

For several generations an enormous stumbling block in reading instruction has been the fruitless attempt to regiment reading instruction—to assume that all pupils are prepared to learn to read upon admission to school, to use the same textbook with all pupils of that fiction called a grade. In today's reading instruction, however, individualized and group instruction are superseding the iniquitous regimented instruction of the past.

At each succeeding level of reading achievement, therefore, pupils present greater ranges of reading achievement and perceptual and conceptual needs. For example, in a typical fifth grade the range is from those who need help in beginning reading to those who do read so-called twelfth-grade materials of interest to them. It appears that the more efficient the reading instruction the greater is the range. But no competent teacher would attempt to teach all the pupils of a grade the same word-perception skills and the same comprehension abilities! To do so produces only mellifluous nothingness or verbalism.

Linguists as well as psychologists need to understand that the big, broad base of effective reading instruction is the quality of differentiated reading instruction. Many factors other than the pupils' production of speech and control over grammar enter into preparation for reading: motivation, visual-motor skills (as revealed, for example, by the ability to copy the letter *K,* or a triangle, or a diamond), visual discrimination skills (for example, letter discrimination and word discrimination), vision and hearing efficiency, ability to deal with levels of abstraction, and so on. These factors tend to be multiplied as the pupils proceed from beginning reading to higher levels.

Reading instruction, based solidly on an effective plan for differentiated teaching, deals directly with three facets of learning: motivation, word perception, and comprehension (thinking abilities). This article will deal primarily with word perception.

Linguists have made substantial contributions to two facets of reading instruction: comprehension and word perception. Their studies of morphology, syntax, and the keystone of grammar, intonation, have given substance to the concept that reading is done by structures. Furthermore, they have contributed basic information on reading as a *thinking process,* especially on learning to read as a process of learning to think in a language.

But psychologists, too, have contributed to these understandings regarding reading as a thinking process:

1. Reading is thinking that results in the formation of attitudes and concepts.
2. Reading is thinking in a language, calling for awareness of levels of abstraction, sensitivity to shifts of meaning, and the like.
3. Reading is a relationship with the author.
4. Reading is the use of skills to serve specific purposes.

Word Perception Skills

With the help of linguists and psychologists the development of word *perception* skills is superseding the ineffective letter phonics of yesteryear. Through the linguists' study of the distinctive sound of speech, called a phoneme, they offer a valid content for the speech sound facet of sound-alphabet (phoneme-grapheme) relationships and for a simplified set of pronunciation symbols in the dictionary. There is no longer a need for the teacher to be an expert in *phonetics,* which is concerned with hundreds of variant sounds of American English; instead, she deals with about thirty-four significant speech sounds, or phonemes.

Furthermore, the teacher no longer gives duality to the teaching of phonic skills and dictionary pronunciations; instead, she uses the pupils' phonic skills as a preparation for the immediate interpretation of pronunciation symbols.

While the linguist is contributing a valid content to the phonics program, the psychologist is providing the necessary basis for methods of teaching phoneme-grapheme relationships in *syllables,* emphasizing the development of relationships in *perceptual* settings. In short, the psychologist's research is putting perception in word perception. When maximum use is made of the conclusions gleaned from both linguistics and psychology, the teaching of word-perception skills is taken far beyond the ineffective "grunt and groan" phonics of yesteryear.

In general, linguists who have either dabbled or made serious attempts to prepare beginning reading materials have found themselves trapped by (1) their lack of understanding of the psychology of word perception, (2) their lack of experience in the teaching of reading, and (3) their failure to evaluate word perception in relation to the intonation of efficient reading. They have not published, for example, a systematic treatise on either the linguistic basis or the psychological basis of word perception.

In the past, educators have been concerned with phonic rules. For example, the "short" vowel rule has been stated: If there is only one vowel in a stressed syllable and it is followed by a consonant (for example, *at, hat*), the vowel is usually "short." This statement, it will be noted, stresses the whole word, the word pattern, rather than the vowel alone.

Furthermore, educators have studied the application/exception ratios for these rules and have found that the above-mentioned rule applies to 53 percent of the "closed" syllables in beginning reading and to 71 percent at the third-reader level. However, many of these words, especially function words, are said one way when stressed as isolated syllables and another way in phrase stress, (for example, *can* as /'kan/ and /kən/).

Under the leadership of Leonard Bloomfield, the linguists, too, have concerned themselves with patterns of relationships between the sounds of words and the letters of words. Instead of phonic rules they deal in spelling patterns, especially those spelling patterns (for example, *it-sit*) that consistently represent patterns of sounds. Although Bloomfield recommended the use of consistent spelling patterns in beginning reading, he was undoubtedly aware of the many pitfalls of writing materials using closed syllables only and ignoring intonation, especially phrase stress. He, therefore, recommended "either to postpone other graphs [irregular spellings] until the elementary habit has been fixed, or else to introduce them, in some rationally planned way, at earlier points" (p. 501). It is the second part of his statement that has been violated by zealots of the word-pattern idea.

Eight Valid Statements

To summarize this situation, the following statements appear to have validity:

1. The word pattern includes both consonants and vowels; therefore, consonants are introduced as systemically as vowels are.
2. There are not three basic patterns emphasized by some linguists, but more than twenty basic patterns.
3. Pattern 1 *(at-sat, set-pep, it-lip, not-stop* and *us-but),* which has intrigued linguists, is for the pupil really five patterns. As a general pattern it is ambiguous for the pupil, because he does not have the linguistic sophistication to make the required overall generalization.
4. A valid word pattern has value to the degree that it functions not only for identifying one-syllable words (for example, *sat)* but also for identifying embedded patterns in the stressed syllables of multisyllable words (as in *satisfaction).*
5. A word pattern is serviceable to the degree that it has a high application/exception ratio, or batting average.
6. Many irregular spellings tend to pattern, as in *right, sight, might,* and *light.*
7. Word perception as an automatic part of the ongoing reading process requires an awareness of both syllable stress and phrase stress.
8. Both word-pattern cues and phonogram cues are used to identify words, such as the *oi* in the unpatterned word *noise.*

Perceptual Learning

Furthermore, the perception of words, as the structuring of stimuli, is a psychological process. Perceptual learning is:

1. *Category learning.* The pupil learns word-pattern and phonogram categories.
2. *Cue learning.* The pupil learns to identify the unknown part of a word (e.g., the *ar* of *cart* or the *Ne* syllable of *Neanderthal)* as a cue to be learned or previously learned.
3. *Probability learning.* The pupil learns, for example, that the usual sound of the vowel is /ī/ in *by, my, why, sky, try.* On the other hand, he learns that the *ow* in *cow* or *crow* probably stands for the sound /aů/ or /ō/.

4. *Relationship learning.* The pupil learns the relationships between regular spellings and sounds and between irregular spellings and sounds. In learning a new skill he is taken from the spoken word to the written word. When the pupil applies his word-perception skill, he "feeds back" from the written word to the spoken word.

5. *Generalization learning.* The pupil learns to make generalizations regarding the relationships between the sound patterns and letter patterns of words and of phonograms.

6. *Mediation response learning.* The pupil learns to use obscure and unobservable processes that operate between the stimulus and the response. For example, in responding to the word *hat,* the beginner may call on preestablished associations with *at* and *cat.* In responding to the word *redound* or *retaliate,* the experienced reader may call on one or more preestablished associations, depending on which part is unknown: the number of places in which he sees vowels as indicative of the number of syllables, the relationship between the phonogram *ou* and the sound /aủ/, awareness of syllable stress, and so on.

Significant Factors

The perceptual process of decoding writing into speech is dependent upon a number of conditions and factors:

1. Motivation, for example, the attitudinal factor *need* to identify the unknown part or parts of a particular word

2. Attention as a powerful selector of stimulus information to be processed and as a constant feature of perceptual activity

3. Set, a determiner of perception, that, among other things, causes the pupil to regard reading as a poverty-stricken word-calling process or as a thinking process

4. Grouping of stimuli into recognizable syllables, phonograms, and other patterns for making optimum use of a limited span of attention

5. Meaning, both structural and referential, needed for the closure of perception

6. Contrast, such as the contrastive letter patterns which represent contrastive sound patterns

7. Feedback, a circular process, from the examination of letter groupings of the written word to the sounds of the spoken word; for example, the *application* of word-perception skills to the written word during silent reading

8. Closure, as in the identification of the word *noise* after the usual sound represented by *oi* is recalled

9. Kinesthesis, as it operates in inner speech and in word learning

In Conclusion

Generally speaking, linguistics is a source of content for the teaching of reading, and psychology supplies information on which to base methodology. These two disciplines have not been wedded as a new discipline, psycholinguistics, but substantial progress has been made to demonstrate they are not out of ardor!

The key to improvement in reading instruction is not only materials which are built on sound linguistic and psychological bases but also the teacher. The chief problem is convincing teachers of teachers and certifiers of teachers that well-defined courses in psychology and linguistics are essential prerequisites to a methods course—that competence is achieved by a firm grasp of the basic disciplines rather than by a proliferation of courses on methods.

References

Betts, E. A. "Excellence in Contemporary Reading Instruction." Boston, Mass.: New England Reading Association, September 1965.

— "Linguistics and Reading: A Critique." In *Innovation and Experiment in Modern Education.* Report on the Twenty-ninth Educational Conference, Educational Records Bureau. New York: American Council on Education, 1964, pp. 130–40.

— "A New Area: Reading and Linguists." *Education* 84, no. 9 (May 1964):515-20.

— "Reading: Linguistics." *Education* 83, no. 9 (May 1963):515-26.

— "Report on Phoneme-Grapheme Relationships: Dictionary." Coral Gables, Florida: Reading Research Laboratory, University of Miami, 1964.

— "Word Perception Skills for Tomorrow." *Education* 85, no. 9 (May 1965):523-28.

Black, E. B. "A Study of the Consonant Situations in a Primary Reading Vocabulary." *Education* 72, no. 9 (May 1952):618-23.

Bloomfield, L. *Language.* New York: Henry Holt and Company, 1933.

Oaks, R. E. "A Study of the Vowel Situation in a Primary Vocabulary." *Education* 72, no. 9 (May 1952):604-617.

Linguists raise questions about the nature of language and the nature of the writing system. They suggest that a fundamental difference exists between the language processes of the beginning reader and the mature reader. If such questions and conjectures are solved, what then will be the effect on reading instruction?

Linguistic Insights into the Reading Process

RONALD WARDHAUGH

Various linguists have put forward proposals for studying the reading process and for teaching reading. Bloomfield and Fries tried to use linguistic knowledge to devise a method of teaching reading based on a belief that children had to learn sound-symbol relationships in order to read. Venezky has proposed a model of the reading process which is something of a bridge between their work and that of Chomsky and Halle. The latter have proposed that present English orthography is an optimal system for the language and that the phonemes of so much interest to

Bloomfield and Fries are no more than methodological artifacts. However, they acknowledge that their phonological model might not be an appropriate one for children. If this is the case, then certain insights from Bloomfield and Fries may still be relevant. The possible applications of linguistics to reading are still uncertain in the absence of empirical evidence to support any of the present hypotheses.

Within applied linguistics the topic of linguistics and reading is of great interest for several reasons which should be stated at the outset.[1] First of all, it forces us to discuss some of the difficulties involved in attempts to use insights from research in theoretical linguistics in the solution of a practical problem, in this case the problem being one of teaching children to read and of understanding the reading process. In other cases the problem may be one of teaching a foreign language, of translating a text, or of choosing a national language. The same difficulties arise in each case: just what linguistic knowledge is relevant to solving the problem and how may knowledge which is considered relevant be used? The teaching of reading is a very real problem almost everywhere in the world and often a controversial one. Those linguists who have looked at it have adopted a variety of different approaches because they have viewed the nature of the problem differently and because they have also held different views about the proper nature of linguistic inquiry. In this paper, therefore, I will try to indicate some of the different views of the reading process held by different linguists and some of the solutions that they have proposed.

The second reason which makes this topic interesting is that it allows us to observe some of the limitations of linguistic knowledge in solving a practical problem. In the course of the paper, some indication will be given of specific areas in which the limits of linguistic knowledge are reached and in which other kinds of knowledge are called for. It is apparent that certain linguists have confused nonlinguistic matters with linguistic ones, possibly to the extent of overreaching themselves. Such overreaching is not unique to linguists: experts from many disciplines are accustomed to speaking on topics outside their field of competence with the same air of authority they assume within that field!

The third reason is no less important than the first two: it is to show how linguistics itself is changing in its concerns, its techniques, and its rhetoric. This last statement should become clearer when the approaches to the reading process taken by Bloomfield and Fries are compared with those taken by Chomsky and Halle. There is a vast difference in both the content and the style of their discussions of the problem; however, there is some reason to say that the conclusions of Bloomfield and Fries on the one hand and those of Chomsky and Halle on the other may not actually be so very far apart.

The earliest proposals to use modern linguistic knowledge in the teaching of reading apparently came from Leonard Bloomfield, who was disturbed by certain aspects of school instruction, particularly the instruction given in language and in reading. For example, in a statement published in the very first volume of *Language* in 1925 explaining in part why the Linguistic Society of America had been founded, he wrote as follows:

> Our schools are conducted by persons who, from professors of education down to teachers in the classroom, know nothing of the results of linguistic science, not even the relation of writing to speech or of standard language to dialect. In short, they do not know what language is, and yet must teach it, and in consequence waste years of every child's life and reach a poor result.[2]

Bloomfield felt that the methods being used to teach his son to read were unenlightened and revealed a lack of knowledge about language. Consequently, he devised his own method of teaching his son to read and shared his opinions, methods, and materials with those of his friends who had like interests. These later became known as the Bloomfield system for teaching reading when they found their way into *Let's Read*.[3]

Bloomfield rejected the "code-breaking" approach known as phonics as a way of teaching reading, claiming that the proponents of phonics confused statements about speech with those about writing to the point that they often appeared to be teaching children to speak, whereas all they were really doing was teaching them to associate written symbols with already known words. He objected to practices such as breaking up words into smaller parts corresponding to letters, crediting individual letters with having sounds; sounding out words (e.g., *cat* as [kᵊ æ tᵊ]), and blending sounds in an attempt to decode written words. Not only did Bloomfield reject a "code-breaking" or phonics approach, but he also rejected the competing "whole-word" approach, claiming that it ignored the alphabetic nature of the English writing system in that it treated English as though it were Chinese.

Bloomfield believed that children learning to read should first be trained in visual discrimination and then be taught to associate visually discriminated objects (letter and word shapes) to already known sounds and meanings. The story line (the meaning of the reading materials) was, he believed, far less important than the regularity of the connection between sounds and symbols, the phoneme-grapheme correspondences. In order therefore to guarantee that children should easily acquire a mastery of these correspondences, Bloomfield insisted that they be trained to discriminate in a left-to-right direction and also to name the letters of the alphabet without error. He believed that requiring children to name the letters in new words from left to right guaranteed both visual discrimination and correct word attack. Just as linguists, and presumably children (intuitively in their case), could segment an utterance into phonemes, beginning readers had to learn to segment words into graphemes, and the teacher systematically had to teach children to relate the two discrimination abilities. The Bloomfield approach is, therefore, one which is based on the introduction of regular sound-symbol, or phoneme-grapheme, correspondences so that children can acquire the fundamental understanding they must acquire in order to read, the understanding that writing is a representation of speech and, on the whole, quite a systematic one.

Bloomfield was also concerned with the notion of contrast, seeing a need to teach whole written words such as *can, van,* and *fan* in contrast with each other and to introduce all the contrastive details of the English writing system gradually and systematically, so that the child learning to read would realize, as Bloomfield wrote, that *"printed letter = speech sound to be spoken."*[4] It is not surprising therefore that the resulting lists, exercises, and testing materials look something like the old "word family" lists in many of the old-fashioned nineteenth century readers. Here is an example of some testing materials from *Let's Read:*

> ban, can, Dan, fan, gan, . . .
> bat, cat, fat, gat, hat, . . .
> bad, cad, dad, fad, gad, . . .
> bap, cap, dap, gap, Hap, . . .
> bag, cag, dag, fag, gag, . . .[5]

According to Bloomfield, the basic task the child learning to read had to master was that of understanding the spelling system of English not that of understanding the meanings of English words and sentences. Therefore, it was quite possible for teachers to use nonsense syllables and nonsense words in order to allow their students to achieve such mastery. He wrote as follows on this point:

> Tell the child that the nonsense syllables are parts of real words which he will find in the books that he reads. For example, the child will know *han* in *handle* and *jan* in *January* and *mag* in *magnet* or *magpie*. The acquisition of nonsense syllables is an important part of the task of mastering the reading process.[6]

Later, Robert Hall gave very much the same kind of advice, claiming that the "ultimate test of any method of teaching reading is whether the learners can deal with nonsense syllables. . . ."[7] Both Bloomfield and Hall are really advocating an emphasis on a "code-breaking" approach, but not the particular "code-breaking" approach known as phonics. In his work, Bloomfield was concerned almost exclusively with monosyllabic words, and polysyllabic words received very little attention. In defense of this emphasis, he claimed that his son found no difficulty in transferring to polysyllabic words once he had achieved a mastery of the monosyllabic patterns. This observation is a very interesting observation to which I shall have further occasion to refer in connection with the work of contemporary linguists.

Believing that the major task the beginning reader must master is one wholly concerned with the interpretation of words and not one concerned with guessing at the meanings of words by using accompanying illustrations, Bloomfield rejected the use of illustrations in reading materials on the grounds that they are either irrelevant or misleading. Some of the materials for teaching reading that Fries and his followers were to develop following Bloomfield's example likewise do not contain pictures so that children may be left free to focus their attention on the words themselves rather than on the illustrations accompanying the words. The results of applying Bloomfield's theories to reading are reading materials like the following.

A rap. A gap.

Dad had a map.
Pat had a bat.

Tad had a tan cap.
Nan had a tan hat.
Nan had a fat cat.
A fat cat ran at a bad rat.[8]

There is much that is admirable in Bloomfield's ideas on reading. First of all, his work on English phoneme-grapheme correspondences was based on a good knowledge of the important surface phonological contrasts in English. Bloomfield also stressed the fact that the English writing system is basically an alphabetical one and that it is not as inconsistent as it is often made out to be, particularly when it is approached from the viewpoint of *how sounds are represented in writing* and not from that of how letters are pronounced or, even worse, *should* be pronounced. Then, too, there is in his work on reading a welcome insistence that the proper content of reading and the basic insights necessary to understand the reading process are to be found in linguistic rather than in social and psychological factors. However, the Bloomfield method has much more to say about the linguistic *content* of reading materials than about an actual *method* of teaching reading. What comments on methodology there are in Bloomfield's writings seem to be based on an extrapolation of some procedures, such as contrast, which linguists have found useful in their work as linguists, and not on procedures derived from teaching reading. This type of extrapolation is characteristic of much work in applied linguistics in general. It is certainly not unique to the problem of using linguistic insights in understanding the reading process or in the teaching of reading!

A more recent proposal than Bloomfield's to use linguistic insights in reading was made by Charles Fries in *Linguistics and Reading*,[9] undoubtedly the most influential book on linguistics and reading published to date. Like Bloomfield, Fries took the position that reading experts are quite unfamiliar with linguistics and in general exhibit little knowledge of language at all; consequently, he set out to correct this defect and to offer an outline of a method for teaching reading that drew heavily on linguistic insights in a manner reminiscent of the approach behind his well-known book on second-language teaching, *Teaching and Learning English as a Foreign Language*.[10]

One important distinction that Fries insisted on is in the use of the terms *phonics, phonemics,* and *phonetics,* and a whole chapter in his book is devoted to the problem of clarifying the differences among these terms and setting the record straight. The chapter contains example after example of the confused use of the three terms in the literature on reading and is a telling indictment of most writing on the subject of phonics, that is, most writing on the "code-breaking" view of reading. Like Bloomfield before him, Fries emphasized that written English is alphabetic in nature and that English spelling is not inconsistent if statements about speech and statements about writing are clearly distinguished and if letters (graphemes) are regarded as representations of significant speech sounds (phonemes). Fries pointed out the regular spelling patterns in English and said that it was the reading teacher's task to teach these to beginning readers by presenting them in carefully arranged sequences and by giving beginning readers considerable practice in recognizing them in contrasting words.

Fries considered that in learning to read, children had to master a new visual task, in which they had to associate quite automatically visual responses with previously discriminated auditory responses. He believed that this process, which he regarded as a transfer process, required visual training, for example training in left-to-right eye movements and in the discrimination of the important features of letters and words. For this reason Fries rejected the concurrent introduction of both upper- and lower-case letters in beginning texts in favor of the exclusive use of uppercase letters so as to reduce the burden of discrimination for the child who was learning to read. He apparently rejected the argument that the elimination of ascenders and descenders and the resultant uniform "block" shapes of written words might result in the loss of many useful visual clues and would reduce the amount of visual information available to the child. Instead, Fries believed that children would find written words composed out of twenty-six uniform letters easier to perceive than the corresponding words composed out of twice that number of letters. Later he modified this view.

Fries also insisted on the use of contrastive word patterns since for him the principle of contrast was basic to both linguistic structure and visual perception. He rejected the spelling out of words that Bloomfield recommended, insisting instead that the critically important skill for children to acquire is one of being able to make visual discriminations between whole words and

between whole patterns or units of meaning. He sought, therefore, to minimize any factor which would tend to require children
to focus on units smaller than whole words. Although Fries recognized that written English is alphabetic and the alphabet is a
contrastive system, he claimed that the more important system
of contrasts was the one associated with words and meanings;
consequently, his method was essentially a "whole-word" method
rather than a "phonics" method of the traditional kind. Fries
also stressed the importance of oral reading in the belief that the
written message is but a representation of the oral message; however, his goal was still most definitely silent reading in the later
stages of the program. The following is an example of a page from
one of the Fries readers, as these were later developed from his
ideas.

The Cat on the Van.

Dan is on the van.
Nat is on the van.
The pan is on the van.

The cat can bat the pan.
Dan can pat the cat.
The man ran the van.[11]

Like Bloomfield, Fries had very little to say about comprehension: both apparently regarded comprehension as a basically
passive activity which is highly dependent on oral language
skills. Children must learn to react instantly to the contrasts
between *mat* and *mate* and between *bit* and *beat*. They already
react to the differences between these words when they are
spoken. What they must do in learning to read is to associate a
visual pattern which they have learned to discriminate from
other visual patterns to a speech pattern which they already
know and can discriminate from other speech patterns. A child
who is learning to read is already subconsciously aware of the
different kinds of meanings and patterns in his language or he
could not communicate in that language. What he needs to have
unlocked for him is the code that is writing, so that he can have
access to these different kinds of meanings and patterns through
the medium of print. Fries went so far as to claim that this code
can be unlocked for the beginning reader within a year of his
learning to "talk satisfactorily," an age which he put at four or
five. Needless to say, this claim has appeared to be rather extrav-

agant to many who actually teach reading. Fries, therefore, did not regard the problem of teaching reading comprehension as a serious one. He obviously took issue with wide-ranging definitions of the reading process which relate that process to social, psychological, and physiological factors in favor of a view of the reading process as a kind of high-speed visual recognition of meanings that are already familiar to the reader. Reading comprehension is, therefore, a specific instance of general linguistic comprehension.

In both the Bloomfield and Fries approaches there is a strong insistence that a particular kind of linguistic knowledge is of paramount importance in gaining insight into the reading process and in determining the content of a reading series. There is also an assumption that principles of linguistic analysis, such as patterning and contrast, can by extrapolation become useful principles in reading pedagogy. Henry Lee Smith has pointed out[12] that there are certain valid pedagogical points which linguists have tended to ignore when they have talked about reading. In listing a number of these, he specifies such matters as typography, choice of illustrations, some repetition of patterns and words, and attention to both story line and characters. Smith cautions that it would be unwise for linguists who take an interest in reading to assume that reading teachers have learned nothing about teaching reading from their experiences, either individually or collectively. His words have been heeded to some extent in recent writings on linguistics and reading. They were obviously motivated in part by the hostility which characterized some of the original linguistics-reading discussions. That such hostility, particularly on the part of the reading experts, should have been aroused is not surprising when one reads some of the statements made by linguists about reading. For example, the statements by Bloomfield and Hall that there should be no illustrations in reading texts and the one by Fries that reading is a passive activity run counter to what most authorities on reading consider to be pedagogically sound observations. It must be emphasized that linguistics as a discipline has nothing at all to contribute to the discussion of whether or not there should be illustrations in a reading text: the inclusion or exclusion of illustrations is entirely a pedagogical decision. Likewise, any definition of reading which makes it out to be a passive activity indicates a certain lack of awareness of the many problems inherent in the teaching of reading.

It would not be unfair to say that what has become known as the linguistic method of teaching reading in North America is one which relies heavily on the work of Bloomfield and Fries. In essence, the method entails little more than the presentation of regular phoneme-grapheme, or sound-spelling, relationships in beginning reading texts, in many ways a kind of neo-phonics. The materials developed by the followers of Bloomfield and Fries reflect this concern: there is almost no indication in these materials that the possible linguistic contribution to reading involves anything more than the systematic introduction of the regularities and irregularities of English spelling. There is, in fact, scarcely more than an occasional passing reference to any other than this one solitary point that linguists have made about English.

The concern for phoneme-grapheme correspondences and for the importance of these in teaching reading has led to many studies, some quite sophisticated, of the relationships of various phonological segments to various graphological segments. These studies vary in quality and purpose. One of the best studies has come from Richard Venezky, particularly because he has attempted to relate his correspondence studies to a model of the reading process.[13] Venezky has done more than count phonemes and graphemes, compute frequencies of correspondence, and attempt to program a logical sequence of correspondences. Rather, he has attempted to construct a set of rules for translating orthographic symbols into speech sounds, because he considers it useful to characterize the reading process in those terms. His work is, therefore, an attempt to construct a model of the reading process which recognizes the distributions of phonemes and graphemes, the frequencies of occurrence, and the patterns of correspondences. Central to the model is a set of rules which relates all of these. Venezky writes of the process of learning to read as follows:

> Learning to read . . . requires primarily the translation from written symbols to sound, a procedure which is the basis of the reading process and is probably the only language skill unique to reading . . . . The patterns summarized here represent an ideal system for translating from spelling to sound. . . .[14]

He describes how the model works as follows:

> As examples of how this model organizes spelling-to-sound rules,

the processes for predicting the pronunciation of *social* and *signing* are shown below.

social would be mapped into *//sosɪæl//* by the grapheme-to-morphophoneme rules for the separate units *s, o, c, i, a, l.* On the first morphophonemic level, the main word stress would be placed on the first syllable, resulting in *//sōsɪæl//.* Then, through vowel reduction, *//ɪæl//* would become *//jəl//* and the resulting *//sj//* would be palatalized to *//š//.* The form *//sóšəl//* would then be mapped onto the phonemic level, giving */sóšəl/.*

signing would first be broken into *sign* and *ing* and then each of these graphemic allomorphs would be mapped onto the morphophonemic level, yielding *//sɪgn//* and *//ɪng//.* Upon combination of the two forms and the application of stress and certain phonotactical rules, the form *//signɪŋg//* would result. By rules for leveling consonant clusters, final *//ŋg//* would become *//ŋ//* and *//gn//* would become *//n//* with compensatory alternation of *//ɪ//* to *//ai//.* These operations yield *//sáɪnɪŋ//* which is automatically mapped into */sáɪnɪŋ/.*[15]

There are some very interesting differences between such an approach and that of Bloomfield and Fries. First of all, there is a concern with a level of representation called *morphophonemic,* a representation which looks very like the standard orthography. Then there is a set of ordered rules which, for example, assign stress and convert morphophonemes sometimes into morphophonemes but always eventually into phonemes. This last phonemic level is important in Venezky's work. He makes no attempt to eliminate it. Nor are the conversion rules necessarily made to conform to the demands of the kind of evaluation measure that the generative-transformationalists insist on in their work. In the *signing* example, the morphophoneme *//ɪ//* becomes the phonemes */ai/* (through an intermediate morphophonemic stage) in an apparently idiosyncratic way that a computer can handle which is apparently unrelated to the way in which certain other morphophonemes are given their phonemic realizations. However, Venezky's work does recognize some important patterns of English orthography as, for example, in the following comment on the *a* grapheme and on the possible pedagogical consequences. Venezky points out that the letter *a* has two primary pronunciations in stressed position, */æ/* and */e/*, and he notes the orthographic and phonological relationships of pairs of words like *annal* and *anal, rat* and *rate,* and *sane* and *sanity.* He adds this comment:

The Bloomfieldian sequencing begins with the /æ/ pronunciation for *a*, introducing the /e/ pronunciation at a later time with no special emphasis on the relation between /æ/ and /e/ when derived from *a*. An alternative to this approach is to present both pronunciations at once, working with such pairs as *rat:rate, mat:mate, fat:fate, hat:hate,* and *man:mane.* Both the associations of *a* to /æ/ and *a* to /e/ and the discrimination of the graphemic environments would be emphasized. Whether or not a child first learning to read can handle this task probably depends upon the pedagogy employed. The potential generalization derived from the differentiation approach, however, certainly is greater than that from the simple-sequence method.[16]

Venezky has added a further dimension to understanding the reading process beyond that of the contributions of Bloomfield and Fries. As is indicated in Diagram I, Bloomfield and Fries were concerned with a model of the process in which the beginning reader was required to establish a set of visual contrasts and then to associate this set of visual contrasts to a set of already known phonemic contrasts. Venezky is less concerned with such simple sets of contrasts and associations. As indicated in Diagram II, he favors drawing up a set of conversion rules rather than a set of association rules. Moreover, he is very much concerned with proceeding from writing to speech rather than in the opposite direction.

In addition to postulating such a model of the process, Venezky also points out the way in which pairs of lax and tense, or, in his terms, "checked" and "free," vowels relate to each other in English, in such words pairs as *fat:fate, met:mete, sit:site,*

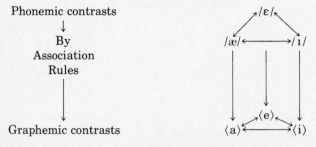

Bloomfield and Fries

Diagram I

Venezky

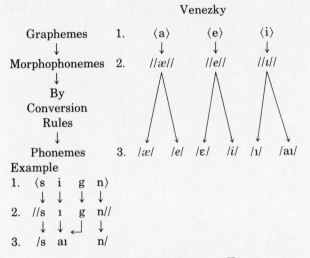

Phonemes   3. /æ/   /e/   /ε/   /i/   /ɪ/   /aɪ/

Example
1. ⟨s i g n⟩
    ↓ ↓ ↓ ↓
2. //s ɪ g n//
    ↓ ↓ ⤶ ↓
3. /s aɪ   n/

Diagram II

rob:robe, and *run:rune.* He stresses the fact that English ortho-graphic conventions require the use of the same vowel letter in certain orthographic patterns, as with the *a* in *sane:sanity,* the *e* in *concede:concession,* and the *i* in *collide:collision,* but he makes no attempt to account for the patterning synchronically.

As is well known, the phonemic level of representation of so much interest to Bloomfield, Fries, and Venezky holds no attrac-tion to Noam Chomsky and Morris Halle, who regard it as no more than the methodological artifact of a particular kind of lin-guistic inquiry which they have attacked repeatedly. Chomsky and Halle favor a level of representation which they call *system-atic phonemic,* a level which they claim the standard orthography captures quite well. They write as follows on this point in *The Sound Pattern of English:*

> There is, incidentally, nothing particularly surprising about the fact that conventional orthography is . . . a near optimal system for the lexical representation of English words. The fundamental principle of orthography is that phonetic variation is not indicated where it is predictable by general rule. Thus, stress placement and regular vowel or consonant alternations are generally not reflected. Orthography is a system designed for readers who know the language, who understand sentences and therefore know the surface structure of sentences. Such readers can produce the correct phonetic forms, given the orthographic

representation and the surface structure, by means of the rules that they employ in producing and interpreting speech. It would be quite pointless for the orthography to indicate these predictable variants. Except for unpredictable variants (e.g., *man-men, buy-bought*), an optimal orthography would have one representation for each lexical entry. Up to ambiguity, then, such a system would maintain a close correspondence between semantic units and orthographic representations.[17]

According to this claim, therefore, English orthography is a good orthography for a speaker who "knows" the language. Chomsky and Halle proceed to describe the reading process in the following terms. Diagram III attempts to model what they say.

[The] process of reading aloud . . . might . . . be described in the following way. We assume a reader who has internalized a grammar *G* of the language that he speaks natively. The reader is presented with a linear stretch *W* of written symbols, in a conventional orthography. He produces as an internal representation of this linear stretch *W* a string *S* of abstract symbols of the sort that we have been considering. Utilizing the syntactic and semantic information available to him, from a preliminary analysis of *S,* as well as much extralinguistic information regarding the writer and the context, the reader understands the utterance, and, in particular, assigns to *S* a surface structure Σ. With Σ available, he can then produce the phonetic representation of *S* and, finally, the physical signal corresponding to the visual input *W*. Clearly, reading will be facilitated to the extent that the orthography used for *W* corresponds to the underlying representations provided by the grammar *G*. To the extent that these correspond, the reader can rely on the familiar phonological processes to relate the visual input *W* to an acoustic signal. Thus one would expect that conventional orthography should, by and large, be superior to phonemic transcription, which is in general quite remote from underlying lexical or phonological representation and not related to it by any linguistically significant set of rules. . . . [Conventional orthography] can be read only when the surface structure (including the internal structure of words) is known, that is, when the utterance is to some degree understood.[18]

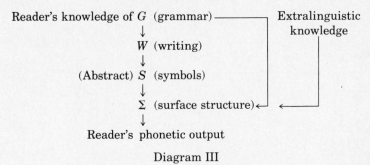

Diagram III

The Sound Pattern of English is primarily concerned with two problems. The first is the search for the optimal set of abstract phonological units to represent meaning units, that is for the best set of underlying lexical representations for English. The second is the search for the optimal set of rules to realize these lexical representations as phonetic output in order to convert a level of systematic phonemics into one of systematic phonetics. The result of the first search is the postulation of a set of systematic phonemes which look remarkably like the set of phonemes one needs to postulate for Early Modern English. For example, the set of systematic vowel phonemes contains only monophthongal representations and uses both tense and lax and round and unround as distinctive features. The symbolization used by Chomsky and Halle looks very much the same as that of standard English orthography and neatly draws together both phonetically quite different vowels, such as those in *deduce* and *deduction, Canada* and *Canadian,* and *divine* and *divinity,* and variant pronunciations such as the well-known variant pronunciations of *ration, level, sinecure,* and *progress.* The result of the search for the optimal set of phonological units or systematic phonemes is an extremely elegant and attractive system. The result of the second search for generative phonological rules is the postulation of a set of such rules which resemble, even in their clothing in distinctive features and a generative phonology, that set of rules more traditionally minded linguists must postulate to account for such phenomena as the Great Vowel Shift and other well-known sound changes. *The Sound Pattern of English* is a rather convincing demonstration that it is possible to describe a vast amount of English phonology within the system the authors postulate. The demonstration of the importance of two types of cluster, strong and weak, in determining stress placement, the generality of the transformational rules, and the importance of ordering and cycling in the application of the rules are undoubtedly important contributions to linguistic theory. However, there are many *ad hoc* decisions and exceptions and certainly the main vocabulary discussed in *The Sound Pattern of English* is of Romance origin. Moreover, the authors make few claims either for the truth of the system, stating only that *The Sound Pattern of English* is a report on "work in progress,"[19] or for its psychological reality. The interesting question to ask oneself then is of what use is the system for understanding the processes involved in reading, and in particular in beginning reading.

It is possible to make some observations about the proposals put forward by Chomsky and Halle. The first one is that this type of theoretical work may really be of little or no use for gaining any insights at all into the reading process. One might observe that since Chomsky and Halle are largely concerned with vocabulary of Romance origin, what they have to say about such vocabulary adds little to any understanding of the processes involved in beginning reading. A beginning reader neither knows nor needs to know this vocabulary, and he certainly should not be taught it as part of the task of learning to read. His reading materials should be filled with vocabulary of Germanic origin, possibly of a simple monosyllabic variety. Certainly, it should not be words like *policy, politic, politicize, politico-economic, polyandrous, polyandry, polygamous, polygamy, polyhedral, poly-hedrous, pond, Pontiac, pontificate,* and so on, which is one randomly selected sequence from the World Index to *The Sound Pattern of English.*[20] It is an interesting fact that most of us can pronounce these words correctly without even knowing what some of them mean, but they are, except for *pond,* not the words we would expect a six-year old to know or want him to read. Rather, they are just the words we expect him to be able to read later when, as a result of learning to read, he is in the position of being able to read in order to learn. Much of Chomsky and Halle's description is valid only for a particular kind of person, a highly literate one. The crucial question is how much of such a rich system of phonology as that postulated in *The Sound Pattern of English* can we ascribe to a six-year old. Undoubtedly we must ascribe a great deal, for certainly a six-year old can assign stress correctly, does reduce vowels automatically, and does make the majority of surface phonetic contrasts without difficulty. A six-year old undoubtedly possesses much of the basic phonological competence he will have as an adult. At the same time though, it is likely that the sets of transformational rules that he uses and of lexical representations that he has at his disposal are more limited than the sets discussed in *The Sound Pattern of English*.

A second observation about the system concerns what may be called its direction. The system put forward in *The Sound Pattern of English* is one which appears to focus on how meaning is encoded into sound, in spite of the claims to neutrality between speaker and hearer which Chomsky has made repeatedly. For example, Chomsky and Halle point out that an awareness of surface structure is necessary if one is to assign certain stress patterns correctly and to make the rules operate properly in the production of sentences. However, the task which confronts a reader is one of decoding print to discover meaning. His task is one of somehow getting to meaning through print. The beginning reader must use the visual cues he has on the page to reconstruct the meaning, must somehow give a syntactic reading to a phrase such as *American history teacher* ([*American history*] *teacher* or *American* [*history teacher*]) before he can pronounce it correctly. The writing system does not mark surface structure except in certain gross ways such as by word spacing and punctuation marks. The beginning reader's task is apparently one of relating symbols to sounds at an age when such abilities as the ability to assign a surface structure may be quite different from those of sophisticated adults. Chomsky and Halle comment as follows on some of the problems:

> There are many interesting questions that can be raised about the development of systems of underlying representation during the period of language acquisition. It is possible that this might be fairly slow. There is, for example, some evidence that children tend to hear much more phonetically than adults. There is no reason to jump to the conclusion that this is simply a matter of training and experience; it may very well have a maturational basis. Furthermore, much of the evidence relevant to the constructure of the underlying systems of representation may not be available in early stages of language acquisition. These are open questions, and it is pointless to speculate about them any further. They deserve careful empirical study, not only

because of the fundamental importance of the question of
"psychological reality" of linguistic constructs, but also for
practical reasons; for example, with respect to the problem of the
teaching of reading.[21]

The comment is a most interesting one because if empirical evidence confirms the suspicion that Chomsky and Halle have, then
it would tend to justify much of the approach taken to reading by
Bloomfield and Fries. It would justify an approach which utilizes
a taxonomic phonemic, or broad phonetic, level of representation
and which relates such a level to orthographic patterns, an approach, too, which excludes work with derivational patterning in
favor of work with sound-letter associations and which, by some
kind of happy default, does not get itself involved with patterns
of stress assignment in polysyllabic words, patterns which one
can assume a six-year old already controls to a great extent by
virtue of the fact that he is a native speaker.

It could well be that the basic problem a child has in learning
to read is really one of learning the association between written
symbols and surface rather than deep phonology. For example, he
must learn that *hatter:hater; petter:Peter; dinner:diner; comma:
coma;* and *supper:super* show a systematic spelling difference
associated with a systematic surface phonological difference. In
the terminology used by reading teachers he must learn that a
double consonant indicates a "short" vowel and that a single consonant plus vowel indicates a "long" vowel. Even though the use
of the letters *a, e, i, o,* and *u* in the above words is "correct" in
Chomsky and Halle's terms in spite of the very different phonetic
realizations, the child's problem is one of cueing in to the visual
task involved in decoding, a task which even the generative-
transformationalists refer to as the problem of identifying the
visual response. Likewise, with a set of words like *metal, rebel,
civil, Mongol,* and *cherub,* it is important that the child have
available to him a strategy for approaching these words so that
he can attempt to pronounce them as *metal* or *meetal, rebel* or
reeble, and so on. It helps him very little to be told that the spellings are the best ones for English because there are also English
words like *metallic, rebellion, civilian, Mongolian,* and *cherubic.*
A six-year old is even less likely to know these derivatives than
the base forms and any knowledge about the "best" spellings for
the second vowel in each word is more appropriate to teaching

him to spell than to read. Perhaps *The Sound Pattern of English* is a better book for those interested in teaching spelling than in teaching reading, tasks which appear to be rather different!

What the child basically needs in beginning reading is a set of strategies for decoding print. No one is really sure what strategies successful beginning readers do employ. There is reason to suspect that they do not use the strategies which teachers who believe in the various phonics approaches attempt to teach. These latter strategies, sometimes called phonic generalizations, have been severely attacked by linguists. However, a few of them seem to contain germs of truth, particularly recognizable after reading *The Sound Pattern of English,* as, for example, statements about final *e*'s making preceding vowels "long," about an *i* before *gh* having its "long" sound, about *c*'s before *e*'s or *i*'s being "soft," and so on. But then such is likely to be the case. Phonics instruction cannot be all wrong—rather it shows evidence of considerable confusion in its general orientation and the need for a transfusion of linguistic insights, not euthanasia.

This discussion of the work of Bloomfield, Fries, Venezky, Chomsky, and Halle leads to certain conclusions. The first very obvious one is that some linguists do have an interest in applying their theoretical knowledge to the solution of practical problems. However, the second is that the proposed applications vary considerably and the results are sometimes contradictory. Linguists have different ideas about linguistics and about the nature of the problems to which linguistics might contribute a solution. Some linguists are also more definite in their proposals than others. It is possible to contrast the attempt by Fries at what appears to be a definitive attack on the reading problem to the extremely tentative suggestions put forward by Chomsky and Halle. Furthermore, the reading process itself is not an easy one to understand. Linguists have different notions about what language is, about how it may be described, about what its fundamental units are, about how these are related, and about what processes may operate. All these are linguistic matters quite properly and all have some relevance to understanding the reading process and teaching reading. But there are also nonlinguistic matters which must be taken into account when one turns to problems in learning and teaching, and help must be sought from psychologists and educators as well as from linguists. The greatest need at present is for empirical work in which linguists, psychologists, and educators combine their insights in an attempt to improve our understanding of the reading process and the teaching of reading.

Notes

1. This is a revised version of a paper presented at the autumn meeting of the British Association for Applied Linguistics, in Edinburgh on September 28, 1968.
2. Leonard Bloomfield. "Why a Linguistic Society?" *Language* 1 (1925):5.
3. Leonard Bloomfield and Clarence L. Barnhart. *Let's Read.* Detroit: Wayne State University Press, 1961.
4. Bloomfield and Barnhart, p. 36.
5. Bloomfield and Barnhart, p. 101.
6. Bloomfield and Barnhart, pp. 41–42.
7. Robert A. Hall, Jr., *Introductory Linguistics.* Philadelphia: Chilton Book Company, 1964, p. 432.
8. Leonard Bloomfield and Clarence L. Barnhart. *Let's Read,* Part I. Experimental edition. Bronxville, N.Y.: C. L. Barnhart, 1963, p. 37.
9. Charles C. Fries. *Linguistics and Reading.* New York: Holt, Rinehart & Winston, 1963.
10. Charles C. Fries. *Teaching and Learning English as a Foreign Language.* Ann Arbor: University of Michigan Press, 1945.
11. Charles C. Fries, Agnes C. Fries, Rosemary G. Wilson, and Mildred K. Rudolph. *Merrill Linguistic Readers, Reader I.* Columbus: Charles E. Merrill Books, 1966, p. 36.
12. Henry Lee Smith. "Review of *Let's Read.*" *Language* 39 (1963):67–78.
13. Richard L. Venezky. "English Orthography: Its Graphical Structure and Its Relation to Sound." *Reading Research Quarterly* 2, no. 3 (1967):75–105.
14. Venezky, p. 102.
15. Venezky, pp. 94–95.
16. Venezky, p. 103.
17. Noam Chomsky and Morris Halle. *The Sound Pattern of English.* New York: Harper & Row, 1968, p. 49.
18. Chomsky and Halle, pp. 49–50.
19. Chomsky and Halle, p. vii.
20. Chomsky and Halle, p. 458.
21. Chomsky and Halle, p. 50.

> **False dichotomies abound. Here it is suggested that the current debate over "code-emphasis" instruction versus "meaning-emphasis" instruction is invalid.**

Decoding and the Quest of Meaning

Discussions of reading sometimes assume a contradiction between decoding a passage and discovering its meaning. If decoding is interpreted as converting graphemes into phonemes, then there is indeed a fence on whose two sides partisans of two opposed points of view can range themselves: code-breakers vs. meaning-pursuers. The decoding advocate can argue that speech is common property, even among nonreaders, and that writing is a set of clues designed to elicit in the reader's mind the spoken language; since native speakers already know the greater part of the spoken language before they come to school, the teaching of reading is simply a matter of clueing the student into the system for turning printed hieroglyphics into the already-familiar language of speech. The pursuer of meaning, on the other hand, can argue that the capacity to pronounce haltingly a page of prose is a far cry from understanding what one is pronouncing — that the principal problem in promoting literacy is not to teach the empty mouthing of sounds but to foster an intelligent approach to the significance of the passage, including a capacity for judgment, appreciation, and lively animated response.

The question I wish to raise is whether there is any real justification for the opposition — and indeed mutual contempt — which seems to exist between these two points of view. The function of the present article, then, is a modest attempt at peacemaking. It seeks to place "both" objectives in a common framework with a common objective compatible with both points of view. The advantage of the framework I have in mind is that it leaves plenty of room for all honest toilers in the field of language instruction. Indeed, the chief problem may be that there are so few people to man so wide a territory that we may all be out of shouting distance from one another.

The term "decoding," it seems to me, has often been narrowly interpreted as applying to the process of producing a sequence of sounds that corresponds in some way to a sequence of written marks. The ability to perform this type of decoding — sometimes known as "sounding out" a passage — is, of course, a civilized and valuable skill. It is, indeed, so valuable that any adult in the United States who cannot do it with most of the printed matter he encounters is a severely handicapped person; whoever — for whatever reason — cannot perform this sort of decoding with ease, confidence, and a fair accuracy, must necessarily lead a life that is full of complications, embarrassments, and more seriously circumscribed possibilities than most "normal" readers can even imagine. Furthermore, there is no reason to suppose that, in spite of certain "irregularities" in English spelling, the skill to perform this phonological decoding is too arcane and abstruse for the vast majority of children to acquire with reasonable competence in a fairly short period of time. Finally, there seems to be mounting evidence both that the irregularity of the language has been viewed too pessimistically and that phonological approaches to beginning reading have a benign influence on measurable achievement. In the latter connection, of course, Chall's massive review of the literature (1967) and the report by Bond and Dykstra (1967) on the so-called First-Grade Reading Studies, embracing twenty-seven separate projects, constitute evidence that cannot be lightly dismissed. In the former connection, the work of Venezky (1967) and the large-scale study of phoneme-grapheme correspondences by Hanna, Hanna, Hodges, and Rudorf (1966) provide a substantial contribution to a perhaps belated defense of our oft-maligned spelling system. In discussing the last-mentioned study, a prominent dialectologist remarks:

> If the algorithm tested in the later chapters, which is mainly phonological, can produce the correct spellings of almost 90 percent of the sounds in a corpus of 17,310 words, it seems likely that recognition of morphemic boundaries and diaphonemes might push the percentage of accuracy near 100 percent and reduce the list of really unpredictable spellings near zero. (Reed, 1967.)

Whether the instructional efficiency of phonological decoding approaches to reading and the current high estimates of regularity in phoneme-grapheme correspondences are accepted at the values suggested by these researchers may, of course, remain controversial; but the value of early and systematic alphabetic instruction for readers of English—that is, instruction in the relation between spelling and sound—can hardly any longer be a matter of serious controversy. There is very little prospect of success in the pursuit of meaning by students who cannot decipher successfully the words that contribute so substantially to the meaning of any piece of prose. The confusion and controversy among teachers about this kind of decoding must derive not from its obvious values but from overstatements on its behalf by those who would insist that no other procedures are necessary in order to extract the meaning from a passage.

By "other procedures" I do *not* have in mind an unsystematic "combination of methods" by which—it appears—the simple obligation to acquaint students with the system of their language becomes diluted and diffused into an aura of "good feeling" and irreparable confusion and dependency. I have in mind, rather, the fact that meaning is conveyed not by an indiscriminate succession of phonemes (or their graphemic counterparts), but by a hierarchical structure of units and processes starting with the linguists' morpheme and proceeding through the most sophisticated concepts of modern rhetoric and literary analysis. From the point of view which I am suggesting, most insights concerning the interpretation of English prose are contributions to the teaching of reading. These would include not only studies in depth—such as those at the research level in literary criticism (*e.g.,* a "key" to *Finnegans Wake* or an interpretation of the symbolism in *Moby Dick* and *Pierre*), but also treatments from the point of view of the "competent" reader, suggesting how he may glean more meaning in less time (*e.g.,* Adler's *How to Read a Book* or Spache and Berg's *The Art of Efficient Reading*).

The procedures by which meaning is extracted from a passage (i.e., by which decoding is done) occur at several widely recognized levels of structure, of complexity and organization, within a piece of writing. The first of these is morphemic—i.e., at a level *lower* in complexity than that of the word. A student cannot be said to read very successfully—or *to know how to decode a passage competently*—unless he can not only cope with the various graphemic units in which the letter *s* participates phonologically (e.g., *sh* or the /z/ sound at the end of *goes*), but also understands the meanings contributed morphemically by this *same* letter and its *various* phonemic counterparts in such differing instances as *goes, takes, despises, friends, bricks,* and *mazes* (i.e., respectively, as the third person singular inflectional morpheme designated by the phonemes /z/, /s/, and /iz/, and the morpheme *plural* designated by the same phonemes). It has been argued (Osgood, 1964) that the morpheme is "psychologically nonexistent"—on the basis that in *boys* and *noise,* there is "no sense of the morpheme boundary in the former"; but the point is not whether the listener or reader recognizes the morpheme as an entity (he almost certainly *won't* unless he has studied linguistics!) but that he gets the message conveyed by the *s* of *boys* in a quite different way from that in which he gets the message of the final sound in *noise.* In *noise* this last sound is necessary in order for him to make any sense at all of the immediately preceding sounds of the word, whereas in *boys* the two morphemes contribute intelligibly and independently to the denotation of the word: without the *s* the word is still meaningful.

The next level, of course, is the word itself—involving the reader's understanding (in action—not of course consciously or explicitly) of the distinction between a free and a bound morpheme—whereby, for instance, the so-called plural morpheme, while quite meaningful, cannot occur in the absence of a *base* to which it is applied (i.e., if the reader were to see an isolated *s* in a piece of prose, he would—in spite of his familiarity with its general meaning as a plural—*not* so interpret it, but would search for some other meaning, as, for instance, in the expression *s-curve,* which he would not interpret as a synonym of *curves).* Evidence that even in speech, and in spite of the specific lexical meanings attaching to morphemes, the word is clearly recognized as a meaning-bearing unit in some different sense from that of the morpheme was adduced a generation ago by Sapir (1921).

The next level essential to decoding is very complex indeed — and here, far more than with morphemes or words, the teacher of reading or the adult student of a new language needs to take into account a vast amount of information that is totally distinct from "lower" levels of organization in—and of contribution to the meaning of—a piece of writing. This is, obviously, the level of syntax. The range of syntactic structures, of course, extends from the phrase (or, perhaps, even more simply from the residue of "deletion" transformation—*e.g.,* a single adjective—or, for that matter, from the form-class in which a given word participates in a given context) to the vast grammatical riches of discourse, sustained and as yet—even in the most advanced theoretical literature—not very well analyzed.

The reason syntax poses such a special problem for students' decoding of written English is that, in countless instances, it presents complications which are simply not to be found in the spoken language. It is not that the written language is totally different, in gross ways, from the spoken language—but that in varying degrees it becomes more dense, more formal, less redundant, and less embroidered with the concurrent nonverbal language of expression, gesture, and so on. There are even some minor but significant qualitative differences—as, for instance, between this rather dated poetic language and current standard speech:

> Breathes there the man, with soul so dead,
> Who never to himself hath said
> This is my own, my native land!
> Whose heart hath ne'er within him burn'd
> As home his footsteps he hath turn'd,
> From wandering on a foreign strand.

The problem here, for the unsophisticated reader, goes well beyond questions of vocabulary (and would apply equally if *hath* were changed to *has, ne'er* to *never,* and *strand* to *shore).* Very puzzling to the naive reader is the occurrence of the nonstandard question *breathes there* in lieu of *does there breathe,* the baffling inversion of *he has turned his footsteps home* into *home his footsteps he has turned,* and the startling remoteness of *whose* from its antecedent eighteen words earlier.

The sheer quantitative burden of adult prose syntax (encountered in ninth-grade civics if not earlier) is suggested by the following challenge to the struggling reader:

> Every order, resolution, or vote to which the concurrence of the Senate and House of Representatives may be necessary (except on a question of adjournment) shall be presented to the President of the United States, and before the same shall take effect shall be approved by him, or being disapproved by him, shall be repassed by two-thirds of the Senate and the House of Representatives, according to the rules and limitations prescribed in the case of a bill.

If the reader is asked to process more syntax than he has any previous skill in handling, he is likely to be defeated by the problem of having too many unresolved variables to keep in mind. The psychologists' rule of "seven plus or minus two" (Miller, 1956) contributes importantly, it seems to me, to the decoding problems posed by this kind of prose. Unless the reader can cope syntactically with the structure of the sentence (so that, for instance, he sees in the last example *what* it is that "shall be repassed"), then he is being asked to hold in mind more isolated ideas at once than he knows what to do with. If, however, the structure itself is readily understandable to the reader (as from extensive reading of comparable material), then what might have been a confusing variable becomes instead a reasonable contributing part of a quite sensible *single* phenomenon. Since, again in the last example, the vocabulary is not especially formidable, the decoding problem is clearly at a higher level than phonemic-graphemic relations, morphemes, or words.

We are far, of course, from a complete technology of syntax, even in the most advanced linguistic quarters—and further yet from anything really suitably predigested for wide dissemination in the public schools. This is merely one dramatic locale in the "wide territory" mentioned above which is all too hard to staff with present knowledge and personnel. We have grammarians laboring hard in the jungle of syntax—traditionalists, structuralists, transformationalists, tagmemicists, stratificationalists—attempting to clear the ground for future occupants (but all too often prone—like reading experts—to pick on one another instead, in spite of vast unfinished business of a more serious nature). We have verbal behaviorists and psycholinguists approaching the understanding of a sentence through models derived and resynthesized from those of the grammarians (*e.g.*, Osgood, 1964). We also have—perhaps at this level, or perhaps (for at this altitude levels are poorly defined) at a different level best described as rhetorical—a burgeoning "science of writing" whose obverse is a key to the reading of an author's subtler rhetorical strategies. The pages of *College English* and of *College Composition and Communication* have, for several years, reflected this growing specificity about what, exactly, a good writer does to achieve his impact (especially in the work of Christensen, 1963, 1965, 1968).

Finally, at two levels which are perhaps "higher" yet—available through stylistics (*e.g.*, Sebeok, 1960) and literary criticism—the advanced reader's growing sensitivity and appreciation need to be matched by the highest levels of reading instruction if he is to pursue the meanings of a piece of writing all the way to its grandest purposes and its shyest subtleties.

At all of these levels, I would like to suggest, decoding takes place. When the great symbolic novelist imbeds a deeply intricate design into his masterpiece, the reader's problem is to observe the means and to grasp the message. This is no less a decoding problem (and perhaps no *more*) than that facing the elementary-school student who has just come upon his first "silent initial *g*" (*gnome, gnaw*), or who is beginning to realize that sentence intonation differs appreciably from that of the same words in lists or in isolation.

The writer, who usually has nothing to help him communicate his meanings to the reader except parallel lines of black type, must invest those lines with signals for his meanings—not just for the discrete sounds of particular words. The reader who knows how to pursue meanings in a piece of writing also knows, at least in action, the various tactics and strategies adopted by writers for the expression of those meanings. And, unless we are to suppose ESP as standard equipment for good readers, then the reader must be able to get all of his clues to the meaning of the passage from the sequence of words, the parallel black lines. The fact that he brings his own knowledge of the world (content) and of the language (expression) to the task of reading does not alter the fact that he must decode the writer's message from the available text. (In fact, only his prior experience with both makes this essential task possible.) This decoding presupposes the identification of the smallest denotative units (morphemes) from still smaller (nondenotative) units (letters, and indeed from the distinctive features of letters by which one instance of one is distinguished from one instance of another). But it also presupposes the identification of the higher-level units of expression emerging from lower-level units—since meanings are conveyed (far more than additively) by larger as well as smaller units, from the "spirit" or style or symbolism of the work as a whole down to its humblest morpheme.

In terms established by our present knowledge of language, these levels of units which carry meaning seem to be, in the order of complexity, the morpheme, the word, the phrase, the clause, the sentence, the "metasentence" (a group of mutually dependent sentences), the paragraph and other rhetorical structures, the overriding style of the piece of writing, and perhaps certain larger "literary" entities in the case of substantial pieces of writing.

There is no "approach" to any of these levels which can be construed as genuinely incompatible with a reasonable interpretation of "decoding." Neither can there be any cryptography, applicable by a reader to a passage of prose, which could possibly fail to provide information vital in the pursuit of meaning. In view of this compatibility—indeed, total interdependence—of decoding and the quest of meaning as processes in reading, I submit that any realistic description of successful reading behavior must find the reader to be engaged continuously and simultaneously in both.

Furthermore, if this is the case, then the various disciplines and points of view which can shed light on the nature of meaning (and meaners!), and on the nature of decoding (and decoders!) cannot be safely ignored by anyone interested in the meaning of decoding or the decoding of meaning.

References

Bond, G. L., and Dykstra, R. "The Cooperative Research Program in First-Grade Reading Instruction." *Reading Research Quarterly* 2, no. 4:5–142, Summer 1967.

Chall, J. *Learning to Read.* New York: McGraw-Hill, 1967.

A child learns to recognize written words. What enables him to do so? Stages of perceptual organization, as suggested by Piaget, may help answer the question. Beyond this, they may suggest indirectly some optimal techniques for aiding word perception.

Piaget's Theory of Perceptual Development: Its Application to Reading and Special Education*

DAVID ELKIND

This paper will describe an application of Piaget's theory of perceptual development to the process of reading. Before proceeding, however, it might be well to make a few general remarks about Piaget and education.

*Revised from an invited address delivered to Division 16 of the American Psychological Association, New York, 1966.

Although a great deal has been written on education in the name of Piaget, he himself has never been very much concerned with pedagogical issues—and this for at least two reasons. First of all, he tends to feel that practical applications of his work are somewhat premature—that we need to have much more information about the mental development of the child before we begin tampering with educational practice. Secondly, and perhaps more significantly, Piaget sees himself primarily as an epistemologist rather than an educator or psychologist and is more concerned with resolving philosophical issues through the experimental study of the child than with advancing psychological theory or improving educational practice. Accordingly, what follows here is an interpretation of the implication of Piaget's perceptual theory for reading and is not necessarily the view of Piaget himself of these matters.

The paper is divided into four parts. In the first part Piaget's developmental theory of perception will be briefly summarized. In the second and third parts two lines of research on this theory will be interpreted with respect to the process of reading. The concluding section will deal with some implications for remedial education.

Piaget's Developmental Theory of Perception

According to Piaget (1961), perception is developmental in nature, which is to say that it changes significantly with age through the interaction of maturation and experience. Unlike the development of intelligence, which is marked by qualitatively distinct stages related to age, the development of perception is continuous and must be assessed quantitatively rather than qualitatively. The essential characteristic of this development is a gradual shift from perception that is controlled by peripheral sensory processes to perception where central processes play the leading role. Let me be somewhat more specific.

In Piaget's (1961) view, the perception of the young child is *centered* in the sense that it is caught and held by the dominant aspects of the visual field. In each case, the dominant aspects of the field are determined by Gestalt-like principles such as *closure, good form,* and *continuity* which Piaget calls *field effects.* With increasing age, however, and the development of *perceptual activities* (internalized actions), perception becomes increasingly *decentered* in the sense that it is progressively freed from its earlier domination by the field effects. These general ideas need to be amplified in several ways.

First of all, perceptual activities differ in kind and function, and include *perceptual exploration, schematization, reorganization, anticipation,* and *transport.* Secondly, recent research suggests that these activities do not appear all at once but rather emerge in a sequence which is related to age. A corollary to this observation is that *decentration* — the behavioral evidence of perceptual activity — is not a once-and-for-all phenomenon but rather is always relative to the particular activity in question. That is to say, a child whose perception may be decentered with respect to exploration may not display decentration on a task requiring reorganization. Finally, the extent to which a subject can decenter in any given situation is always a joint function of the level of maturity of the perceptual activities in question and the nature of the stimulus itself. For those configurations where field effects are strong, decentration may appear at a later age than it will for those configurations where the field effects are weak.

Although this theory would seem to have relevance for a wide range of perceptual phenomena, Piaget and his colleagues have limited their research almost exclusively to the study of geometric illusions. In our work, on the other hand, we have attempted to apply this theory to the perception of meaningful materials. In the following sections two aspects of our research will be described which seem to have particular relevance for the problem of reading, namely, our work on schematization and reorganization.

Perceptual Schematization and Reading

The activity which Piaget calls *schematization* involves the coordination of wholes and parts in such a way that both retain their unique identity without losing their interdependence. To study this activity, we constructed a set of drawings in which wholes were made out of parts with independent identities (Elkind, Koegler, & Go, 1964). For example, we had a man made out of fruit with an apple for a head, a pear for a body, bananas for legs, and bunches of grapes for arms. When we showed these drawings to children at different age levels we found that nursery school children saw only the parts, kindergarten and first grade children saw primarily the wholes, and children at the second grade and beyond saw both the parts and the wholes in an integrated fashion. A common response among the older children was: "A man made out of fruit."

What do these findings mean with respect to reading—or, more particularly, to the *look-say* method of reading instruction? As the writer understands this method, it teaches the child to recognize the whole word without analysis of its parts. Successful reading, on the other hand, would seem to require a true whole-part schematization; a good reader must be aware both of the independence of the individual letters and of the whole word while remaining cognizant of their interdependence. Only a true whole-part schematization of words will enable the child to spontaneously discover and recognize new words. The *look-say* method would seem to work against such schematization. A more fruitful approach might be to train children directly on this perceptual activity.

A similar conclusion will be reached after a consideration of a second perceptual activity of importance to reading skill, namely, *perceptual reorganization*.

Perceptual Reorganization and Reading

In the Piaget sense, *perceptual reorganization* means acting upon a given configuration so as to produce a new organization without corresponding modification of the stimulus. A simple example of such reorganization is figure-ground reversal. When looking at an ambiguous figure such as the classic Rubin Vase-Profile, one can see either two profiles or a vase without any change in the stimulus. While some psychologists (e.g., Kohler & Wallach, 1944) attribute such reversals to sensory dynamics such as the firing and recovery rates of neurons, Piaget attributes figure-ground reversal to a perceptual activity which is, in some respects, similar to the process of logical multiplication on the plane of conception.

According to Piaget (Piaget & Morf, 1958), the ability to reverse figure and ground depends upon the child's readiness to mentally detach the contour line from one area and reattach it to another. For example, to see the *vase* in the Rubin Vase-Profile, the child must mentally attach the contour line to the center area while mentally detaching it from the surrounding area. To see the *profiles* the child must do just the opposite—he must attach the contour line to the surrounding area and detach it from the center area. For the young child, the essential difficulty is the recognition that one and the same element can give rise to two different forms depending upon the context.

The young child's difficulty in reversing figure and ground is directly comparable to his difficulty in multiplying logical classes. It is not until the age of 8 or 9, for example, that children recognize that they can be Protestant and American at the same time (Elkind, 1963). With respect to figure-ground reversal, the same holds true. In a number of studies (e.g., Elkind, 1964; Elkind, Koegler, & Go, 1962; Elkind & Scott, 1962) we have shown that it is not until the elementary school period that children begin to spontaneously reverse figure and ground when presented with ambiguous figures of the Rubin variety. These findings, it seems to me, are especially relevant to the teaching of English phonics.

It is probably fair to say that the major difficulty in learning English phonics lies in the fact that one and the same letter can represent more than one sound while one and the same sound can be represented by different letters. Similar problems are posed by the equivalence of upper- and lowercase letters and of script and printed letters. In all of these instances, the real problem lies in the recognition that the same element can represent different things and that different elements can represent the same thing. The problem is then directly analogous to that faced by the child in reversing figure and ground when viewing an ambiguous figure. That such an assumption is not fortuitous is shown by the fact that slow readers are deficient in the ability to reverse figure and ground in comparison with average readers of comparable mental ability (Elkind, Larson, & Van Doorninck, 1965).

In this connection, the apparent success of the Pitman International Teaching Alphabet may very well lie in its elimination of the need for perceptual reorganization. If this hypothesis is correct, an alternative might be to train children directly in perceptual activity of the reorganization type. Our experience (Elkind, Koegler, & Go, 1962) has been that children can profit from such instruction.

Implications for Special
Education

The significance for special education of the perceptual-activity approach to reading would seem to lie in two major areas — diagnosis and remediation. With respect to diagnosis, the measures of perceptual activity which have been constructed (Elkind, 1964; Elkind, Koegler, & Go, 1962; Elkind & Weiss, 1967) may well have diagnostic significance. We have already shown, for example, that measures of perceptual organization can discriminate between brain-injured and familial retarded children (Elkind, Koegler, Go, & Van Doorninck, 1965) and between speaking and nonspeaking children with limited hearing (Binnie, Elkind, & Stewart, 1966). We are currently testing kindergarten children with a battery of perceptual-activity tests to see whether we can predict success in reading during the first grade and whether we can select those kindergarten children who will encounter difficulty in learning to read.

Reading difficulties, of course, stem from many factors besides perceptual handicaps, and measures of perceptual activity should be employed only as part of a more inclusive assessment procedure. The particular value of the perceptual-activity measures in such an assessment procedure lies in their specificity. When a child does poorly on any one of our measures, we immediately have some idea of the processes involved and can direct our remediation effects accordingly.

With respect to remediation, we are currently engaged in a large-scale study to determine the effects of nonverbal training in perceptual activity for slow-reading urban children. Work with individual children with severe reading handicaps is also being undertaken. With the severely visually-retarded child we use many sensori-motor methods including sandpaper letters, letter-form boards, and movement exercises. In many ways our approach is similar to that of Fernald (1943) and for parallel reasons. Perceptual activities are, from a developmental standpoint, internalized actions. Such actions become internalized only after they have been mastered and perfected on the sensori-motor plane. This internalization, moreover, is automatic, and as soon as the child becomes proficient at the sensori-motor level, this proficiency is transferred to the perceptual realm.

Accordingly, any materials and procedures that aid the child in reorganizing arrays or objects, exploring patterns in a systematic fashion, and schematizing figures and patterns on the plane of action will be beneficial for the development of visual perceptual activities. For this reason teachers who forbid their pupils to follow words with their fingers are probably making a mistake. With some children, such pointing is a necessary prerequisite to completely unaided visual scanning, and the pointing will drop out by itself when this occurs. Thus allowing the child to use his fingers is not perpetuating a bad habit but, on the contrary, is fostering a perceptual skill. This is but one of the many practical implications to be drawn from a consideration of the role of perceptual activities in reading.

Conclusion

This paper has presented a brief sketch of Piaget's theory of perceptual development and attempted to convey some of the implications of research on this theory for the process of reading and remedial-reading instruction. Two perceptual activities – perceptual schematization and reorganization – are considered as essential components of the reading process. These activities, however, are by no means the only perceptual activities required for reading. Some of our recent work on perceptual exploration (Elkind & Weiss, 1967), for example, suggests that this activity is particularly relevant to the early stage of reading when up-down and left-right scanning patterns are being acquired. Likewise, some of our current work on perceptual anticipation and transport suggests that these activities are of importance for the more advanced stages of reading skill.

Without going into detail on these most recent phases of our work, it is hoped that what has been presented will suffice to convey the fruitfulness of the Piaget approach to perception for the problem of reading. On the practical plane, this approach has already led to new remedial teaching methods (Elkind, 1966) and may well lead to improved reading-readiness measures. The unique advantage of these practical applications of the Piagetian theory to the problem of reading seems to lie in the fact that they are based upon a consideration of the varied and complex perceptual acts the child must perform if he is to learn to read.

References

Binnie, C.; Elkind, D.; and Steward, J. "A comparison of the visual perceptual abilities of acoustically impaired and hearing children." *International Audiology* 5 (1966):233–41.

Elkind, D. "The child's conception of his religious denomination: III, The Protestant child." *Journal of Genetic Psychology* 103 (1963):291–304.

Elkind, D. "Ambiguous pictures for study of perceptual development and learning." *Child Development* 35 (1964):1391–96.

Elkind, D. "Non-verbal exercises for remedial reading instruction." *Colorado School Journal,* 1966.

Elkind, D.; Koegler, R. R.; and Go, E. "Effects of perceptual training at three age levels." *Science* 137 (1962):755–56.

Elkind, D.; Koegler, R. R.; and Go, E. "Studies in perceptual development: II, Part-whole perception." *Child Development* 35 (1964):81–90.

Elkind, D.; Koegler, R. R.; Go, E.; and Van Doorninck, W. "Effects of perceptual training on unmatched samples of brain-injured and familial retardates." *Journal of Abnormal Psychology* 70, no. 2, (1965):107–10.

Elkind, D.; Larson, M.; and Van Doorninck, W. "Perceptual decentration learning and performance in slow and average readers." *Journal of Education Psychology* 56 (1965):50–56.

Elkind, D., and Scott, L. "Studies in perceptual development: I. The decentering of perception." *Child Development* 33 (1962):619–30.

Elkind, D., and Weiss, J. "Studies in perceptual development: III. Perceptual organization." *Child Development* 38 (1967):553–61.

Fernald, G. M. *Remedial techniques in basic school subjects.* New York: McGraw Hill, 1943.

Kohler, W., and Wallach, H. "Figural aftereffects: an investigation of visual processes." Proceedings of the American Philosophical Society 83 (1944):269–357.

Piaget, J., and Morf, A. "Les isomorphismes partiels entre les structures logiques et les structures perceptives." In *Etudes d'épistémologie génétique,* vol. 6, edited by J. Piaget. Paris: Presses Universitaires de France, 1958, pp. 51–116.

Piaget, J. *Les mécanismes perceptifs.* Paris: Presses Universitaires de France, 1961.

High importance must always be attached to physical factors in the pursuit of literacy. Here as elsewhere specific diagnosis is needed. "He doesn't feel well" and "He doesn't see clearly" may indicate a problem, but they do not go far toward finding a remedy. Hence, the careful weighing and defining of physical factors must be accomplished.

Physical Factors in Reading

THOMAS H. EAMES

When education first suspected physical factors as causes of reading failure it naturally turned to medicine for the answer but medicine could offer only alexia as a probable explanation. Therefore, the early concept of reading failure was a neurological one. It soon became apparant, however, that many children who failed to learn to read or who had great difficulty in doing so were not aphasics, although some were. This led to a search for a possible physical cause in the nature of a specific lesion, either in the nervous system or in the sensory organs.

Suspicion first centered on *vision*. Obviously, if a child can not see the print, he can not read, so it was supposed that the cause of reading difficulty was inability to see. Research soon showed, however, that while actual blindness precludes visual reading, partial blindness does not necessarily do so, since both vision and reading are perceptive processes. One child might be greatly handicapped by a visual defect while another might perceive adequately on the basis of very poor retinal images. Statistically, it has been shown that defective visual acuity is not much more frequent among reading failures than among nonfailures, although individual cases occur in which failure is definitely the result of impaired vision. Such cases are greatly benefited by glasses *if* the poor vision is due to refractive error (eyes out of focus), but glasses are of no benefit when the visual deficiency is of an amblyopic (insensitivity) nature. The mere existence of low visual acuity is to be regarded as a possible but not invariable cause of poor reading.

School testers often miss important visual handicaps by making their tests at twenty feet rather than at the reading distance. The reading distance is usually deemed to be that in which the arm holding the book makes a right angle with the forearm. This criterion makes it unnecessary to allow for the child's size and build. *Near* visual acuity is often different from *far* visual acuity, and tests, such as the Snellen, made at twenty feet are inadequate for the evaluation of visual acuity in reading. The *Eames Eye Test*[1], *Keystone Visual Survey*[2], *Jaeger*[3], *Reduced Snellen*[4], and other appropriate tests may be used for measuring visual acuity at the reading distance. If *near* visual acuity is reduced, the possibility of interference with reading is greater but still not positively established. The principle of individual differences in perception still applies.

When the eyes are out of focus, as a camera is when set for the wrong distance, the condition is known as *refractive error*. There are several types, each of which has been studied with relation to reading. Generally, *myopia* (nearsightedness), unless of extreme degree, is rarely associated with poor reading. Many feel that a moderate myopia favors rather than hinders reading. Certainly myopic pupils, as a class, enjoy book- and deskwork. Few myopic reading failures have appeared among my cases.

The situation is quite different in *hypermetropia* (farsightedness). Visual acuity is impaired *only in extreme cases* of this condition because the individual can compensate for it by using his ciliary (focusing) muscles, the act being called *accommodation*. This function normally adjusts for near vision, but the hypermetropic child uses it for both near and far vision and consequently is under constant strain. Since he has to compensate for distant vision and then must add more effort to adjust to the reading distance, he is making a much greater-than-normal effort to hold clear vision during the reading act. Hypermetropia of significant degree occurred *30 percent more often* among my reading failure cases than among other comparable pupils.[5] Low to medium degrees are of greater importance to reading than higher ones because the latter produce so much discomfort and often low vision that they are detected, while the lower degrees are not. The hypermetropic pupil typically dislikes schools and teachers, preferring outdoor play to book- or deskwork.

Glasses for reading (book and desk tasks) or for constant use, according to the eye doctor's recommendation, usually relieve strain in hypermetropia and increase the efficient reading time. However, they make little or no difference in the visual acuity of low- to medium-degree hypermetropic cases and may even cut it down a bit. Pupils complain bitterly about wearing glasses under such circumstances, arguing that since they can see just as well with or without glasses, there is no point in using them. Many hypermetropic cases in low to medium degrees have shown marked improvement in reading as a result of the use of correct glasses.

Low to medium hypermetropia is seldom, if ever, picked up by the Snellen test. Other tests, such as the *Eames Eye Test, Keystone Visual Survey,* and *Massachusetts Vision Test,*[6] differentiate many more of those who have such degrees of hypermetropia from those who do not, and they should be used for screening suspected cases.

Astigmatism is a condition of uneven focus of the eyes, partaking of hypermetropic, myopic, or mixed characteristics. It sometimes interferes with learning to read or with reading comfortably but is not a very common cause of poor reading. As in the other refractive conditions, corrective lenses are used to overcome its effects.

Another condition, early suspected of causing some reading difficulty, is *heterophoria* (imperfect fixation). Much confusion resulted in early studies because many of them were based on tests made in distant vision rather than at the reading distance. Heterophoria existing at either distance may or may not exist at the other. Studies have shown that heterophoria in distant vision has little or no relationship to reading ability, but when certain types occur in near vision, difficulties often result.

The most significant type is *exophoria at the reading distance.*[7,8] This means a tendency to *inadequate convergence* of the eyes when fixating on texts or other close material. It is the result of muscular weakness or poor muscular innervation. Children who have this condition can compensate for a variable length of time but as fatigue builds up there is a tendency for fixation to be impaired. The image from one eye may overlap that of the other or disappear momentarily; the child loses his place and experiences confusion of various sorts. Here again, there are individual differences in the degree to which this handicaps the pupil in reading. The condition occurred 11 percent *more often* among my reading-failure cases.[9] Fatigue may be a prominent factor in some instances, while other children may not be aware of this element.

Another type of heterophoria that is definitely related to some cases of poor reading is *hyperphoria*. Here the tendency is for one eye to drift above the other when the child is tired. It is not often observed by pupils or teachers, but it is frequently the cause of *line shifts*. Pupils with the condition complain that after reading a while they no longer understand what they read. This results from fixation shifts from one eye to the other while one is aimed at the line to be read, and the other at the line above it. Continuity of meaning is broken at each shift.

Both of the heterophoric conditions discussed here are variously treated by eye doctors. Exercises, glasses, prisms, and even occasional surgery have been noted as remedial approaches. Neither condition is detected by the common Snellon Test but the other tests mentioned in connection with hypermetropia will usually detect important degrees of heterophoria.

Fusion deficiency, the imperfect mental combination of one eye's image with that of the other, has been considered as a possible cause of reading difficulty but appears not to be very closely associated with it.

There is a direct relationship between the size of the lateral *visual field* and eye span. The center of the field is at the point of most distinct vision in the eye. When the field is broad, more letters and words can be perceived at each fixation. Various investigators have demonstrated that the average person can take in from five to seven words at a single fixation, which means that the field is big enough to permit reception of that number of words. The field varies with pathological, traumatic, and hysteric processes.

Restrictions along the horizontal diameter result in fewer words being perceived, the extent ranging from letter-by-letter perception in extreme restriction, often encountered in hysteria, to moderate or slight impairment, resulting in perception of perhaps two or three words at a time. When restrictions exist, more fixations per line are necessary and the mechanics of reading take more of the reader's effort, leaving less energy for interpretive and comprehensive activity. Although restrictions of the visual field are always a medical problem, there is no reason why the teacher should not apply the usual pedagogical techniques for developing greater eye span unless a physician advises against it.

Investigation centered largely on *lateral dominance* in the early years of the study of reading failure. First left handedness, then left eyedness, crossed dominance, and finally confused dominance were blamed for reading failure. Distinctions were made between the sighting and the leading eye, and variations between them were also considered. Unfortunately, after more than sixty years the picture has not been clarified. The literature presents as many reports denying any relation between reading and lateral-dominance variations as reports attributing reading failure to this physical cause. I have observed some reading difficulty cases which appeared to be due to lateral-dominance variations but also many more with the same dominance conditions but no difficulty in reading. An open mind must be preserved toward this area until some significant evidence builds up.

Certain *brain areas* are known to be related to various kinds of memory. Both civilian and military injuries and neurosurgical experience have demonstrated that loss of such areas results in loss of the corresponding memories or skills. For example, damage or extirpation of the *angular gyrus* (Brodmann 39) invariably results in some reading disability, its degree being somewhat proportional to the amount of tissue damage. No doubt other parts of the brain participate in the reading function but it is plain that the angular gyrus must be functioning reasonably well if the individual is to read with average facility.

When the tracts connecting the angular gyrus with the *peristriate area* (Brodmann 19) are severed, the individual can recognize words as such but can neither name nor understand them. When interruption occurs between the *area striata* (Brodmann 17) and the *parastriate area* (Brodmann 18), the subject sees words as shapes but does not recognize that they are words nor does he associate symbolic meaning with them.

Sometimes damage to various bundles or tracts of *association fibers* in the central nervous system results in characteristic disabilities.[10] Interference with the *fronto-occipital fasciculus* is likely to affect auditory memory and make a phonic approach to reading inefficient or impossible for the child. Auditory and visual memories are likely to be impaired when anything interrupts the nerve flow through the dorsal superior longitudinal bundle of the superior frontal fasciculus. Disturbed function of the posterior longitudinal bundle of the median longitudinal fasciculus sometimes interferes with eye movements and can make it hard to read. The same is true of conditions affecting normal operation of the fibers of the superior cerebral peduncle or the aberrant pyramidal fibers. Eye span can be reduced by trouble in the optic radiations as well as by the visual field restrictions described earlier.

Brain damage is a very broad, inclusive term, covering a multitude of injuries from a great many causes. Within the last few years there has been an increasing interest in learning difficulties resulting from them. Generally, brain-damaged children are likely to give poor attention and to be distracted by nonessentials. They often lose the thread of what they are trying to read and divert their attention to pictures rather than text. Motor activity, such as tracing, writing, and drawing, helps to keep such people from wandering away from the task in hand. A great deal of overlearning is necessary if forgetting is to be prevented.

Smith has recently developed a theory of severe reading disability based on *nerve conductivity* through junctions between neurons (synapses).[11] Teachers should familiarize themselves with it, the better to understand the physiology of reading.

Many investigations of the effect on learning of *endocrine gland defects and deficiencies* have been made,[12] and there is general agreement that some of these sometimes interfere with the process of learning to read. Many of my own reading-difficulty cases have been of this sort. Deficiencies of the anterior part of the *pituitary gland* sometimes produce mental retardation. Tumefaction of this gland often causes visual field defects with reduction in eye span. This in turn may make reading increasingly difficult and require the child to make an excessive number of fixations per line. Some children with general pituitary dysfunction are practically unable to use texts at all.

The great majority of my endocrine reading-difficulty cases were of the hypothyroid type, particularly mild to moderate cases which had gone undetected for some time. They usually presented such manifestations as increasing preoccupation, apparent laziness, daydreaming, lack of interest, poor attention, slowing down of word perception, and inability to complete assignments. Fatigue was a common complaint. Some of the more serious cases had trouble in fixating on their texts because of impaired convergence. Probably such children, if they have no other condition interfering with reading, respond dramatically in school, once successful medical treatment is instituted, especially in subclinical to moderate cases.

The relationship to reading of difficulties of the four *parathyroid* glands is not thoroughly understood but it appears likely that under certain circumstances a predisposition to fatigue in book- and deskwork may result from spasm of accommodation. Cases of this kind are more common in secondary and college classes.

The *adrenal* glands, like the thyroid, affect drive, but deficiencies are not as closely related to the functions necessary to good reading. Fatigue, lack of aggressiveness, and occasional psychological problems are seen among pupils with adrenal difficulties.

Diabetes mellitus is a disease of the endocrine part of the *pancreas*. Diabetic children are usually school problems only when their disease has not been detected or when they are not reacting favorably to treatment. Visual defects are common and cataract is not unusual, even among diabetic children. The refractive condition of the eyes is likely to change somewhat in proportion to the blood-sugar level and it is often almost impossible to get adequate relief through glasses for such children. Holding fixation on the book is sometimes very hard for diabetic pupils. Confusions, regressions, and loss of place stem from some of their eye defects. Once the diabetic child is under treatment and is responding well, he is not likely to be a school problem.

No relationship to either good or poor reading has been traced to the *thymus gland* but several studies have suggested that undescended testes (male sex glands) may have some relationship to reading difficulties, probably through emotional disturbances and lack of drive.

I have recently investigated claims that children's eyes are too immature for them to start reading safely at the usual ages of school entrance. Children five years of age were found to have *more* accommodative power than at any subsequent age. The poorest *near* visual acuity found among the pupils studied was quite sufficient for reading the usual texts. These results do not support the contention that reading should be deferred to a later grade than the first.

Summary

Various physical handicaps have been discussed but the reader should not assume that they are the only causes of reading failure.

We know now that there is no single cause of reading failure and that not only physical but also emotional, environmental, pedagogic, and other factors play variable roles in the etiology of reading failure. The wise teacher will bear this constantly in mind and try to evaluate each poor reader's case in the light of broad knowledge of as many contributory fields as possible.

References

1. Harcourt Brace & World, Tarrytown, New York.

2. Keystone View Company, Meadville, Pennsylvania.

3. Any optical supply house.

4. Any optical supply house.

5. Eames, T. H. "Visual Handicaps to Reading," *Journal of Education* 141 (February, 1959):1–35.

6. American Optical Company, Southbridge, Massachusetts.

7. Eames, T. H. "Comparison of Eye Conditions Among 1000 Reading Failures, 500 Ophthalmic Patients, and 150 Unselected Children." *American Journal of Ophthalmology* 31 (June 1948):713–17.

8. Park, G. E. "Reading Difficulty from the Ophthalmic Point of View." *American Journal of Ophthalmology* 31 (January 1948):28–34.

9. Eames, T. H. "Comparison of Eye Conditions."

10. Eames, T. H. "Some Neural and Glandular Bases of Learning." *Journal of Education* 142 (April 1960):1–36.

11. Smith, D. E. P. "A Synaptic Transmission Theory of Severe Reading Disability." *University of Michigan School of Education Bulletin,* 29 (November 1957):25–28.

12. Eames, T. H. "Some Neural and Glandular Bases of Learning."

> To be accepted and valued for what
> you are, and for what you can be-
> come — that is a factor prerequisite
> to learning to read. This author tells
> why.

The Self-Concept
of the Young Child
as He Learns to Read

JEAN T. KUNZ

Introduction

In our culture the young child approaches the formal project of learning to read when he is approximately six years old. During the few years he has lived, he has learned to handle his body, to speak a language, to find his way around his home and neighborhood, along with innumerable subtle learnings having to do with values and patterns of problem solving. He will bring all of his previous learning with him as he approaches the new challenge. The manner in which the child learns and the outcome of the attempt to read print will depend on the interaction between the child and the entire learning situation at school such as the teacher, the physical surroundings, the peer group, reading materials, methods of teaching, and so forth.

Since this Reading Conference is concerned with the self and society, a review of how the self develops will bring into focus the child approaching a beginning reading program. We can then discuss some of the research concerning the self-concept of children.

Interpersonal Relationships and Self-Concept

In the beginning, a child is aware only of his physical comfort and discomfort, for he lives his life largely at a biological level. However through the close, personal relationship with his mother and, perhaps, other nurturing adults, the relevant world gradually takes shape.[1] As feelings, desires, goals, values, and ideas emerge, the behavior of the child indicates how he perceives, feels about, and thinks about his world and himself.

Before language and higher thought processes are well established, the conceptual value of self is determined.[2] The significant people in the child's environment have put a "price tag" on him as they have fulfilled his survival needs. He senses whether they can increase or decrease his sense of helplessness; whether they can promote or diminish his sense of well-being.[2] The child learns ways and develops capacities for meeting the expectations of the people on whom he is dependent.

The individual security of the significant people raising the child and their ability to give love rather than promise love, communicates to the youngster his worth and value as an individual. When acceptance and love at any price is sensed to be futile, the child uses his nuisance value to insure his not being ignored. It is more threatening to have no attention paid to him than to be punished. The young child accepts the assumptions and standards of significant adults, as he perceives them, without critical judgment, and he does what he has to do in order to maintain the relationship.

Erickson states that the individual's physiological-psychological makeup—including intellectual potential, energy level, body shape, and temperament—are the basis for building a self-structure. The reciprocity or interplay that occurs between the child with his capacities form the milieu out of which the child structures his concept of self.[3]

As the child grows from infancy to toddlerhood, to preschool and school age, he is structuring a self-image out of the day-by-day life he lives. Individually, each child differentiates specific and somewhat stable characteristics of himself out of a phenomenal field. The structure of the specific and stable characteristics become the self-image.[4] In time, the self-image is the child's guide to his behavior. He strives to maintain the image; for, as long as he can function according to anticipation, he is relatively free from disturbing feelings of helplessness.[5]

A child about three-and-one-half-years old came into her new nursery school the first day to look around and become acquainted with her teacher. She was in the room only a few minutes when she asked the teacher:

"Where do you put the naughty children?"

The teacher replied, "You know, we don't have any naughty children in our school."

The child walked away, looked at the toys on the shelf and returned again to the teacher. Her face was tense, her voice determined, as she asked again, "Where *do* you put the naughty children?"

The teacher stooped down to the youngster's level as she said, "Do you think we need a place for naughty children?"

"Yes."

"I wonder why?"

"Because, I'm one!"

Many times daily during the following weeks at school, the child would come to check with the teacher as to whether or not it was "naughty" to open the clay bucket, get on the climbing equipment if other children were there, and so on. In the new setting, the child was not able to predict or anticipate the reactions of the adults to her behavior so she became very restricted and careful in what she did.

Hopefully, the child approaching a beginning reading program comes with a self-image which will allow him to enter into it with eagerness, confidence, and some degree of realism. The child who is behaving in such a manner will have the physical maturity and the experience and background necessary for successful reading. During the early years when much of a youngster's behavior was motivated by his physical maturation, "significant others" in his life reacted positively to his growth attainments. As the gradual shift from the force of maturation to the push for learning occurred, there were still adults who were willing and able to answer the child's constant questions, to adjust to his curiosity, and to provide materials, equipment, and time for him to learn skills, organize information, and develop ideas. To the educator this is the concept of readiness. The child, through his behavior, indicates that the essential conditions have been achieved so that he can learn.[6] The self-image at this time is most pliable. Significant relationships can influence growth toward either a positive or negative self-concept as the child is working toward building skills necessary for reading.

Realistically, however, there will be children in every group who will come with privations of one kind or another—some severe, some slight. A youngster who has never felt a sense of being a trustworthy and able individual is not going to find the printed page exciting or challenging. It may be that some children come to school with such limited experiences that they have not learned the language necessary for reading print. One teacher took her students to see some cows and calves three different times before the children could give the animals labels. Even then the cows were referred to as horses and the calves as puppies.

Crow and colleagues[7] predict that by 1970, one out of every two children under six in the United States will come from impoverished backgrounds. Children from a ghetto area often have low self-concepts and little or no sense of allegiance to authority, social order, or social institutions. The child's experience has taught him that his nuisance value is about the only way he has to make contact with significant adults. The teacher and the peer group are now significant others to the child and, positively or negatively, they will reflect back to him their perception of him. The expanded relationships within the school setting can enhance the child's sense of trust, autonomy, initiative, and industry, or they can intensify his feelings of mistrust, doubt, guilt, shame, and inferiority.[3] The "price tag" placed on the child at this time is again dependent on the degree of personal security and adequacy felt by his teacher and his friends. When children are starting school the teacher is the bridge across which children relate to one another and to learning materials.

The Teacher's Challenge

No two individuals have the same intellectual capacities nor do they have the same self-image. The challenge to a teacher is to plan and carry out programs for learning for every individual who comes into his class.[7] For children from impoverished backgrounds, the beginning reading program may consist of building a broad background for reading through many firsthand experiences. The teacher may find it necessary to reach far beyond her basic reading series to challenge other children. You might respond that individual teaching is impossible. There are so many reasons why—classes are too large, it is too expensive, some children can't learn, administrators are not willing to provide materials, even the custodians will not tolerate moving the furniture. However, it is necessary to find a way to help every child learn if the social ills of the United States are to be remedied. If our democratic way of life is to be preserved, it is necessary to consider the social ills as they now exist in our society.

A close human relationship is the basis for all learning. The learnings which are of prime importance are the ones that influence behavior.[8] The successful teacher is the one who strives to set the stage so that every child can feel the desire to learn and not only feel a responsibility for his own learning, but for that of his fellow students. The teacher has a three-point goal in teaching. Such a teacher will be aware of (1) the student's self-image, (2) the skills necessary for reading, and (3) the subject matter being taught.

The Self-Concept of Children
in a Classroom Setting

On the premise that the self-concept is a learned structure growing mainly from reactions and comments made by others and inferences drawn by children out of their experiences, Staines[9] set up a study to investigate the possibility of teaching so that the self-concept would improve. Both the experimental and control group were scholarship classes with highly rated teachers. The teacher of the control group had no awareness of the self-picture as an outcome of education, and she made many more negative comments to children about their performance, status, and potential. Her students showed a significant decrease in certainty about self.

The teacher of the experimental group studied the self-ratings of her class and attempted to teach so that her students might positively change their feelings about themselves. There were statistically significant changes which occurred in self-traits.

Subject-matter gains were slightly higher in the experimental group, but they were not statistically significant. Staines states that the self is a factor in all learning experiences and the development of self should become one of the major teaching aims for education.

Davidson and Lang[10] have examined how the self is influenced in a classroom setting by a study of the relationship between the children's perception of their teacher's feeling toward them and the children's perception of themselves, academic achievement, and classroom behavior. On all three measures there was a positive correlation. The investigators conclude that the teacher's feelings of acceptance and approval are communicated to the child and perceived by him as a positive appraisal. The teacher's positive feelings are the beginning of a circular reaction—the child achieves and the teacher's feelings cause the child to strive for further approval by behaving as a "good" student.

In an attempt to discover whether or not there were differences in the self-concepts of overachievers and underachievers in reading, Lumpkin[11] matched groups on chronological age, mental age, sex, and home background. Overachievers revealed significantly more positive self-concepts, higher levels of adjustment, saw themselves as liking reading, and they were viewed positively by peers and teachers. The underachievers had low academic-achievement measures, negative perceptions of self, showed a desire to be different from self as seen, expressed more feelings of conflict, and they were viewed by their teachers as having high problem tendency. The investigator concludes with confidence that in the group studied, the self-concept of the individual influences his behavior and may determine the direction and degree of his expression in academic work and social relationships.

Bodwin[12] found a significantly positive correlation between immature self-concept and reading disability. A study completed by Hamarchek[13] revealed a relationship between high intellectual and achievement self-images and reading age, mental age, and educational age.

Wattenberg and Clifford[14] set up an exploratory study to determine whether the relationship of low self-concept and reading difficulties was caused by poor self-concepts leading to reading difficulties or unfortunate experiences in reading undermining self-concepts. During the first semester in kindergarten, ratings were obtained relative to (1) self-concepts, (2) ego strength, and (3) intelligence. Two years after completion of kindergarten, the children were again measured and rated in self-concept and ego strength. Progress in reading was measured on the test for the book in which they were reading as prepared by the publisher. Generally, the measures of self-concept were the measures of mental ability (*The Detroit Beginning First Grade Intelligence Test*). The authors recommend further study in this area.

The research of Thompson-Hunnicutt and Perkins[15] indicates that a teacher's awareness of a child's self-image and the conscious teaching for enhancement of the self results in a general enrichment for more effective human relationships and living.

Beginning Reading Materials and Self-Concept

There is a growing concern on the part of those preparing materials for a beginning reader to provide books and stories related to the child's life experiences. Reading materials must reflect an appreciation for and an understanding of language in the child's life.[16] A child can experience a feeling of self-acceptance from the teacher when the reading materials presented to him reflect his life and his language. The creative teacher finds many ways of teaching and a variety of materials to use in a beginning reading program.[16] In planning for the teaching of reading skills and enhancement of self, learning to read through experiences can be most effective.[17]

A first grade teacher discovered soon after school started that she had a youngster, Rulan, who was not at all interested in reading. He was a polite, shy youngster who stayed by himself most of the time. She also found that he was in school daily until recess and then he was missing. Her concern for the child led her to try many ways to make friends with him and to interest him in school and reading, but nothing seemed to work.

She enlisted the help of a sixth grade boy who was instructed to wander off with her charge when he left school — not to bring him back but to see where he went, what he did, where he stopped to look, and what he looked at. The older boy returned to report his findings. Rulan went into the foothills close to the school to look for lizards. He was also interested in rocks and seemed to know a great deal about them. Once in a while he stopped to talk about the plant life on the hillside also.

The sixth grader became a teaching assistant in that he gathered specific information on lizards, rocks, and plants for the teacher. The teacher wrote the stories and it was not long until Rulan was asking his teacher to write a story about how mountains were formed and what happened to Lake Bonneville. All of the youngsters were eager to read the stories written for Rulan and he was perceived by both teacher and students as the idea person in the room.

Another first grade teacher in a different location had a group of fifteen children who were not one bit interested in reading print. They had lived their lives within a four-block radius where there was not much to see or experience which might relate to a beginning reading program. By listening to their conversation before and after school, on the playground, she learned that they talked about food a great deal along with some odd kinds of things. With her electric frying pan and a hot plate she started cooking in her classroom. If one cooks, one must read to find out how. Before too long, each of the fifteen students had a basic reading vocabulary. The word list included *flour, sugar, salt, milk, stir, mix,* and so on. Soon there were stories about getting ready to cook. Through an individualized reading program, everyone was reading at least at grade level by May. School was a pleasure, the teacher a most significant person to the children. They arrived in the morning when she did and they left with her after school. Children can feel competent and valuable as individuals when they "know" they have some knowledge.

With the growing body of information having to do with self-concept and its relationship to behavior and learning, schools need to provide opportunities for experiences which will enable people to develop as individuals rather than as stereotyped conformists. It is not only what a person knows, it is the way he feels about a situation that causes his behavior. Children need an education which will aid them in increasing their sensitivity to, and perception of, their own self-concepts and those of others. Teachers are indeed significant adults who can be instrumental in accomplishing this goal as they teach children the tools for reading.

"What is honored in a country will be cultivated there."

Plato

References

1. Stone, J. L., and Church, J. *Childhood and Adolescence*. New York: Random House, 1957, p. 456.

2. Anderson, C. A. "The Self-Image: A Theory of the Dynamics of Behavior." In *The Self in Growth, Teaching, and Learning*, edited by Don E. Hamache. Englewood Cliffs, N. J.: Prentice-Hall, 1965, pp. 1–13.

3. Erikson, Erik H. "Growth and Crises of the Healthy Personality." In *Symposium on the Healthy Personality*, edited by Milton J. E. Senn. New York: Josiah Macy, Jr. Foundation, 1950, pp. 91–146.

4. Snygg, D., and Combs, A. W. *Individual Behavior*. New York: Harper and Brothers, 1949.

5. Ausubel, D. P., and Ausubel, P. "Ego Development Among Segregated Negro Children." In *Education in Depressed Areas*, edited by A. Harry Passou. New York: Teachers College, Columbia University, 1964, pp. 109–36.

6. Hymes, J. L., Jr. *Before A Child Reads*. New York: Row, Peterson and Company, 1958, p. 96.

7. Crow, L. D.; Murry, W. I.; and Smythe, H. H. *Educating the Culturally Disadvantaged Child*. New York: David McKay Company, 1966, p. 298.

8. Rogers, C. R. *On Becoming a Person*. Cambridge, Mass.: Riverside Press, 1961, p. 420.

9. Staines, J. W. "The Self-Picture as a Factor in the Classroom." In *The Self in Growth, Teaching, and Learning*, edited by Don E. Hamache. Englewood Cliffs, N. J.: Prentice-Hall, 1965, pp. 404–23.

10. Davidson, H. H., and Lang, G. "Children's Perception of Their Teachers' Feelings Toward Them Related to Self-Perception, School Achievement, and Behavior." In *The Self in Growth, Teaching, and Learning*, edited by Don E. Hamache. Englewood Cliffs, N. J.: Prentice-Hall, 1965, pp. 424–39.

11. Lumpkin, D. D. "Relationship of Self-Concept to Achievement in Reading." Ph.D. dissertation, University of Southern California, 1959, p. 120.

12. Bodwin, R. F. "The Relationship Between Immature Self-Concept and Certain Educational Disabilities." In *Dissertation Abstracts* 19 (1959):1945–46.

13. Hamarchek, D. E. "A Study of the Relationship Between Certain Measures of Growth and the Self-Images of Elementary School Children." Ph.D. dissertation, University of Michigan, 1960, p. 210.

14. Wattenberg, W. W., and Clifford, C. *Relationship of the Self-Concept to Beginning Achievement in Reading.* Project of Office of Education, United States Department of Health, Education, and Welfare. Detroit, Mich.: Wayne State University, 1962, p. 58.

15. Perkins, H. V. "Changing Perception of Self." In *The Self in Growth, Teaching, and Learning,* edited by Don E. Hamache. Englewood Cliffs, N. J.: Prentice-Hall, 1965, pp. 449–53.

16. Austin, M. C.; Morrison, C.; Kenny, H. J.; Morrison, M. B.; Gutmann, A. R., and Nystrom, J. W. *The Torch Lighters, Tomorrow's Teachers of Reading.* Cambridge, Mass.: Harvard University Press, 1961, p. 157.

17. Lee, D. M., and Allen, R. V. *Learning to Read Through Experience.* New York: Appleton-Century-Crofts, 1963, p. 153.

study questions

1. Jenkinson suggests that we need more than one model of reading behavior. What, for example, might be the differences between a model of beginning-reader performance and mature-reader performance? Are these differences a matter of *degree* or of *kind*? In other words, is a beginning reader's performance merely a miniature of a mature reader's performance, or do we expect him to perform in a unique way?

2. Why does Jenkinson limit her specific concerns about reading to "assimilation of meaning"? How does Wardhaugh's tentative conclusion differ from this view? Which of the other authors in this chapter would you expect to support Jenkinson in this matter? What support do they offer?

3. As you read the summarizing points at the end of each section in the Betts' selection, see if you can translate each point into *Advice for Teachers of Reading*. Which of these points would most significantly modify practice as you know it?

4. Are Elkind's suggestions as applicable to beginning reading as to remedial instruction? Explain. How might you apply the Piaget model to factors in reading other than word-recognition or word-perception? Would consideration of these other factors modify Elkind's recommendations? How or how not?

5. Each of the linguistic models for reading reviewed by Wardhaugh suggests a definition of reading. Each of these models would include certain factors as most important for learning to read. Try comparing and contrasting these models on the basis of the factors that they stress in learning to read.

6. What physical factors cited by Eames are most in need of further study? Which should receive greatest attention on the basis of present evidence?

7. One school of thought holds that "writing is talk written down" and "reading is talking from a book." Martin disagrees. What is the basis of his disagreement? A school of thought regarding reading instruction holds that "first you learn to read and then you read to learn" and "teach decoding first, then teach comprehension." *You* be R. G. Martin and react to *that* school of thought.

8. What does Kunz's self-concept factor suggest to makers of conceptual models for explaining the reading process?

THREE

organizing for instruction: procedures

objectives

As a result of reading these articles and answering the questions at the end of the chapter you should be able to:

▣ specify alternatives for solving procedural problems related to phonics, grouping, primary-class organization, and comprehension

▣ list ways of evaluating the effectiveness of procedures involving phonics instruction, grouping, primary-class organization, and comprehension

rationale

Differences between the theoretical *what* and *why* and the procedural *how* in teaching reading are partially matters of emphasis. But procedure carries the immediacy of action, which sometimes necessitates going beyond our present stages of theory. To do so requires writers and teachers with creative and critical ability. Selections in this chapter seem to exemplify this ability.

introduction

The gulf between theory and practice is often a deep one. Theorists and researchers appear to many practitioners to be out of touch with the realities of teaching. And, according to some theorists, reading teachers prefer fads and cure-alls to sound procedure based on experimental evidence.

The breach is perhaps inevitable. Theory of so complex a process as reading grows slowly and, as we have witnessed in the preceding chapters, is still far from complete. Ideally, the two pursuits, theory and practice, should be complementary. As theory improves, so should practice. Better understanding of the reading process suggests better procedures. In this sense, present methods of teaching reading comprise a vast field test for application of theory.

Nevertheless, practitioners often grow impatient with theory. "Look—I'm on the firing line. What should I do tomorrow, next week, all year, to make my reading class a success? Give me some sure-fire applications!" The impatience is understandable; used to best advantage, it places healthy immediacy on theory.

The results, however, can be damaging. Incomplete theory can be a bad teacher; on occasion it ignores important factors in the interest of those under scrutiny. Likewise, the quest for certainty, the urge to find and use a "best way to teach reading," can lead us to grasp materials and procedures whose only merit is the enthusiasm of their originators.

There is a tendency to oversimplify the vast area of procedure. A set of materials, no matter how explicit the directions for use, does not comprise a complete procedure. Careful description of a reading *approach* (language-experience, individualized reading, basal reader, and so forth) likewise omits many facets of procedure. There is increasing evidence that results vary widely even when teachers use identical materials and approaches. Since this is true, it is not surprising to find studies of teacher personality, reward systems, interaction, and pupil learning style now receiving attention as components of reading instruction theory. What is more, the future promises more attempts to synthesize all these elements so that, by the end of the decade, we are likely to find a more cohesive theory and, hence, stronger implications for procedure.

For the time being, we are fortunate to find reading specialists whose writings and teachings help to bridge the gulf. Many are especially skilled in converting passive theory into means of active procedure. This is not a simple task, for it requires knowledge and experience beyond the narrower confines of particularized research. The best of the specialists know that knowledge is limited, that promising operational ideas can never be fully communicated or copied. You will find, therefore, that the best of these writers advance suggestions for practice and defend these suggestions — but beyond this, they maintain a marked respect for the individuality and creativity of those who directly carry out procedure in the classroom.

> **Early attitudes and early self-con-
> cepts are more permanent than we
> know. What is the ultimate payoff,
> for example, of read-around-the-
> rosie procedures?**

Have You Disabled a Potential Read'n' Dropout Lately?

VIRGINIA G. GOLDSMITH

I hate read'n'. It ain't my thing, and I don't dig it. And as soon as I'm old enough I'm gonna quit school. Then I'll git out of that old read'n'. Yes, nobody, but nobody, will ever catch me read'n' a book again. I hate my teacher, too. She thinks she's so smart jest because she can read real good, and she thinks read'n' is the most important subject in the world and it ain't, I betcha. Jest wait, I'll show her how I can git along without read'n'. I'll go to the moon where there are no books or teachers. Then I won't have to read in a dumb circle.

I don't want to be a bluebird anyway with all those dumb girls. But I hate my sparrow group, too. I hate those dumb birds. I could read if I wanted to—jest as good as the bluebirds, but teacher keeps pick'n' on us sparrows.

"Johnny, you left out a word. Johnny, you must read more smoothly. Johnny, this. Johnny, that."

She gits you so mixed up that I can't read a word. Then the other kids laugh or show off when I make a little mistake. I hate read'n' in a circle. I hate read'n'. I hate it, hate it, hate it!

How many Johnnies are there in this country who hate reading? Do you have one or more in your room? Does your Johnny hate you too? Are you guilty of having round-robin circle reading?

Although a barbershop or round-robin oral reading ("Next, please read") is a vicious reading technique, it is by far one of the most widely practiced. A number of reading authorities including Bond,[1] Hildreth,[2] and Smith[3] strenuously object to the method, yet year after year thousands of children in the United States are subjected to this humiliating and ego-deflating way of teaching. The group with low reading ability, which usually has more boys than girls, suffers most from this practice, but even among stronger readers its virtues are dubious at best.

Let us examine what happens and why. In barbershop reading each child in the group sits with the same reading book, each open to the same page, and one by one the children read sentence after sentence slowly, often with a feeling of drudgery and confusion. Frequently the teacher interrupts to insist that the children keep their eyes on their books, listen, and not read ahead. Most of the time there is no enthusiasm, little understanding, and little involvement. Lloyd[4] reports that the oral reader is so busy concentrating on pronunciation, enunciation, and other aspects of reading that he is unable to grasp the meaning of the passage.

When a child in the group loses his place, either because he is bored or because he reads ahead, he may be chastised verbally or, at worst, he may have some privilege taken away. The child who reads faster than the class fares no better. Because he is forced to slow down ("to keep up with the class"), he soon loses any enthusiasm he might have had for the material. The probable result of this practice, as Durrell[5] observes, is that silent reading reduced to a slow oral rate encourages lip movements and silent pronunciation (5:150) and little else. Perhaps the most negative outcome is that the child who is supposed to be listening and waiting his turn is daydreaming — a far more pleasant pastime than listening to his peers as they mumble and stumble over difficult words and phrases. What the child is really learning, of course, is to tune out while waiting his turn. Thus the teacher is faced with a condition in which each child spends one or two minutes in oral reading and another twenty pretending to listen. Such an environment simply does not foster learning to read.

But there is more mischief to reckon with. Dull reading groups, in which pupils read, listen, wait, wait, and wait are injurious to the poor reader. Instead of getting group approval and a sense of personal worth, he is most likely meeting with rejection and failure. His experience with failure day after day reinforces his negative image of himself. In a prestige subject like reading, it is an established fact that poor readers suffer severe feelings of inferiority.[6,7]

We know little about the side effects, but we may conjecture that they manifest themselves in restlessness, disobedience, disorderliness, aggressiveness, defiance — all typical forerunners of juvenile delinquency.

These children are learning to hate reading, school, and their teachers. When children cannot meet the expectations of school, they react unfavorably to it, especially to the subjects that have caused them the greatest humiliation. Many will never find books stimulating. More than likely they will carry these negative feelings with them to their graves.

Barbershop reading is frustrating not only to the child, but also to the teacher. Even the most conscientious teacher becomes frustrated and discouraged when some children seem to make no progress in oral reading despite her most valiant efforts. She may "love children and teaching," but as we all know too well her sense of personal responsibility for snail-pace readers is the most painful cross she has to bear. Many times she lacks the knowledge to diagnose reading disabilities through the oral method so that poor reading may persist month after month. Depression and self-doubt regarding her ability to teach begin to assail her. Her own attitudes become remarkably like those of her pupils. The danger, as Slobodian and Campbell[8] aptly observe, is that children tend to value themselves as their teachers do. The children's academic achievement, moreover, is directly influenced by the children's perceptions of self which really mirror the teacher's perceptions of her pupils.

Few teachers would feel comfortable or excited about reading aloud in a group-learning situation where their colleagues pass judgment on them as they follow along paragraph by paragraph.

Are children immune to the same kind of feelings? While an adult might hesitate to criticize another adult for the mispronunciation of a word, children do not so readily spare each other's feelings. John Holt in his book *How Children Learn* has given us the strongest indictment of this method:

> When a child at school makes a mistake, say in reading aloud
> in a reading group, he gets an instant signal from the
> environment. Perhaps some of the other children in the group, or
> class, will giggle, or cover their mouths with their hand, or
> make a face, or wave their hand in the air — anything to show
> the teacher that they know more than the unfortunate reader.
> Perhaps the teacher herself will correct the mistake, or will say,
> "Are you sure?" or will ask another student, "What do you
> think?" (9:100)

The chances are that by now the pupil is intellectually confused and emotionally shaken, but neither the teacher's sympathy nor her kindness manifested by her sweetest smile will undo the mischief. Indeed, such tactics, as Holt goes on to explain, may be "The severest punishments the school has to offer, since it shows him (the pupil) he has hurt and disappointed the person on whose support and approval he has been trained to depend." (9:100). His environment tells him not only that he has "goofed," but that all about him know it. Even if, in the "face of public failures," he has enough presence of mind to correct his error on his own power, he is rarely given time to do so, for under such harmful and idiotic conditions, "teachers not only like right answers, they like them right away." (9:100).

Alternatives to the insidious practice of round-robin reading are readily available in a dozen professional journals and books. Why don't teachers take the trouble to learn what these alternatives are?

References

1. Bond, G., and Tinker, M. *Reading Difficulties — Their Diagnosis and Correction.* New York: Appleton-Century-Crofts, 1967.
2. Hildreth, G. *Teaching Reading.* New York: Henry Holt and Co., 1958.
3. Smith, N. B. *Reading Instruction for Today's Children.* Englewood Cliffs, N. J.: Prentice-Hall, 1963.
4. Lloyd, B. A. "The Chimera of Oral Reading." *Education* 86 (October 1965): 106–8.

5. Durrell, D. *Improving Reading Instruction.* New York: World Book Co., 1956.

6. Taberlet, B. E. "Poor Readers and Mental Health." *Elementary English* 35 (December 1958):522–25.

7. Gillham, I. "Self-Concept and Reading." *The Reading Teacher* 21 (December 1967):270–73.

8. Slobodian, J. and Campbell, P. "Do Children's Perceptions Influence Beginning Reading Achievement?" *Elementary School Journal* 67 (May 1967):423–27.

9. Holt, J. *How Children Learn.* New York: Pitman Publishing Co., 1967.

"Reading," states the author, "is a
solitary act." Do grouping practices,
then, run counter to the needs of the
reader? The question is examined
and suggestions are made for improving grouping procedure.

Grouping for Reading or for Reading Instruction

MIRIAM E. WILT

Reading, however one wishes to define it, is not an act that can
be performed in a group. Reading is communication between an
author and an individual.

The title of this article may imply a misconception, for while
individuals can be grouped together to learn and practice skills,
share ideas, and orally interpret printed material, the reading
act itself is a visual-mental activity between the writer and his
audience of one. The reader internalizes the symbols he sees and
finds in the symbols meanings drawn from his own experiential
background. Teachers can help children learn to read in groups

or individually but reading itself cannot be a group activity. Let us then consider the topic to be "Grouping for Reading Instruction and Interpretation."

Prior to 1930, grouping for reading instruction was almost unheard of, although from the beginning of education, learners have been grouped by age levels, interests, needs, abilities, or what have you.

The growth in size of public schools in large population centers brought more and more children together so that divisions had to be made. Sex, academic ability, economic levels, vocational interest, and a multitude of other discriminating techniques were applied until finally one could find school placement based solely on a child's reading level.

Today it is not unusual to find children of a narrow age range or grade level divided into many reading ability groups. When, as so often happens in education, the movement gained momentum, the practice became a prison. The three-ability-reading-groups pattern, self-perpetuating, inflexible, and fragmenting, became a ritual worshipped by many supervisors, coordinators, and superintendents and followed slavishly by teachers. Several generations of children have been labeled in first grade and have carried that label with them throughout their school years, possibly beyond. Let it be noted, however, that humane and creative teachers have ignored the stereotyping throughout these thirty some years.

Studies of Grouping

Most of the research studies on grouping have been quite inconclusive, although Halliwell[1] shows some statistical significance and some favorable-though-not-statistically-significant implications for nongraded grouping. However, this researcher notes that the findings were confused by concomitant changes in the school. Evidence concerning grouping seems to be in peripheral implications from a wide variety of researches established to assess teaching methods and materials.

Grouping is not a method of teaching reading. Any method can be used in any group. Grouping, like individualizing instruction, is an organizational technique that is designed to facilitate learning. Basal, phonic, i.t.a., linguistic, experience-content, these are methods. Teaching children individually and/or in groups does not preclude the use of any method. It seems rather obvious that method and organization should not be measured one against the other. In looking at the research in method, one is impressed by certain conclusions and implications that appear and reappear in a wide cross section of research and from which some conclusions for grouping can be drawn.

In examining the titles of the 264 reading research studies listed in *The Reading Teacher,*[2] researchers have found that less than two percent dealt with the thorny question of grouping, and yet this is one of the major problems of teachers of reading. Grouping in reading may be as flexible as three children brought together to practice some specific reading skill. On the other hand, grouping in reading can be as highly organized as the Joplin plan, in which children scoring within certain intervals on standardized and/or informal reading tests go daily to a reading teacher who organizes the children into groups as homogeneously as possible.

A review of twenty of the twenty-seven reports of First Grade Reading Studies, funded by the U.S. Office of Education, published in the May 1966 issue of *The Reading Teacher*[3] also revealed an astonishing number of these studies reporting method but not organization for teaching reading. One is led to believe that with two exceptions the children (26–35) in a class were taught as a whole or in ability groups.

Some of the most positive findings, however, were stated by Doris U. Spencer[4] in summarizing her study, "Individualized First Grade Reading versus a Basal Reader Program in Rural Communities." Again one might conclude from these brief descriptions that organization may be equally as, if not more important than, method. Classroom organization and the teacher seem especially significant since the attitudes, knowledge of various methods, and general interest in improving the teaching of reading appear again and again as implications in many of the studies.

The Hawthorne effect may skew results undesirably in research studies but this peripheral benefit in improved educational programs needs to be fostered in ongoing innovative programs in which teachers and children are experimental in trying out new ideas.

It is not grouping that is wrong, but what has been done in the name of grouping that has held teachers and children in a vise.

On the positive side, the individualized reading instruction move-ment, which never really got off the ground although it was a severe threat to the status quo, has catapulted some teachers into thinking about the serious harm that rigid, inflexible grouping has imposed on some children. Yet individualized reading could not expunge the need for grouping, nor did it try. Variety, ex-pediency, common needs, and interests provide a kaleidoscope of reasons for establishing and disbanding groups as the needs of children are being met.

In the early grades, when children are introduced to the com-plexities of our phonemic-graphemic systems, it would seem that children in quite small groups could profit by working together in discovering the regular, semiregular, and irregular ways in which phonemes pattern. When this is learned, it would seem that the word-analysis drills that seem to continue endlessly in some of the reading programs could be discontinued. When these mechanics are under control, the teacher's role changes. Now the teacher becomes a discussion leader, a diagnostician of needs, and a planner. All three roles should be shared with children some of the time.

Independence in reading cannot be programmed for groups. The very fact that children achieve independence at varying rates and at varying levels seems to deny the value of rigid A, B, and C grouping.

A Solitary Act

Reading is a solitary act and whether the same story is read by one child or by many, or whether every child reads a different piece, they do it alone. Only at the very beginning do children need to read orally so that they know they are reading, and even then, they do not really need an audience. Oral reading is speak-ing and interpreting the author's words to an audience. There are and should be many opportunities for children to read aloud but this is not the reading act, but rather a sharing experience.

In the process of education and specifically English education, speaking, listening, reading, and writing skills are the founda-tion of all learnings and are our most useful tools. The mechanics of these skills can be mastered early but the fine polishing re-quires years of practice in real situations that grow out of the total curriculum. In English impression and expression the "learning to" is only the beginning of a long and exacting program. Knowing about language and how it works; knowing how to write, learning to appreciate writing, being able to evaluate writing, and learning to improve one's own writing; knowing how to read the literature of English; and finally being able to use language in its very best sense, these are the purposes of English language education.

How does grouping for reading fit into this statement of goals? There are social, emotional, and intellectual reasons for putting learners into groups. Common needs, age, sex, interest, and acculturation are a few of them. There are probably some occasions when masses can profit from the same exposure such as seeing plays, storytelling, oral reading, choral speaking, poetry reading, and others. Even some of these at times should be shared in small intimate groups where the teacher can get very close to the learners to help them in their evaluation of content, performance, and appropriate treatment.

In "grouping for teaching reading," flexibility is probably the major condition. It is doubtful that there are definitive steps to excellence in reading that can be parceled out month by month and year by year. Many people do not believe that there is such a person as a first grade reader or a fifth grade reader. New and expanded skills should be taught as the need for them occurs regardless of age or grade. The curriculum makers are the arbiters of what content shall be taught. The needs of the children are the dictators of when certain skills are needed.

One child, or six or twelve or more, may need to be introduced to new skills, put into situations where they can practice, and finally use these skills in the content of literature or other subject-matter areas. If this can be done most efficiently in programmed, computer, or other individual ways, so be it. If not, probably quite small groups will be most effective: small groups that are set up and disbanded as the needs are met; small groups in which neither age nor ability level are the major determiners but rather "Who can profit from the experience?"

A true reading group is one in which the child brings to the discussion table the attitudes, understandings, facts, and perplexities he has experienced in reading. Here in a life situation he learns what reading really means. Size of schools or organizational patterns vary but, within any framework, the grouping of children can and should be planned as needs arise and interests require. Placement in educational levels for extended periods of time should not be determined by reading ability alone but rather by age or maturity levels.

Notes

1. Joseph W. Halliwell. "A Comparison of Pupil Achievement in Graded and Nongraded Primary Classrooms." *Journal of Experimental Education* 32(1963): 59-64.

2. Helen M. Robinson, Samuel Weintraub, and Carol A Hostetter. "Summary of Investigations Relating to Reading, July 1, 1963, to June 30, 1964." *The Reading Teacher* 18(1965):331-428.

3. *The Reading Teacher* 19(1966):563-675.

4. Doris U. Spencer. "Individualized First Grade Reading versus a Basal Reader Program in Rural Communities." *The Reading Teacher* 19(1966):595-600.

> An antidote to "textbook pacing," a
> highly practical idea to try . . ..

Individualizing Instruction through "Ad Hoc" Grouping

JAMES E. HAGERTY

Problem

How to teach a difficult idea or skill to a class of 30 students with a few who are ahead of the rest, some who are performing at grade level, a couple of discipline problems, a new arrival, and several performing at lower levels.

Solution

Individualize your teaching through "ad hoc" grouping!

"Ad hoc" grouping is based on the realization that small-group teaching techniques are not necessarily based on the size of the groups or the number of learners involved.

Students *can* learn in all sizes of groups, but each one of them learns independently because of differences in interest, ability, and experience.

One way to take advantage of individual differences is to arrange your students into "ad hoc" groups according to levels of performance for the particular purpose at hand.

The basic steps follow:

1. State the idea or skill to be learned in terms of behavioral objectives that each individual in the class can readily understand.
2. Let each student evaluate himself according to these objectives to determine what he needs to learn further to attain them.
3. Diagnose the different learning requirements among the students and group them according to the similarities of their needs.
4. Make available diversified materials and learning activities that best suit each group's needs.
5. Let each student evaluate his progress in terms of his own group's progress.

Your success with "ad hoc" grouping will improve as you improve your diagnosis of those students who need the same prescription for a given learning objective.

Students can learn more effectively in a classroom situation if they are performing in groups that are contrived to meet their specific needs for a specific learning objective. As the objectives change during the year so will the needs of each member of the class. Each new learning objective will require new "ad hoc" grouping.

With this approach, group-paced learning will eventually replace textbook pacing and your role as a teacher will be more meaningful to you and more valuable to your students.

Primary-school procedures relevant to reading need rethinking. The English primary-school model is helping to stimulate such thought. Here a noted educator describes, synthesizes, and evaluates his extensive visit to English primary schools.

English and American Primary Schools

VINCENT R. ROGERS

Ideas that American educators have been talking about for a long, long time are being put to practice in a large percentage of English primary schools. Education for life, basing instructional activities on the interests and problems of children, integration of subject matter, emphasis on *learning* rather than *teaching* and on *process* rather than *product,* development of independence and responsibility in children, concern for the creative aspects of learning — all of these are standard phrases in the lexicon of American education. But in England they are more than phrases. They are being brought to life daily in the primary classrooms which I visited during my stay in England as a Fulbright scholar in 1966.

When I made known my desire to get inside some schools, my English friends and advisers guided me initially to Oxfordshire, where I visited the Bampton, Brize-Norton, and Tower Hill primary schools. I have never been quite the same since. Seventy-two schools later I still found myself wondering if what I saw was real, if such schools and teachers do exist. Four cartons of notes taken on 3 × 5 cards give material support to my impression that these schools do indeed exist, and that they are becoming increasingly influential not only in England but in other countries as well.

I must note here that only about 25 percent of England's primary schools fit the model described in the following paragraphs. Perhaps 40 percent can be described as quite traditional, while another third or so are in various stages of transition. Nevertheless, 25 percent is a significant number of schools when one looks at the size of the total educational enterprise in England, and even more significant is the obvious movement toward this new kind of education among schools which cannot as yet be included among the exciting and innovative 25 percent.

What is there that is so unusual about these schools? To begin with, it seems as if the new English primary school is committed to the notion that children should live more fully and more richly now, rather than at some ill-defined time in the distant future. Education, then, is not preparation for life; education is life, with all of its excitement, challenge, and possibilities. This is happening here and now in perhaps 20 to 30 percent of the primary schools in England.

English teachers and headmasters conceive of the curriculum as a series of starting or jumping-off places. An idea, a question, an observation — child's or teacher's — acts as a stone thrown into the middle of a quiet pond. The ripples begin, one idea leads to another, and a study is under way. In contrast, American educators seem far more concerned from a curricular point of view with identifying and then covering a series of ideas, concepts, generalizations, or skills that (theoretically) form the backbone of the curriculum in any area. We shall discuss this in greater detail later. However, it seems worth mentioning that there appears to be very little subject matter that is perceived of as "basic" and "essential" in the eyes of the English teacher or head-master. The curriculum emerges through the mutual interests and explorations of children and their teachers, working together occasionally in large groups, sometimes in small groups, and often as individuals.

Another characteristic of the emerging British primary school, and one that is closely related to the preceding point, has to do with the eagerness of teachers to cut across disciplinary lines in their handling of any study that may evolve in their classrooms. Art, music, history, poetry—all are brought to bear on a given problem or topic, and it is often difficult to tell whether children are studying history or geography, art or science. This, of course, tends to give a wholeness to learning that must be lacking in more compartmentalized curricula, and it helps support and build the image of the school as a place where lifelike questions are investigated as opposed to questions that are narrowly academic.

A fourth observation is that the English teacher is concerned with *learning* as opposed to teaching. Rarely will one find such a teacher standing in front of the room teaching a "class" lesson. Rather, the teacher is largely a stagesetter, a stimulator, who encourages and guides but who does *not* direct. It is often difficult to find the teacher when one first walks into a typical classroom, since she is likely to be working with a child here and a child there, moving around the room and among the children.

Having said all of this, a fifth conclusion is inescapable: The English teacher accepts the significance of *process* over *product* in the education of the child. There seems little doubt that English teachers are greatly concerned with *how* a child learns, the kinds of questions he asks, and the ways in which he goes about resolving them. Over the long haul, English teachers believe these learning "strategies" will prove to be infinitely more valuable than the subject matter.

Similarly, English teachers seem greatly concerned about the development of independence and responsibility in children—often to a far greater extent than American teachers. In the best of English primary schools, a degree of individual freedom, flexibility, and responsibility exists in a way that is virtually unknown in most American elementary schools. Teachers do not hang over their children, supervise them in every conceivable activity, watch them on the playground, in the halls, in the buses, and in the washrooms. All of this is done, of course, in a calculated way, recognizing that such qualities as independence and reliability need to be "practiced" as well as spoken about.

Finally, one might say that the teachers in the kinds of schools I visited seem to care deeply, perhaps passionately, about *children*. Children are to be taken seriously, not laughed at or ridiculed in the staff room. Children are to be watched; children are to be listened to; children are to learn from; children are the essential ingredient in the teaching-learning process; children make one's job exciting, challenging, and truly professional. This point cannot possibly be exaggerated. It is, in fact, the day-to-day practical implementation of the intellectual rationale for a very real revolution in education.

As one reads about these exciting developments in English schools, one cannot help but wonder why such ideas have never really caught on here on the scale they have in England. There is, of course, much talk about creativity, the needs of children, and the importance of the student taking responsibility for his own learning. Indeed, bits and pieces of the educational processes described in the preceding pages do exist all over America. It is, rather, the complete expression of, and commitment to, a set of educational ideals that seems to be missing in this country.

Let us examine some possible reasons for American reluctance to move in similar directions. One must say at the beginning of such an analysis that a number of American teachers, writers, and teachers-turned-writers are passionately involved in a movement to bring a looser, more relevant, more child-centered and experience-based kind of education to American children. One thinks immediately of Jonathan Kozol, Herbert Kohl, James Herndon, and John Holt as examples of the turned-on, deeply concerned teacher who, on the basis of his experiences in classrooms, has something to say about American education. In addition, journalists like Joseph Featherstone and Charles Silberman are also joining the crusade, and even as influential a group as the Educational Development Center in Cambridge, Massachusetts (the base for Jerome Bruner's curricular operations) has recently hired an Englishman or two to help plan the center's various projects.

Because of the pressures brought to bear by this new breed of educational critic, changes are being made in some public schools; and a few private schools have been founded here and there that are more completely faithful to the educational point of view described in this article. Nevertheless, and in all fairness, it must be said that these disparate efforts are hardly an organized, well-directed, and advancing movement.

Perhaps one reason for American failure to move more rapidly in this direction can be traced to the curricular and methodological impact of the launching of the Russian Sputnik in 1957. The event was perceived as an educational humiliation, and the curricular developments that followed it during the next decade all gave a push to a kind of education that was vastly different from the movement that was already under way in England.

It is no news to American or English educators that the search for "structure," for "basic concepts and generalizations" in mathematics, science, social studies, literature, and other fields, has dominated curricular activity in the United States during the years following Sputnik. This has led, quite logically, to an emphasis upon separate subjects rather than upon the integration or wholeness of the curriculum; it has led to further support for a traditional educational disease which we will call "the covering syndrome," i.e., one *must* deal with certain "basic" ideas, topics, or problems, or else one is clearly derelict in one's duty; therefore, one must avoid those diversions, those sidetracking situations that often lead to relevant and exciting learning, even though they *do* interfere with "coverage."

In an attempt to be as faithful as possible to what we perceive of as the "work-ways" or methods of the various disciplines, American educators have spent a great deal of time and energy in organizing the new curricula so that children will not merely memorize and repeat concepts and generalizations as they memorized and repeated the much despised "facts" of the old. Therefore we talk a great deal about inquiry and discovery approaches to learning. However, a careful examination of the materials and methods that comprise many of the new curriculum projects and packages reveals (with some exceptions) that the kinds of questions raised, the problems studied, the discoveries or generalizations arrived at are rarely the children's. We try valiantly; we smile, entreat, and cajole. Some of the kids are caught up in it some of the time—perhaps an unusually challenging topic catches their fancy or perhaps an unusually dynamic teacher draws them out through the force of his personality. More often than not, however, we end up with something Vincent Glennon has described as "sneaky telling." We know where we're going; we know what the questions should be, what the "big ideas" are, and the conclusions one should come away with, if the teacher's manual is followed.

Perhaps, in the final analysis, this is the best way to teach. Perhaps we cannot afford the luxury of exploring children's questions in whichever direction they may take us. Certainly there is little evidence which demonstrates empirically that the less structured, more child-centered English teacher is producing a "better product" than is the tighter, more discipline-centered American teacher. At the moment, the best evidence I can offer is simply watching children at work and at play over extended periods of time in schools. If their reactions, their activity, their art, music, and poetry, their attitudes toward teachers and toward school are valid criteria, then we have a great deal to learn from the English.

Perhaps another reason for our reluctance to move in the same direction as the English is our comparative affluence, which enables us to develop and pay for mechanical panaceas, with whatever educational hardware happens to catch our fancy. In both countries "to individualize" is thought of as a good thing. Increasing numbers of conferences and workshops are devoted to this theme in America, yet American teachers seem not to have learned the lesson that is grasped so well by many English primary teachers: One individualizes, as Philip Jackson* put it, by

> . . . injecting humor into a lesson when a student seems to need
> it, and quickly becoming serious when he is ready to settle down
> to work; it means thinking of examples that are uniquely
> relevant to the student's previous experience, and offering them
> at just the right time; it means feeling concerned over whether or
> not a student is progressing, and communicating that concern in
> a way that will be helpful; it means offering appropriate praise
> . . . because the student's performance is deserving of human
> admiration; it means in short, responding *as* an individual *to* an
> individual.

*P. W. Jackson. *The Teacher and the Machine: Observations on the Impact of Educational Technology.* Mimeographed. Univ. of Chicago, 1966.

This conception is much, much more than allowing for differences in speed when moving through some particular "program"; it is more than telling us automatically, if politely, that "you are wrong, please turn to page fifteen for another explanation."

In other words, one individualizes by watching and listening to *children*. Mechanical aids are useful, but there is no substitute for the conception of individualization expressed so ably by Jackson in the preceding paragraph. Many American teachers have been seduced by the promise of technology; their less affluent English counterparts know that individualization will come to their children only if they make a concerted effort to bring it about under classroom conditions that are not likely to change radically soon. So they collect, construct, beg, borrow, and, I suspect, steal materials of all kinds to provide the kind of learning environment they know is good — and they often do so for classes of forty children or more. Most English teachers are willing to agree with Mort Sahl that "the future lies ahead." They are not banking on an educational promised land that may lie just around the corner. They are addressing themselves to solving the individualization problem in terms of their own intelligence and energy — now.

A third invidious comparison one is forced to make with American elementary schools when he visits an English primary school is in the area of aesthetics. Aesthetics — arts, music, movement — is in a dismal state in American schools as compared with their English counterparts. Even for our very young children, many schools have music and art teachers who conduct twenty-minute, weekly lessons that become *the* art or music program. Aesthetic activities generally take a back seat to the more academic components of the curriculum.

Perhaps this is a problem inherent in American culture rather than a school program. These things are considered effete; they are not valued in the same way that reading and mathematics are. It would be rare, indeed, to see an American teacher seriously encourage children to use their bodies as a mode of expression. It would be even more rare to find the teacher herself joining the children and participating in the creation of a dance pattern. (Perhaps a new generation of teachers, reared on the less inhibited use of their bodies that has developed with the universal acceptance of rock, will see possibilities in movement that their predecessors did not.)

In my judgment, aesthetics plays an infinitely more important role in the education of English children than in that of American children, and the hesitancy of American teachers to utilize these means of reaching children is a major difference between primary education in England and in the United States.

Another curious factor that gets in the way of American movement toward a more free and less structured school may lie in our dichotomous treatment of kindergarten and primary children. In England, children are treated as individuals from the moment they enter school at the age of five until they leave the primary school. Teachers of "reception classes" (five-year-olds) move children into reading, for example, if the child seems ready to read. Similarly, a *six*-year-old child in an English primary school is not pushed, hounded, and bullied, ready or not, into reading when he reaches that magical age. In other words, we have created a very unreal and unwise division between what learning ought to be for five-year-olds and what it ought to be for sixes. One might call this the kindergarten-primary grade dilemma. We usually find a far greater degree of freedom, child-centeredness, looseness, or lack of structure in our kindergartens than we find at any other level of elementary school. Many American children begin their education enjoying learning, being happy in school and contented with themselves. For many of these children, however, first grade becomes a cruel awakening. No more time now for learning as fun; now we must "work"; now we must put away dress-up clothes, blocks, and spur-of-the-moment curricular explorations.

In a good English primary school, this dichotomy does not exist. A child comes to school initially to learn, and to learn at his own pace. This point of view is carried continuously through the primary years.

Finally, we might mention one other factor that may play a role in discouraging the adoption on a large scale of the sort of primary school we have been describing in these pages. I refer to the relative freedom that English teachers and headmasters have to develop the kinds of educational programs that they, as professionals, deem right—with minimum concern for outside pressure groups. Conversely, American teachers and principals are subject to tremendous pressures from the community, and no state-supported school can casually ignore them. This means that some changes will be easier to bring about than others; that what the lay public conceives of as "good" education may be adopted in the schools more readily than other changes. At this point, the American public seems to see "good" education as a hard-driving, highly competitive academic race, and educational innovations fitting that image stand a better chance of acceptance than do other innovations.

In England, which has traditionally had an exceedingly competitive education system, the movement toward drastic change in the education of young children originated and was carried out largely by professionals and often *against* the wishes of parents. This is not to say that English teachers and headmasters can do as they please. It does mean, however, that they are more independent of, and more protected from, outside pressures of all kinds than American educators. Vulnerability to public pressures probably causes American school people to be reluctant to adopt a child-centered approach to teaching.

Having examined and compared English and American primary-school programs, I turn now to criticism. This will be difficult, since I have not attempted to hide my considerable admiration for what I see happening in the modern English primary school. Nevertheless, what seems good can no doubt become better, and perhaps some of the following questions may serve to further that purpose.

The first point is really not a criticism of classroom practices at all. Rather, it is a plea for some form of systematic evaluation of the achievements of the schools described in these pages. Those of us fortunate enough to have visited good English primary schools recognize almost intuitively that what we are seeing is mostly right, mostly effective, mostly sound. On the other hand, many educators have a way of asking questions that cannot be adequately answered by referring to one's personal observations. How, in fact, do children in such schools perform on various objective measures when compared to children who have had quite a different sort of school experience? Obviously, academic achievement is not the basic goal of such schools, but since it is not, what effects do these schools have on children's attitudes toward school, teachers, and peers? How does this experience affect their approach to learning, the problem solving strategies they adopt, their persistence, their curiosity?

A more direct criticism is exemplified, perhaps, by a description of an afternoon spent in what was, in many ways, a fascinating primary school in rural Leicestershire. During the entire afternoon the children were free to carry out projects that were of interest to them. There was a great deal of arts and crafts activity – carpentry, weaving, block printing, and so on. The children were obviously well behaved, busy, and interested in their work. Yet I couldn't help but feel that this happy, involved group of children were somehow existing in the middle of what we all know to be a terribly complex, rapidly changing world – divorced from its reality, protected from its problems, and uninvolved in its conflicts and dilemmas.

Somehow, the "real" world that children explore in such schools is often a rather limited version of reality. It is a real world of fields, streams, trees, rocks, stones, flowers, birds, and insects, if it is a country school. If it is a city school, it is a real world of traffic patterns, nearby shops, local museums and libraries, parks and gardens. The "real world" is often conceived of as that world which is nearby and, more precisely, that world which can be seen, felt, smelled, touched, or listened to.

One might suggest, then, that there are, after all, limits to how far one can go with personal, concrete experience as *the* essential teaching technique. Children can study only a small part of the world by direct observation and experience, and one must question the hours that are spent in making, building, and physically "doing" that could, conceivably, be used in other ways as well. One wonders, for example, if in studying the wool industry, the process of making wool does not get treated all out of proportion to some of the related economic, social, and political problems that might be implied in such a study – granting, of course, that much of this "activity" would be intellectual rather than physical, vicarious more than direct.

If one largely limits the objects of one's study to those found only in the local environment, it is difficult to see how the school can play a significant role in helping children understand the broader world in which they live. Conflict exists about Rhodesia and about the immigrants who have recently settled in sections of English cities such as Wolverhampton and Bradford. These problems are important to all English people. The fact that they do not lend themselves to direct or "concrete" experience does not render them any the less important.

The real world of social conflict exists, and no school, no teacher, no syllabus will ever completely isolate children from it. Yet the schools' responsibility would seem to include some attempts at

increasing children's awareness of the inadequacies and inequalities that exist in both their local and their wider environments. Failing this, children will, of course, muddle through,
picking up ideas and attitudes wherever they find them and becoming more and more aware (perhaps through harsh personal
experience) of the conflict that exists between the school world
and the world of social reality.

Similarly, one might question the degree of curricular egali-
tarianism that exists in the emerging British primary school.
Obviously, only the simplest of societies can hope to teach its
children "all they need to know." Therefore, it has become increasingly important to ask, what knowledge is of the most worth
to *our* society at this particular moment in time? Which ideas
will help the nonspecialist citizen to understand the world in
which he lives? Which ideas are fundamental enough to have
transfer value? Which ideas will help one to better understand a
unique phenomenon that has not been formally studied before?

My English colleagues will immediately argue that only the
child can know what knowledge, what information, what understanding, is important and necessary to him. Identifying significant ideas seems to smack of predigested academic luncheons
that have little relevance to children's interests or needs. I would
also agree. I would indeed argue further that this appears to be
the major weakness in many of the American curriculum projects
which were developed during the Brunnerian revolution of
the 60s.

However, this does not negate the argument that there *are*
some things worth knowing, that some ideas help to order and explain our lives and the lives of others while other ideas do not. It
seems to me that the great weakness one observes in both English
and American schools is the lack of knowledge about and understanding of such ideas among *teachers*.

It would be foolish indeed to suggest that a discipline like
anthropology has developed no ideas that are really worth teaching to children, no concepts that help order, classify, and explain
the social world in which we find ourselves. The real value, the
ultimate utility of such ideas, however, lies *not* in the creation
of prepackaged "teacher-proof" curricula; rather, it is the classroom teacher who must grasp them and utilize them at the appropriate moment. In other words, "structure" belongs in the
minds of teachers.

One might mention other arguments, other "weaknesses"; these, however, seem to me to be among the most fruitful to discuss and perhaps are among the questions most likely to be raised by American educators.

Robert Emans clarifies the forces
and issues in the phonics field, then
suggests an alternative.

Phonics:
A Look Ahead

ROBERT EMANS

In a previous issue of *Elementary English* (Emans, 1968), I presented a history of the teaching of phonics. Between the time the article was written and when it was published, two important studies were reported, one by Bond and Dykstra (1967) and one by Chall (1967). Both studies seem to indicate that there should be an early emphasis on decoding in reading, with possibly a revived interest in phonics. Bond and Dykstra in summarizing the Cooperative Research Program in first-grade reading instruction came to the conclusion that "word study skills must be emphasized and taught systematically regardless of what approach to initial reading instruction is used" (Bond and Dykstra, p. 122). In reviewing the research from 1912 and 1965 Chall concludes "that a code-emphasis method—i.e., one that views beginning reading as essentially different from mature reading and emphasizes learning of the printed code for the spoken language

—produces better results, at least up to the point where sufficient evidence seems to be available, the end of the third grade" (Chall, p. 307). In addition to the studies indicating a critical look at phonics, recent books and articles, for example, Hodges (1966), Fries (1963) on linguistics, suggest that phonics instruction may be going through a period of change. This article will present some views on the direction that phonic instruction may take in the future.

My purpose here is not to give a blanket endorsement to all kinds of phonic instruction. Such an endorsement would be meaningless since phonics take many different forms. My purpose is to present some ideas about phonics in the hope of encouraging discussion. Too often in the past those concerned with phonic instruction have emphasized various procedures, not always giving the underlying reasons for using them other than that they appear to work. When others have attempted to implement the suggested procedures results have varied. There has been little basis for examining why the various procedures have or have not worked. This article will examine some of the forces operating in the implementation of phonic instruction, some of the theories behind a number of different procedures for teaching phonics, and suggest a program for teaching phonics.

Forces

Numerous forces probably influence what phonics are taught and how they are taught. Chall describes a number of such forces (Chall, pp. 288–300). Many forces seem to come from society, what and how children learn, and research involving reading and reading instruction. Each one of these forces will be described briefly.

Society

Probably one of the most important sources of influence on phonic instruction is the goals that society, or influential segments or individuals of society, deem important. For example, during the colonial period in the United States hearing the Word of God read was considered important. Later, learning a universal American English dialect was a major goal. At various times in our history the ability to spell was considered a mark of the educated man. Thus during such periods, when oral reading and spelling were considered of paramount importance, instruction in phonics received much attention. More recently, when readers were to react reflectively to the meaning of what was written, phonics was considered of less importance. Today reading precociousness of young children and the acquisition of information for college seem important. Therefore, instruction which facilitates early achievement in reading seems to have become increasingly important.

Children Learning

Viewpoints regarding what children are capable of learning and theories as to how children learn are also important influences on phonic instruction. For example, many teachers and reading specialists have thought that children under seven years of age find the learning of phonics difficult. This view may be changing. In respect to how children learn, one school of psychology has stressed that children learn by responding to certain stimuli. Those teachers supporting these stimulus-response theories of learning have tended to teach phonics through procedures stressing various forms of drill. On the other hand, some teachers have believed that children should understand why they are learning what they are expected to know. This group of teachers has tended to stress the importance of establishing purposes for learning. Other teachers take the view that both schools of thought have merit and have stressed practice exercises, but only in situations where children have goals for learning what they understand.

Reading Research

The research involving reading may have had less influence than some other forces. This reduced influence probably has had a number of causes. Researchers have probably not been in a position to put into practice some of their findings. Many years normally pass before findings from research find their way to the classroom. In addition, much of the research has been carelessly done, resulting in conflicting findings. The tendency for researchers attempting to *prove,* rather than *find out,* something has also had a negative effect.

Still other forces influencing phonic instruction have come from other sources. For example, studies of linguistics appear today to have an increasing influence. Other areas include neurology, optometry, psychiatry, and communicative theory.

Theory of Past
Phonic Programs

Theory is an important aspect of any phonic program because it presents the reason or reasons why the procedures should contribute to children learning to read. Theory can be reexamined or revised to suggest further advances in procedures as evidence arises. Procedures based only on a belief that they work, and not on theory, cannot be altered rationally and cannot be examined in respect to long-range effects or broader implications. Fortunately, most practices in reading instruction can be supported by some type of theory, even though the theory may often be expressed only implicitly. However, because the theory is often stated implicitly, it is difficult to examine it. Nevertheless, in the next few paragraphs I will present what appear to be theories upon which several of the past procedures seem to have been based. What appear to be some of their strengths and weakness will also be discussed.

Spelling Approach

In a spelling approach the child is to recognize a word by spelling it first. By giving the names of the letters a child is to associate the letter names with the visual details of a word. One advantage of such an approach is its simplicity. Only twenty-six names need to be recalled and associated with less than twice that number of visual shapes. Although some of the names have no resemblance to the sounds they represent (for example: *w, h*), most of the letter names contain frequently used sounds represented by the visual symbol (for example: *g, b, d, t*). A number of letter names are similar to often heard sounds the visual symbols represent, for example, the long vowel sounds. Therefore, a knowledge of letter names may give a clue to the sound of some words. On the other hand, the spelling approach often fails to give a close enough approximation of the sounds to the visual symbols to really give much help. There are more sounds in our language than there are visual symbols. Often critics claim that spelling a word is different from procedures mature readers use when they recognize words. Although the spelling approach may produce good spellers, it may also produce slow, laborious readers if used alone.

Synthetic-Phonic Approach

In the synthetic-phonic approach the child learns to associate sounds with letter shapes, as opposed to letter names in the spelling approach. The child recognizes words by associating sounds with the letter symbols and blending the sounds together into words. Such an approach appears to have the advantage over the spelling approach since recognizing letter sounds may give a closer representation of the words than just the letter names. As with the spelling approach, an advantage of the synthetic-phonic approach is its simplicity. Teachers and children can give much concentrated attention to it. On the other hand, knowing the sounds that letters represent may give little idea as to the word, for example, *eye.* In addition, the sounds represented by letter symbols may be quite different when pronounced than the sounds that are represented by the symbols as they appear in actual words. As is generally recognized, some sounds (for example: *b, d, g*) cannot be sounded in isolation and must be accompanied by a vowel sound. For example if a child is taught the sounds represented by *b* and *g* he may learn to say "bŭ" and "gŭ." Some children when trying to recognize the word represented by the symbols *big* will blend the sounds together as "bŭ-i-gŭ," which has little approximation to the actual word.

Sight Approach

In the well-known and controversial sight approach, the child learns to recognize a word through repeated exposures to it. Although it is seldom found in today's school in its purest form, it is used in most programs at some point. The child uses no sound clues, but may be expected to glean the pronunciation of the word from context. The sight approach is often used to help children recognize words which are largely nonphonic and to help them build a stock vocabulary from which they may later draw phonic generalizations. The sight approach came about, at least in part, as a result of research on eye movements which indicated that mature readers tend to recognize words as wholes, not parts (Judd and others). It also was supported by the findings of some schools of psychology that indicated that children learn best when meaning is involved. Words, not sounds, it was argued, are the smallest units that carry meaning in themselves.

The sight approach has been challenged because it gives little clue, other than configuration and context, to help children recognize words on their own. Lefevre (1964) has criticized it, along with other approaches stressing words, because he contends that the smallest language unit to carry meaning is the sentence and not the word.

Analytic-Phonic Approach

The analytic-phonic approach is the one found in many present-day reading programs. It is more eclectic in that it uses visual, auditory, and meaning clues in word recognition. Consequently, it uses both sight and phonic learning activities. Because it is eclectic some people feel that it has no theory of its own. However, it does possess theory which can be examined. Very simply the theory is that readers recognize words as wholes until they come to words that they cannot recognize instantaneously. At this point, the reader stops and examines the word more closely. He uses various clues. One of these clues is from the meaning of the other words that surround it. Another clue combines meaning with recognizing parts of the words visually as in structural analysis. Still other clues may be the sounds that various letters or combinations of letters represent. Of course, a number of clues may be used simultaneously, and if none work, a dictionary can be consulted. To learn phonics, a child develops a stock vocabulary from which he is to generalize the sounds that the letters represent in conjunction with words, and not in isolation. Therefore, sounds are not distorted as they may be in synthetic phonics. Meaning can be stressed within the limits of a controlled vocabulary. Phonics is taught, but it is not presented as intensely as it is in a synthetic-phonic approach. To illustrate, say that a child has learned to recognize the words *boy, baby,* and *better.* He also has learned the words *cat, look, hold.* When the child comes across the words *bat, book,* and *bold* and has not seen them before, he is to recognize them by substituting the initial sound of *b* that he learned in *boy, baby,* and *better,* taking off the first letters of the already familiar words of *cat, look, hold,* and then blending the various sounds together. Such a procedure does seem complicated. Although phonics is taught as the child is learning to read for meaning, practice on phonics is sometimes given aside from actual reading.

Linguistics

The most recent to receive attention in reading circles are programs based on various linguistic principles. Although some linguists have attempted to disassociate their approaches from phonics, they do seem to have similar objectives to those of previous phonic programs. Fries has criticized phonics for teaching sounds in isolation and claims, because his linguistic techniques do not do this, that his program is not a phonic program (Fries, p. 146). However, as had been pointed out previously, a pure analytic-phonic approach also does not teach sounds in isolation and, therefore, is similar to Fries' linguistic approach in this respect. When phonics is broadly defined as a process of applying phonetics to reading, the recent linguistically based programs may also be viewed as another phonic system.

The authors of linguistically based programs assume that reading is the "transfer from the auditory signs for language signals, which the child has already learned, to the new visual sign for the same signs" (Fries, p. 120). Therefore, "one can 'read' insofar as he can 'respond' to the language signals, now represented by contrastive spelling patterns, as completely and as efficiently as he has learned to respond to the same language signals formerly represented by sound patterns" (Fries, p. 187).

To teach beginning reading using a linguistically based approach, children are to develop habits of responding to contrasting aspects of spelling patterns. The words selected are only those for which spelling patterns have been previously presented or those that are being introduced. For example, in the first lesson of Fries' first reader (Fries and others, 1966) the child is expected to learn *cat, fat,* and *mat,* with *is* and *a* introduced as sight words. The story is as follows:

> Nat is a cat.
>
> Nat is fat.
>
> Nat is a fat cat.

Although the linguistically based programs have been received with great interest, some of the theory can be challenged. Written language may be based on oral language; but it is not identical to it. For example, intonation is only approximated in written language. Perhaps more importantly, the milieu for reading is different from the milieu for oral language. Most of the oral language for young children takes place in conversation where what is said may be repeated and questions asked when the meaning is not clear. In reading, the child may stop reading and reread and think as he wishes, whereas in conversation, language continues to flow.

There are other aspects of the linguistically based teaching procedures which may be questioned. Although the practices may be sound in respect to linguistics, there are psychological principles which may be violated. In respect to the words *cat, fat,* and *Nat* given as examples previously, experiments involving associative learning (Muehl, 1961) would indicate that the child is not learning the sound *at* as the instructional objective, but is learning to distinguish the words visually through recognizing the letters *c, f,* and *N.* Therefore, the child may later make such confusions as *cat* for *can, for* for *fat,* and *Ned* for *Nat.*

Whereas it may be an advantage not to confuse the child by introducing him to inconsistent spelling patterns such as *mother* and *to* where the *o* represents different sounds, there is the question concerning the use of similar spelling patterns as the *technique* for teaching children to read. If the linguists were to be consistent in representing highly predictable spelling patterns, the practice of introducing such letters as *c* may be challenged since it represents two different sounds which, in fact, can be presented by two other letters—*s* and *k.*

Another practice of the linguists which may be questionable is the one of not teaching the letter-sound correspondences directly. Bishop (1962) found that half of the children in her experiment receiving linguistic-type training could not induce the letter-sound correspondence without direct instructions. As Chall (Chall, p. 118) stated, "The best results probably came from using some control of spelling patterns and directly teaching their sound values." One must wonder if the verbalizing of phonic generalizations, such as those taught in many phonic programs, do not also have value. Moreover, the area of structural analysis, with its body of word identification clues, is apparently given little emphasis in linguistically based programs.

Another Plan

The purpose of the next few paragraphs will be to propose a plan for teaching phonics. Such a plan should not be viewed as set, but one that can be modified through discussion, experimentation, and practice.

First, the starting points for the plan will be stated. Chall states, "We must closely examine the foundation upon which it (the existing truth regarding theory and practice) was built before replacing it with a new set of truths. The foundation for the new truths must be studied carefully as well. Otherwise we build on sand" (Chall, p. 305). The purpose for the first part of this article has been to examine the theory upon which previous phonic instruction has been based. The purpose of the last part will be to state a plan carefully enough so it too may be examined critically and thoroughly. Among the starting points for the proposed plan are the following:

1. The teaching of reading is influenced by many forces from many sources and disciplines, including linguistics, psychology, sociology, optometry, neurology.

2. Linguistics, as a field of study, will be of special significance to reading instruction in the immediate future.

3. Presently, early childhood reading precocity is valued.

4. Although research will probably not provide clear-cut directions, it can influence practice if carefully examined.

5. In an area such as reading instruction where so much controversy is present, it is likely that persons with conflicting viewpoints are observing half-truths and few people are observing the whole truth. No one theory or set of practices can be adopted per se. Chall states, "I cannot emphasize too strongly that the evidence does not endorse any one code-emphasis method over another" (Chall, p. 30). She goes on to say, "Every school that introduces a new method still retains a good deal of the old one. Who is to say that retention of some of the old way of doing things is not a crucial factor in improved results?" (Chall, p. 282).

6. Children should be motivated to read through both an interest in learning to read and an interest in what is being read. Chall is advocating a switch from a meaning emphasis to a code emphasis in the first grade. This writer believes the evidence is that, although it may be possible to defer the development of comprehension skills until a later time, children will best learn the code when meaning is present. In short, the problem is probably not decoding versus meaning. Instead, the problem is to make decoding more meaningful or, conversely, using meaning to help children learn the code.

7. Finally, if conflicting evidence is available concerning the value of a specific goal, the ease which children have in achieving that goal should also be considered.

Based upon the above starting points this writer suggests the following plan for consideration, discussion, and experimentation. The plan is based upon the premise that much of the controversy concerning reading instruction in the past has been because the various practices advocated have merit in some instances but not in others. This is not to say that anything goes. Conversely, what may be a good practice in one case may be a bad practice in another. The task is to be analytical so as to determine when the various approaches should be put into effect and when they should be avoided. For example, two different and opposing practices may be used for teaching the sounds represented by *m* and *b*. The plan is as follows:

1. Children may be taught early the letter names and to relate the letter names to the visual symbols. Bond and Dykstra concluded that "the knowledge of letter names gained prior to initial instruction alone would account for approximately 25 to 36 percent of the variation in reading ability found at the end of the year under the various methods of instruction used in this study" (Bond and Dykstra, p. 117). Although such a procedure may be controversial, many children have some such knowledge before coming to school. Such a goal may be easily achieved by many children. Most of the letter names contain the sounds which the letters frequently represent. (Children may not need to learn the alphabet in order until they need it for work with the dictionary and other reference reading. Neither should children be taught in school the names of letters infrequently used or those letters which are dissimilar to the sounds they represent, e.g., *h*.) Some people who believe that such a procedure should not be followed are at the same time advocating the teaching of sounds in isolation. There is probably little difference between learning that the letter *b* has a name of "bē" or the sound of "bŭ." The sound "bŭ" may be viewed as another name for "bē" and may be no less confusing to the child. Letter names could possibly be used within the readiness programs and closely tied in with visual discrimination.

2. There are probably some advantages for teaching certain sounds in isolation near the beginning of reading instruction. However, extreme care should be taken to include in this part of the program only those letters for which the sound they represent can be pronounced in isolation and to be sure that the sounds are purely made, e.g., "m" not "mŭ." Such a procedure would have the advantage of giving intensified practice on learning sounds, especially the vowel sounds which children seem to have much difficulty learning. Such procedures may be closely related to the auditory-discrimination objectives of a readiness program.

3. Children could develop a stock of sight words early. Such a group of words are quickly learned by many children and would teach that words often can be recognized instantaneously and not always recognized through phonics. This procedure could be used so that materials which interest children and have an element of meaning could be used early in the program. Thus it would introduce the concept that reading is to get meaning and not merely the pronunciation of words. As is the practice in the analytic-phonic approach, the stock of words could be used for analysis in the learning of additional words. Of course, highly useful words and words which do not follow common spelling patterns could also be learned by this approach.

4. The analytic-phonic approach could be reserved for the accomplishment of very specific goals and not be used for the teaching of all sounds. For example, it could be used to teach only those sounds (such as those represented by *b* and *g*) which cannot be pronounced in isolation. In addition it could be used in helping children to verbalize certain clues that may be helpful in phonics and structural analysis such as: Words having double *e* usually have the long *e* sound. Perhaps most importantly, it can be used to teach a procedure for recognizing unfamiliar words in actual reading and to help children apply the phonic knowledge they have learned.

5. Children should also learn how to recognize unfamiliar words by combining phonic knowledge with context clues, thus bringing decoding and meaning together. Context clues, used in conjunction with other clues, help children to apply their phonic knowledge and to use meaning in the recognition of words.

6. Information from linguistics can be used for developing materials which have words that follow common spelling patterns. In this regard, linguistic knowledge would be useful for writing materials, but not solely as a basis for a method of teaching phonics. One of the conclusions of Bond and Dykstra supports this practice:

> Indications are that the initial reading vocabulary should
> be selected with a greater balance between phonetically
> regular words and high-utility words. It is likely that
> introducing words solely on the basis of frequency of use
> presents an unusually complex decoding task for the
> beginning reader. On the other hand, it appears that
> presenting only phonetically regular words makes it very
> difficult to write meaningful material (Bond and Dykstra,
> pp. 123–24).

As is true in the present analytic-phonic procedure, side exercises related to readers and class reading material could be used to teach sounds in more-or-less contextual settings. Care would need to be taken in developing such exercises. For example, in the teaching of the short *a* sound such words as *man, dad,* and *hat* could be used in practice exercises or stories. The practice today of some linguistically based programs of teaching such words as *ban, fan,* and *man* (or *bad, bag,* and *bat*) may be discontinued so as to avoid the use of irrelevant clues. As was previously pointed out, children have a tendency to use the visually distinguishing features (in this event *b, f,* and *m* in *ban, fan, man*) and may not learn that *an* represents a given sound pattern, which is the objective for such exercises. Other considerations, such as selecting words which have letters, sounds, and meanings that are difficult to distinguish, would need to be taken into account in developing the supplementary exercises.

Summary

This article has summarized a number of theories and practices which appear to underlie various phonic programs and has suggested how they may be used together in a more eclectic approach. The premise has been that theory and practice should be closely examined to determine how they may be most effectively used.

Bibliography

Bishop, C. "Transfer of Word and Letter Training in Reading." Unpublished Master's thesis, Cornell University, Ithaca, N.Y., 1962.

Bond, G. L., and Dykstra, R. "The Cooperative Research Program in First Grade Reading Instruction." *Reading Research Quarterly,* 2 (Summer 1967), entire issue.

Chall, J. *Learning to Read: The Great Debate.* New York: McGraw-Hill, 1967.

Emans, R. "History of Phonics." *Elementary English,* 45 (May 1968):602–607.

Fries, C. C. *Linguistics and Reading.* New York: Holt, Rinehart & Winston, 1963.

Fries, C. C., and others. *Merrill Linguistic Readers.* Columbus, Ohio: Charles E. Merrill Books, 1966.

Hodges, R. "The Case for Teaching Sound-to-Letter Correspondence in Spelling." *Elementary School Journal* 66 (1966):327–36.

Judd, C. H., and others. *Reading: Its Nature and Development.* Chicago: University of Chicago Press, 1918.

Lefevre, C. A. *Linguistics and the Teaching of Reading.* New York: McGraw-Hill, 1964.

Muehl, S. "The Effects of Visual Discrimination Pretraining with Word and Letter Stimuli on Learning to Read a Word List in Kindergarten Children." *Journal of Educational Psychology* 52, no. 4 (August 1961):215–21.

> Too often the procedures for aiding comprehension have stopped with *passive* understanding. What might we do to promote *active* understanding? The author provides specific suggestions for raising the level of comprehension training above the literal and passive.

Guidelines for Teaching Comprehension

HELEN J. CASKEY

The importance of developing pupils' abilities in reading comprehension is not questioned. There may well be uncertainties about the contributions of this or that approach to beginning reading, or differences of opinion among those who support programmed texts, teaching machines, individualized reading, or ability grouping, early or delayed instruction. Few persons question that the ultimate objective of teaching a child to read is to make him able to read with maximum power to comprehend what the writer intended to have understood by his readers.

Teachers are generally aware that comprehending a given passage, or indeed an entire book, can be on different levels. At a simpler level the reader is expected to recall the facts given in the selection he has read, and to make a decently accurate summary of the gist of the passage. He is expected to tell how many boys in the troop went on the overnight hike, and to tell in his own words what happened after they reached their destination. This level of comprehension has sometimes been referred to as passive understanding (Covington, 1967). At another level, reading comprehension which involves making evaluative judgments, making inferences about what is not directly stated in the selection, and drawing conclusions based upon the information given has been referred to as critical reading, or active reading, or creative reading, or more simply as a higher level of comprehension skill. As far as teachers are concerned, the nomenclature used is not of great importance. Whether these aspects of comprehension are termed critical, active, or creative, some kind of reading activity exists which goes beyond both the grasp of literal meaning of the passage and the recall of specific details. Of course, the grasp of the central idea and the clear understanding of basic details is essential; no analytical or evaluative procedures by the reader are possible without such basic understanding. The important consideration is to decide whether or not more than passive understanding is to be developed, and how the development of such higher levels of understanding is to be brought about. The choice is an important one and is based upon the values held concerning reading and concerning education of the young.

In the present state of society the choice to develop the highest possible level of comprehension seems inescapable. Problems of stunning magnitude press for effective solutions if man is to survive, let alone prevail, and a good deal of the information needed on which to base decisions is found in print. Thus the passive reader who is limited to simple recall of detail, or even the recognition of the main content of a message, is not able to cope with the reading tasks he is likely to face. The good reader, perhaps even more in the future than at present, will be the one who is able to hold a sort of "summit meeting" with the writer, engaging in an alert dialogue as he encounters an author through the printed page.

Achieving Higher Levels
of Comprehension

It is one thing, of course, to indicate an ideal outcome for teaching, and another thing to accomplish it. Two questions particularly come to mind. First, are the higher levels of comprehension in reading teachable? Does such comprehension depend almost completely upon the reader's background of experience (about which the teacher can do some things, but certainly not all things), or the intellectual ability of the learner (about which the teacher can do considerably less). For children limited in these areas, must teaching of necessity be limited largely to developing a more passive kind of reading? Secondly, if higher levels of comprehension are thought to be desirable, what factors in the reading situation should be of chief concern to the teachers? Reduced to its simplest terms, the problem of improving comprehension involves three interrelated factors: the pupil himself, the items he reads, and the kind of instruction in reading which he receives. The teacher in any subject area, as well as the teacher of reading, is vitally concerned with all three of these if power in comprehending is to be enhanced.

With respect to the pupil himself, it is clear that there are some fundamental skills that are basic to his effective comprehension. These include sufficient skill to handle word-recognition problems, experiences which he can relate to meanings of words in their present context, and a meaning vocabulary sufficiently accurate and extensive to enable him to cope with his reading materials. Further, he is helped by having a disposition to seek additional information when he feels uncertain as to the accuracy of his present interpretations. These factors influencing power of comprehension are evident both in research and in everyday teaching experience.

There is, however, some uncertainty respecting the relationship of mental abilities and higher levels of comprehension. A high level of comprehension involves thinking activities that are more complex than those required in passive reading. Assume that you as a reader are at some time asked to respond to such questions as: "Why do you think the author repeated the word *green* in this description of the fields and mountains?" or, "If the person in this story of colonial times were living today, how do you think he would earn his living?" or, "How do you think Jim felt when Mr. Jones discovered the missing boat?" or, "What did Launcelot mean when he said, 'Diamond me no diamonds'?" In responding you are evidently expected to go beyond what is specifically given in the selection in order to project the ideas into a different setting, to relate what is said there to what you already know or what you have felt yourself in a similar circumstance. You are asked to infer why a deliberate choice of words was made and are expected to expand or to translate a cryptic remark into language which reveals the same idea, put into idioms equally revealing, but in a currently conversational tone. Perhaps Launcelot in a baseball uniform, and putting on a catcher's mitt instead of an azure and silver shield, might well have said, "Don't give me any of that stuff!"

It is possible that many teachers feel that questions like these may be suggested only for the most able pupils, since they obviously require ability to take a kind of forward mental leap and to perceive relationships that are far from obvious. Should those of us who teach the "average" or the "below average" pupils in any age group be discouraged from making efforts to help these children to comprehend in this more complex set of situations?

Fortunately, there is evidence that achievement in higher level comprehension skills is not limited to gifted pupils only. The nature of the stimulation and guidance which has been received by the pupil appears to be more important. In the teaching of critical reading at the elementary level Wolf, et al. (1968) noted, for example, the importance of the teacher in "determining the depth of pupils' thinking." In comparing the responses of two subgroups of good and poor readers in a twelfth grade to questions posed by the investigator, Smith (1967) found that subjects whose intelligence quotients were within approximately the same range differed in success in reading, and that difference appeared to be more closely related to reading achievement than to the mental ability of the students. Covington (1967) reported that a group of pupils in grade five with lower I. Q. scores (below 100) was not specifically handicapped in what was termed "creative understanding." The conclusion was drawn that "the fact that these same low I. Q. children were reading on the average almost two years below grade level strongly suggests that students can benefit from such instruction (in creative understanding) in reading proficiency, provided, of course, that the reading level of the materials is adjusted accordingly."

Thus it appears that if the pupil has skills adequate for dealing with the material at his level, a higher level of comprehension is dependent not so much upon intellectual ability as it is upon the kind of instructional assistance that is given him.

Guiding Pupils' Reading

What kinds of instruction and guidance are most likely to be helpful in bringing about higher levels of comprehension? The first step is to note the range of skills involved in comprehending. Fortunately, information on this point is readily available; lists of comprehension skills exist in abundance, as every teacher who has used a workbook, looked into a teacher's manual for a reading series, or consulted a book on the teaching of reading at any level will quickly tell you. A helpful recent analysis of eight comprehension skills by Davis (1968) showed two significant and separate abilities: "memory of word meanings," and "drawing inferences about the content of material read." While no aspect of reading skill necessary to the best development of the reader may be neglected, here are two particular reading abilities in which specific help given the pupil will be likely to yield results in development of comprehension at higher levels.

Acquiring a broad and accurate vocabulary, one rich in depth and range of meanings is a life-time job. The language grows, new terms are added, and meanings shift or become current in a new context. Yesterday *Medicare* came into the language, and the words to be used wherever possible were *charisma* and *relevant.* Tomorrow—who knows what words will be in a newly minted, or repolished, verbal currency? The speaker and listener, the writer and reader, will have to know them and to use them in their new settings.

Field trips call attention to new words and develop concepts, particularly if both planning for the experience and subsequent discussion are assured. Such experiences give pupils at all levels a chance to learn new terms and to use them with precision and accuracy. Such first hand experience can also lend vitality to the "book bait" that teachers have used for a long time: "You were interested in the fossils we saw yesterday . . . here are some books you might like to read that tell a good bit more about fossils."

Self-help devices also help the learner to acquire greater precision in using words. Many teachers and pupils develop class word lists to help with words they are likely to need in their writing at a given time. A pupil's own word list is also useful. Furthermore, wide reading has a great deal to offer in this area. The reader finds many words which have recently been introduced to him, and meanings are more likely to be retained than would be the case with one or two exposures. Also, words are used in instruction and in general conversation for the express purpose of adding to the pupils' stock of word meanings. The youngster who hears quite frequently such transitional phrases as "on the other hand," "on the contrary," "in addition to," especially if attention is called to them specifically, finds that he can use them as aids in structuring his own ideas in speaking or in writing.

Word meanings, important as they are in developing higher levels of comprehension that go beyond remembering and restating factual details of the content, need to be supplemented by additional learnings. What do teachers consider important respecting levels of thinking and reading in elementary and secondary classrooms? Guszak (1967) examined nearly two thousand questions asked by a dozen teachers in grades four, five, and six. Over one-half of the questions asked required the pupils to recall some specific detail mentioned in the selection. This proportion may not reflect the situation in classrooms familiar to the reader, but it tallies pretty closely with the candid evaluations of many teachers with whom the writer has worked during recent years.

Since pupils master early the art of doing what they think teachers are going to ask them to do in class, or more particularly on written examinations, it appears that many of them stand a good chance of getting thorough preparation in avoiding any kind of thinking that would lead to habits of judging, evaluating, or drawing inferences or conclusions from their reading. The secondary pupils are also likely to be in the same condition. Smith (1967) comments that: "This study showed that the teachers' questions and examinations are important determinants of the manner in which students read. It further pointed out that the preponderance of questions asked by teachers were those requiring students to recall details or factual information."

It is not too helpful to say merely, "Don't ask so many questions requiring the recall of specific details." A more positive approach is called for. If pupils are to increase their power in making inferences, they must have guided practice in doing so.

It is especially useful to think about the kinds of assignments that are made in any subject area involving reading. They can be managed so as to set up situations that require judging, evaluating, and making inferences. For example, pupils may be asked to respond to this situation: "Many people who have read this short story consider the author a master in choosing and describing incidents which add, bit by bit, to our understanding of the character. Do you agree? Can you give some examples of how the author proceeds to make us better understand the persons in the story?" Or another: "Is there any indication in this story as to what season of the year it is? Does the time of year make any particular difference in the story? Why do you think so?"

A social studies class is challenged to discover what is involved in the statement "The frontier had ceased to be a factor in American life." A science class may try to describe a plan for a simple, workable, and easily visible demonstration of convection.

Another fruitful area for development of thinking is in guided classroom discussion, or in individual conferences that are a planned part of instruction. A good "first step" may be to seek a cure for the "right-answer syndrome" — the hardened conviction that any question must have a quite visible answer directly stated in the text. There are two reasons why such a fixed idea needs to be overcome. First, reliance upon questions of such factual nature establishes the habit of the teacher's preparing evaluations which rely solely upon easily verifiable questions. Such items can be undeniably right or wrong, with no possibility of haggling argument, a thing to be dreaded as papers are returned to their writers. Admittedly, it is difficult to phrase questions which require judgment, evaluation, and inference and still avoid ambiguities.

In the second place, pupils thoroughly conditioned to responding with an easily verifiable "right answer" are likely to be afraid to make any bolder attempts to speculate, to inquire, to test out the possibilities of understandings that go beyond involvement in the literal sense meaning. The final results of such conditioning appear in college students who complain bitterly that they "don't make the grades" because their responses do not exactly agree with those expected by their instructors.

Furthermore, the learner can acquire an unfortunate habit of needing to lean on the teacher's question: "Don't you think the boy felt lonely?" or, "Look again; that's not what the story tells us." There is not very much to be done in situations like this other than to guess as quickly as possible the response that will meet with approval.

A possibility for the more fruitful guidance of development in reading comprehension is in the use of a question that widens the range of possible response. "Did Jim feel different, in some way, at the end of the story?" may induce some pupils to think whether there was or was not a difference. Once this small response is unearthed, another probing must follow. "How different?" "Why?" Good enough, but perhaps a better tool would be a question that tickles the imagination as well as calls for recall of a set of related circumstances. "Suppose you were the illustrator for this story. What expression would you show on Jim's face as the story ends?" The "Why," of course, follows as a most important adjunct. Hopefully, the net result of such stimulation is to involve all children in the group in the thinking that must accompany any reasoned responses. There is a strong temptation, however, to feel that the situation will be challenging to Bob and Sue and Harry, but that it is not really right for poor Jane and Willard. They, it is feared, will be left out entirely as unequal to the task of what is hoped to be some fairly high-powered thinking. These pupils who are "slower" than others can also be a part of the thinking and responding. Any experience background possessed by any in the group can also be Jane's or Willard's if they share the same conversations and discussions, if they see the same pictures and talk about them, or if they manipulate the same tools or hold the same objects in hand.

All our concern for the individual and his guidance will be of little help if materials read are not chosen wisely and carefully. The level of difficulty of a given reading selection can be lowered markedly, while the level of thinking about it can be genuinely evaluative and interpretative. Beginners can cope with such problems as "Does this story have too many persons in it to make a good dramatization for our small group?" "Would this be a good story to read aloud? Do you think other children would enjoy hearing the parts we think are especially funny?" Older pupils can deal with such questions as: "Is the author accurate and realistic in describing a tense moment in the basketball game?" "How does the author foreshadow the tragic ending of the play?" Any of these questions can be considered about relatively short and easy selections and in all of them the implicit next item is

"Why?" The objective is not only to respond in some fashion. To be "involved" is commendable, but to sort out reasons, to note relationships, to predict consequences, and to substantiate judgments with a statement of the reasons why they are held is indeed to grow in the acts of reading and thinking.

References

Covington, M. V. "Some experimental evidence on teaching for creative understanding." *The Reading Teacher* 20 (1967):390-96.

Davis, F. B. "Research in comprehension in reading." *Reading Research Quarterly* 1968:400-543.

Guszak, F. J. "Teacher questioning and reading." *The Reading Teacher* 21 (1967):226-34.

Smith, H. K. "The responses of good and poor readers when asked to read for different purposes." *Reading Research Quarterly* 1967:53-83.

Wolf, W.; King, M. L.; and Huck, C. "Teaching critical reading to elementary school children." *Reading Research Quarterly* 1968:495.

study questions

1. Examine the answers to the question: Why do I do this? Each answer is taken from the responses of a large sample of teachers of reading:

   a) Because it keeps the children quiet and teaches them work habits.
   b) Because the teacher's manual tells me to.
   c) Because there's a certain amount of _____ everybody has to know, and I'm going to be sure my pupils get it.
   d) Well, the children just love to do it this way.
   e) In this school, it's required.
   f) I do this because it looks to me as if it needs to be done. Why do I think it needs to be done? Ah, well, I'll tell you . . . .

   Specify three or more procedures suggested by any one selection in this chapter. How will *you* respond to the question "Why do I do this?" in defense of each of the procedures you select. What evidence can you give (perhaps using material from chapters 1 and 2) that your defense for the procedure is solidly grounded in theory?

2. Reexamine the question and answers listed in 1 above. What reading-instruction procedures have you observed recently that might receive no better justifications than those stated? Specifically related to those procedures, what do the authors of the selections in this chapter have to offer as alternatives?

3. Do children always dislike "barbershop reading"? What harmful effects does Goldsmith attribute to this procedure regardless of the pupils' attitudes toward it?

4. After reading the Wilt selection, can you identify three situations in which grouping is a most desirable form of organization for reading instruction?

5. How well does Hagerty's ad hoc grouping meet conditions for effective grouping as discussed by Wilt? Do recent reading materials facilitate ad hoc grouping or do such materials await development?

6. What procedures observed by Rogers in the English primary schools could produce desirable changes in American reading instruction? Which of these procedures could be adopted by primary teachers regardless of the overall school organization and philosophy? Which are likely to require substantial alteration of total school systems?

7. Why are Rogers' observations limited to primary school? Are there suggestions here for intermediate and upper grades? If so, what are they?

8. How do the phonics-instruction suggestions given by Emans evolve from the survey of phonics forces discussed earlier in his article? Are his suggestions compatible with procedural suggestions given by other authors in this chapter?

9. Early in her article Caskey cites three types of comprehension above the level of "passive understanding." What are they? How do the procedures discussed subsequently in her article illustrate each of these types?

FOUR

organizing
for instruction:
materials

objectives

As a result of reading these articles and answering the questions at the end of the chapter you should be better able to:

- explain the general uses and limitations of instructional materials

- suggest some concrete ways that instructional materials can be used in the classroom

rationale

In education there is a good deal of sharpening of tools but little agriculture. We hear continually about school programs that propose radical changes. Close examination of many radical programs too often reveals that few, if any, changes have occurred in teaching itself. A major reason for the lack of basic change is the assumption that a change of reading materials means a change in reading teaching. We are not so naive in buying groceries. We do not assume that a change in the art work on a cereal box automatically indicates that the cereal itself has changed. The articles in this chapter provide some understanding of how materials can be used effectively.

introduction

We recall being amused by a three-year-old who was holding a copy of *Life* upside down and "reading" with great solemnity, "Go, Tom, go."

Humor is often accomplished by changing the context in which an action occurs, so that what is appropriate in one setting is amusingly inappropriate in another. The boy's behavior would not be humorous if he were holding a beginning reader in his hand; moreover, the changed situation could be taken so seriously that it might serve as an advertisement for an innovative reading program. A case in point, a recent full-page advertisement for a new reading program showed a little girl reaching for a book. The caption read: "Susan's 4 and she's reading third-grade books. Shouldn't your child too?" The program turns out to be no more innovative than a book and record that together say, "R..R..R.. Run, Rover, run." The same level of hyperbole, and without a hint of humorous put-on, is reached by a leading publisher of children's reading materials with the promise that "every child shall read" and a claim to the effect that never in the history of publishing has such a dramatic presentation been available for the classroom.

That so many people seem to believe these extravagant claims is evidence of their faith in using materials — meaning such non-human devices as books, bells, and teaching machines — to extend man's limited abilities. In great quantity they purchase devices to do work formerly done, presumably not as well, by man: popcorn poppers, carving knives, and can openers. Classrooms are becoming increasingly crowded with self-instructional materials in the form of self-correcting workbooks, simple machines, and typewriters connected to computers, on the assumption that the devices are more effective, patient, and attentive than human teachers.

The lack of faith in the ability of teachers to think and act may be increasing, to judge by the trend in that most popular form of reading material, the basal reader. Jeanne Chall,[1] in a study of forty years of development of the basal-reading series that was most widely used in 1962 (Scott, Foresman)[2] found that teacher's manuals are getting larger. Chall reported a study of the first-grade readers and teacher's manuals for the Scott, Foresman editions of 1920, 1930, 1940, 1956, and 1962. While the 1920 edition contained about 561 words of directions for each lesson, the 1956 edition had about 2300 words. The 1920 edition suggested one comprehension question for each 47 words the child read, and the 1962 edition suggested one question for every 12 words, almost a four-fold increase.

A critic of teachers might conclude that teachers have increased their dependence on materials because that absolves them from blame for children's reading failures. If children do not make satisfactory progress with program X, then the fault lies with the program, not the teacher; the teacher just followed directions.

One of the more unfortunate effects of the heavy reliance placed on materials is the retarding of much real substantive progress in education. That little progress has occurred in the last twenty years is documented in a study by John Goodlad,[3] who along with others visited 260 kindergarten and first-grade classrooms in one hundred schools in thirteen states. They concluded that things were much as they had been twenty years ago, and in some ways were not so good as they had been forty years ago. That the lack of progress is attributable wholly or in part to the reliance on materials is, admittedly, conjecture. But some support for the thesis can be gained from examining studies of the comparative effectiveness of materials.

The Cooperative Research Program in First Grade Reading Instruction[4] is the largest comparative investigation of beginning reading instruction yet made. The massive study was supported by a grant from the United States Department of Health, Education, and Welfare, Office of Education, under the provisions of the Cooperative Research Program. Twenty-seven individual first-grade projects were initiated in 1964–65. Each project was designed to study the effectiveness of two or three different approaches to first-grade reading instruction. The most characteristic difference between approaches was the materials used. The study was viewed as a means of finally answering the nagging question about the best approach for teaching beginning reading. What the study found was that the particular approach used did not seem to matter. Children learned or failed to learn about equally with each approach. The best predictor of how well a child reads by the end of the first grade turned out to be his ability to recognize letters of the alphabet prior to the beginning of reading instruction: in other words, it is not the materials used in instruction that matter, but how much preparation for first grade was provided by parents. Bond and Dykstra concluded that future improvements in reading instruction should concentrate on teacher training rather than on materials.

A similar finding has come from studies of the comparative effectiveness of educational television versus live teachers. The promises for educational television have been great. In 1957 Alexander Stoddard[6] predicted that it would supplement and enrich many of the functions heretofore performed by teachers and, more importantly, would be responsible for raising the level of teaching. The facts do not support the rhetoric. Walter Schramm, after reviewing over four hundred quantitative studies of educational television, concluded in 1962 that the average student is likely to learn only about as much from a TV class as from a live teacher.[7]

One of the signs of the 1970s is the growing disenchantment with technology. The fact that man has the ingenuity to build machines that enable him to walk on the moon is interesting, but not as consequential as the fact that man has yet to solve the more pressing social problems that face him on earth. Teachers seem increasingly aware that instructional materials have thus far offered more gimmickry and packaging than substantive changes. Havelock Ellis once suggested that the largest task for civilization is to make man rather than machines, the master.

In being honest and forthright about our biases, we have started the chapter with this introduction and concluded it with Jeannette Veatch's *Sign and Significance: The Jabberwock Rides Again.* Materials can be very helpful when properly used. The articles in this chapter suggest specific ways you might use materials effectively.

Notes

1. Jeanne S. Chall. *Learning to Read: The Great Debate.* New York: McGraw-Hill, 1967.

2. Scott, Foresman: Glenview, Illinois.

3. John Goodlad. "Thought, Invention, and Research." In *The Schools and the Challenge of Innovation,* Supplementary Paper no. 28, Committee for Economic Development, 1969.

4. The results of the first year of the study were reported in the *Reading Research Quarterly,* Vol. 2, the entire edition. The report was written by Guy Bond and Robert Dykstra. Half of the studies were conducted through second grade, and six followed the children through third grade.

5. Alexander Stoddard. *Schools for Tomorrow: An Educators' Blueprint.* The Fund for the Advancement of Education: New York, 1957.

6. Walter Schramm. "Learning from Instructional Television." *Review of Educational Research* 32 (April 1962):156–67.

The new gadgets will solve kids'
reading problems. Or, will they?
Tinker summarizes research on the
effectiveness of machines, devices,
and gadgets used to improve the
speed of reading. He suggests some
implications for reading teachers.

Devices to Improve Speed of Reading

MILES A. TINKER

Examination of the book and materials exhibits at the national
meetings of the International Reading Association reveals a be-
wildering array of gadgets promoted to improve the speed of
reading. In addition are the advertisements in both scientific and
popular magazines plus the visits of persuasive salesmen. The
claims made for these devices are enticing and more often than
not, appear valid to the teachers and others who want to improve
the reading speed of pupils or of themselves. It is high time to
make an objective evaluation of the usefulness of these devices
or machines or gadgets.

All or most of these devices have their origins in attempts to improve reading speed by training (i.e., pacing) eye movements. In these attempts, stress was placed upon the difference between the eye movements during reading of poor and good readers. The good readers tended to make few fixations and regressions per line of print, while poor readers usually made many fixations and regressions in their reading. This observation eventually led to the practice of attempting to improve the rate of reading by training eye movements. Early procedures "trained" a reader to fixate three times on vertical marks equally spaced across lines of the length of ordinary printed lines. Presumably, after this habit was perfected, the reader would use only three fixations for each line of print in reading. Another variation was to print or type phrases separated by extra spaces and to encourage the reader to make one fixation on each phrase. But individuals vary greatly in the number of fixations employed in reading a line of print, even after training such as described above. Any statements that superior readers make only three or four fixations per line are misleading generalizations of the facts. When a line of twenty-four to twenty-six picas (commonly used in printing books) is used, six to eight fixations per line are employed by a good reader, according to data cited by Anderson and Dearborn[1]. In fact, it has been shown that after the training described above readers continue to make more than three fixations per line. Buswell[4] also notes that few subjects ever achieve three fixations per line.

Soon gadgets or devices appeared on the market designed to pace eye movements so that only three fixations would be employed to read a line of print. One of these machines is the metron-o-scope, a triple-action electrically operated tachistoscope (short exposure apparatus) which exposes successive thirds of a line of printed matter. (Although this apparatus is no longer on the market, hundreds of them are owned by schools and clinics.) After the first line of a selection has been exposed in this manner, the second line is exposed similarly. This continues with successive lines until the whole selection has been read.

Using the metron-o-scope gives rather uniform results in promoting faster reading. The question arises as to whether the use of the apparatus is necessary to achieve speedier reading. Whether dealing with children or adults, the answer is no. Cason[5], working with third grade children, found significant gains: *(a)* by use of the metron-o-scope, *(b)* by well-motivated reading in the library, and *(c)* by use of special phrases marked up into phrase units. The gains proved to be just as good by one method as by any other. Her analysis indicated no special benefit from use of the machine. And Westover[11] found that college students who used ordinary materials and methods in a well-motivated speedup program made just as good gains in speed of reading as students using a modified metron-o-scope.

Another device which has found wide usage is the Harvard Reading Films or modification of the principle such as the High School Reading Training Films (State University of Iowa). These are motion-picture techniques in which phrases, grouped in thought units, appear on a screen in boldface type on a faint printing of the whole page of connected material. The rate at which the phrases succeed one another can be varied by adjusting the speed control of the projector. The alleged values of the films are that they *(a)* give a mechanical stimulus which focuses attention and aids concentration and the rapid association of meanings without verbalization, *(b)* provide practice in reading by thought units, and *(c)* give students objective evidence that improvement is possible.

Glock[6] evaluated the film technique by studying the effect upon eye movements and reading rate of three methods of training: *(a)* using Harvard films, *(b)* employing a new film which exposed two successive lines simultaneously, and *(c)* reading printed material while motivated to read fast and comprehend. Four weeks of training was given to six sections of college students. The students made significant improvements in eye movements and thus in rate of reading under all three methods of training. But there were no significant differences between results of the three methods, i.e., the technique that paced eye movements (Harvard films) was no more effective than either of the others in increasing speed of reading.

Other pacing machines are in common use. Some devices pace the reader by moving a shutter, line by line, over the material being read. The reader is expected to keep ahead of the shutter. The rate of moving the shutter may be varied from slow to fast. In one variety of this type of machine, a shadow from a wire moves down the page of printed material. The reader tries to keep ahead of the shadow. The trade names of some of these machines are: Controlled Reader, Reading Accelerator, Reading Rate Controller, Rate Reader, and Reading Board. The same end may be accomplished by a push-card method. The teacher pushes a large card from top to bottom of a page while the reader is supposed to keep ahead of the card. The rate of moving the card can be varied to suit the needs of the particular pupil.

Reading speed is increased for many but not for all pupils by use of the pacers just described. But there is no assurance that the gains are lasting after the pacing is stopped. Also, the improved rate is not transferred to other types of reading materials without special training. Proponents argue that the machines improve rate of reading because of the increased motivation of the reader while using the gadget. Spache[9] states: "The answer that research gives to this question is that gains in reading rate or speed of word recognition can be achieved equally as well by ordinary motivated practice or carefully planned classroom activities." He also states that the use of these pacers when other methods fail to provide sufficient motivation or impetus will help some students to read faster. And he notes that the pacers are not successful with all students and cannot be used indiscriminately.

Should the teacher use the reading-accelerator type of pacer to improve the speed of reading? One argument usually advanced for use of pacers is that pupils are tremendously interested in the use of the device and thus highly motivated. This is true. But even so, such children make no greater gains than do those taught by regular methods. Any skilled teacher should be able to provide the incentives that promote good motivation. There is always a possibility that some child will improve with machine training but not by good classroom methods. However, no investigation has shown this to be so.

Another difficulty is that, when speed per se is taught by machine, the pupil may be prevented from becoming a versatile user of rates of reading, i.e., from becoming flexible in the use of different rates according to the kind and difficulty of the material to be read and the purpose for which the reading is done. Too frequently, a teacher may consider that a machine will solve all her problems and will use it not as a supplement but to the exclusion of proper emphasis on more fundamental aspects of reading instruction.

The Flashmeter, the Tach-X, and other short exposure devices known by the general name *tachistoscopes* are employed to flash number series and words upon a screen for a brief interval. The aim of this technique is to develop quick perception and increase the span of recognition and hence, speed of reading. Flash cards may be used instead of a tachistoscope. However, Anderson and Dearborn[1] are doubtful that tachistoscopic training has value in increasing speed of reading. They conclude that the time might be better spent on promoting growth in comprehension. But Brown[3] on the other hand, describes and supports the alleged advantages of using the tachistoscope to improve reading, including rate. His report and others like it apparently fail to take into account the role played by other factors in an experimental program, such as motivation to improve vocabulary, comprehension training, and so forth. In a carefully controlled experiment Manolakes[8] checked the influence of tachistoscopic training on improvement of eye movements and hence on speed of reading. When the effects of other factors were isolated, he found that the use of the tachistoscope had no effect upon reading performance. In a more recent study Bormuth and Aker[2], using sixth grade pupils, investigated the influence of tachistoscopic training on reading performance. All other factors in the experiment were carefully controlled. They found that the tachistoscopic training over a period of twenty weeks was ineffective in improving rate of reading, comprehension, or vocabulary. Jones and Van Why[7] also found that tachistoscopic training over a period of three months had no effect on reading rate and comprehension with fourth and fifth grade pupils. An evaluation of the entire body of relevant literature by Tinker[10] suggests that tachistoscopic training to improve rate of reading is of no, or at least of questionable, value.

A summary for the evaluation of machines, gadgets, and devices used to improve speed of reading follows:

1. Many so-called procedures for training eye movements or for controlled reading result in improved speed.
2. The improvement obtained by eye-movement training, with or without elaborate apparatus, is no greater than that resulting from motivated reading alone.
3. Experiments concerned with pacing eye movements and controlled reading usually involve other techniques and are never divorced from increased motivation. Buswell[4] flatly states that "training eye movements does not increase reading ability."
4. The use of pacing devices too often becomes a ritual tending toward an over-emphasis upon the mechanics of reading to the sacrifice of adequate attention to the more important processes of perception,

apprehension, and assimilation. This mechanical training may result in a decrease in the flexibility and adaptability of reading habits that characterize good readers. According to Buswell[4], "the exploiting of machines and gadgets" to control reading "by persons who do not understand the psychology of reading seems at present to be adding greatly to this mechanistic folly."

5. The tachistoscope is without value for increasing speed of reading. And the tachistoscope and rate-controller devices are relatively expensive equipment. The money might be better used for books and other more worthwhile supplies.

6. It is the view of this writer that as long as gadgets and comparable devices are used by those with an inadequate understanding of the psychology of reading, we shall continue to have the undesirable emphasis upon oculomotor mechanics.

References

1. Anderson, I. H., and Dearborn, W. F. *The Psychology and Teaching of Reading*. New York: Ronald Press, 1952.

2. Bormuth, J. R., and Aker, C. C. "Is the Tachistoscope a Worthwhile Teaching Tool?" *Reading Teacher* 14 (1961):172–76.

3. Brown, J. I. "Teaching Reading with the Tachistoscope." *Journal of Developmental Psychology* 1, no. 2 (1958):8–18.

4. Buswell, G. T. *Remedial Reading at the College and Adult Levels*. Supplementary Educational Monographs, no. 50, 1939.

5. Cason, E. B. *Mechanical Methods for Increasing the Speed of Reading*. New York: Bureau of Publications, Teachers College, Columbia University, 1943, no. 878.

6. Glock, M. D. "Effect upon Eye Movements and Reading Rate at the College Level of Three Methods of Training." *Journal of Educational Psychology* 50 (1949):93–106.

7. Jones, R., and Van Why, E. "Tachistoscopic Training in the Fourth and Fifth Grades." *Journal of Developmental Reading* 6 (1963):177–85.

8. Manolakes, G. "The Effects of Tachistoscopic Training in an Adult Reading Program." *Journal of Applied Psychology* 36 (1952):410–12.

9. Spache, G. D. *Toward Better Reading*. Champaign, Ill.: Garrard Publishing Co., 1963.

10. Tinker, M. A. "The Study of Eye Movements in Reading." *Psychological Bulletin* 43 (1946):93–120.

11. Westover, F. L. *Controlled Eye Movements versus Practice Exercises in Reading*. New York: Bureau of Publications, Teachers College, Columbia University, 1946, no. 917.

> "Bland" and "pollyannaish" are the
> ways Busch describes most first
> grade reading texts. But of even
> greater concern to Busch is the fact
> that these texts may communicate to
> the child that reading is to be feared
> and avoided.

Basals Are Not for Reading

FRED BUSCH

In the past decade there has been a growing dissatisfaction with the content of first grade reading textbooks. The crux of this dissatisfaction revolves around the lack of relatedness of these textbooks to the developmental concerns and interests of most children in America who are learning to read. Various authors have indicated that on an *a priori* basis, the predictably polly-annaish, affectless, suburban life depicted in first grade readers is either alien or inappropriate to the experiences and lives of most first-grade children. The assertion of inappropriate content in first grade readers has received support from systematic studies as well.[1] In a content analysis of the twelve most frequently used first grade reading series, Blom *et al.*[2] found the themes of stories to be bland and pollyannaish, with very few character types except parents and young children (ages six and below), whose behavior was influenced mainly by trivial external events, with sex role differentiations being conspicuously absent. There is evidence that attempts to overcome these deficiencies in the more recent "multi-ethnic" readers have not met with any greater success.[3] That bland stories with little relevance to the experiences of first graders are also uninteresting to them is shown in studies of children's free choices of library books to read.[4] Here one finds a marked discrepancy between the story content children choose to read and the content of first grade readers.

The question must be asked, though, why interest and relevance should play a role in learning to read. McCracken and Walcutt,[5] in their definition of reading, do not seem to consider the content of what is being read of particular importance in the child's learning to read. It is the thesis of this paper that content is of crucial significance in the process of learning to read, and that interest and relevance are significant content variables. Even McCracken and Walcutt,[6] while emphasizing the importance of their instructional process in learning to read, imply that there is a need for the young learner to read stories that include rewarding content. In an attempt to specify the importance of interest and relevance in learning to read, each will be treated separately for the purpose of clarity. However, these must be considered interdependent issues.

Interest   It would seem *a priori* that content of interest to a child (i.e., content of importance that excites curiosity and attention) would facilitate the process of learning to read. This in itself is not convincing, though, and the one study in this area is encouraging but not conclusive.[7] Although in the Whipple study[8] a new multi-ethnic reader compared favorably to a traditional primer on various tests of reading skill and interest appeal, the small actual differences and lack of follow-up to determine long range effects make the data inconclusive.

In order to look at the role of interest in learning to read, one must first look at the motivations of a child in learning to read. Namnum and Prelinger[9] point out that motives for learning to read are conspicuously absent in most writings dealing with the teaching of reading, and for the most part, the concept that a child will be motivated to learn to read is usually taken for granted. In their review of the literature on why children learn to read, the authors do mention, however, two motives implicitly discussed by various writers. The first of these can be broadly defined as the child's relationship to adults. That is, due to the social pressure adults put on the child to learn how to read, and the child's need to win approval from adults and to strongly identify with adult activities, the child will want to learn to read. The second motivational factor mentioned by those writing on why children learn to read has to do with the child's need for mastering his surroundings. In other words, the child faced with a new situation like reading will, because of his particular developmental stage, want to master the unique task. While not disagreeing with these motivations as important factors in learning to read, there are dangers in depending upon these as the child's only motives when teaching him to learn how to read.

If the child's motives for reading are viewed only as a reaction to external pressures or intrapsychic needs, while the motivational qualities inherent in the reading process are ignored, then the *process* of learning to read can become an end in itself. The complex job of translating perception of symbols into vocalizations and thoughts is something that can totally involve the child. Thus if "learning to read" is presented to the child as an autonomous process that is unrelated to anything in particular, once this challenge is past, loss of interest should occur. That is, if by "learning to read" one has met the expectations of society and satisfied the need for mastery, then reading could become unimportant or irrelevant.

Capitalizing on Content   What if one tried to stimulate and then capitalized on the child's interest in the content of what is to be read, and this was made an inherent part of learning to read? The purpose of learning to read then would not only be "learning to read," but also the satisfaction and excitement of engagement with the whole range of experiences available through reading, including obtaining information. That this is where the child starts his involvement with reading can be seen by observing a toddler's introduction to books. His involvement is not with *how* the material is communicated from the printed word, but with the interest the content provides for him. By teaching the child to learn how to read with material of little interest or with a total emphasis on mechanics, it would seem that we are clearly delineating between work and play, school and nonschool experiences. This is of questionable worth both educationally and psychologically. More than fifty years ago Dewey[10] warned against the danger of isolating the child's experiences in school from those outside the school, especially in the early years. In similar terms to the discussion above, he cautioned against the problems inherent in material unrelated to immediate and direct experience, and also warned against media of representation becoming an end in themselves. From a psychological point of view, to arbitrarily separate work from play (in its broadest sense) is not to use the child's developmental involvement with each.[11] Furthermore, for the child only recently able to put off need gratification for any length of time and just discovering means of receiving gratifications in modified fashion,[12] the demand to put off pleasure in the task of reading for some unspecified future gain is, at best, inconsistent with the child's developmental readiness to meet such a demand.

Reading Given a Purpose   In a recent study of children who are successful readers,[13] the authors point out that these children most often come from homes where reading is an important aspect of the parent's life, and where the children are included in numerous experiences involving books (i.e., they are frequently read to, books are given as gifts on special occasions, the library habit is established early, and so forth). While most educators have probably suspected this for a long time, its full implications seem never to have been realized nor capitalized upon. It would seem that the most heuristic interpretation of the McCarthy *et al.* data[14] would be that these children have already been shown the purposes behind learning to read, both through adult example and their own experience. If a child has already been shown how books can be interesting and of value to him through previous experience, then important motivational factors for learning to read are there from the beginning. It then becomes the school's task to stimulate the child to learn how to read who has not come from the type of background identified above, by interesting him in the content as well as the process of reading, and thus specifying the purposes. Again, if the child can see the value of books for him through content, the process of learning to read then becomes more meaningful.

It does not seem to be a very bold prediction to state that other media beside the printed word have, and will increasingly take over, the role of disseminators of information and conveyors of intellectual enjoyment and emotional experience. As this occurs, it will become clear to schools that they must first interest the child not only in the process of reading but in its purposes, or reading will become the Edsel of the school system. In looking at McLuhan's discussions of television,[15] one can see that its attraction to children when compared to first grade reading texts is that television's purposes are inherent within the process itself. The boundary between the *how* and the *why* of television simply does not exist as it does in present day means of learning to read. *How* to learn to read is taught, but *why* seems left to the child's previous experiences—experiences that may be slowly disappearing.

Relevance   Implicit in the fact that the content of first grade reading texts are bland and pollyannaish is that the child learning to read is a precariously balanced object who will tip if touched even lightly. That is, the child will be harmed in some way if confronted in books by the issues he is experiencing and living in his daily life. That nothing is further from the truth can be documented by the writings on the needs and developmental tasks of latency-age children.

Erikson[16] discusses the importance in this stage of the need for mastery and how the child's personality crystalizes around the idea, "I am what I learn"[17] What the child needs to master and has to learn during this stage are not only the rational, practical techniques and means of behavior that allow for a feeling of being part of the adult world, but also a means of dealing with one's inner world. For example, Erikson, in discussing play, talks of the importance of a child mastering objects in the toy world and how this becomes associated with the mastery of conflicts, resulting in an experiential feeling of prestige for the child. This allows the child to advance to new stages of mastery not restricted to toys and objects, but which "includes an infantile way of mastering experiences by meditating, experimenting, planning, and sharing."[18] What Erikson is saying, then, is that the child needs to have the feeling of mastery of conflict at this stage of development to facilitate future growth. The outcome of this process and the means by which it is accomplished have much to do with future development. Most important, though, is that the child's normal developmental concerns during this period lead him to be both interested and involved in working on mastery of his inner as well as his outer world. The results of each are inextricably intertwined.

Other psychoanalytic writers,[19] while not discussing latency in the descriptively illuminating language that Erikson uses, view the crucial aspects of the latency-age period in an essentially similar way. For them the most important issue for the latency-age child is the development of mechanisms which allow for adaptive behavior that is increasingly oriented toward reality. The child is driven to find means of dealing with the conflicts of the present and earlier stages of development in order that growth may occur. Although external factors certainly exist, this process is primarily viewed as determined by internal factors that drive the child toward mastery that will allow both for the unfolding of the socialization process and for the child's becoming progressively less dependent upon the external world for controls. The key for these writers, as with Erikson, is the development of healthy mechanisms (i.e., ego functions) for the child's ability to cope with what is going on inside of him and with the realities of the external world, as well as with the interaction of these two.

Developmental Concerns   From what is known about the child learning to read, it would seem that the content of first grade reading texts should include the developmental concerns of children and the mastery of issues that are crucial to them. That this type of content is not something that will frighten the child, but to the contrary will intrigue him, is not just a hypothesis based upon knowledge of latency, but receives support from others. Although Zimet[20] has pointed to the difficulties in research on children's reading preferences, two studies seem relevant here.[21] These authors, in discussing children's stories which have successfully endured over time, mention two important factors in these stories. They are: the stories are related to the developmental concerns of latency-age children;[22] and at the core of each story there is a universal daydream containing within it the conflicts with which each child must struggle.[23] It would seem, indeed, that the child is drawn to stories that include within them the conflicts of the type he is experiencing and which current first grade reading texts strenuously avoid. While Friedlander and Peller stress the importance of instinctual gratification in the stories they identify as enduring, this seems to be only a partial answer. Although it is true that areas of conflict contain elements of gratification, the essential nature of conflict is that it is painful. A more complete conceptualization of the child's interest in stories with conflictual themes can be viewed in Eriksonian terms. As in the child's play where he projects conflicts on toys and uses these in the mastery process, the child can use the story characters in conflict to identify with, utilizing the pain itself as well as the solution to aid in mastery.

Successful Stories Peller[24] has pointed out how stories which have been read and enjoyed by successive generations of latency-age boys repeat, on a larger scale, everyday experiences that are difficult to cope with. One recurrent theme in these stories is that of the latency-age boy, apart from his parents, who encounters adult figures representing the whole spectrum of character types in situations of varying degrees of danger. This theme depicts, in an exaggerated fashion, the quality of experiences that are common to most latency-age boys. First of all, the latency-age boy is starting, on a consistent basis, to leave the protective influence of home for increasingly extended periods of independence. Secondly, he is coming in contact with numerous types of authority figures in school, community, and church. Thirdly, if nothing else, the uniqueness of the many new situations that the latency-age boy must face causes much anxiety and perceived danger. In the exaggerated situations the story's hero is usually portrayed as clever, resourceful, and virtuous, with his actions resulting in triumph. One can see, then, how the story communicates to the latency-age boy that he does have come control over and power in his environment and that he has qualities that are uniquely his own which allow him to successfully adapt. In summary, a simple theme related to developmental concerns of latency-age boys can be extremely beneficial. There is the sharing of a series of anxiety-provoking, painful experiences common, in a qualitative fashion, to most latency-age boys. This in itself can prove to be helpful. Most important, there is the main character's ability to cope with difficult experiences. The latency-age boy can thus gain the impetus for dealing more actively with his own conflicts, both through identification and example. The problems he is facing no longer have to seem so ominous or insurmountable. Although solutions aren't offered, the process of resolving conflict is presented as a possibility that should intrigue the child desirous of mastery.

What are the dangers involved in first grade reading texts avoiding areas that are germane to the developmental concerns of children learning to read? Pearson,[25] using a psychoanalytic model to discuss learning problems, points to the difficulties that arise when an external situation does not hold the attention of a child. He states, "An important function of the ego is to direct attention to a particular situation or stimulus in order to master it."[26] When the child is faced with a stimulus that he can invest in, the multitude of other stimuli which exist at the same time, but which do not have investment, can be deflected. However, if no such situation or stimulus of importance is present, the child appears distractible and uninterested. First grade reading texts, by not addressing themselves to the content appropriate to the ego functioning of the latency-age child and the need to get on with the process of mastery of the external and internal world, further complicate "learning to read."

Probably the most important weakness in the current content of most first grade reading texts revolves around the whole growth and maturation process. Various authors[27] have pointed out that certain tasks in latency are important for further development in adolescence and adulthood. Certainly books could be helpful to the first grade child in dealing with the conflicts he is primed to master during this stage. This hypothesis has been supported in general terms by numerous investigators.[28] However, the bland, pollyannaish content found in most first grade reading texts not only stifles the growth process, but more importantly may communicate to the child that this must be something to be frightened of and avoided. Why else would the characters not show emotion that is negative as well as positive, feel anxiety and pain, or experience conflicts?

Notes

1. Gaston E. Blom, Richard R. Waite, and Sara G. Zimet. "A Motivational Content Analysis of Children's Primers." In *Readings in Child Development and Personality,* edited by P. Mussen, J. Conger, and J. Kagen. New York: Harper & Row, 1969.

2. Ibid.

3. Gaston E. Blom, Richard R. Waite, and Sara G. Zimet. "Ethnic Integration and Urbanization of a First Grade Reading Textbook: A Research Study." *Psychology in the Schools* 2 (1967):176–81. Richard R. Waite. "Further Attempts to Integrate and Urbanize First Grade Reading Textbooks: A Research Study." *Journal of Negro Education* Winter, 1968:62–69.

4. R. C. Smith. "Children's Reading Choices and Basic Reader Content." *Elementary English* 39 (1962):202-9. J. L. Wiberg and Marion Trost. "Comparison of First Grade Primers and Free Choice Library Selection." *Elementary English,* in press.

5. C. McCracken and C. Walcutt. *Basic Reading.* Philadelphia: J. B. Lippincott Co., 1963.

6. Ibid.

7. G. Whipple. *Appraisal of the City Schools Reading Program.* Detroit: Detroit Public Schools, Division for Improvement of Instruction, Language Education Department, 1963.

8. Ibid.

9. A. Namnum and E. Prelinger. "On the Psychology of the Reading Process." *American Journal of Orthopsychiatry* 31 (1961):820-27.

10. J. Dewey. *Democracy and Education.* New York: Macmillan Co., 1916.

11. Anna Freud. *Normality and Pathology in Childhood.* New York: International Universities Press, 1965.

12. Panel Report. "The Latency Period." *Journal of the American Psychoanalytic Association* 5 (1957):525-28.

13. P. McCarthy, L. Gillotey, and G. Wagner. "Let's Get Together." *Education* 83 (1963):564-66.

14. Ibid.

15. M. McLuhan. *The Medium Is the Massage.* New York: Random House, 1967.

16. E. H. Erikson. "Identity and the Life Cycle." *Psychological Issues* 1 (1959): 82-88.

17. Ibid.

18. Ibid.

19. P. Blos. *On Adolescence.* New York: The Free Press of Glencoe, 1962. E. Buxbaum. "A Contribution to the Psychoanalytic Knowledge of the Latency Period." *American Journal of Orthopsychiatry* 21 (1951):182-98. F. S. Friedenberg. "Thoughts of the Latency Period." *Psychoanalytic Review* 44 (1957): 390-400. Panel Report, op. cit.

20. Sara G. Zimet. "Children's Interest and Story Preferences: A Critical Review of the Literature." *Elementary School Journal* 67 (1966):122-30.

21. K. Friedlander. "Children's Books and Their Function in Latency and Prepuberty." *American Imago* 3 (1942):129-50. L. Peller. "Reading and Daydreams in Latency, Boy-Girl Differences." *Journal of the American Psychoanalytic Association* 6 (1958):57-70.

22. Friedlander, op. cit.

23. Peller, op. cit.

24. Peller, op. cit.

25. G. H. Pearson. "A Survey of Learning Difficulties." *Psychoanalytic Study of the Child* 7 (1952):322-86.

26. Ibid.

27. Blos, op. cit.; Erikson, op. cit. R. J. Havighurst. *Developmental Tasks and Education.* New York: David McKay Co., 1952.

28. L. Bender and R. Lourie. "The Effect of Comic Books on the Ideology of Children." *American Journal of Orthopsychiatry* 11 (1941):540–50. P. J. Cianciolo. "Children's Literature Can Affect Coping Behavior." *Personnel and Guidance Journal* 43 (1965):897–903. C. Martin. "But How Do Books Help Children?" *Junior Libraries* 1 (1955):83–87. C. Mattera. "Bibliotherapy in a Sixth Grade." Unpublished doctoral dissertation, Pennsylvania State University, 1961. P. A. Witty. "Meeting Developmental Needs through Reading." *Education* 84 (1964):451–58.

Simple steps for constructing and using an informal reading inventory with whatever reading series may be available in the classroom are suggested by Cheyney.

The Informal Reading Inventory: How to Construct It, How to Use It

FRAZIER R. CHEYNEY

Third-grader Johnny B. is reading in an intermediate level reader . . . and having a hard time of it. His classmate, Joey S., is bored to tears by the same volume. It's just too easy.

These are usual problems dealt with effectively every day by teachers. Johnny goes back a level in his reading. Joey moves up a volume.

But what about the child who isn't so obviously ahead of or behind the demands of the book? How can you be sure of where to place him? How can you be sure that he's working at his optimum level?

The answer is to take a reading inventory. And for teachers on the spot and pressed for time, the informal reading inventory is probably the answer. But, although much has been written about informal reading inventories in textbooks and journals, little of the published information has been immediately helpful to the teacher. The procedures for constructing informal reading inventories have seemed so detailed and time consuming. Or, alternatively, the methods have been presented so sketchily as to be almost meaningless.

Your first step is to select a basal reading series, from preprimer to sixth grade, that is not commonly used in your school. It is extremely important that the stories be unfamiliar to your students.

Now choose 20 words from the basal vocabulary index of each level. The words should be picked at random and should not include proper names. These words will make up the vocabulary section of your inventory.

Next, select a story from somewhere near the end of each reader in the basal series you have chosen. These stories will constitute the silent-reading part of the comprehension section of the inventory. Each story should contain from 50 to 100 words for the preprimer through the third-grade levels, and from 150 to 300 words for levels 4, 5, and 6.

If a story has a word count above these recommended numbers, simply use part of the story.

For each story chosen, write 10 comprehension questions. Draw up your questions this way: two main ideas, two details, one inference (a "why" or "how" question), one sequence (placing three to five events in proper order), and four vocabulary questions (what does this word mean in the story?).

Once you have completed these steps, you are ready to begin testing.

You can usually test the children, one at a time, at your desk, while the rest of the class is engaged in a seatwork assignment. But you may find it necessary to meet outside the room if the conversation can be heard by the other children.

Starting at the preprimer level, have the children read the words on the vocabulary lists. Mispronunciations and hesitations of longer than two seconds are counted as errors. (You can time responses by saying to yourself, "one-thousand-and-one, one-thousand-and-two.") Continue to work upward from the pre-primer level until at least four words are missed at any given level.

Four or more mistakes is considered a child's *frustration* level — the reading level that most often produces failure. Zero or one mistake is the *independent* level. Two or three mistakes, therefore, is the *instructional* level — the level at which the child should be reading in school.

At this point, you have determined the child's ability to read words. But how well can he comprehend those words when they are in sentences and paragraphs? This is where the comprehension section of the informal reading inventory comes in.

After you have found the child's instructional level in vocabulary (for example, grade 3), have him read the comprehension section for that level. There is no need to time him while he is reading the story. When he has finished reading, ask him the 10 questions you have prepared, but do not permit him to reread any part.

You "score" the comprehension test the same way you did the vocabulary test: four or more mistakes, frustration level; two or three mistakes, instructional level; and zero or one mistake, independent level.

There is nothing very complicated about evaluating the results of the inventory; however, a great deal of care must be taken. What you do, or fail to do, at this stage may be the difference between a child progressing satisfactorily in his reading or floundering to the point of failure.

Don't overload the child The cardinal rule to remember in grouping is never to give a child more than he can handle. If, for example, his vocabulary test shows that he can recognize words independently on a fifth grade level but his comprehension test indicates that he will be frustrated reading on that level, don't make the mistake of grouping him so high. Play it safe and give him the fourth grade book.

Perhaps the best way to explain the evaluation procedure is to look at the hypothetical cases of two children who have been tested by an informal reading inventory:

1. When Carl was given the vocabulary test, he made no errors at all until he reached the third grade, second-semester level. He made three mistakes at the fourth grade level indicating he had reached

his vocabulary instructional level. In the fourth grade comprehension test, Carl missed five questions—well into his frustration level—and his teacher correctly decided that fourth grade reading was too difficult for him. She grouped Carl at third grade, second semester.

Her evaluation can be represented like this:

Vocabulary: Fourth grade, three mistakes, *instructional level*.

Comprehension: Fourth grade, five mistakes, *frustration level*.

Grouping: Third grade, second semester.

2. When John took the vocabulary test, he made either one error or no errors on every level until he reached fifth grade, at which point he missed two questions. The teacher then gave him the fifth grade comprehension test and John responded by getting all 10 questions right. Had the teacher been careless in her evaluation, she would have assumed that John was ready for the sixth grade, that fifth grade was just a waste of time. Instead, she went back to the vocabulary test and tried John out on sixth grade words. He missed four of them. The teacher, taking no chances, evaluated John's grouping as fifth grade, despite his excellent scores.

The evaluation:

Vocabulary: Fifth grade, two mistakes, *instructional level*.
Sixth grade, four mistakes, *frustration level*.

Comprehension: Fifth grade, no mistakes, *independent level*.

Grouping: Fifth grade.

Simple logic dictated both groupings: It is better to give children books they can read comfortably and confidently than it is to have them flounder out of their depth. In short, success is better than failure . . . for reading *teachers* as well as their students!

The attitudes of children can be significantly affected by the supplementary use of paperback books. Lowery and Grafft support that conclusion with a study, and in the process give some suggestions on how you might make use of paperback books.

Paperback Books and Reading Attitudes

LAWRENCE F. LOWERY
WILLIAM GRAFFT

Considerable time and effort have been expended to discover the most efficient way to teach the basic mechanics of reading. Less attention has been devoted to the question of whether or not a child will read on his own once he knows the mechanics and is able to read. Certainly the goals of reading programs must include the development of positive attitudes toward reading, attitudes which will insure self-direction. Yet little work has been aimed at the vast area of testing attitudes. This study is of a growing trend in reading and its effect upon children's attitudes. Paperback books are appearing more frequently in schools throughout the country. Although secondary classes have relied on paperbacks for several years, the appearance of the paperback as a reading resource in the elementary school is relatively new.

As more and more titles are made available every year by publishers, more and more schools are becoming faced with the decision of investing or not investing funds in paperback volumes. One of the factors which schools must consider in the decision is whether or not paperbacks make any difference to or develop any changes in the attitudes of boys and girls in the elementary school.

If paperback books can serve to get children more interested in reading, if these are books that children will read on their own, and if the use of these books results in an improved attitude toward reading, then they become a vehicle to promote learning.

Purpose of the Study

In the fall of 1965, packets of paperback books were purchased for elementary classrooms in Oakland, California. These paperbacks were placed in classrooms with the hope that they would appeal to boys and girls and improve their attitudes toward books and reading. The primary purpose of this study was to measure the effects of these paperback books upon the attitudes of fourth grade students.

Sample

The study was conducted over an eight-week period in six fourth grade classrooms in the Oakland Unified School District. Three comparison groups were used. One control class, one Experimental I, and one Experimental II were selected from schools in the middle socioeconomic areas. The other half of the sample came from low socioeconomic area schools. Selection of the schools was made from income, education, and unemployment data from the 1963 Federal Bureau of Labor Statistics Publication on Oakland's Census Tracts.

In the two Experimental II classes, fifty-eight students were supplied with forty clothbound books which had the same titles as the paperback books used by the first group. In the two control classes, fifty-three boys and girls used the libraries at their schools. The same titles were available among the thousands of books in the library, but no supplementary books were placed in the control classrooms.

The titles of books for the Experimental groups were selected from a list approved by the Elementary Library Book Selection Committee in Oakland. This committee was composed of teachers, principals, supervisors, librarians, and the Director of Elementary Education. Criteria used by the committee include style, taste, and appeal to children. Books are often tested in classrooms with children before they are approved for the list. From this list, titles were chosen that were known to be popular with children and teachers and, in a sense, were "tried and true." The decision to conduct this study was made three months after the selection of the paperbacks.

In the Experimental I and Experimental II classes, library tables were arranged. Boys and girls were encouraged to browse and to read books from the tables. The control classes went to their school libraries to obtain books on a regular basis. The use of the clothbound, paperback, and library books was supplementary to the basic reading textbooks, and all teachers used the same methods suggested in the teacher's manual (Russell, 1961) to help children become interested in reading on their own. Book reviews were shared regularly by both teacher and students in all classes. Some sharing took the form of oral or written reviews. Others took the form of illustrated summaries, dioramas, sales posters, or pantomimes. None of the schools had librarians.

To measure attitudes, a variation of the *Projective Tests of Attitudes* (PTOA) was given as a pretest and posttest. This test device consisted of three interwoven projective techniques—a *Word Association Test,* a *Thematic Apperception Test,* and a *Sentence Completion Test* (Lowery, 1966). The PTOA was administered orally to students, one at a time. Responses were tape-recorded.

The *Word Association Test* contained two key stimulus words which were placed at random among some generally neutral words. The key words were: *book* and *read.* Ten words were read aloud, one at a time, to the student. The student was instructed to respond as rapidly as possible with the first three words that came to mind.

The *Thematic Apperception Test* consisted of a series of four drawings. The drawings showed a child sitting at a desk reading a book. No expressions or influencing actions were put in the pictures. They were made as neutral as possible. Each student was shown only one of the pictures, but four drawings were made to check on several variables. When the student was male, the drawing shown had a small boy reading a book; when the student was female, a small girl was in the drawing. When the student was Caucasian, the drawing showed a Caucasian child reading a book; when the student was Negro, a Negro child was reading the book. The purpose for the various drawings was to enable the student to relate as closely as possible to the child in the picture. Each student was asked to say what was going on in the drawing, what led up to the situation, and what would happen after it.

The *Sentence Completion Test* was administered as the last of the three tests. It consisted of three unfinished sentences to which the students orally supplied an ending. The first sentence, "Reading a book is . . . ," was designed to be open-ended and neutral. The second sentence, "Most [boys, girls] like books that . . . ," guided the student into revealing positive feelings. The third sentence, "One thing that puts some [boys, girls] against books is . . . ," guided the student to reveal negative feelings.

Analysis of the data

The interview responses to the PTOA were submitted to a descriptive analysis to uncover specific attitude changes. Because of the similarity among many of the responses, it was possible to establish categories in which to place them. Five response categories were established. Placement was done as follows:

1. Ideas considered to be overriding or common were selected from the data. These ideas were used as category headings.
2. Judges were given the pretest and posttest data, unmarked as such, and asked to place each response into an appropriate category. The judges worked independently and separately. They were instructed to categorize the unmarked data and to handle each projective test separately. If the judges felt that a significant idea for a category was overlooked, they were allowed to establish an appropriate one. Placements made by the judges were then compiled.

   It is important to note that the established categories were the same for each key stimulus word on the *Word Association Test*.

This commonality may suggest that the words *book* and *read* elicit synonymous associations in the minds of fourth grade children. The established categories are as follows:

Category 1 contained words or descriptions which were clearly negative in connotation. Some of these responses tended to refer to books or reading in a destructive sense (e.g., *tear, break, throw away*). Some pertained to a difficulty associated with books or reading (e.g.: *hard, difficult, touch*). Others were generally unpleasant in connotation (e.g.: *hate, dumb, boring*).

Category 2 contained words which pertained to school- or work-oriented thought. Many of the responses showed an association between books or reading with assignments and homework activities (e.g.: *study, homework, memorize*). Some responses pertained to the names of school subjects (e.g.: *spelling, arithmetic, science*). Some described aspects of the school environment (e.g.: *school, teach, teacher*).

Category 3 contained words which described the characteristics or usage of books. Responses often described the physical properties of books (e.g.: *dictionary, magazine, encyclopedia*). Some indicated the usage of books (e.g.: *read, learn, study*).

Category 4 contained responses which tended to be library oriented. Some respondents associated books and reading with the word *library*. Many of the responses indicated various storybook interests (e.g.: *mystery, adventure, horses*).

Category 5 contained responses which were clearly positive in connotation. These words all associated pleasant or enjoyable terms with books or reading (e.g.: *fun, interesting, nice*).

Table 1 reports the categorized pretest and posttest responses to the *Word Association Test;* Table 2, to the *Thematic Apperception Test;* Table 3, to the *Sentence Completion Test.* Because of the nature of the forced positive and negative completion sentences the inappropriate categories are not shown.

The decision rule established for the descriptive analysis was to consider a change of 20 percent or more in a category between pretest and posttest responses as significant. The elimination of responses in a category or the appearance of responses in a category for the first time was also considered to be significant.

On the pretest it can be seen that there were no important differences in the number of responses in each category among the control or experimental groups. On each of the PTOAs, the responses tended to be uniform.

On the posttest the Control and Experimental I groups showed no significant (20 percent) changes. Significant changes occurred in the Experimental II group. These changes showed a significant decrease in the responses in category 1 (clearly negative) and a significant increase in category 5 (clearly positive) on each of the PTOAs except for the third sentence on the *Sentence Completion Test.* On the *Thematic Apperception Test* and the *Sentence Completion Test,* significant decreases in category 2 (school- or work-oriented responses) are also apparent.

TABLE 1

PRE-POST TEST RESPONSES TO THE *Word Association Test* CATEGORIZED BY SIMILARITIES IN THOUGHT (STIMULUS WORDS: *Book* AND *Read*)

Groups	Control (N–159)		Exper. I (N–168)		Exper. II (N–174)	
Categories	Pre	Post	Pre	Post	Pre	Post
	Book		*Book*		*Book*	
1	37	37	26	27	32	0
2	49	46	61	57	62	53
3	72	73	75	81	77	78
4	1	3	6	3	3	21
5	0	0	0	0	0	22
	Read		*Read*		*Read*	
1	37	30	38	35	31	1
2	58	57	52	54	55	19
3	57	65	67	67	77	76
4	7	7	9	11	11	46
5	0	0	2	1	0	32

TABLE 2

PRE-POST TEST RESPONSES TO THE *Thematic Apperception Test* CATEGORIZED BY SIMILARITIES IN THOUGHT

Groups	Control (N–53)		Exper. I (N–56)		Exper. II (N–58)	
Categories	Pre	Post	Pre	Post	Pre	Post
1	16	13	20	10	14	0
2	18	21	14	20	19	6
3	14	16	15	17	17	9
4	4	3	4	6	7	8
5	1	0	3	3	1	35

TABLE 3

PRE-POST TEST RESPONSES TO THE *Sentence Completion Test* CATEGORIZED
BY SIMILARITIES IN THOUGHT

Groups Categories	Control (N–53) Pre	Post	Exper. I (N–56) Pre	Post	Exper. II (N–58) Pre	Post
"Reading a book is . . ."						
1	32	26	28	24	25	3
2	5	4	5	6	4	0
3	15	23	18	20	28	14
4	0	0	0	0	0	0
5	1	0	5	6	1	41
Most people like books that . . ."						
2	5	9	0	3	4	1
3	13	16	21	18	23	12
4	29	25	26	26	22	20
5	6	3	9	9	9	25
"One thing that puts some people against books is . . ."						
1	31	27	38	30	27	24
2	13	14	10	13	15	14
3	7	12	4	8	14	11
4	2	0	4	5	2	9

Summary and Recommendations

The results of this study led to the conclusion that the attitudes
of the tested children were significantly affected by the supple-
mental use of paperback books. Boys and girls who used the
paperbacks showed significant increases in their number of pleasant or positive attitudes and a decrease in their number of negative attitudes.

Both experimental groups had the same titles and the same
ready access to books in their classrooms, but the Experimental
I group, with the clothbound books, showed no significant change
in their posttest attitudes. It seems that there is something about
the paperback book which has an important and positive effect
upon the attitudes of fourth grade students.

Specific causes for changes in attitudes cannot be determined
by this study. Only a gross change was measured so that further
studies could be suggested:

1. Perhaps clothbound texts become symbols of scholastic failure to many students. Perhaps such books impart negative feelings because they represent assignments and homework rather than items of choice and pleasure. In the case of disadvantaged students, the clothbound books certainly are not a real part of their world outside the school, and the classroom, and as such are not looked upon with favor.
2. Perhaps the attitudes toward reading and books are affected by the colorful covers, smaller size, and/or ease of handling of the paperbacks. Clothbound library books do not lend themselves to being tucked into a pocket for easy carrying. Perhaps paperback books encourage a feeling of possession and are symbols of casual reading.
3. As further study it may do well to investigate the permanency of any attitudinal changes and the effects of such changes upon general achievement and interests.

References

U. S. Department of Labor. *Income, education, and employment in neighborhoods —Oakland, California.* Washington, D. C.: Bureau of Labor Statistics, 1963.

Russell, D., *et. al. Finding new neighbors.* New York: Ginn, 1961.

Lowery, L. F. "Development of an attitude measuring instrument for science education." *School Science and Mathematics,* 1966, 64, (5).

Nicolich and Canepa provide an
overview of how teachers might use
a variety of audiovisual aids to supplement and improve a reading
program.

AV in the Total Reading Program

GLORIA F. NICOLICH
DOMENICK CANEPA

In a society such as ours, with its many complexities and increased dependency upon scientific technology, mastery of the
printed page is a prime essential for personal adjustment and
individual economic security.

That reading is of great importance becomes obvious when we
stop to consider what happens to those who fail to read well. In
the school, the ability to read well is a prerequisite to learning
in every subject area. Consequently, as early as the elementary
school, the child who does not read up to grade level may find
himself a holdover and a failure. Repeated failure breeds frustration and boredom. Thus the child may become a discipline prob-

lem and a potential delinquent. If he does reach the high school, he is almost certain to join the ranks of the dropout. Later on many desirable occupations which require a high school or college diploma will be closed to him. He may find that his inability to read will isolate him from a variety of cultural activities, and he will discover that he will not be included in groups frequented by educated people. Consequently the reading problems of childhood may very well beget the social, emotional, and economic problems of adulthood.

It is imperative for us to institute a comprehensive reading program which will adequately fulfill the needs of all the children in all areas of the city. Although there is a high proportion of reading disability among the children living in deprived areas, it does not necessarily follow that a low socioeconomic environment is the sole cause of reading retardation.

Specialists agree that a child can read only as well as he can relate his reading to his experience. Research indicates that there is a close correlation between good auditory discrimination, good vocabulary, and concept development and reading achievement.

Weiner and Feldman measured the reading skills of lower socioeconomic children and found them defective in basic skills related to listening, speaking, and concept development.[1] In deprived areas children may have such a limited environment that the basic essentials for effective communication are denied to them, e.g., lack of parental interest, lack of opportunities to speak, lack of opportunities to share experiences, and lack of economic security.

Audiovisual devices can play a major role in providing experiences for the child. They can sharpen impressions. A well-integrated program of audiovisual instruction can help build concepts. The child is exposed to real and vicarious experiences which provide motivation for discussion and the sharing of ideas.

What Are Audiovisual Aids? Simply stated, audiovisual aids appeal to all our senses, particularly those of sight and sound. Some appeal only to sight, e.g., filmstrips, flat pictures, and transparencies. Phonograph records, magnetic tapes, radio, and so forth, have auditory appeal.

Many types of equipment are available to the schools from industry. Each type has a special strength and a distinct advantage. The use of a variety of media in schools for a reading program is, of necessity, a matter of selection. The teacher will be better able to utilize the equipment if *(a)* she is familiar with the specific strength of each piece, *(b)* she has a definite lesson in mind, and *(c)* she is familiar with the equipment in her particular school.

If we are to offer a language-arts program which meets the needs of the individual child, we must know the potential of the media with which we are concerned. Schools all over the country are vitalizing language-arts programs by the creation of listening-viewing centers.

What is a listening-viewing center? It is a section of the classroom where audiovisual equipment is placed for the use of the teacher and the pupils. This center usually includes a phonograph, a tape recorder, 12 headsets, a connecting box, a filmstrip projector, and a screen or a large desk viewer. Records, tapes, and filmstrips should be accessible to the children and be placed in the center.

Listening, observing, and speaking are basic to the language-arts program. The listening-viewing center provides opportunities for developing these skills. In such a center children can *(a)* learn to work independently, *(b)* gain self-confidence in completing their assignments, and *(c)* listen and observe and then evaluate what they have seen and heard.

Certain routines must be established with the children before actual use of the center is initiated. These routines, which should include standards for completing assignments in the center and instructions for the proper care and use of equipment, should be posted within the center itself so that the children can refer to them while they are working. After sufficient training most children can gain proficiency in the handling and operation of the listening-viewing center. As teachers become familiar with the various techniques and strengths of the center they become increasingly enthusiastic about the possibilities it affords them to improve their teaching techniques. It offers the instructor opportunities to work with small groups in the classroom while other children are at the listening center.

Research findings show that mental age is neither the only nor the most important factor in the child's ability to read for the first time.[2] All children will benefit from planned experiences in listening, observing, and speaking. Some children enter school with less of these experiences because of language barriers or environmental limitations. Consequently, the school must pro-

TYPE OF EQUIPMENT	READING READINESS	BEGINNING TO READ	GROWTH IN READING	EXTENDED READING SKILLS
TAPE RECORDER	Recognizes and identifies sounds on tape. Listens to rhyming words on tape. Listens to show and tell experiences. Listens to stories and poems.	Continues to identify sounds in the school and community. Records stories, tales, radio programs— Discuss sequence of events. Find the main idea. Recall details. Predict outcomes.	Records choral speaking. Allows children to engage in independent activities at the listening-viewing center. Develops word banks on tape. Records interviews and comments on a field trip with portable tape recorder. Records oral reading for analysis.	Tape record book reports. Tape parent interviews. Committee reports can be put on tape. Organize tape-pal programs with schools in your district. Tape school dramatization—use special sound effects. Continue to use tape recorder to improve listening acuity.
PHONOGRAPH	Records are easily available and generally inexpensive. They are available in all curriculum areas and on all grade levels. Classroom phonographs should have variable speeds. Phonograph can be utilized in much the same way as the tape recorder.			
FLAT PICTURES	Identifies familiar objects by name. Identifies colors. Arranges pictures in the proper sequence. Becomes familiar with the vocabulary of picture reading, e.g., near, far. Listens independently to stories in the listening-viewing center and looks at pictures in the story. Associates symbols with word meanings.	Interprets pictures by making simple references. Compares size and shape in pictures. Estimates distance in a picture, e.g., near, far. Writes captions for pictures. Predicts what will happen next in a picture story.	Extends picture interpretation. Uses pictorial clues to identify temperature, time, and environment. Uses a picture dictionary. Reads pictures to gain the main idea in a story. Uses pictures to identify vocabulary for contextual clues.	Begins to interpret simple abstractions. Engages in individual study utilizing study prints. Collects pictures and begins a simple picture file. Extends picture reading skills to maps, graphs, etc. Can draw pictures from word descriptions.

OVERHEAD PROJECTOR	Show silhouettes of various shapes and sizes. Show color lift transparencies of animals and homes. Make colorful illustrations on acetate to accompany storytelling time. Introduce simple line drawings.	Use to introduce manuscript writing. Prepare overlays using prefixes and suffixes. Prepare overlays using compound words. Prepare transparencies of initial consonants and blends.	Use to introduce cursive writing. Use to teach outlining and letter writing. Prepare phonetic rules on acetates. Use projector as tachistoscope.	Assign compositions on acetates. Teach map skills, e.g., interpreting symbols. Add motion to still transparencies. Illustrate stories developed by children.
FILMSTRIPS	Many inexpensive filmstrips are available in these areas. Children read, discuss, listen, dramatize, and predict outcomes of stories. They gain in auditory and visual discrimination. Numerous film companies produce picture stories for reading readiness.		The child is able to evaluate filmstrips and is able to work independently at the listening-viewing center. Viewing stories stimulates creative expression and provides a basis for dramatization.	
16mm SOUND FILM	Identifies and locates the immediate and surrounding community, e.g., farm, city. Provides vicarious experiences. Stimulates oral communications.		Correlates with reading in other curriculum areas. Extends vicarious experiences and vocabulary experiences. Uses kinescopes of television programs. Looks for facts and details in a film. Rewrites and makes a simple outline of events of the film.	
REALIA	Uses realia to allow child to find out about his environment through his senses, e.g., blocks, dolls, fish tank, turtle. Children can draw simple conclusions from observations. Uses play corner to relate to real-life experiences, e.g., setting the table. Communicates likenesses and differences in concrete objects.	Uses realia to develop readiness in map skills. Uses realia to clarify distortions.	Makes dioramas of scenes in a story and uses realia. Uses realia and other media to extend concepts and vocabulary. Realia help to express an idea, an interest, or a feeling of an individual. Guest speakers can be brought in to demonstrate materials for special programs, e.g., an author discusses his book.	

vide a rich program of experiences for these children. The activities should lead to better auditory and visual discrimination, as well as concept building and vocabulary development. Further experiences can be provided through planned field trips, dramatization, creative bulletin boards, flat pictures, prerecorded tapes, and so on.

Many teachers are hesitant to permit the kindergarten child to operate audiovisual equipment. However, experience has shown that with adequate preparation, and after a short training period, young children are not only capable of handling audiovisual equipment, but are enthusiastic about demonstrating their abilities to their peers.

Perhaps one of the most stimulating approaches to building a healthy self-confidence in the child is by teaching him to successfully utilize a variety of audiovisual materials and equipment. We can begin with those ordinarily found in the classroom. These range from the reading of simple pictures to the more sophisticated use of materials and equipment. The use of this equipment creates situations in which the child will *(a)* communicate with others, *(b)* learn to follow directions, and *(c)* develop an oral vocabulary related to the handling of equipment. The accompanying audiovisual-skills chart suggests possible uses of audiovisual material and equipment in developing a language-arts program with particular emphasis on reading skills.

Just as in any classroom concept-building situation the ability to use the audiovisual materials and equipment will be a developmental process where each lesson is dependent upon previously learned skills. Part of the preparation requires development of meaningful vocabulary; e.g., *knob, focus, large, small, high, low,* and so on.

The basic ingredient of any successful instructional program is the experienced classroom teacher. We believe that an intensive program of audiovisual instruction, when utilized by a creative teacher, is not a supplement but an integral part of the entire curriculum.

Notes

1. M. Weiner, and S. Feldman. *Measurement of Reading Skills of Lower Socio-economic Children.* Paper presented at American Psychological Association, August 1963.
2. Margaret McKim. *Guiding Growth in Reading.* New York: Macmillan Co., 1955, p. 39.

Bibliography

McKim, M. G. *Guiding Growth in Reading.* New York: Macmillan Co., 1965.

Lamoreaux, L., and Lee, D. *Learning to Read Through Experiences.* New York: Appleton-Century Inc., 1943.

Sequential Levels of Reading Growth in the Elementary Schools. Publication of the Division of Elementary Schools, Board of Education of New York City, February 1963.

In a most interesting way, Veatch expresses a concern about the effect of the marketplace on developments in reading instruction.

Sign and Significance: The Jabberwock Rides Again

JEANNETTE VEATCH

You may well wonder what the Jabberwock has to do with the field of reading. The key is in the theme of the Conference — SIGN AND SIGNIFICANCE — . Let me read you the whole poem and then tell you how I see it fitting into the picture.

JABBERWOCKY
(From *Through the Looking Glass*) *Lewis Carroll*

'Twas brillig, and the slithy toves
    Did gyre and gimble in the Wabe
All mimsy were the borogoves
    And the mome raths outgrabe.
"Beware the Jabberwock, my son!
    The jaws that bite, the claws that catch

Beware the Jubjub bird, and shun
    The frumious Bandersnatch!"
He took his vorpal sword in hand:
    Long time the manxome foe he sought —
So rested he by the Tumtum tree
    And stood awhile in thought.
And, as in uffish thought he stood,
    The Jabberwock, with eyes of flame
Came whiffling through the tulgey wood
    And burbled as it came!
One, two! One, two! And through and through
    The vorpal blade went snicker-snack!
He left it dead, and with its head
    He went galumphing back.
"And has thou slain the Jabberwock?
    Come to my arms, my beamish boy!
Of frabjous day! Callooh! Callay!
    He chortled in his joy.
'Twas brillig and the slithy toves
    Did gyre and gimble in the wabe:
All mimsy were the borogoves
    And the mome raths outgrabe.

As you know, this is a poem about nonsense. In fact, it raises nonsense to quite a high literary level, and the Jabberwock is slain, killed dead, among much rejoicing. Now, I propose that we apply a SIGN to the Jabberwock, and then discuss its SIGNIFICANCE.

To me, the JABBERWOCK is nothing more or less than the commercialization of the field of reading; the gadgetry, the materials, the machines, the hardware of all sorts. To the extent the gross aspects of commercialization are nonsense, it is Jabberwocky. The SIGN then is the profit motive and the SIGNIFICANCE is that excessive commercialization is interfering with the proper education, in its highest sense, of our young.

"Beware the Jabberwock, my son!" says to me, "Beware of all of the materials that exist for the major purpose of making money." Note that word, *major*. It is an important emphasis. My point is that the vast majority of materials are manufactured first for profit and second for their educational purposes. Great is the rejoicing when educational professionals come up with ideas that are both educational AND profitable. The sickness that is now so obvious on all sides in American society comes, in some part, from the sickness within the majority of classrooms in our

nation, with the seemingly inescapable dependence upon inanimate materials, particularly the children's texts, in every
conceivable aspect of the curriculum.

As I would show that most materials are interfering with the
best education of our young, let me define the word "commercial."
I mean it to describe those materials that are intended for use,
if sales would allow, by every child in every school all over this
nation. As it is patently impossible for single pieces of material
to perform such a monumental task, the hard sell must take place.

Obviously there are few things that do not make money for
the manufacturer. Chalk yields profits, chalkboards yield profits.
So do paper and pencils as do the most beautiful of all books,
the trade books. In the case of chalk and paper, the profits are
small. In the case of trade books, the numbers are so extensive
that it is difficult for any one of them to be used by every child
in every class in the nation. Trade books are the best of children's books. They exist on charm. They dare to take their
chances in the market place. The good ones will sell in the tens
of thousands. The poor ones fall by the way-side in sales. This
is the way it should be. Monopoly capital has no place in the
realm of childhood. Yet it is here. It has been here for decades,
and unless we expose its terrible consequences it will continue
to exist.

Dangers to Democratic Principles

Eisenhower, it must be recalled, issued a warning in the last
days of his presidency against the danger to freedom, democracy,
and our way of life inherent in the military-industrial complex.
I am only a professor, but I hope this audience will not deny me
the right to take a leaf from Mr. Eisenhower's book and warn,
in just as serious terms, that our way of life, our society's happiness, is in desperate peril from the tidal waves of educational
material and hardware that inundate our teachers at all levels,
in all parts of the country.

One month after his resignation as President of San Francisco
State College, Robert Smith spoke not far from here on the Bill
of Rights.

I quote from his text:

> Our society and our educational system has managed . . . to
> teach increasing numbers of its young the antithesis of
> democratic concepts . . . (the) massive failures in the nation's

efforts to measure up to, and live by, its humane ideals, provide
an ample context in which the young learn at the gut level the
antithesis of democratic principles. Educational institutions
contribute their share to these baleful outcomes. I believe that
young, fanatical totalitarians are increasing in number and
rapidly gaining in sophistication and capacity for liaison and
alliance and disruption . . ."

The sickness in this country is too widespread. The role of the
schools is too prominent in producing this sickness. We have no
more time. Tax monies are involved here, and some kind of controls, some kind of checks are necessary. The extent of inane,
noneducational, expensive gadgetry suggests that there is more
than innocence abroad in the land.

Nor are the manufacturers really to blame. They have consistently said that they will fill a marketing vacuum, if it can
be proven to exist. I am sure that is true. But I cannot help but
wonder why they are dragging their feet at filling the over-
whelming dearth of trade books, the best of books, in the nation's
classrooms. It is strange that manufacturers do not move more
quickly into this wide-open market. I think they will, but not until the monopoly of basal texts in all fields is truly broken. And
that is our job. We are the professional educators. We must clean
our own house and expose the nonsense that is being foisted on
the American school child. I propose to proceed with the job.

It is tempting to go more deeply into the totalitarian personality and how it develops, but others must take over that task.
This conference deals with reading, and I have been asked to
interpret in my own way the continuing theme of the Claremont
Conference: "Reading is the process of making discriminative
responses." The sign of the Jabberwock is the profit motive that
interferes with rational, relevant education. And the field of
reading is the worst offender in the whole curriculum on this
point. It is the most material-ridden and irrelevant of all.

Materials pour from the manufacturers. We claim to be interested in reading achievement. Note that the *Stanford Primary Battery* correlates .95 with the vocabulary of five of the big
selling basal primers. This, I submit, is professional incest.

"'Twas brillig and the slithy toves . . ."

For the truth of the matter is that materials are not the answer
at all. The secret to good education is what happens between

human beings, the teacher and the child. Yet, producers of educational materials have been, and still are, in a state of alarm over a practice called "Individualized Reading." This is the only practice, in its original, self-selective conception, that has nothing to sell in a single package. Yet the basic idea was and is so frightening, so powerful to vested interests that efforts to mechanize individualization, to package it, are still going on. Anything, it would seem, except a child and his teacher sitting down together to talk about a book the child has chosen, because (1) he likes it, and (2) because it is just right for him.

You see, materials are the answer to nothing, educationally speaking. But teachers have been trained to panic when they are not provided. It is quite possible that American elementary children can be taught all of the reading, writing, math, and so forth, to the peak of their ability, with no children's texts *whatsoever* available. Teacher's texts, yes. But not children's texts.

> "And as in uffish thought he stood,
>   The Jabberwock, with eyes of flame
> Came whiffling through the tulgey wood
>   and burbled as it came."

Well might the commercial interests whiffle through the tulgey wood. I am using my vorpal sword in the only way I know how. For my vorpal sword is belief in the educational strength of one human being teaching another, human to human, and the inanimate relegated to a very minor, ancillary position.

The Sword Cometh

Using the sword in this way, we might start with those machines called "Controlled Readers" available under several manufacturing labels. The theory, once the verbiage of the manual is stripped away is that if the retarded reader's eyes look at moving words (with occasional pauses, often unrelated to the meaning of the phrases involved), then by some magical operations, those same eyes will be better able to deal with honest-to-goodness reading in some book somewhere. Even the Old West gambler knew that the hand was quicker than the eye because the eye can see NOTHING when it is moving. So an enormously expensive machine is bought by the sickening thousands to do a job it can never possibly do.

Film Strips Instead of Books

Another twist of the sword might be made in the body of the machines that have a film strip, with story and pictures, which is read over earphones from a central tape. Each child, isolated in a booth, is supposed to keep turning the picture in order to keep up with the story. A more major indictment of the wreckage caused by traditional materials can hardly be imagined. Such children have been taught to hate books so much that it takes an expensive gadget to revive—if it works—an interest in reading. It would be funny if it were not for the spectre of the Jabberwock overhead. Profit making. ANYTHING except good books for children. ANYTHING except contact with a human being with whom you might exchange thoughts about reading.

Misused Hardware

The sword should also swing a bit, although perhaps not so vehemently, against the misuse of some hardware such as the overhead projector. In a city near Phoenix I have seen classroom after classroom, with chalkboards covered with—you know—flowers —"Welcome to Spring," and other such slogans and decorations —where the teachers are teaching, of all things, penmanship, on the overhead. I have seen dozens of times when teachers were screwing up their faces deciding how their marker was going, when the chalkboard beckoned by their side. Put it down to my being of the older generation. I just hope that the public never catches on to how we are squandering money on misused hardware. If they do, we will all be out of a job.

An Analysis of Some Materials

Let us take some developments and see how they might be analyzed.

A recent workshop on a systems approach to communication in Phoenix hit the front page of the local paper* thusly, and I quote in part:

> Donald E. Miller, assistant superintendent of schools in San
> Mateo County, California said a "systems" approach to
> problem-solving in education would improve communications in
> school districts.

*Arizona Republic, February 2, 1969.

Miller . . . offered an 18-page paper on the "systems" approach which contained the following sentences:
"The (systems) concept has been expanded, . . . and . . . validated as a meaningful logic construct through its historical use and subsequent appraisals."
"These early scientists explored every available method and means which might aid them in their attempts to conceptualize interrelationships among complex phenomena and enable them to integrate these interrelationships into a systematic body of knowledge."
Mrs. Pauline Dorsett of Tempe, a first grade teacher . . . and president of the Arizona Classroom Teachers Association, was asked by a reporter what she thought about the two sentences. "Why, I think the two sentences are just fine," she said. "Conceptualize is a great word."

So much for the systems analysis. You take it. I don't want it.

"Beware the Jubjub bird, and shun
The frumious Bandersnatch."

Individualized Prescribed Instruction

There is the Oakleaf Project in Pittsburgh in which highly structured programming is being carried on. Dr. Louis Bright, at a conference in Mesa, Arizona in describing how children could proceed at their own pace through unit after unit of programmed material, with the privilege of skipping that which they already knew, nevertheless confessed: "We don't do very well with creative communication." This is precisely the problem with Individualized Prescribed Instruction. It freezes the child and teacher into an Orwellian pattern of mechanized uncreative lessons. In another center for Individualized Prescribed Instruction, The Rocky Mountain Educational Laboratory, this paragraph appears in their material:

> . . . It is planned that a series of specific learning episodes are to be developed to help the child overcome his specific deficits. Certain clusters of checked remedial procedures which *the classroom teacher can select from until one is found to work best with a given child* . . . (Italics added)

This, I believe, is a gross prostitution of the concept of individualization. It is material centered to the ultimate degree. I suggest that if such practice becomes nationwide the current turmoil in our schools will be child's play. Or we will have an elected totalitarian government that will spell the demise of democracy as our founding fathers conceived of it.

An Analysis of Some Current Programs

Let me analyze some more programs on the market in terms of their educational and social validity. For example, take the visual-perception materials. At this moment there are doctoral studies at the University of Southern California and perhaps elsewhere that demonstrate the ineffectiveness of these materials and activities. They not only do not improve reading, they don't improve visual perception. Sidney Shnayer reports a study at Chico where children, pretested by the *Frostig Test,* then subjected to the program as described in the manual, were found to do worse on the *Frostig Post-Test!* Patently, what has physical movement to do with the process of gaining meaning from a printed page? Oh, I know, the process of left to right is a physical progress. Yet Klausmeier[1] states:

> Research on rigidity and set in problem solving shows conclusively that when an individual experiences repeated success in solving problems with a certain method or instrument, he clings to that method or instrument *even when it is inappropriate for solving new problems for which other methods and/or instruments are appropriate.* (Italics added)

In short, one learns to read by reading, and not by identifying differing shapes and sizes of nonwords to teach word recognition, or to hope that movement from left to right in a nonreading situation will lead to progression from left to right in a reading situation. The transfer of training is nil, as the efforts to validate all perceptual materials is rapidly proving.

The Role of the S-R Bond

Not surprisingly, at the root of such commercial systems is the Pavlovian strategy of stimulus response. The behaviorists are the enemy and, perhaps more than any other group in education, are responsible for the hatred of learning in this country. Behavioral psychology was most certainly used by Hitler and Stalin for the subjugation of their peoples. Many of the less violent techniques are prevalent in many classrooms today, however innocently and unknowingly they are used.

For example, one technique to subjugate the masses to the will of authority is monotonous repetition. All I have to say to illustrate how prevalent monotonous repetition is in American classrooms is to quote:

> "Oh, Oh, Oh.
> Look, look, look."

Another strategy for totalitarian methods is that of forceful interrogation. We have the Bereiter and Engleman example gaining ascendancy so that it is one of the four accepted programs for national *Follow Through* funding. Who here has not heard their classic lesson? "THIS IS A CUP! SAY IT! THIS IS A CUP!"

While there is certainly something to be said in favor of not boring children by yelling at them in contrast to the teachers who demand deathly stillness, nevertheless, this program is an extreme expression of totalitarianism and is so admitted, with pride, by the authors.[2]

Another technique to enforce unquestioning obedience is that of the seeming logical syllogisms. That is, if something SEEMS logical then it must be so. For example, the teaching of sequence in the manuals of the basal readers is presented over and over again. That is, children should know the plot of a story. Therefore to know it, they must be trained in the proper sequence of the story. This, of course, completely ignores the automatic understanding of a story's plot by children who are captivated by the story. In short, a poor story needs its sequence taught. A good story's plot sequence is learned automatically.

Further strategies can be found in the isolation of human beings from each other. "Sit in Rows." Do not look at each other's papers." The list goes on.

You will notice that my vorpal sword has not even drawn blood from the most vulnerable commercial materials of all—the basal readers and their workbooks. This has been a subject of attack by others than myself. I remember some lovely articles on the matter around 1948 and 1950. To this day, there is no research evidence of educational validity of basal readers and their omnipresent workbooks. One child called one publisher's efforts "The Unthinkables." Over and over there have been attempts to prove the worth of these materials. But, alas, the Jabberwock rides again. They exist only because of his sign.

The Directed Reading Lesson

Let us take the most prevalent reading practice there is: the directed reading lesson. It is straight S-R bond behaviorism, as are all materials that require a response as stated in the manual. The directed reading lesson begins with step 1 called "Developing Interest." Briefly, the merit of the teacher's performance depends on how she can persuade children to become interested in the story chosen for the day. How does this persuasion take place? By charm—"This is a very exciting story," and so forth, by force —"I want everyone to turn to page 10," or by guilt, convincing the child that he SHOULD be interested in this material. In short, every aspect of "Developing Interest" is a form of obedience training. The American Kennel Association does it better. But obedience training is not education.

The remaining steps of the directed reading lesson are designed to drill, by repetition of course, so that the desired material will be learned. Not that the child will learn to think, mind you, but that he will learn the material. This audience is surely sophisticated enough to know that monotonous repetition is a tool of the brainwasher. So teachers proceed through succeeding steps of this practice: 2, anticipating problems; 3, reading silently; 4, reading orally; and then 5, doing follow-up exercises. Of course, the monotony of the tasks are such that each teacher must again resort to persuasion, charm, guilt, and/or force to secure concentration to the task—more obedience training.

Nonmeaning "Reading"

Another interesting piece of material, found in a teacher's manual accompanying a basic reading series states that reading is the process of turning printed symbols into sounds. As soon as we say this, however, someone is sure to ask . . . What about *meaning?* Do you propose to define reading as mere word calling, without regard for meaning? Yes, *we do.* (Emphasis mine)

This type of statement could be found in many places, and particularly in manuals for commercial phonics systems. What is so wrong about it? It is wrong because it makes no sense to the learner to make meaningless sounds. When a child is asked to do something that makes no sense to him, he must be conditioned to trust the authority. Conditioning is obedience training. Instead of conditioning a child to reality, to relevance, to sensibleness, he must be conditioned to accept meaningless symbols, slogans, catchwords, jargon. "Can Dan fan man" certainly fits in that category. Nonsense, nonwords, mumbo-jumbo must, sooner or later, be turned into sense. So why do it *senselessly* in the first place? There are many, many similar kinds of printed offerings. As such approaches are deeply rooted in the S-R bond, I think there must be a connection to our young totalitarians. The schools do have some responsibility, I do believe.

Boxed Individualized Materials

There is another commercial program long on the market, called SRA Individualized Reading boxes. As most of you know, it is composed of a series of folders purportedly to be of graduated difficulty. Its virtue is that children may proceed through the folders at their own pace. This is true of all programmed material. But its vice is that it teaches children that reading is only for the purpose of answering questions. But whose questions? The child's? Of course not. The questions are the product of the developer of the material, as are all of the questions to be found in workbooks in teacher-made exercises. Endless questions. None of them are from the inner being of the child.

Inquiry

Yet, we know from studies of totalitarian societies that the one activity that cannot be tolerated if a given population is to remain under the sway of an authoritarian regime is open-ended, freely asked and answered questions. Democracy cannot exist without inquiry. But teachers often mistrust the child's study skill and intention so that they fall into the trap of questioning him on the content of what he is studying. He is not allowed to examine the philosophical aspects of what he is reading. He must answer what the material wants him to answer. He cannot inquire independently. Study of Pavlov's dogs showed that all of the conditioning, ingrained laboriously into the animal, broke down when the dog's master came into the room. We know prisoners of war become "*un*brainwashed" after months of effort if, by chance, they hear just one word from the "outside." American textbooks are built upon a systematic, rigorously planned, graduated program of question asking, and rarely are those questions genuinely the child's. Only the individual-conference approach allows inquiry.

Humanistic Learning

I cannot close my presentation on such negativism. I insist that it is easy to teach FOR democracy if we only avoid S-R bond obedience training as educational method. We must teach so that learning is instantaneous, as it is with Sylvia Ashton-Warner's key vocabulary. We must avoid monotonous repetition, as in a self-selection program of reading and, most of all, we must encourage the process of unfettered inquiry—wherever it may lead. The development of thought units comes from within the child. Skills are not a thing apart. We learn *through* experience, not, as Skinner erroneously states, *from* experience.

Learning words in order to read is backwards. Learning sounds in order to learn words is a further step backwards. We read in ORDER TO LEARN WORDS. We write in ORDER to learn sounds. Involving children in learning must necessarily involve working with whatever it is he wants to express. We must perfect ways of getting him to want to verbalize not what we want him to say, but what *he* wants to say. It may be that the manufacturers, after all, can provide us at a profit with pieces of equipment that encourage children to say what *they* want to say. What is better for that, of course, *outside* of a living, breathing, warm teacher, than a tape recorder and a microphone?

But the answer lies, for democracy's sake, in human interaction.

> One, two! One, two! And through and through
>> The vorpal blade went snicker snack!
> He left it dead, and with its head
>> He went galumphing back.

The Jabberwock should not ride any more. Or we, as a democratic society, are done. The sign of the profits that interfere with education must be the significant fact for the decades to come. Whether or not you agree with me is not the point. What is the point centers on the health, the sanity, the human values of our society.

Notes

1. Herbert J. Klausmeier. *Psychological and Classroom Learning.* Mimeographed material.
2. See: *This Magazine Is About Schools* Fall 1967, p. 96 (P. O. Box 876, Terminal A, Toronto, Ontario, Canada).

study questions

1. In one sentence, how would you summarize the bias the authors express in the introduction to this chapter?

2. What might be a suitable one-sentence summary of the position expressed by Veatch?

3. Are the authors and Veatch explaining the same position in different terms, or have they expressed different positions? Explain your answer.

4. If you were on a committee assigned the task of suggesting instructional materials that should be purchased for grades four through eight, how would you support or reject one teacher's suggestion that the bulk of the available funds should be used to buy reading pacers because he personally has seen the great progress children can make with controlled readers? Justify your answer, and explain any counter proposal.

5. The stories in most basal-reader series are intended to reflect the child's "expanding environment," on the assumption that children will enjoy and benefit from reading about experiences similar to their own. Consequently, the first grade basal reader contains stories about school and home. Busch considers these stories to be "bland and pollyannaish." What alternative suggestions does he make for producing children's readers that are relevant and interesting, even though they are limited to the number of words required in a beginning reader? What suggestions do you have?

6. For a group of interested teachers, explain the steps in constructing and using the informal reading inventory.

7. How do Nicolich and Canepa support their conclusion that, "the basic ingredient of any successful instructional program is the experienced classroom teacher"?

FIVE

organizing for instruction: personnel

objectives

As a result of reading these articles and answering the questions at the end of the chapter you should be better able to:

- specify the roles that parents, principals, reading specialists, and tutors can play in helping the classroom teacher establish and maintain an effective reading program

- identify the characteristics of the reading teacher that contribute to successful learning

rationale

A major conclusion of the last two chapters is that the crucial variable in the classroom is what the teacher is and does. Now, how do you live up to that kind of advanced billing? This chapter attempts some answers. Among the topics discussed are changes in teacher preparation and certification, effectiveness in teaching, and working with parents and tutors.

introduction

Changes are coming in the preparation and certification of personnel responsible for teaching reading. The change is inevitable in our society, for, as Stephen Vincent Benét once noted, "Americans are always moving on." As long as they do we need not despair unduly about the future. Change is needed in education. After a thorough study of reading in elementary schools, Austin and Morrison[1] concluded that the teaching of reading today is mediocre at best. Moreover, the public is coming to accept the notion that teachers are largely, if not wholly, responsible for the large numbers of children who fail to read up to their potential. If General Motors can be held responsible for a faulty brake system, if physicians can be held responsible for prescribing the wrong medicine, then teachers can surely be held responsible for the high failure rate of their students.

That change is indeed coming can be seen from studies conducted within the last ten years that cause one to raise the serious question, "What is it that certificated reading teachers can do that other people cannot?" One such study, conducted by Greenleigh Associates[2] for the Office of Economic Opportunity, compared the effectiveness of four reading programs and three types of teachers in teaching reading to welfare recipients who were eighteen years and older and reading below the fifth grade level. The four reading programs were highly prescriptive, that is, "cookbook" programs where the teacher does just exactly what the directions say. The three types of teachers were certificated teachers, college graduates not trained as teachers, and high school graduates. The effectiveness of reading programs and teachers was determined solely by measuring the achievement-test score gains made by students: the greater the gains the more effective the program or teacher. The high school graduates were significantly more effective as teachers. The four programs were equally effective. The conclusion: When using a highly prescriptive reading program, where effectiveness is narrowly determined by student performance on achievement tests, high school graduates with no training might well be more effective than certificated teachers; and further, the particular reading program used does not matter. The effectiveness of uncertificated teachers is supported by studies of tutoring. Schoeller and Pearson[3] found that untrained volunteers from the community, working under the guidance of a reading specialist, could effect significant improvement in children's word-recognition skills. Robertson, whose article was written for this book, found that fifth graders significantly effected the sight word learning of first graders.

An understanding of the factors that retard change is a critical prerequisite to understanding the direction the changes in certification and preparation will take. While lack of sufficient classroom experience is often cited as a cause of teachers being unwilling to change, the fact is that teachers have spent about 10,000 hours as students in classrooms before reaching college. But the experiences have been largely in what teachers do, not in what teachers should do. Unless the teacher-preparation program is so effective that it can alter the effect of those many hours spent in classrooms, teachers will teach largely as they remember being taught.

Another significant factor retarding change has been the tendency among teacher educators to confuse the introduction of materials with the learning of strategies usable with any materials. A case in point, all of the "exemplary" inservice education projects funded through the Title III PACE program and reported in *Pacesetters in Innovation,* USOE, 1966, constitute nothing more than "publisher's tryouts." Published sets of materials were tried out by groups of teachers. Following a different set of directions does not involve new teaching skills any more than cooking a pie today and cooking a cake tomorrow requires significant improvement in cooking skills. The utilization of most of the hundred approaches to beginning reading, summarized so well by Robert Aukerman,[4] requires only that the teacher be able to read well enough to follow the explicit directions provided in the teacher's guides. The sad fact about this confusion between materials and teachers is that recent studies have suggested that it is the teacher who matters, not the material. (Recall the discussion from the last chapter of the Office of Education study of first grade reading and the earlier mention in this chapter of the Green-leigh study.)

The direction of change in teacher preparation and certification can be predicted from the growing public feeling that teachers should be held accountable for the failures and successes of their students, and the profession's increasing awareness that the teacher is a more significant variable in student learning than the material. Teachers in the future will probably be trained and certified for demonstrating competency in achieving certain identified changes in students. In a review of research on teacher effectiveness, Biddle and Ellen[5] defined competency as the ability of an individual to produce agreed-upon results. Teachers will be held accountable not for using a certain reading approach or material, but for demonstrating that each child under their tutelage has made significant gains as a direct result of their efforts.

Few teachers are presently prepared to demonstrate competency in effecting significant changes in individual students because they are oriented to materials and grade levels. The Austin and Morrison[6] study indicated that most elementary teachers have been unable to ignore the idea that they are third or fourth grade teachers. They feel compelled to teach the reading skills considered suitable for their grades irrespective of the real differences existing among the children. All the children in their classes are expected to read from the same page of the same book.

The reading teacher will be prepared to demonstrate competency in effecting changes in individual students only when he is able to identify and provide for the specific reading needs of children. Many teachers have recognized their inabilities in diagnostic teaching better than their reading supervisors. In studying questionnaires of persons applying for an NDEA reading institute, Marcus[7] found that, while teachers most often asked supervisors for help with diagnosis of disabled readers and objectives in reading, the most prevalent type of help given was in the provision of supplementary materials. The demonstration of competency in teaching reading must occur with all types of reading personnel, not just classroom teachers.

Three articles in this chapter describe the roles that effective reading personnel can play. One article describes how teachers can work productively with parents.

NOTES

1. Mary Austin and Coleman Morrison. *The First R: The Harvard Report on Reading in Elementary Schools.* New York: Macmillan Co., 1963.

2. Greenleigh Associates, Inc. *Field Test and Evaluation of Selected Adult Basic Education Systems.* New York: Greenleigh Associates, Inc., 1966.

3. Arthur Schoeller and David Pearson. "Better Reading Through Volunteer Reading Tutors." *The Reading Teacher* 23 (April 1970):625–36.

4. Robert C. Aukerman. *Approaches to Beginning Reading.* New York: John Wiley & Sons, 1971.

5. B. J. Biddle and W. J. Ellen, eds. *Contemporary Research on Teacher Effectiveness.* New York: Holt, Rinehart & Winston, 1964.

6. Austin and Morrison, op. cit.

7. Marie Marcus. "The Status of Reading Instruction—Greater New Orleans Area." *Journal of The Reading Specialist,* 7(1968):153–63.

How does an effective teacher behave? What does he do? Artley reviews research that can give some
indication of the characteristics that
constitute the effective teacher of
reading. He identifies some conclusions from this research and suggests areas of further study.

The Teacher Variable in the Teaching of Reading

A. STERL ARTLEY

Certainly all educators are committed to increasing the level
of achievement of their clients whether they be children, young
people, or adults, and whether the area be mathematics, science,
or foreign language. But with reading, a high level of performance is so important that no stone can be left unturned in our
search for ways of facilitating growth and development. Society
may raise only an eyebrow for one's inadequacies in spelling,

mathematics, or ability to speak a foreign language; but, in one way or another, it castigates an individual who cannot read or read effectively.

It is no surprise, then, that to improve reading we have instituted research in all directions. Instructional materials have been examined and improved and new ones developed. Reading methods have been searched and researched, and the search continues for ways of improving instruction. Teacher-education institutions have sought to strengthen their reading program by adding courses, modifying course content, or providing learning experiences that will strengthen the preparation their graduates are receiving. And above all, government funds have been poured into studies, programs, and projects designed to discover ways of improving the level of reading attainment on all academic levels.

One of the best-known government sponsored studies is the Cooperative Research Program in First Grade Reading Instruction, reported in detail in the *Reading Research Quarterly* (Bond and Dykstra, 1967). The master study, you recall, involved twenty-seven individual studies carried on in various places in the United States, and attempted to discover if there were an approach to initial reading instruction that would produce superior reading and spelling achievement at the end of grade one. Instructional approaches currently in use, including the linguistic, basal, language-experience, and i.t.a., were evaluated in terms of objectively measured reading achievement.

Though the study has some inherent limitations, its findings and conclusions are significant in relation to pupil achievement, and its implications for teacher education are cogent. It is to the issue of teacher education that I would like to direct attention, starting from the recommendations of the First Year Study.

In the first place the study points out that children seem to learn to read by a variety of materials and methods. Accordingly, the authors state, ". . . no one approach is so distinctly better in all situations and respects than the others that it should be considered the one best method and the one to be used exclusively" (Bond and Dykstra, 1967). In other words, improved reading achievement does not appear to be a function solely of approach or method. And then the authors (1967) continue,

> Future research might well center on teacher and learning-
> situation characteristics. . . . The tremendous range among
> classrooms within any method points out the importance

of elements in the learning situation over and above the methods employed. *To improve reading instruction, it is necessary to train better teachers of reading rather than to expect a panacea in the form of materials.*

A similar statement has been made by others. Ramsey (1962), in an evaluation of three grouping procedures for teaching reading concluded, "The thing that the study probably illustrates most clearly is that the influence of the teacher is greater than that of a particular method, a certain variety of materials, or a specific plan of organization. Given a good teacher, other factors in teaching reading tend to pale to insignificance."

A very recent study reported by Harris and Morrison (1969) reiterated the conclusions of the two other studies. These authors reported a three-year study and a replicated two-year study of two approaches to teaching reading, basal readers vs. language experience. They found, as did Bond and Dykstra, that differences in mean reading scores *within* each method were much larger than differences between methods and approaches. They write,

> The results of the study have indicated that the teacher is far
> more important than the method. Costly procedures such as
> smaller classes and provision of auxiliary personnel may
> continue to give disappointing results *if teaching skills are
> not improved.* It is recommended, therefore, that in-service
> workshops and expert consultive help be provided for all
> teachers and especially for those with minimal experience.
> (P. 339)

In other words, these studies seem to be saying clearly—to improve pupil achievement in reading, one should look first at the teacher and his training. This, then, puts the responsibility squarely upon the shoulders of those who are engaged in teacher education, both pre- and in-service—teachers of methods courses, supervisors of practice teaching, and school- and systemwide reading supervisors, both elementary and secondary.

But to look at the teacher and his training poses a question in need of an answer. What teacher characteristics or teaching behaviors appear to differentiate the effective teacher of reading from the ineffective one? What seems to make a difference between "good" and "poor" reading teaching? Knowing the answers to such questions as these would make it possible for us to select as reading teachers those with certain characteristics or to prepare teachers with certain skills and understandings that appear to be associated with maximum pupil growth.

The writing and research in the areas of teacher education, teacher effectiveness, and teaching behaviors are voluminous, almost as voluminous as those in reading. And, like the research in reading, their findings frequently leave much to be desired. I can certainly agree with Jackson (1966) who writes,

> . . . Almost all of the noble crusades that have set out in search of the best teacher and the best method . . . have returned empty-handed. The few discoveries to date . . . are pitifully small in proportion to their cost in time and energy. For example, the few drops of knowledge that can be squeezed out of a half-century of research on the personality characteristics of good teachers are so low in intellectual food value that it is almost embarrassing to discuss them. . . . (P. 9)

Part of the reason for the disappointing results, at least insofar as reading is concerned, is that the researcher was attempting to identify the good teacher and good teaching rather than the good teacher and good teaching of *reading*. And I have good reason to believe they are not the same. As a result they have described for us a kind of invisible, ghostlike person who, in fact, may not exist. She (he) has been found to be cooperative, sympathetic, and poised. She is well groomed, healthy, imaginative, and cooperative. She gets along well with her coworkers and her principal, and she gets her reports on time. As one of my friends said, "She has the same characteristics we would expect to find in a good bar-girl." We know nothing of what this person does in a reading class nor do we know anything about the achievement of her pupils. In short, the studies tell us little that we can put into the context of reading or that gives us helpful clues in planning programs of teacher education. Let me illustrate from several studies.

A widely quoted and certainly monumental study of teacher characteristics is the study reported by Ryans (1960). Ryans attempted to identify the general personal or social characteristics that would distinguish groups of teachers receiving high and low assessments as indicated by a self-report inventory and observations of classroom behavior by trained observers. Three dimensions of teacher classroom behavior were identified; namely, X — warm, understanding, friendly vs. aloof, egocentric, restrictive; Y — responsible, systematic vs. unplanned, slipshod; Z — stimulating, imaginative vs. dull, routine. Further studies with the

Teacher Characteristics Scale indicated that the "highly assessed" teachers received more favorable opinions of pupils and administrators than "low assessed" teachers, and that pupil behavior was rather closely related to teacher behavior, at least on the elementary school level.

A group of studies growing out of the work of Flanders and his coworkers (Flanders, 1960; Amidon and Flanders, 1963) deal with the development and use of a system of interaction analysis. Verbal behavior of teachers in the classroom was studied by trained observers and categorized as indirect (eliciting creative and voluntary pupil behavior) or direct (eliciting conformity and compliance). An indirect-direct (I/D) ratio was derived for each teacher studied. The rationale for the study of classroom interaction rests on the assumption that certain kinds of teacher statements, those that indicate acceptance, encouragement, and praise, encourage student participation; while other kinds indicating commands, criticism, statement making, and the like, inhibit student participation. The degree and quality of student participation, in turn, affects achievement. In verification of these assumptions Flanders was able to show that in seventh and eighth grade social studies and mathematics, students who were taught by teachers with a high I/D index achieve to a greater extent than those taught in a direct manner.

In another study conducted by Amidon and Giammatteo (1965) the authors were able to show that elementary teachers selected as "superior" by their supervisors and administrators showed a higher incidence of indirect teacher-talk when teaching language arts than that used by a randomly selected group of teachers. The authors conclude that, "The results . . . would seem to indicate that verbal behavior patterns of superior teachers can be identified and that these patterns do differ markedly from the verbal behavior patterns of other teachers." (P. 285)

Meux and Smith (1964) have developed still another approach to identifying significant teaching behaviors. They classify teaching behavior in terms of its logical qualities through observation of the teacher in the classroom. Classroom interaction is categorized into "logical dimensions of teaching" involving such functions as defining, describing, stating, explaining, and so forth, on the assumption that classroom discourse may be identified and analyzed in terms of rules of logic. On the basis of their analysis procedure they are able to show that increased pupil understanding and improved thinking ability are outcomes of instruction where teachers are taught to handle the logical operation involved in teaching.

The studies to which we have referred make important contributions to our understanding of what is involved in teaching and could be justified solely on that basis. Teaching on any level is multi-dimensional and we need studies that will enlighten us as to the nature of the process. Yet looking at these studies for information relative to ways of improving reading instruction, and thereby pupil attainment, provides little that would be helpful.

In the first place, the teacher is being studied as a generalist, nonspecific to any teaching area or any grade level — elementary or secondary. Yet we know that there are differences among teachers in the way they handle given instructional areas and levels. A third grade teacher teaching in a self-contained classroom may be a very effective science teacher, but leave much to be desired in the way she handles reading. Or an eighth grade teacher may very skillfully teach reading through his literature, but would be completely lost as a teacher of second grade reading.

In the second place, such studies as those mentioned have failed to give us any information about the teacher's teaching procedures, the content she teaches, the understandings she must have, or the commitment she has made to clinic teaching. It is conceivable that an observer might make use of one of the interaction analyses and derive for a fourth grade teacher a high score while observing an oral-reading-round class. The teacher-talk is at a minimum, she asks questions, she is accepting of the child's responses, she praises and encourages, yet who would accept this as an effective way of conducting a reading lesson? Or in another situation, the teacher may be well groomed, poised, efficient, gracious, and get along well with her coworkers and principal, and yet never have had a course in the teaching of reading.

In the third place these studies are concerned only indirectly with the product of teaching, that is, changes in pupil behavior, or with the cognitive aspects of learning in the way of skills, abilities, understandings, and so forth. It is not until we have seen the results of teacher characteristics, or interaction, or behavior, or whatever, on pupil development that we will have something that we can use in teacher education.

Not for one minute are we deprecating the value and significance of the studies to which we have referred. They have made and are making a contribution to our understanding of the teaching process. I am certain that the researchers, themselves, would say that the studies are not designed to provide the kind of teacher-education help to which we have referred. This being true we need, then, a different research approach. At least we need to ask different kinds of questions that will give us different kinds of answers, answers that we can use in developing our pre- and in-service teacher-education programs.

Coming somewhat nearer to the type of studies we need in reading are those being carried on by Turner and Fattu (1960) at the University of Indiana. These investigators see teaching behavior as problem-solving ability involving the use of learning sets and specific responses relevant to the teaching situation. In reading, a "Teaching Tasks in Reading" test was developed, assessing a teacher's understanding and application of skills in such areas as selecting appropriate instructional materials, grouping children, judging improvement, diagnosing word perception, and the like. The authors found that the test differentiated between preparatory teachers, student teachers, and experienced teachers. It was interesting to find that their studies substantiated the observation that teaching skill in one area (reading) was not necessarily indicative of the level of performance in another (arithmetic). Moreover, they found that a given teacher may not perform evenly in a single curricular area when different problems were encountered.

A more recent side study was reported by Turner (1967) who found that an analysis of the data derived from a Teacher Characteristics Schedule (measuring nine selected personal-social characteristics such as friendly, organized, stimulating, child-centered, emotional adjustment, and so forth) and a combined Mathematics Teaching Task and Teaching Tasks in Reading scale made possible the identification of teacher characteristics associated with given types of problems of beginning teachers (discipline, management, forming instructional groups in reading, pupil expectancy, and so forth). For example, teachers who had problems in reading appeared to be disorganized, to lack warmth or friendliness and a high level of imaginative behavior, and failed to have a favorable attitude toward democratic procedures. Turner suggested that a set of measures could be assembled by which problems of beginning teachers could be identified, and through counseling and in-service activities, steps could be taken to alleviate them.

The work of Bush and Gage (1968) at the Center for Research and Development in Teaching at Stanford University should be watched with interest, in view of the fact that one of the areas they are investigating is that of teacher behaviors and characteristics and their relationships to pupil achievement and changes. In fact, they indicate that one of their long-term goals of one project is to define a set of skills for effective teaching, to determine the effects of those behaviors, and to determine how to train teachers to use those skills. As a project effort this approaches the thing that I am concerned about. It will be interesting to note whether their "skills for effective teaching" will be general or whether they will be differentiated for various instructional areas and levels.

Lacking information about teacher competencies and related student behavior that could be translated into the context of reading, I would like to suggest a study or series of studies that might provide the needed information. I think we would have to admit that without research evidence all of us in teacher education have been operating pretty much on a series of hunches, on empirical evidence rather than objective. It may well be that if and when we do have the research evidence that clues us in on what "good" reading teachers do that "poor" ones do not, we may find only that our hunches have been confirmed. But at least we will know that.

Thinking about the two basic undergraduate courses, one for elementary teachers, the other for secondary, offered at our institution, here are the areas in which I would like information that would provide an objective base for what we try to do. First, I need consensus on the skills, abilities, understandings, and behaviors that we expect a mature reader to possess. Next I need to know the abilities, skills, knowledges, and competencies that a teacher will need to have if she is to promote sequential growth toward those desired learner competencies. Finally, I need to know the teaching procedures, the course content, the learning activities that I should use in my education classes in order to develop those teacher competencies.

To secure these kinds of information obviously requires a series of studies, each with the necessary research design that will yield appropriate findings from which conclusions may be drawn. It will be a prodigious task, but I am as certain as I am of anything in the reading area that Bond and Dykstra, Ramsey, and Harris and Morrison are right in saying that to improve reading achievement our efforts must be placed on the improvement of our teacher-education program. This is our frontier for exploration. Believe me, I am not unaware of the problems to be encountered, but they should not deter us from action.

Let me try to indicate the broad steps the studies may take:

1. *Formulating a broad and inclusive concept of reading maturity.* By this I mean goals, or more appropriately, a series of goals, toward which reading instruction and guidance should be directed. I say "broad and inclusive" because the goals must be more than ability to perceive words and comprehend meaning. I used the term "maturity" not as a final point to be attained as an adult, but rather as a series of maturities, for a third grader may be a mature reader (i.e. meet the normal expectations for a child completing his third year in school), or he may be a mature reader going into high school, with yet a distance to go on a scale of maturity. Maturity is considered a process, a series of expanding concentric circles, rather than a final fixed point on a scale.

    Coming to a decision with regard to what is involved in reading maturity will be no small problem, to begin with. However, spade work in this area has been done by Gray and Rogers (1956) and described in their *Maturity in Reading—Its Nature and Appraisal.* If you have read this monograph, you will remember that the authors defined reading maturity in terms of five dimensions: interest in reading, purposes for reading, recognition and construction of meaning, reaction to and use of ideas, and kinds of materials read. Each of these five dimensions was broken down into specific criteria which in turn, were assessed on a five-point scale. The authors of this study applied their scale to adults. Obviously if the idea is used with elementary- and secondary-aged children, intermediate maturity points would need to be established. Determining objectives for a reading program is little different from deciding where one is going on a vacation trip. One needs to know his destination before he backs the car out of the garage.

2. *Making a series of decisions with respect to how the several correlates of reading growth referred to in number one will be measured.* Apparently some of the areas may be measured by objective tests, others by observation, others by rather subjectively determined points on a scale. Suffice it to say that the ultimate criterion of the adequacy of a reading program and the effectiveness of teaching will need to be in terms of changes in the individual, with changes very broadly construed as indicated, but quantitatively assessed none the less.

    I am cognizant that learner change as a measure of teaching effectiveness has been avoided in the studies of teaching chiefly for the reason that it is difficult to measure. Substituted for it have been evaluations by principals, supervisors, peers, and even pupils. But in reading instruction we cannot compromise. The teacher is either good or poor in terms of what happens to the child. The principal as an evaluator is likely to be a questionable one, for he evaluates the generalist rather than the teacher of reading. Frequently he has never had work in reading, and his assessment of the goodness of instruction may be in terms of his own biases and misinformation.

3. *Ascertaining teacher characteristics and teaching practices assumed to promote in the most expeditious and effective manner the kinds of changes and types of growth decided on in number one and measured as in number two.* Here the researcher's efforts will be in identifying the teacher variables that might differentiate the effective from the ineffective teacher. This could be done by making a series of kinescopes of reading instruction on a given label taught by a number of different teachers. Experienced observers would examine the tapes in terms of the concept of maturity established in number one to see if they would be able to identify and classify such factors as teacher talk, competencies developed, teaching style used, provision for individual needs, and the like.

4. *Subjecting to measurement each assumed factor or teacher variable determined in step number three, and through experimentation determining its relation to pupil changes or growth in the various dimensions and levels of the mature reading act as established in number one and measured in number two.* One might attempt in this step to identify groups of high- and low-achieving children, holding constant such factors as intelligence, socioeconomic background, and so forth, and observe the teachers and their teaching to see if in truth the assumed variables determined in step number three differentiate the teachers of the high-achieving pupils from those of the low achievers and to what degree. Or one could identify groups of teachers having and failing to have the variables derived in step number three, and determine if the pupils taught by those teachers were differentiated in terms of reading maturity. It is through step number four that we should be able to indicate that a teacher who possesses certain characteristics, who uses certain techniques and certain types of instructional media, and who provides in certain ways for the differentiated needs of children will stand greater chances of having learners who are higher on a scale of reading maturity than teachers who do not have these characteristics and understandings and who do not perform these instructional acts.

5. *Using the information provided through step number four to improve the program of teacher education in reading.* Since one now

has objective evidence that certain teacher characteristics and understandings and certain teaching practices are productive of a higher level of pupil maturity than others, he can now begin to employ this evidence in his teacher-education program in reading. One may discover that he needs to give more or even less emphasis to certain instructional areas than he did before. He may need to provide certain kinds of learning experiences to develop needed teaching competencies. In fact, a new dimension of research opens up for the teacher educator. Having evidence that teachers need to possess certain understandings and do certain things in certain ways to bring a desired level of achievement in their pupils, the teacher of the "methods" course finds it incumbent to discover the best ways to prepare his teachers in training. Answers will be needed to such questions as the following: How effective is lecturing in relation to other procedures? Will a four-minute single-concept audiovisual tape be as much help as a thirty-minute film? How effective is microteaching in producing a particular understanding? Can one use effectively a group of students from his methods class to serve as a simulated group of third graders to demonstrate a given technique? Armed with the kinds of information described, one can begin to say with some degree of assurance that as teachers of reading teachers we have taken significant and objectively derived steps toward improving the quality of teaching and thereby the quality of reading that children, young people, and adults are able to do. Teacher education is a rich and rewarding area within which to work. As for myself I would choose no other. We know now that the reading that children and young people do will not be improved by the administration of a capsule, by facilitating their creeping and crawling, by the use of a machine, or by method x. We can give up these searches and concentrate on what we surmised was the case all along—that improved reading is the result of improved teaching, and in that pursuit many of us have a major stake.

References

Amidon, E., and Flanders, N. A. *The role of the teacher in the classroom*. Minneapolis: Paul Amidon and Associates, 1963.

Amidon, E. J., and Giammatteo, M. "The verbal behavior of superior teachers." *The Elementary School Journal* 65 (1965):283–85.

Bond, G. L., and Dykstra, R. "The cooperative research program in first grade reading." *Reading Research Quarterly* 1967, 2.

Bush, R. N., and Gage, N. L. "Center for research and development in teaching." *Journal of Research and Development in Education*, 1, (1968):86–105.

Flanders, N. A. *Teacher influence: pupil attitudes and achievement, final report, 1960*. (Project 397) Washington, D.C.: U.S. Office of Health, Education, and Welfare, 1960.

Gray, W. S., and Rogers, B. *Maturity in reading: its nature and appraisal*. Chicago: The University of Chicago Press, 1956.

Harris, A. J., and Morrison, C. "The CRAFT project: a final report." *The Reading Teacher* 22 (1969):335–40.

Jackson, P. W. *The way teaching is*. Washington: Association for Supervision and Curriculum Development, 1966.

Meux, M., and Smith, B. O. "Logical dimensions of teaching behavior." In *Contemporary research on teacher effectiveness,* edited by B. J. Biddle and W. J. Ellena. New York: Holt, Rinehart, & Winston, 1964.

Ramsey, W. Z. "An evaluation of three methods of teaching reading." In "Challenge and experiment in reading," edited by A. Figurel, *International Reading Association Conference Proceedings* 7 (1962):153.

Ryans, D. G. *Characteristics of teachers*. Washington, D.C.: American Council on Education, 1960.

Turner, R. L., and Fattu, N. A. "Skill in teaching: a reappraisal of the concepts and strategies in teaching effectiveness research." *Bulletin of the School of Education*. Indiana University 36 (1960):1–40.

Turner, R. L. "Some predictors of problems of beginning teachers." *The Elementary School Journal* 67 (1967):251–56.

Children really can learn from each other. When low-achieving fifth-graders tutor first graders in reading, both groups of children can make significant progress. Moreover, the fifth graders develop more positive attitudes toward both reading and school. Robertson describes an intergrade tutoring project, and explains in some detail how the children were taught to be effective tutors.

Intergrade Tutoring: Children Learn from Children

DOUGLAS J. ROBERTSON

This article reports the results of a study of an intergrade tutoring program and describes procedures in training the tutors. Intergrade tutoring is where children at one grade level tutor children who are at another grade level. In the intergrade tutoring program fifth graders who had been identified as low achievers in reading were trained to tutor first graders in sight word recognition. The major purpose of the study was to determine what effects a tutoring experience had on the attitudes of the tutors toward (1) *reading*, (2) *teachers*, and (3) *self* (themselves). A second purpose was to determine whether fifth grade students performing as tutors made significant gains in reading achievement as a result of the tutoring experience. A third purpose was to determine the effect that intergrade tutoring had on the sight word recognition ability of the first graders who were tutored.

The tutoring program was based on the premises that: (1) students who are low achievers in reading tend to have negative attitudes toward reading, teachers, and themselves; (2) the responsibility of tutoring a first grader in reading might provide a fifth grade student with a means of developing positive attitudes toward reading, teachers, and himself; (3) the responsibility of tutoring a first grader in prescribed reading tasks might provide a fifth grade student with incentive to improve his own reading skills; (4) fifth grade students are human resources having great potential for enhancing the quality of reading instruction for primary grade children; and (5) first grade children might achieve significant reading gains as a result of being tutored by fifth grade children.

Selecting the Tutors

Five fifth grade teachers from Wilbur Avenue Elementary School in Tarzana, California, were asked to list the students from their classes who were in the lower 50 percent in reading achievement. Ninety-three students were identified. The ninety-three fifth graders were pretested and posttested on the *Stanford Diagnostic Reading Test* to assess reading achievement, and three semantic differentials to assess their attitudes toward (1) *reading*, (2) *teachers*, and (3) *self*. The ninety-three subjects were organized into three equivalent groups on the basis of sex, pretest score on the *Stanford Diagnostic Reading Test*, and pretest score on the semantic differentials. One group was randomly chosen to receive tutor training followed by actual tutoring experience with first graders. A second group received tutor training, but did not tutor. The third group served as control subjects and were merely pretested and posttested. Each group had thirty-one subjects.

Selecting the First Graders

Five first grade teachers from Wilbur Avenue Elementary School selected a total of thirty-one first graders to receive tutoring in sight word recognition. The first graders were chosen on the basis of needing individual help in sight word instruction. An equivalent control group was secured from a neighboring school. Both groups were pretested and posttested on the *Primary Word Recognition* section of the *Gates-MacGinitie Reading Test.*

Tutoring

Each first grader from Wilbur Avenue Elementary was assigned to work with a trained fifth grade student tutor. The assignment was random in an attempt to control for any possible effects of tutor-learner interaction.

The actual tutorial sessions were held three days a week. Each fifth grade tutor worked with his first grader 30 minutes per day over a two-month period. Little instructional time was lost from the classroom as the fifth graders tutored during their morning recess period. Actual tutoring took place in hallways and outdoor patios.

Results: Fifth Grade Tutors

Fifth grade student tutors developed significantly different and more positive attitudes toward the concepts (1) *reading,* (2) *teachers,* and (3) *self* than did the equivalent groups of fifth grade students who did not tutor. Also, the fifth grade student tutors attained significantly different and higher reading-achievement scores on the *Stanford Diagnostic Reading Test* when compared to the subjects who were trained to tutor, but did not tutor, and the control subjects.

A one-way analysis of variance and the Scheffé post-hoc multiple comparison method were applied to statistically evaluate the posttest data. The .05 level of significance was utilized.

Results: First Graders

First graders who were tutored by trained fifth grade tutors in sight word recognition made significantly higher reading gains than an equivalent group of control subjects who received normal classroom reading instruction. A *t* test for uncorrelated data was applied to the posttest scores on the *Gates-MacGinitie Reading Test*. The .05 level of significance was adopted.

What Made It Work?

The findings indicate that this intergrade tutoring program was highly successful. Tutoring experience would appear to have a positive effect on the development of some important school-related attitudes as well as increasing the reading achievement of fifth grade tutors and first grader learners. The results realized in this tutoring program were not automatic nor were they accidental.

Tutor Training: A Key Factor

Prospective fifth grade tutors were trained by this writer to provide sight word instruction to the first graders. The training consisted of four one-and-one-half-hour sessions which were completed in four consecutive days.

The first tutor-training session consisted of informal discussions concerning: (1) the function of a tutor; (2) the nature of the learner; (3) means of developing rapport with first graders; (4) the purposes and expected outcomes of the tutoring program; and (5) specific tutoring behaviors and procedures.

The second session included an introduction, explanation, and demonstration of how to use the *Dolch Picture Word Cards* representing 95 common nouns. The principles covered in the first session were incorporated in the demonstration.

In the third session, the fifth graders practiced using the *Dolch Picture Word Cards* by interacting with the writer in role-playing situations. The fifth graders and the writer alternated roles as first grade learner and as a tutor. At the conclusion of this session, each fifth grader was given his own box of the *Dolch Picture Word Cards*. Each tutor's goal was to help his first grader learn to recognize and pronounce as many sight words as possible in two month's time.

The fourth session consisted of having the fifth graders pair up and role play. The fifth graders took turns tutoring using the *Dolch Picture Word Cards* or acting the part of a first grader. By the end of this session, the fifth graders were ready to commence tutoring actual first graders.

A question and review period followed each tutor-training session. The tutor trainer supervised the tutoring program and met with all the tutors once a week to discuss any problems that developed. It is important to mention that both the tutors and the first graders enjoyed the tutoring experience.

Specification of Tutor Behaviors

The fifth grade tutors practiced specific behaviors with the first graders. The tutoring behaviors were designed to provide: (1) continuous active response, (2) immediate knowledge of results, (3) positive reinforcements, (4) appropriate pacing of instruction, and (5) correction of errors before proceeding. The tutor behaviors consisted of two interrelated components, each emphasizing different types of skills. The tutors were taught to use: (1) *interaction skills,* consisting of such interpersonal communication actions as smiling and praising; and (2) *product-referenced procedures,* which emphasized the effective employment of the *Dolch Picture Word Cards* in teaching sight word recognition.

The *interaction skills* were specified as follows:

1. During the tutorial interaction the tutor will act in an encouraging and friendly manner. Observable indices of such behaviors are:
   a) Tutor smiles frequently—especially at the beginning of each session.
   b) Tutor calls student by his first name.
   c) Tutor talks with student about something other than the lesson, e.g., "Do you have any pets at home, Bruce?"
2. Whenever the student gives a correct response to a verbal or picture stimulus, the tutor will immediately give a verbal confirmation, e.g., "That's right," "Fine," "OK." He will do this every time.
3. Several times during a session, the tutor will do more than provide simple confirmation following a correct response. He will praise the student in sincere and varied ways, e.g., "You're doing a great job today. Keep it up."
4. Whenever the student gives an incorrect response to a verbal or picture stimulus or fails to answer, the tutor will tell the student the correct answer and then require him to respond correctly before going on, e.g., "Look at this word, Bruce. It is *book.* What is this word?" The tutor will *not* attempt to elicit the correct response by prompting.
5. The tutor will *avoid* punitive verbal behavior with the student, e.g., he will not say something like, "No, that's not it. Can't you remember? We just had that word a minute ago."

6. At the end of the session, the tutor will make a positive comment on the student's performance, e.g., "You did well today, Bruce. Good work."

The *product-referenced procedures* were specified as follows:

1. The tutor will hold each picture word card up individually so that the learner has a clear view of it.
2. The tutor will read and pronounce correctly all words on the picture word cards.
3. The tutor will sit near the learner as he reads aloud the printed words that appear on each picture word card.
4. Following step number three, the tutor will show the picture to the learner and ask such questions as "What is the word for this picture?"
5. The tutor will introduce five to nine picture word cards each week depending on the learner's apparent readiness and learning rate. The tutor will practice until the first grade child can correctly pronounce each word when presented with the printed word.
6. The tutor will keep a daily progress report on how well the child did and record the words covered each week on a *Tutor Record Card*. The tutor will also evaluate his own performance on the *Tutor Record Card*. The *Tutor Record Cards* were turned in to this writer following the last tutoring session of each week.
7. From day to day, the tutor will recycle for review and mastery purposes.
8. Once a week each tutor will read a story to his first grader.
9. Once a week each tutor will listen to the first grader read from his reading or library book.

Conclusions

The following factors would appear to have contributed largely to the significant results realized in this intergrade tutoring program. The fifth grade tutors were (1) thoroughly trained in specific tutoring behaviors and procedures; (2) given prescribed tasks to accomplish; (3) given demonstrations in how to employ the program materials; (4) provided with opportunities to role play the part of the tutor as well as the part of the first grader; (5) informed regarding the purposes and expected outcomes of the tutorial program; and (6) directly involved in the process of evaluation.

The interaction between the tutor and the learner was well defined and specific, and adequate controls were maintained. It seems essential that at least one key person be available to motivate and train the tutors and supervise all aspects of an ongoing intergrade tutorial program. Further, it is vital to gain the support of the community and the cooperation of the principal and teaching staff before attempting to implement an intergrade tutoring program.

If the above conditions are met within an elementary school attempting to implement an intergrade tutoring program, it seems highly probable that positive effects will be realized for both the tutor and the learner regardless of the content or complexity of the subject matter or learning tasks. As more tutoring programs of this kind are implemented, more children may be (1) actively involved in meaningful activities, (2) contributing and being useful to others, and (3) developing positive self-concepts.

Shouldn't children be helping other children learn to read instead of competing against them?

Many teachers know they should improve the line of communication between the school and the home, but they don't know how to start the conversation. Davis believes that children will benefit when school personnel make a concerted effort to communicate *with* parents and not *at* them. She suggests procedures for establishing a meaningful line of communication.

Parents and School Should Share

S. ELIZABETH DAVIS

Probably the most important and most difficult job in the world today is that of parenthood. It also is one of the few for which there is no prerequisite except biological maturity.

It is the opinion of this author that most parents are the best kind of parents they know how to be. In everyday life they are bombarded with advertisements of what they should buy for their children from the best diaper, infant bottle, and baby powder to the best of lotions, creams, and bell bottoms for the teenager.

Pressures and Their Effects

Pressure is also exerted to prepare for a child's future education. This pressure stems from many different sources. Numerous insurance plans are available for saving money for a college education. Attractive advertising campaigns for educational toys and materials to assure that the child will be able to read when he enters school are to be found everywhere. Popular magazines carry stories of miracle methods that cure a child's problems whatever they may be. There appears to be little or no thought given to the differences in children or to the fact that giving expensive gifts to them has little to do with their learning.

Stories and articles are written for the lay public which in essence put full "blame" for a child's problems upon the parent. One fault as stated or implied to parents is that they have been overly directive. The next article a parent reads may very likely state or imply that the same type of problem stems from a parent's being overly permissive. Unless the parents have a great deal of insight, background, and experience with child development and a fair amount of ego strength, it is very difficult to try to determine what may best help the child in his development.

Many parents cannot afford the expensive educational toys even if the use of these toys actually would accomplish that which the advertisers say they will accomplish. They do not know if the child will be able or will want to go to college and often they cannot afford the insurance plans, but they do try to put the money aside.

A child is naturally an ego-extension of the parent. Parents are, therefore, naturally proud of their children and consequently fearful of criticism or of the observable fact that the child is not doing well in school or society.

Until the child reaches the age at which he enters school, few parents have a chance to observe his behavior in a large group. In many cases the parents do not see him with a small group outside the family. The school setting is probably the first place where the child enters a comparative situation. Here he is made aware of working and playing with others of his age group. He is expected to persist in some activities and change in others. The term *persistence* is often thought of as the ability to attend to a task. The lesson of persistence is often an exceedingly difficult task for children. When the child has difficulty adjusting to the wide range of behavior which is required by the combination of persistence and change, he usually reacts in the same manner he did in the primary social group (the family). These reactions may or may not be appropriate in the larger secondary social group (the school setting).

In too many cases, the parent is the last one to be told of a child's inappropriate behavior. This is usually done after the behavior has limited the ability of the child to learn or the ability of his classmates to benefit from the learning situation.

It is imperative for teachers to know something of child development and adjustment if help is to be given both to the child and to the parents. The school personnel must have knowledge of the concept of readiness and how it is developed at any age.

This knowledge must then be shared with the parents. Parents can and should in turn share knowledge of their children with the teachers. According to Smith (1965), one of the most important things to be remembered by parents and teachers in helping a child in the adjustment process is consistency. When the adult world surrounding the child is consistent, he can learn to adjust more easily because he knows what to expect. The author believes it is necessary for the school and parents to communicate with each other early in a child's school life to help both understand the child's adjustment.

Heilman (1966) believes that one of the factors which affect a child's learning is the pressure which is put upon him. This pressure appears to come from three major sources. One source would be the home. The numerous advertisements, stories, and articles with which the parents are bombarded put a tremendous amount of pressure upon the parents. They, in turn, overtly or covertly put pressure on the child to learn, especially to learn to read. Much of this pressure starts with the child's first day in school. It continues with the first report card sent home or the first conference held. This is particularly true if the child in question does not do as well as an older sibling. A second source of pressure is the school. Grades and nonpromotion are often used as a threat to children. Certain grouping procedures, or comparison of and contrast to another child's work, will put undue pressure upon him. The materials for learning, too, are often of an inappropriate nature. The third source of pressure is the child himself. When he cannot adjust or is unable to do the work, he feels he has disappointed his parents and teacher and he begins to feel the pressure. He can either digress or rebel. Teachers and parents must enter into a cooperative effort to be aware of the signs of pressures.

Suggestions for Communication

The usual reporting system (report card, conference, PTA meetings) is inadequate. There must be more communication with the parents. Small group conferences can and should be held with parents of children who have similar problems and/or strengths. In this way, the parents can realize more easily that the child is not unusual and the teacher is not "against" them or him. The conferences should be lead by the teacher but should not be lectures. The teacher will then be able to learn more easily the dynamics of the home, what the parents would like to see done, and that the parents and child are not "against" the school.

Individual conferences should also be held where parents and teachers become alert together to the child's adjustment to different situations. This should not be done only after inappropriate behavior patterns have arisen.

Other school personnel should be involved in presenting the reading program to parents. This can be done through parent-school meetings, conferences, television programs, bulletins, and workshops. Both parents need to be involved in these programs.

What can be said to parents beyond what has been mentioned above in this article?

1. The time a parent spends with a child is invaluable. Talking *with* the child and listening *to* the child will express more love and attention than any number of gifts given. This will also give the child a sense of ease in using his language.
2. Both parents should read with the child, read silently for pleasure as well as for practical life problems, and allow the child to read to them. If he cannot pronounce a particular word, tell him what it is. Guard against telling a child to "sound out" a word—if he could do so, he would have done it and while he is struggling, the sense of the story is lost.

3. Take the child to the library. The librarian will help in the choice
   of books. Be sure to choose some books for you to read, also. This
   will show the child that libraries are not just for kids. It is necessary that fathers choose books, also.
   If the father does not have the time, the mother can choose books
   for him. This will help avoid a child's perception of the library as
   being a place for women. Most libraries have a story hour for children of different ages. Take the child and enjoy reading while he is
   involved in the listening.
4. Set aside a quiet time in the evening. This should probably last
   about half an hour. During this time there should be no television,
   no record playing, no radio, no friends of the child present. The
   family is quiet, with the parents reading and plenty of reading material for the child available. The child should not be forced to read
   but if the "quiet" standard is kept, he will read.
5. The level 2 on a basal reading book or on a report does not mean
   second grade reading. It means that this is the book which follows
   successful reading of level 1. It would be much better to talk in
   terms of skills needed and skills accomplished rather than in terms
   of levels since there is such wide misunderstanding of levels.

Each year standardized achievement tests are given to children
in the schools. Often the results of these tests are given to the
parents in terms of grade norms or percentile ranks. It is the
belief of this author that this practice should not be continued.

The reasons for testing of this type should be given to the parents by someone skilled in testing procedures — the counselor or
school psychologist. An interpretation of the results can be given
by the same individuals. Test results alone are rarely understood
by parents or by many of the personnel within a school.

Hopefully, if there is a concerted effort put forth by the school
personnel to communicate *with* parents not *at* them, the child
will benefit from the coordinated effort.

References

Heilman, A. W. *Principles and practices of teaching reading.* Columbus, Ohio:
Charles E. Merrill Books, 1966.

Smith, H. P. *Psychology in teaching.* Englewood Cliffs, N.J.: Prentice-Hall, 1965.

> The International Reading Association has established a definition of the roles, responsibilities, and qualifications for four types of reading specialists.

Roles, Responsibilities, and Qualifications of Reading Specialists

The revised statement of the roles, responsibilities, and qualifications of reading specialists has been formulated by the Professional Standards and Ethics Committee and approved by the Board of Directors of the International Reading Association. It is intended that these minimum standards will serve as guides to:

1. Teachers and administrators in identifying the reading specialist.
2. State and provincial departments of education in certifying specialists in reading.
3. Colleges and universities offering professional programs in reading.
4. Individuals planning to train as reading specialists.

These standards are under constant study and are periodically revised by the committee. This 1968 guide is a revision and extension of the brochure, "Minimum Standards for Professional Training of Reading Specialists," published in 1965.

Copies of a brochure including this information and the Code of Ethics are available from IRA Headquarters.

The Need for Establishing Standards

Reading is a complex process that develops within an individual throughout years of formal schooling and adult life. As a result of expanded knowledge, the demand for trained personnel in reading at all levels has increased tremendously. With the demand high and the supply relatively short, the danger of unqualified persons attempting those tasks which only a trained reading specialist should undertake has become a very real one. One means of preventing such occurrences is by establishing minimum standards for the professional training of reading specialists.

The reading specialist may be designated as that person (1) who works directly or indirectly with those pupils who have either failed to benefit from regular classroom instruction in reading or those pupils who could benefit from advanced training in reading skills, and/or (2) who works with teachers, administrators, and other professionals to improve and coordinate the total reading program of the school.

Definition of Roles

Special Teacher of Reading

A Special Teacher of Reading has major responsibility for remedial and corrective and/or developmental reading instruction.

Reading Clinician

A Reading Clinician provides diagnosis, remediation, or the planning of remediation for the more complex and severe reading disability cases.

Reading Consultant

A Reading Consultant works directly with teachers, administrators, and other professionals within a school to develop and implement the reading program under the direction of a supervisor with special training in reading.

Reading Supervisor
(Coordinator or Director)

A Reading Supervisor provides leadership in all phases of the reading program in a school system.

Responsibilities of Each Reading Specialist

Special Teacher of Reading

- Should identify students needing diagnosis and/or remediation.
- Should plan a program of remediation from data gathered through diagnosis.
- Should implement such a program of remediation.
- Should evaluate student progress in remediation.
- Should interpret student needs and progress in remediation to the classroom teacher and the parents.
- Should plan and implement a developmental or advanced program as necessary.
- Complete a minimum of three years of successful classroom teaching in which the teaching of reading is an important responsibility of the position.
- Complete a planned program for the master's degree from an accredited institution, to include

1. A minimum of 12 semester hours in graduate-level reading courses with at least one course in each of the following:
    a) Foundations or survey of reading
       A basic course whose content is related exclusively to reading instruction or the psychology of reading. Such a course ordinarily would be first in a sequence of reading courses.
    b) Diagnosis and correction of reading disabilities
       The content of this course or courses includes the following: causes of reading disabilities; observation and interview procedures; diagnostic instruments; standard and informal tests; report writing; materials and methods of instruction.
    c) Clinical or laboratory practicum in reading
       A clinical or laboratory experience which might be an integral part of a course or courses in the diagnosis and correction of reading disabilities. Students diagnose and treat reading-disability cases under supervision.

2. Complete, at undergraduate or graduate level, study in each of the following areas:
   a) Measurement and/or evaluation.
   b) Child and/or adolescent psychology.
   c) Psychology, including such aspects as personality, cognition, and learning behaviors.
   d) Literature for children and/or adolescents.
3. Fulfill remaining portions of the program from related areas of study.

Reading Clinician

- Should demonstrate all the skills expected of the Special Teacher of Reading and, by virtue of additional training and experience, diagnose and treat the more complex and severe reading-disability cases.
- Should demonstrate proficiency in providing internship training for prospective clinicians and/or Special Teachers of Reading.

Reading Consultant

- Should survey and evaluate the ongoing program and make suggestions for needed changes.
- Should translate the district philosophy of reading with the help of the principal of each school into a working program consistent with the needs of the students, the teachers, and the community.
- Should work with classroom teachers and others in improving the developmental and corrective aspects of the reading program.

Reading Supervisor

- Should develop a systemwide reading philosophy and curriculum and interpret this to the school administration, staff, and public.
- Should exercise leadership with all personnel in carrying out good reading practices.
- Should evaluate reading personnel and personnel needs in all phases of a schoolwide reading program.
- Should make recommendations to the administration regarding the reading budget.

Qualifications

General (Applicable to all Reading Specialists)

- Demonstrate proficiency in evaluating and implementing research.
- Demonstrate a willingness to make a meaningful contribution to professional organizations related to reading.
- Demonstrate a willingness to assume leadership in improving the reading program.

Reading Clinician

- Meet the qualifications as stipulated for the Special Teacher of Reading.
- Complete, in addition to the above, a sixth year of graduate work including

  1. An advanced course or courses in the diagnosis and remediation of reading and learning problems.
  2. A course or courses in individual testing.
  3. An advanced clinical or laboratory practicum in the diagnosis and remediation of reading difficulties.
  4. Field experiences under the direction of a qualified Reading Clinician.

Reading Consultant

- Meet the qualifications as stipulated for the Special Teacher of Reading.
- Complete, in addition to the above, a sixth year of graduate work including

  1. An advanced course in the remediation and diagnosis of reading and learning problems.
  2. An advanced course in the developmental aspects of a reading program.
  3. A course or courses in curriculum development and supervision.
  4. A course and/or experience in public relations.
  5. Field experiences under a qualified Reading Consultant or Supervisor in a school setting.

Reading Supervisor

- Meet the qualifications as stipulated for the Special Teacher of Reading.
- Complete, in addition to the above, a sixth year of graduate work including

  1. Courses listed as 1, 2, 3, and 4 under Reading Consultant.
  2. A course or courses in administrative procedures.
  3. Field experiences under a qualified Reading Supervisor.

study questions

1. In his review of research on teaching Artley looks more toward needs for additional research than to conclusions that can be made from present research. What are some characteristics of effective teachers that can be identified from the research studies that Artley reviews?

2. In what ways might Artley agree with the authors of this book? In what ways might he disagree with them?

3. Summarize the suggestions Davis gives for improving communication between the school and the home.

4. What are the four types of reading specialists identified by the International Reading Association? How might each type of specialist help the classroom teacher improve the effectiveness of the reading program?

5. Robertson found that tutoring is an effective learning experience for both the child being tutored and the child doing the tutoring. Summarize the suggestions he gives for initiating a tutorial program in reading.

6. If Robertson, Davis, and Artley were asked to agree on five suggestions for increasing the effectiveness of reading instruction, what might they be?

7. What do you consider to be the three most important characteristics of an effective reading teacher?

SIX

guiding responses to reading

objectives

As a result of reading these articles and answering the questions at the end of the chapter you should be able to:

- ▣ explain the theoretical viewpoint that reader response is the central focus of communication through print

- ▣ cite reasons for including selections dealing with social problems, humor, poetry, exposition, and various other topics in a response-to-literature program

- ▣ list recently explored techniques for measuring literary response

rationale

Without response, there is essentially no reason for a communication. Reading theory and procedural recommendations have quite justifiably turned attention toward response. The importance of response, the means of stimulating it, and suggestions for evaluating response are discussed in this chapter. Beneath the surface lies a sense of urgency—that unless the response goal is more fully implemented, reading in the future may become an anachronism.

introduction

Complete communication requires a receiver as well as a sender. It is the role of the receiver in reading that has recently come under scrutiny. Picture a lone man on a hilltop sending a message by smoke signal: I am hurt. Help me. There is no communication unless someone sees the message. Suppose the message is seen and is read but with no result. The people in the valley, let us say, read the message but go on about their business, and tomorrow the message is forgotten. Perhaps we would maintain that communication did take place, but by now the term gives a hollow ring, as in the Zen query about the sound of one hand clapping.

Or suppose that you sit at home with this book. You begin to read, but the sound of the ice cream wagon drifts through your window. You recall a time three years ago when that sound led to a neighborhood get-together and that was when you—but by now you have read a whole page and cannot recall a thing it said. Did communication occur? Did reading take place? Now you go over the page again. The meaning appears fairly clear this time. But, really, it seems to add nothing to what you already know. It seems to make no change in your thinking or what you intend to do. So—is this communication? Is this reading?

Whatever the dimensions of meaning we ascribe to communication or to reading, the *active* response of the reader must concern us. In the past our concept of comprehension has often neglected this aspect. Our tests of comprehension ability, for example, have not gone far beyond the level of *passive* understanding. The discrepancy was noted early by William S. Gray, who included a utilization factor in his definition of reading outcome, and more recently by David H. Russell in his posthumously published *The Dynamics of Reading*.[1] The nature and nurture of reader response has been the subject of an increasing number of research studies, some of them reviewed by Doris Young in this chapter.

Response to literature entails initial acceptance of the author's presentation, including generally a grasp of his interpretation of reality communicated through *theme*. Henceforth the reader is stimulated to examine his own beliefs in light of this theme. Eventually, if he is an active recipient of the literary message, he is led to make some judgment of the total experience. Along the way, he experiences enjoyment or realization of benefit—a justification for reading the literary work in preference to using the time for some other activity.

To encourage such response to literature, studies and opinion suggest various procedures: care in matching interests and developmental level of the reader with appropriate literary works; questioning and discussion strategies designed to call forth active interpretation from the reader; dramatization, role playing, and oral interpretation of a literary text. Recent children's literature dealing with current problems highlights the path to active response. Humor as a surefire ingredient for arousing response is another factor worth considering. The teacher's role in guiding literary response is central, as Iverson has indicated.

Expository material, designed to explain or to argue a point of view, asks a response quite different from literature. Here the emphasis may be on following directions, acquiring information —or determining whether a writer's opinion is substantiated to the point of acceptance. Whatever the objective, the reader's stance as an active participant in the expository communication process is requisite. And because active response entails making choices, critical reading looms all the more important as a guide to active response.

The challenge of defining and designing reading strategy as an active-response process is all the more apparent when we note the need. Americans, compared with other nationalities of equivalent literacy, do not comprise a nation of avid readers. There may be some positive, relativistic reasons for this. American living patterns seem to preclude a stampede to the book store or library. But there may also be reasons involving our failure to view reading as a response-arousing occupation. ("Don't sit around reading all morning—get up and *do* something," says the exasperated parent.) A recent Roper poll indicates, too, that Americans place less *trust* in their reading for news than in their television watching for news. The comparative merits of these two media are still debatable, but one may conjecture that part of the distrust of print springs from undeveloped, unrealized critical reading abilities. Perhaps the most amazing condemnation of our attitude toward reading as an influence on attitude and action is an indirect indictment: the recent opinion of a federal commission that "illicit" reading material can cause no harm. The corollary—that reading can cause no "good"—reflects how far we have to go in realizing that reading entails active response, leading to altered attitudes and/or behavior.

Considering the recent attention to response and apparent need for such attention, it is not surprising to find this aspect of reading at the center of new proposed theories for explaining the entire process. Frank Smith's *Understanding Reading*[2] suggests that reading be regarded on all levels as "the reduction of uncertainty." The reader actively responds to print by considering information of visual, orthographic, syntactic, and semantic dimensions. He brings to the reading task the reservoir of information from which the reaction, the "reduction of uncertainty," derives. Total involvement is necessary in order to integrate the communication with the information already possessed by the reader. If translated into teaching procedure, this communications-based theory might significantly alter reading instruction and its results, drawing together the various components of the act with response as its keystone.

The importance of the topic, therefore, seems vouchsafed. Each of the readings included in this chapter examines a particular aspect of eliciting response, suggesting procedures to be tried. No other topic requires so much of teacher and pupil individuality and spirit. The key to response-getting may lie in selection of material, in inspired presentation and sharing of humor, or in explicit attention to the high scarce art of critical reading. It may lie in improved objective setting and evaluation of response. One can be certain that emphasis on response to reading is not misplaced. The lone man on the hilltop and the writer of a message to be read must be responded to.

References

1. Russell, D. H. *The Dynamics of Reading,* Robert B. Ruddell, editor. Waltham, Mass.: Ginn-Blaisdell, 1970.
2. Smith, F. *Understanding Reading.* New York: Holt, Rinehart & Winston, 1971, pp. 12, 20.

If we are to guide response to literature, we need ways to evaluate response. This is difficult when the
potent response is an "unspoken
word," a "look of mutual understanding," or "inarticulate sensitivity." How, pray, do we measure the
light in the eyes that dawns during
the reading of *Charlotte's Web* or
Rosie's Walk? Here are some sensible
answers.

Evaluation of Children's Responses to Literature

DORIS YOUNG

In one of the *Peanuts* cartoon strips, Schulz presented one kind
of response to literature as Lucy summarized Snow White. Lucy
stalks along as she says: "This Snow White has been having
trouble sleeping, see? Well, she goes to this witch who gives her
an apple to eat which put her to sleep. Just as she's beginning to

sleep real well . . . you know, for the first time in weeks . . . this stupid prince comes along and kisses her and wakes her up." Linus then remarks, "I admire the wonderful way you have of getting the real meaning out of the story."[1] Expressing the "real meaning" is but one response to literature. Response to literature is also evident as it satisfies a child's need. For example, in *Home from Far,* Little describes this response: "Usually when Jenny was sent to her room, she felt it was cheating to read. You forgot all about whatever you had done wrong two minutes after you opened a book. But now she jumped off the bed and went to the bookcase. She wanted a sad book. She was not ashamed of crying over people in a story. She chose *The Birds' Christmas Carol* and curled up in the chair next to the window. Soon she was in another world, where Mother, the two Michaels, and the nightmare of fear she had felt when she had been trapped by the fire could not follow her."[2]

Evaluation begins with recognition that the child's "real meaning" and other responses are internal evaluations. He decides to give attention by evaluating his environment; he evaluates as he selects elements to remember, allows feelings to flow, or permits the alchemy of imagination to work its wonders. However, the concern of this paper is external evaluation. A brief definition of evaluation as a process will be followed by examples of four categories of responses. There is no attempt here to summarize research; the intent is to indicate kinds of investigations that have been made. The analysis will lead to questions that need to be answered.

Evaluation as a Process

The first step in the process of evaluation is identification of the kinds of responses that might be observed. Concurrently, it is necessary to make some judgments about the kinds of changes it would be desirable to make as the child spends time in the elementary school. The child does "spend" his time, and educators have no right to insist that he waste this precious coin of life. Thus the objectives we select are of prime importance. Determining objectives is a part of evaluation. Instead of a synonym for measurement, it is considered to be "a continuous process of inquiry, based upon criteria cooperatively developed in the school-community, which lead to warranted conclusions with respect to how successfully the school is studying, interpreting,

and guiding socially desirable changes in human behavior."[3]
Thus the design of instruments to gather evidence and the collection and interpretation of evidence about behavior are but
parts of a total process. Some educators would urge us not to attempt the measure of responses to literature. They are afraid that
the intangible elements, like love, will disappear with analysis.
Others fear written tests of cognitive development may overbal-
ance the objective of enjoyment of literature. There is concern
that procedures designed for research might become the major
teaching strategy. These fears are unjustified if the concept of
evaluation of a total situation is kept in mind. Krathwohl and
others[4] point out the dangerous "erosion" of educational objectives that are not evaluated. Failure to identify objectives in
terms of behavior in both the cognitive and affective domain will
only result in further "time-stealing" school activities.

Evidence of Children's
Responses to Literature

Every teacher or librarian is aware of the varied responses of
children to literature. Children react differently to the very act
of reading or listening. An individual reads for different purposes
at different times. Closely related to these interests and attitudes
is the category of emotional experience of literature. Meanings
and understandings form another category of responses related
to a particular selection. A fourth type of response is in the cognitive domain—knowledge of literature as a field. The child's
creative products reflect further responses to the experience of
literature. All of these responses are components of that elusive
term, *appreciation*.

Interests, Attitudes,
Preference

The Children Respond

The following expressions reveal some of children's interests
and attitudes:

"How many books do you have to read to go to the summer
party?"
"Aw, that's a baby book."
"But horse stories are for girls!"

"Nope. I just read science books."

"The author of my book is Elizabeth Speare. The title is
The Bronze Bow. It's a Newbery book on the list. It has 254
pages. The main character is Daniel. The setting is Galilee. I
like it because it had lots of fights. That's my report."

"I chatter, chatter as I flow,
    To join the brimming river,
For men may come and men may go,
    But I go on forever.

"That's my 100 lines!" (The fourth grader had completed his
memorization assignment in the middle of the poem, and sat
down with a thump.)

Investigators Report

Concerned with the development of citizens who are readers, the
school must ask, "What does the child do?" as well as, "What can
he do?" Many studies of reading interests and preferences have
been made. For example, Norvell's study of 24,000 children revealed that children do not like what adults think they should or
do enjoy.[5] One problem with this study was that there was no investigation of the literature available to the children. Kindergarten children studied by Cappa responded by asking to hear
the story again, by looking at the book, or through creative activities.[6] Interests of boys in grades four through six were obtained through interviews by Starchfield.[7] We do have evidence
regarding content interests according to age and sex. Interests in
poetry have been investigated by Mackintosh in 1932,[8] Kyte in
1947,[9] and recently by Pittmann.[10] In these studies, children
selected favorite poems among those read by the teacher. Wells
found that adolescents' preferences for humorous literature were
influenced by cultural level.[11] In schools having a higher cultural
level, satire and whimsy received greater appreciation. Absurdity
ranked first, slapstick second, satire third, and whimsy fourth.
Gaver developed measures for studying effectiveness of centralized library service.[12] Sixth graders maintained complete reading
records for nearly four months. Concerned with quality, I developed an instrument to determine levels of maturity in reading.

Further Questions

There have been few, if any, longitudinal studies of reading interests and attitudes. What will be the effect of the libraries made
possible by federal funds? What are the opportunities for respond-

ing to literature? How do differences in these opportunities affect attitudes and interests? What would be the effect of more cooperative planning of the school librarian and public librarian? What teaching strategies will create a more open response toward varied types of literature? What poems will children select, read to the class, and memorize when given an opportunity to read from many sources?

These are questions to be investigated about groups. Each teacher and each librarian must be concerned with study of the unique patterns of interest of each reader. What records can be maintained easily? What information about reading and listening experiences should become part of the cumulative record? How shall this information guide their work with boys and girls?

Emotional, Imaginative Response

The Children Respond

The internal response as the child interacts with visual and auditory symbols may be reflected in overt behavior, or it may be recalled through introspection. Yet, introspection cannot be considered a true account of the process. These responses illustrate behaviors that reflect emotional response:

"Oh!"—on a rising note of surprise as second graders see the picture of Tico's golden wings. Surprise, joy, beauty are surmised.

"Read it again!" after hearing, "Once there was an elephant/ who tried to use the telephant/ . . ."

"I cried when Biddy died—She was so wonderful . . . And I really liked Peter," says a child after reading *Mountain Born* by Yates. However, it was the unspoken word, the look of mutual understanding that passed between teacher and pupil that reflected the deeper satisfaction.

"I want to read you this poem—not the class, just you," announced the child who wanted to share McCord's *This is My Rock*.

"It was awful—just terrible when they were beating the greyhound," reported a nine-year-old who reflected some of his horror. Yet he liked the book and commented he felt he had really read a "grown-up" book now.

——. This space can only indicate the sudden intake of breath when a nine-year-old turned a page of *In a Spring Garden* to experience the glowing color of Keats's background for the poem by Issa, "Just simply alive,/ Both of us, I/ And the poppy/ . . ."

"Listen now, I want to tell you about this book, *Island of the Blue Dolphins*. How many have read it? I've read it three times. It's well, sort of a girl's book, but not really. Well, do you *know* about it, what it *really means?*" The fourth grader continued to discuss the plot, characterization, and theme of a book that had deep significance to him.

Evidence of Research

Varied methods have been used to identify and measure emotional response to literature. Hruza used a galvanometer and a pneumograph to note changes as college students listened to fifteen poems.[13] However, introspection indicated some subjects who showed large galvanic reactions were unaware of emotional reaction. This study also showed there was a greater reaction when the subject matter was related to personal experience. Broom also used a galvanometer to determine emotional reactions to specific words.[14] Other investigators attempted to identify responses through recall of feelings experienced as a selection was heard or read. Valentine asked graduate students to recall the degrees of pleasure, imagery, and details experienced while hearing poetry.[15] He found that imagery or a deliberate attempt to create a visual image may interfere with pleasure. Letton also used the retrospective-verbalization technique in a study of ninth graders' oral reports of their thoughts during reading of poetry.[16] After telling what he thought as he read, the student was asked to look at "thought units" from the poems and tell what he thought about and felt when reading that part of the poem. In 1935, Pooley urged that measures of appreciation be devised and noted that "any measuring instrument which rests exclusively upon the student's ability to identify and explain the sources of appreciation without first measuring his inarticulate sensitivity to them is not a valid test."[17] Indeed it is this "inarticulate sensitivity" that has been neglected. Perhaps the work of Hess in measuring dilation and constriction of the pupil of the eye will give a method for study of inner responses.[18]

The effect of the child's stage of development has been explored by Peller.[19] She suggested the importance of literature that supports daydreams for both boys and girls in the latency stage and believed that sex differences are of great importance. Loban's study of social sensitivity among adolescents revealed that the reader tended to identify with the character most like himself.[20]

An example of a study of overt responses of two- to four-year-olds as they listened to stories was made by Smith.[21] Such behavior as laughter, smiling, nodding approval, and annoyance behavior was checked.

There are descriptive accounts but scant research in the area of bibliotherapy.

Collier and Gaier have published reports of investigations of college students' childhood preferences for literature.[22] Cultural and sex roles are apparently influential factors, and literature may affect acceptance of role. Very little is known about the relationship of literature and psychological development. Peller suggested that a child may have a crucial experience through a daydream in a story at a time when he is under stress.[23]

Needed Research

Perhaps our first concern should be that teachers become more aware of emotional responses to literature and provide opportunities for the child to express his feelings in an atmosphere of "psychological safety." We need to know more about the nature of the experience of literature. What occurs in the process of "identification" with a character? What factors lead to empathy, imagination, identification? What is the relation of self-concept to imaginative response?

Responses of Understanding and Insight

Literal comprehension is not essential for response to sensory images, rhythm, or rhyme; perhaps some readers feel they "stand in the shoes" of a character without fully comprehending the situation. However, literal comprehension is the foundation for understanding implied meanings and for perception of relationships. As children gain insight into man's relationships with nature, with other men, and with the supernatural, they gain self-knowledge. There is a very close relationship of the cognitive and affective responses as values are internalized and as understanding of the human condition is applied to life experience.

Children's Responses

The following excerpts are from tape recordings of group and individual discussions of books. Frequently, we can see the child fumbling for words to cage fledgling thoughts: "I just didn't know what it would be like to be deaf. David was lost and he couldn't even tell anybody." The ten-year-old had gained insight into problems of a deaf person through reading *David in Silence* by Robinson. "I think Swimmy had to change, you know, he had to swim slower to be the eye. And I think he worried about, well, some little fish might not stay in that place . . . and, uh, it wouldn't be easy." A second grader was perceiving some problems of leadership as he reflected upon *Swimmy* by Lionni. A sixth grader was thinking through the implications of *Harriet the Spy* by Fitzhugh. "No, Harriet wasn't exactly like anybody I know. Who would need a nurse at her age? And in most schools I think you'd have to do your homework instead of writing. But I know about, well, like telling the truth, even if it makes people mad, and . . . some kids are like that, well—before you learn, and it's, well, hard to decide." In another discussion, of Holm's *North to Freedom,* the same reader said: "David shouldn't have told the younger children about things being so awful—like you can't trust people . . . and, well, that things are bad. They'll find out, but, like—if I told Laurie about awful things, she'd never go to play, maybe—or she'd be afraid."

Findings from Research

To assess children's understandings of literal and implied meanings we can utilize reading-comprehension tests and vocabulary tests, but there is a need for instruments to measure literary meanings. Garrison and Thomas asked sixth graders to write what they thought a poem was about after hearing it read.[24] They found a significant relationship between vocabulary ability and discovery of theme, reader participation, and sensory imagery. Weekes presented forty-one poems in original and simplified versions to 421 sixth graders.[25] Figurative language presented more difficulty than "involved sentence structure." She found that actual experience could be a favorable or unfavorable factor in understanding the poem. Foreman held the view that basic appreciation is "a concept of the reality and humanness of the characters in a story: the awareness of story purpose and trend; the pictures which are stimulated by the author's description and completed through the child's experience."[26] The interview method was used to determine meanings seventh graders obtained from excerpts from three prose selections. He developed scales to classify responses to such questions as, "If you were going to paint a picture, what would you put in? Were there any people you would like to know or be with?" In Skelton's study of intermediate-grade children's interpretations of poems, 49 percent of the responses were denotative interpretations and 35 percent were meanings "read into" the poem.[27] Most of the children did not go beyond reporting of the details of the four poems read to them.

Tests were developed by Logasa and McCoy to determine high school students' ability to discover themes in poetry. A test of literary comprehension and appreciation is available for high school students.[28] The studies of critical reading underway at Ohio State University[29] will provide some instruments that should prove useful.

Further Questions

Most of the investigations have used poetry or excerpts from longer works. We need to study meanings children derive from total works. What selections are appropriate for a measure of literary understandings? When a child returns to a selection in a year or two years, what additional insights will be evident? What is the effect of wide reading upon discovery or understanding of themes? Do particular teaching strategies result in higher levels of insight?

Responses to Literature as a Discipline

The child's reaction to a specific selection is influenced by his knowledge of literature, authors and illustrators, genre, the craft of writing, and criteria for evaluation. Each discipline does have its mode of inquiry, but in literature there is no one "method of literary study."

Responses of Children

The following examples of children's responses indicate the beginning of awareness that each selection is a part of a larger body of literature: "This is a fantasy," announced a third-grade reviewer of *The Borrowers Aloft* by Norton. He was implying certain expectations and criteria in recognizing the literary genre. When a large poster copy of the poem, *Brooms,* was displayed with the poet's name, second graders expressed interest, "Oh, Dorothy Aldis! We know her poems." Familiarity with the poet established a "set" for the new poem. Upon hearing *Baba Yaga,* by Small, a seven-year-old said, "It's like Hansel and Gretel—you know, the children in the oven, and the pot in this story." To the question, "What are you reading today?" Lissa replied, "A Nancy Drew—oh, I know it really isn't good writing—but it's fun, and everybody else reads Nancy Drew." Lissa was aware of criteria as we discussed Nancy Drew plots and characterization, but she also wanted to be accepted by her peers. "I know why the South Wind has to be the baker—because a south wind is warm—and he says 'bites' because the north wind bites your fingers." A second grader volunteered this response to Lindsay's, *The Moon's the North Wind's Cooky.* "This book isn't as good as *The Loner,*" remarked the ten-year-old who had just read Wier's new book, *Easy Does It.* His reasons for the statement were supported by evidence. A critic of *The Spider Plant* by Speevack commented, "It just wouldn't be that way. I don't think everybody would come to the play—they just wouldn't suddenly start being nice." These kinds of responses include what has been called critical reading. The reader separates fact from fiction, draws inferences, recognizes the author's point of view. He evaluates structure of plot, validity of theme, authenticity of setting, depth and realism of characterization, use of figurative language. His awareness of the form and arrangement of symbols in creating the total effect is a part of this kind of response to literature.

Evidence from Research

In the thirties there was a surge of interest in testing "appreciation" of literature. To many of the investigators, appreciation was considered recognition of merit. Carroll's high school subjects were asked to rate prose selection,[30] and Speer's sixth graders ranked poetry according to merit.[31] Howells and Johnson devised a test in which high school pupils selected a line of poetry that most nearly fitted the poem.[32] A test designed by Eppel also asked pupils to select the best line of poetry when one was omitted.[33] In Burton's short-story test three possible endings were presented for student selection.[34] The Logasa-McCoy tests attempted to assess ability to identify rhythm and trite and fresh expressions, for example. Very little attention has been given the problem of assessing the elementary school child's knowledge or awareness of types of literature, sound effects of language, metaphor, plot structure, or characterization.

Huus presented a summary of research related to development of taste in literature in the elementary school.[35] However, many articles cited were descriptive accounts; the majority of the studies were old; there were very few investigations of children in primary grades.

Problems for Investigation

At the present time we do not know what knowledge of literature children possess at the end of elementary school, or at different age levels. What criteria do children use in evaluating the prose and poetry they encounter? What *can* they learn about modes of inquiry? This question should be followed by the question, What *should* they learn about the process of literary criticism in the elementary school? How can a local school system establish guidelines in terms of "standard literary works" children should know, yet provide the flexibility needed for special group and individual needs? An example of a kind of question facing the curriculum makers is that of biblical literature; if children are to be familiar with the body of literature, with literary allusions, should Bible stories be included in the program? What materials could be used?

How children express awareness of literary style is another kind of question. Before an analysis of teaching materials and methods can be made, it will be necessary to develop instruments to assess such responses. At the present time a committee of the National Council of Teachers of English is developing one instrument. Challenged to develop a paper-pencil instrument for grades four to six, the committee has faced the problems of identifying and limiting kinds of responses that could be assessed in this way. We need to know, for example, how responses differ when the selection is read silently by the child and when he hears it read aloud by the teacher. What selections are appropriate for such an instrument? What cues or activities will elicit children's understanding of a selection and their sensitivity to the ways in which the total effect was created by the writer?

Responses to Literature in the
Child's Creative Work

A fourth category of response to literature is the response evidenced in the child's own creative work. The experience of literature becomes part of the child's resources for communicating *his* responses to his environment.

Examples of Children's
Responses

"Creative work" as viewed in this context does not have to be a tangible product. There is creativity in discussion, for example, when children make comparisons, evaluate, and juxtapose ideas in new relationships. Recordings could be analyzed to identify this type of creativity, but the following examples reflect ways literature may become a catalyst for tangible creative endeavors: "I made a hat like Jennie's," said a first grader as she displayed a creation of her own after hearing Keats's story, *Jennie's Hat*. "Once upon a time in a faraway land . . ." begins a child's story patterned after the folk tales he had heard. "Now you're Robin Hood, and I'm Little John," the director of a backyard dramatic play was overheard to say. "Beyond the fence is Sherwood Forest . . ." "This is a haiku poem I wrote. Can you help me make it sound better in the last line?" requests a sixth grader. In a letter to Taro Yashima, "I think you know just how it is to be a lonely little girl."

Needed Research

To respond to literature with deeper awareness, children need to experience the problems and pleasures of attempting to communicate their experiences. In this paper, we can neither explore nor summarize the research related to creativity. It should be noted that the University of Nebraska curriculum project has been concerned, in part, with the effect of literature upon composition. Further studies of children's writing, painting, and dramatizations are needed to identify responses related to experience with literature.

Teachers and Librarians as
Evaluators

Teachers and librarians have always evaluated children's responses to literature in informal ways. Perhaps they have been satisfied to enjoy the comradely glow when a child finds pleasure in a book they enjoyed. They are happy when they observe good readers seeking and discovering "the realms of gold" in literature. Seldom have there been attempts to discover why some children reach out, why others who can read just as well do not really enter the world of books.

Teachers and librarians do not need to wait for the psychologists and educators to present research. In recent years the concept of "action research" has been neglected, but this approach is needed more than ever before. Librarians and classroom teachers can work together to evaluate the various components of appreciation. They can develop and maintain cumulative records of children's reading interests. They can maintain anecdotal records of the child's use of literary models or allusions to literature in his own writing. Analysis could be made of oral and written book reviews at different times during the year. Records can be made of overt responses as a child reads. Anecdotes could include introspective comments as "I know how it feels," "I have done this." Time can be planned for conferences and small-group discussions so that there is opportunity to listen to the child's interpretation of a book. As instruments become available to aid them in gathering evidence about pupil behavior, teachers can use such instruments with wisdom, just as they use intelligence tests, achievement tests, and sociograms to aid in understanding the whole child. The process of evaluation of children's responses to literature must gain priority among the present professional tasks if the school is to plan the kind of literature program needed to prepare the adults of the twenty-first century.

Notes

1. Charles Schulz. *Peanuts*. United Features Syndicate, Inc.

2. Jean Little. *Home From Far*. Boston: Little, Brown & Co., 1965, p. 81.

3. Harold G. Shane and E. T. McSwain. *Evaluation and the Elementary Curriculum*. Revised edition. New York: Henry Holt & Co., 1958, p. 60.

4. David R. Krathwohl, Benjamin S. Bloom, and Bertram B. Masia. *Taxonomy of Educational Objectives. The Classification of Educational Goals. Handbook II: Affective Domain*. New York: David McKay Co., 1956, p. 16.

5. George W. Norvell. *What Boys and Girls Like to Read*. Morristown, N.J.: Silver-Burdett Co., 1958.

6. Dan Cappa, "Kindergarten Children's Responses to Storybooks Read by Teachers." *Journal of Educational Research* 52 (October 1958):75.

7. Jo M. Stanchfield. "Boys' Reading Interests as Revealed through Personal Conferences." *Reading Teacher* 16 (September 1962):41–44.

8. Helen K. Mackintosh. "A Critical Study of Children's Choices in Poetry." *University of Iowa Studies in Education* 7, no. 4 (1932).

9. George C. Kyte. "Children's Reactions to Fifty Selected Poems." *Elementary School Journal* 47 (February 1947):331–39.

10. Grace Pittman. "Young Children Enjoy Poetry." *Elementary English* 43 (January 1966):56–59.

11. Ruth E. Wells. "A Study of Taste in Humorous Literature among Pupils of Junior and Senior High Schools." *Journal of Educational Research* 28 (October 1934):81–91.

12. Mary Virginia Gaver. *Effectiveness of Centralized Library Service in Elementary Schools (Phase I)* New Brunswick, N.J.: Rutgers University, Graduate School of Library Service, 1960. Report of the research study conducted at Rutgers University under contract no. 489, SAE-8132 with the U.S. Office of Education.

13. Thelma E. Hruza. "An Investigation of Some Factors in the Appreciation of Poetry." Unpublished Ph.D. dissertation, George Peabody College for Teachers, 1940.

14. M. E. Brown. "A Study of Literature Appreciation." *Journal of Applied Psychology* 18 (1954):357–63.

15. C. W. Valentine. "The Function of Images in the Appreciation of Poetry." *British Journal of Psychology* 14 (October 1923):164–91.

16. Mildred C. Letton. "Individual Differences in Interpretive Responses in Reading Poetry at the Ninth Grade Level." Unpublished Ph.D. dissertation, University of Chicago, 1958.

17. Robert C. Pooley. "Measuring the Appreciation of Literature." *English Journal* 24 (October 1935):631.

18. Eckhard H. Hess. "Attitude and Pupil Size." *Scientific American* 212 (April 1965):46–65.

19. Lili E. Peller. "Daydreams and Children's Favorite Books." In *The Causes of Behavior: Readings in Child Development and Educational Psychology,* edited by J. F. Rosenblith and Wesley Allinsmith. Boston: Allyn & Bacon, 1962, pp. 405–11.

20. Walter Loban. "A Study of Social Sensitivity (Sympathy) among Adolescents." *Journal of Educational Psychology* 44 (February 1953):102–12.

21. Lois Z. Smith. "Experimental Investigation of Young Children's Interest and Expressive Behavior Responses to Single Statement, Verbal Repetition, and Ideational Repetition of Content in Animal Stories." *Child Development* 1 (March 1930):247–54.

22. Mary J. Collier and Eugene I. Gaier. "Adult Reactions to Preferred Childhood Stories." *Child Development* 29 (March 1958):97–103.

23. Lili E. Peller. "Reading and Daydreams in Latency, Boy-Girl Differences." *Journal of the American Psychoanalytic Association* 6 (January 1958):57–70.

24. K. C. Garrison and M. Thomas. "A Study of Some Literature Appreciation Abilities as They Relate to Certain Vocabulary Abilities." *Journal of Educational Research* 22 (December 1930):396–99.

25. Blanche E. Weekes. "The Influence of Meaning on Children's Choices of Poetry." *Contributions to Education* no. 354. New York: Teachers College, Columbia University, 1929.

26. Earl R. Foreman. "An Instrument To Evaluate the Literary Appreciation of Adolescence." Unpublished Ph.D. dissertation, University of Illinois, 1951, p. 4.

27. Glenn Skelton. "A Study of Responses to Selected Poems in the Fourth, Fifth, and Sixth Grades." Unpublished Ph.D. dissertation, University of California, Berkeley, 1963.

28. Mary Willis and H. A. Domincovich. *Cooperative Literary and Appreciation Test.* Princeton, N.J.: Educational Testing Service, 1943.

29. Charlotte Huck, Martha King, Beatrice Ellinger, and Willavene Wolfe. "The Critical Reading Ability of Elementary School Children." U.S. Office of Education Project OE 2612. Columbus, Ohio: The Ohio State University, in progress.

30. Herbert A. Carroll. "A Method of Measuring Prose Appreciation." *English Journal* 22 (March 1933):184–89.

31. Robert K. Speer. "Measurement of Appreciation in Poetry, Prose and Art and Studies in Appreciation." *Contributions to Education,* no. 362. New York: Teachers College, Columbia University, 1929.

32. Thomas H. Howells and A. A. Johnson. "A Study of Metre-Sense in Poetry." *Journal of Applied Psychology* 15 (1931):539–44.

33. E. M. Eppel. "A New Test of Poetry Discrimination." *British Journal of Educational Psychology* 20 (June 1950):111–16.

34. Dwight L. Burton. "The Relationship of Literary Appreciation to Certain Measurable Factors." *Journal of Educational Psychology* 43 (November 1952):436–39.

35. Helen Huus. "Development of Taste in Literature in the Elementary Grades." *Development of Taste in Literature.* Champaign, Ill.: National Council of Teachers of English, 1962.

Materials designed to teach reading, once confined solely to narrative, now include expository or informational selections. The need for the change is stressed by Cameron. More than that, we should consider contrasting strategies for reading informational as opposed to imaginative selections. Do you agree?

Read Critically — or Join the Mob

JACK R. CAMERON

Perhaps the most emphasized aim of reading education in the schools is to develop "lifetime readers," a phrase which in the minds of the general public and most teachers is interpreted to mean readers of imaginative literature. A Lifetime Reader is a person who, in short, is "at home with books." The rest of the picture is easy to fill in: soft, cushioned chairs, a cozy fireplace, rain on the roof, perhaps an old dog asleep on the carpet, and a hot drink close at hand. Ah, the joys of a Lifetime Reader!

The trouble is that this popular image of reading is a sentimentalized and narrow view of what lifetime reading is really all about. It is an image that is very deep-rooted in our society, and a dangerous image in the big-business, big-government, mass-media age in which people are going to become increasingly involved, and perhaps lost, in the years ahead.

To make clear why this sentimentalized view of reading is dangerous, we should distinguish between two quite different kinds of reading: *informational* and *imaginative*. Obviously, informational reading involves factual prose containing ideas, opinions, judgments; whereas imaginative reading encompasses literature, with its emphasis on narrative, character, mood and emotion. A primary objective of any reading program should be to point out to the student the differences between these two types, the dangers of confusing them, and the need to adapt one's mental set to the kind of material to be read. Reading education in the public schools has concentrated on turning out readers of imaginative literature and has neglected training in informational reading.

In reading informational material, one is expected to be as objective as possible. The emotions are supposed to be under firm control. The reader is analytical, dispassionate, reserved. In imaginative reading, on the other hand, no such objectivity or reserve is necessary; in fact, the reader is expected to let himself go emotionally and to react strongly.

It should be apparent that to *confuse* the different emphases of informational and imaginative reading can be a bad mistake. Unfortunately, such confusion is perhaps the most common reading failure in society as a whole. A frighteningly large percentage of people today fail to make the necessary mental adjustment in moving from fictional to factual prose; they fail to click their mental dials. Their public school education has not stressed the difference between reading that demands emotional *release* and reading that demands emotional *reserve*. People generally have static reading habits, approaching most of their reading with their emotional barriers lowered. As a result, they read virtually everything as if they were reading fiction.

There are two immediate results of this lack of emotional control. First, if what is written fits their prejudices, or agrees with their preconceived notions, they do not read it critically. They simply purr quietly while the author strokes them with opinions; they are not interested in seeking new insights or modifying old biases, but only in reinforcing what they already believe. The second manifestation of this lack of emotional control appears when they read something that does not reinforce their prejudices but rather challenges or contradicts them. Then they read with excessive attention to the smallest details in a constant search for weaknesses. In such cases they are reading only negatively, not sincerely seeking information or new points of view, but only for purposes of criticism and attack.

Since the mass media often encourage people to react at the emotional level to the spoken and written word, the schools must do more to train young people to resist such influences. It is fashionable these days to quote Marshall McLuhan; in the lexical smog of his *Understanding Media* appears this statement: "Just as we now try to control atomic-bomb fallout, so we will try to control media fallout. Education will become recognized as civil defense against media fallout." The daily papers, which the graduates of the schools will read more regularly than any other print medium, cannot be approached with the mental attitude appropriate to a short story. If students finish their schooling as enthusiastic and chronic readers of quality literature, and yet are incapable of reading critically when they pick up the evening paper, then their education has largely been a failure.

That the schools have not succeeded in instilling a critical habit of mind is apparent in the tendency of most people to have firm opinions on most of the major issues of the day. Anyone asked about Vietnam or socialized medicine or race riots or religion in the schools or capital punishment or marijuana or fluoridation is expected to have a clear point of view which he is prepared to defend. It is not popular nowadays to reserve judgment, to hold tentative or qualified opinions, to confess that enough evidence is not available. Such unpolarized thinking is dismissed as wishy-washy neutrality, or fence-sitting. After all, it is always more exciting over coffee or cocktails to run head-on into someone who either fully agrees or fully disagrees with one's own views. The man who doesn't hold his opinions too strongly, and who is willing to concede something on the other side, is not much fun at all.

Since readers are not robots, they cannot totally submerge

their emotional reactions. But reading education in all subjects can do a great deal more to train students to avoid the worst pitfalls of uncritical reading. Teachers can spend less time sentimentalizing about the lifetime-reading habit, and more time preparing young people to resist the lure of mob thinking. There is something in all of us that wants to join a mob; something that tempts us to let the emotions take over the function of the intellect.

The chief job of reading education in an age of media fallout is not to train people to read novels in front of a fire, attractive as such a prospect might be, but to make them critical readers in a world where emotional reading at the wrong time can amount to joining the mob rather than resisting it and will, in the long run, enslave a man rather than set him free.

> If reading is to be a pleasurable experience, then shouldn't reading materials be about pleasurable experiences? Not always, suggests this authority. Not when the response is, "I could have died from bore."

Baby Dolls Are Gone

NANCY LARRICK

If we are to develop lifetime readers among our children, I think we must recognize how our social and economic revolution is affecting our youngsters and what this means to the teaching of reading.

It is a truism to say that we are living in a time of world revolution. We see its most brutal manifestations in such places as Vietnam, Nigeria, Detroit, and even Cambridge, Maryland. Prolonged rioting on our city streets and accompanying police brutality are symptoms of the social revolution in which we live. Children are a part of this, and as a result the whole pattern of their reading is changing—their sense of need, their sense of values, and their taste in books.

The political, economic, and social chaos of our world was analyzed by Max Lerner in an address to students at the University of Florida. He described Five Revolutions in American Life: The Revolution of Weapons-Technology which has hurled us into the Age of Overkill; the Revolution of Access as dramatized in our civil rights movement; the Uprooting Revolution — uprooting from rural communities, from neighborhood solidarity, from religious commitments, from the cohesive family to inner-city despair and protest; the Revolution of Cultural and Intellectual Explosions which have brought us more art museums, more symphonies, more school libraries, and — of special interest to us today — more children's books in both hardcover and paperback. The fifth he calls the Time and Values Revolution, springing from automation and its release of time for deeper involvement in work and play.

Of the five, the Revolution of Access has thus far had the greatest immediate impact on our children and their schools. For, as minority groups (both adults and children) have marched and protested, as they have been attacked by cattle prods, tear gas, and machine guns, as they have been jailed in lots of a hundred or more at a clip, they have dramatized not only the inequities of educational opportunity for minority groups but the shoddiness of the education we provide for millions of our children. Negro protests have shown us that we have educationally disadvantaged children of all races and all economic levels — many of them children who have been uprooted, children who can no longer derive status from their families, children who find themselves labeled failures at school and who develop a feeling of utter hopelessness about themselves. Many of these become children who hate. And as Fritz Redl puts it, "Children who hate are the children who are hated."

One child in six in our country attends public school in the nation's 16 largest cities where schools, for the most part, are in the slums. Sixty-five percent of American Negroes live in urban areas. Of these, 80 percent are in the worst of the inner slums. Desegregation has barely touched these schools. In Chicago, for example, 90 percent of the Negro elementary school children attend schools which have at least 90 percent Negro enrollment.

These children — and their parents and neighbors — are part of the army of the disadvantaged — an army that is not only growing in numbers, but is becoming more and more disadvantaged with each passing year. The complexities of our labor market have created unemployment or, at best, marginal living for vast numbers of our population. When we are told that in the past six years 3000 new job classifications have been added to the roster of vocational openings, we can see what is happening to the would-be-wage-earner with only minimal education and training. For the person who finds it difficult to qualify for jobs which he grew up with, the jobs of the Age of Automation are baffling, if not defeating. So far, our efforts to fight a war on poverty at home have made no appreciable difference. Children who gained through the first summer of the Head Start program have slipped back to their old place in classrooms with poor teachers. It is not surprising that the children of the disadvantaged are rarely the ones who succeed in school.

Yet when we compare the interests of these children with those of their classmates, we find great similarity. Most children choose the same radio and television programs. They turn to books about the same subjects. They know the same TV singing commercials, not the Mother Goose rhymes and songs some of us grew up with. Often they have the same array of facts about such subjects as space travel, jet planes, knives, guns, war, and jazz.

Our Oral-Language Culture

These are children who have grown up in an oral-language culture—the first since Gutenberg froze language on the printed page. They get words by ear that their parents never heard of as children: words like *astronaut, penicillin, orbit, automation, pentagon,* and dozens more.

Even more important, they are attuned to the rhythm of oral language—to the strung-out sentences which mark our casual speech and the studied informality of TV jargon. They listen to the sounds of radio and television language for five or six hours a day; a harsh, dramatic language which is marked by little that is beautiful or contemplative.

The programs our children watch are largely the ones planned for adults and are packed with violence. In adult newspapers and photo magazines children follow the pictures as eagerly as their parents.

And what do they see? A dead Vietcong dragged through the street by a rope behind a U.S. personnel carrier (photo courtesy of the *Washington Post*); a Congolese rebel being stomped to death by soldiers (photo courtesy of the *AP*); or the blood-drenched room in Chicago where eight student nurses were slain a year ago (courtesy of the *UPI*).

It's really no wonder, then, that the toy department of the typical discount center features weapons of all kinds—knives, guns, hand grenades, bombs and bomb sites, along with innumerable games labeled "Terrifying," "Shocking," "Monstrous," and "Hair-raising." For your bike there is a "Lurid Monster Plaque" complete with red reflectors. And for the do-it-yourself child, there is a Creeple-Peeple set with which to make your own monsters or human deviates.

In the doll department, baby dolls are gone. In their place we find the aisles lined with miniature teenagers of the Barbie type, with bangle earrings, high heels, bras, and bikinis. It's a very grown-up world our children play in with their toys—and not one that we can call beautiful, creative, or inspiring in any sense.

In their interests and often in their behavior, our elementary school children are more adolescent than childlike. As Dr. Arthur Pearl of the University of Oregon put it, "If Booth Tarkington were to write *Seventeen* today, he'd have to change the title to *Twelve*."

Even our 12-year-olds seem to have more problems to cope with than the hero and heroine of *Seventeen,* and a greater inclination to cope. Many of them are reaching out for more serious books, for example, than their predecessors. *The Diary of Anne Frank* and *Death Be Not Proud* have become standard sixth- and seventh-grade favorites nowadays. *Lord of the Flies, To Kill a Mockingbird,* and *Catcher in the Rye* are widely read in junior high school—not because they are recommended by teachers and librarians (because they are not), but because the children's grapevine tells them to read these books. And because the crises—the bitter issues—of these books are close to the experience of young readers.

Even four- and five-year-olds are showing the same fascination with books that touch upon the conflicts that are crucial to them. Claudia Lewis of the Bank Street College of Education reports that disadvantaged four- and five-year-olds in New York respond eagerly to Charlotte Zolotow's *The Quarreling Book*. This is a book about quarreling people and angry feeling—just what these children know and can identify with. It is a book about their world and, hence, one to be listened to.

In Detroit, Dr. Daniel Fader and his associates launched a
reading experiment in the Maxey School for Boys — a rehabilitation center for boys who have had trouble with the law. Dr. Fader
opened a paperback library of 1200 titles carefully selected by
adults who thought they knew what these boys would want. More
than half of these books never left the shelves. But some of the
others circulated like mad. Boys who had never read before were
borrowing, and then buying such titles as *Black Like Me, Sex and
the Adolescent, Prison Nurse, The Mad Sampler, 100 Years of
Lynchings, Native Son, Of Mice and Men,* and the *Pro Football
Handbook.* Lush and lusty, violent, even brutal, they are the
utter antithesis of most of those school-recommended books
which one of the Maxey boys dismissed with the pronouncement,
"I could have died from bore."

No one ever "died from bore" when reading James Baldwin,
Ian Fleming, Irving Wallace, and Kyle Onstott. Those teenagers
who do read them may go on to a better understanding of themselves and their world.

From the disadvantaged four-year-olds who choose *The Quarreling Book* as their favorite, and the unruly teenagers who
choose *Black Like Me* or *Native Son* to avoid dying from bore, we
can learn a great deal about those millions of youngsters who do
not fit into either extreme. Advantaged and disadvantaged — preschool or teenage — our youngsters reflect the passion of our
times for that which is bold, strong, vigorous — even violent and
terrifying.

It should not have surprised us, then, when very young children embraced Maurice Sendak's *Where the Wild Things Are.*
Some of their parents and grandparents protested that these
are ugly monsters, unfit for children to see. But remember those
TV monsters the children are watching, those make-your-own-
monster sets in the discount house. Sendak shows a touch of his
own make-a-monster genius, all right, but the antics and the
lilting phrases of his monsters are close to poetry. No wonder that
children like to chant the words of the text

> . . . his ceiling hung with vines
> and the walls became the world all around.

You see this kind of boldness in the theme and art of many of
our newer and more popular books for children. Note the most
recent winner of the Caldecott Award — *Sam, Bangs and Moon-*

shine by Evaline Ness. The situation is fraught with problems: Sam, short for Samantha, is the only daughter of a fisherman who warns against her reckless habit of lying. "Stick to real talk, not *moonshine*," he says.

Sam said her mother was a mermaid, when everyone knew she was dead. When Thomas arrives one day, Sam sends him off to see the mermaid mother in a cave beyond Blue Rock. A storm comes up—one big enough to cover Blue Rock. The air is heavy with violence and impending tragedy.

This is a book that is as bold as it is beautiful. The author doesn't hesitate to say that Sam is lying, although her predecessors of an earlier generation would have called it imagination. Children understand lying better, I believe, but adults talk around the word.

Evaline Ness is bold in her art, too. Sam is shown in muted tones of gray, a strange gray-green, what someone called off-khaki. Her hair is uncombed, her clothes ill fitting, her shoes too heavy for a child. Her face is most expressive when she is troubled —and then such utter misery with only a few gray lines and a bit of the gray-green sponged on!

Tragedy never seemed so close in the earlier picture books for children. Children never seemed so real as Sam, who might be any youngster seeking escape from the loneliness of her life. Children love this book, and I think it is because it is in tune with the needs of today's children.

Fortunately, we have many writers and artists who are operating on today's wave length. They are facing up to the critical issues and the anxieties which beset our children, and they are presenting them in books that youngsters read avidly, once they have a chance.

The Empty Schoolhouse by Natalie Savage Carlson is one of these books. The story is told in all the words of 14-year-old Emma Royall, whose younger sister Lullah is the first Negro to be admitted to St. Joseph's Parochial School of French Grove, Louisiana. When Lullah enrolls, the white children begin to drop out. Abusive phone calls flash through town and the school is bombed. Librarians tell me that Negro children with only second- and third-grade reading skills tackle this book and read eagerly.

Now we have *The Jazz Man* by Mary Hays Weik, the story of a lame Negro boy transplanted from the South to Harlem, where his father's unemployment and mounting strife in the family lead to the boy's being deserted. This is a harsh little drama, but a beautiful one, played against the background of music from the neighboring apartment where the Jazz Man and his friends tear the air with their melodies.

In *Durango Street*, Frank Bonham writes of a young Negro on probation from a rehabilitation center who is drawn into leadership in the gang warfare of Los Angeles where stealing, fighting, and shooting are the way of life. In *The Outsiders*, S. E. Hinton, a teenager herself, writes the story of a 14-year-old boy who lives in the slums with his two older brothers in the midst of bitter tension and extreme violence. These are youngsters who are trapped by their environment. Their audacity is a mask to hide their insecurity and fright. Their violent acts grow out of despair over the hopelessness of their lives and loyalty to those in the same predicament.

For older readers *Jazz Country* by Nat Hentoff tells of a white boy, almost intoxicated by jazz, who finds himself in an all-black world which he tries to penetrate in search of self-fulfillment through his music. The bitterness he encounters is the bitterness many young people feel because they have been rejected in the midst of a Revolution of Access.

Our children read such books eagerly and thoughtfully. They know the ugliness of city living, and they are attuned to the crackling tension of city slums. Fortunately we are getting more and more inner-city stories. Lois Lenski's *High-Rise Secret* is one of the newer ones. One of the most appealing is *Tomás Takes Charge* by Charlene Joy Talbot, the story of a 12-year-old Puerto Rican boy who must provide home, food, and consolation for his strangely withdrawn older sister when they are deserted by their father.

From England we have *The Greyhound,* a grimly realistic story of a lonely boy living in the slums of London. He befriends an old man who creeps out each day with his pedigreed greyhound. Finally Jamie inherits the dog, which he must hide because of his parents' violent objection to a pet. Subterfuge leads to desperation and finally to gang domination.

Again and again we meet this theme of a boy's struggle against unsympathetic parents. Not all are slum dwellers by any means. We find them in *Gentle Ben* by Walt Morey, the story of the lonely son of an Alaskan salmon fisherman. The boy has an Alaskan brown bear as his pet—the most vicious of all wild animals. The father, who resents the boy's pale and listless ways, panics at the thought of what the bear will do to his boy.

In *The Grizzly*, a father, who is a rigid, get-tough perfectionist, takes his 11-year-old son to the wilderness for a weekend of camping and fishing. The boy is terrified. For years his parents have been separated, and the boy remembers his father only as tough, taunting, brutal.

In all of these stories there is a strangely appealing search for understanding—the boy who tries to figure out the probation officer, the one who begins to see why his father is so tough, the one who lies his way into the hands of the police to protect his friend, the one who clings to the image of a successful Negro ball player. These are children of the revolution we are living in.

There is violence in these books—what else in a revolution? But there is tenderness, too. Not all of these young heroes achieve success or even the hope of it. But one cannot read about them without new insights into one's own thinking and new understanding of our social and economic crisis. This is what youngsters are living with. It is what many of them want to read about.

If we are to encourage children to read eagerly, I think we must be ready to help them explore books of all kinds, including those reflecting this period of revolution. It means that we must read constantly and widely ourselves, listening always to the recommendations of children and young people. I am convinced that the youngsters are ready.

Books Cited

Berg, Louis. *Prison Nurse*. New York: Bantam Books, 1963.

Bonham, Frank. *Durango Street*. New York: E. P. Dutton & Co., 1965.

Carlson, Natalie S. *The Empty Schoolhouse*. New York: Harper & Row, 1965.

Davis, Maxine. *Sex and the Adolescent*. New York: The Dial Press, 1958.

Frank, Anne. *The Diary of a Young Girl*. Garden City, N.Y.: Doubleday & Company, 1952.

Gaines, William M. *The Mad Sampler*. New York: The New American Library, 1965.

Ginzburg, Ralph. *100 Years of Lynchings*. New York: Lancer Books, 1962.

Golding, William. *Lord of the Flies*. New York: Coward-McCann, 1962.

Griffin, John H. *Black Like Me*. Boston: Houghton Mifflin Company, 1964.

Griffiths, Helen. *The Greyhound.* Garden City, N.Y.: Doubleday & Company, 1964.

Gunther, John. *Death Be Not Proud.* New York: Harper & Row, 1949.

Hentoff, Nat. *Jazz Country.* New York: Harper & Row, 1965.

Hinton, S. E. *The Outsiders.* New York: The Viking Press, 1967.

Johnson, A. & E. K. *The Grizzly.* New York: Harper & Row, 1965.

Lenski, Lois. *High-Rise Secret.* Philadelphia: J. B. Lippincott Co., 1966.

Lee, Harper. *To Kill a Mockingbird.* Philadelphia: J. B. Lippincott Co., 1960.

Morey, Walt. *Gentle Ben.* New York: E. P. Dutton & Co., 1965.

Ness, Evaline. *Sam, Bangs and Moonshine.* New York: Holt, Rinehart & Winston, 1966.

Salinger, J. D. *Catcher in the Rye.* Boston: Little, Brown and Company, 1951.

Sendak, Maurice. *Where the Wild Things Are.* New York: Harper & Row, 1963.

Steinbeck, John. *Of Mice and Men.* New York: Modern Library, 1937.

Talbot, Charlene J. *Tomás Takes Charge.* New York: Lothrop, Lee & Shephard Co., 1966.

Tarkington, Booth. *Seventeen.* New York: Harper & Row, 1916, 1962.

Weik, Mary Hays. *The Jazz Man.* New York: Atheneum Publishers, 1966.

Wright, Richard. *Native Son.* New York: Harper & Row, 1940.

Zanger, Jack. *Pro Football Handbook.* New York: Pocket Books, Division of Simon & Schuster, 1966.

Zolotow, Charlotte. *The Quarreling Book.* New York: Harper & Row, 1963.

At school age and beyond, the balm
of laughter can heal more readily
than the unguent of tears. Some
writers of children's literature are
especially skilled at arousing laughter. Here is an analysis of their appeal, complete with a host of fine
examples.

Humor in Children's Literature

DIANNE MONSON

Recently, when a sixth grader was brought to the office for help
in reading, the discussion about his reading interests indicated
that he had read most of the C. S. Lewis books. His comments
about the books were extremely intelligent and suggested a
strong interest in reading many kinds of books. He said that he
had just finished reading *Pippi Longstocking* for the third time
and that it had replaced *Henry Huggins* as his favorite book. He

volunteered the information that he liked both books because they made him laugh. He said, in fact, that he liked those books so well that he even enjoyed reading them aloud. Pressed for an explanation of that statement, he explained that he definitely did not like to read anything out loud; however, when a book made people laugh, the reading was worth it.

What are the qualities of humor that amuse? Are they easily definable? Perhaps not. It is likely that much laughter is undefined. A reader is aware of humor in a story but does not readily paraphrase it. Consider, for example, the poem "The Owl and the Pussycat." The poem may not seem to be a particularly humorous piece of literature. Some time ago, however, the *New Yorker* published a cartoon by Richter based on the poem. The picture was of two owls facing each other on a tree branch. And the caption read, "They're never getting me out in a pea-green boat with any pussycat!"[6] That cartoon puts the humor of the poem in focus, in a sense, and uncovers an element of incongruity not readily apparent to an unsophisticated reader.

It is easy to skirt the edge of interpretation when it comes to the discussion of humor. Children are asked whether they think a book is funny, but rarely are they asked to explain why the book is funny or how it is similar to another humorous book. An important aspect of reading instruction involves the analysis of certain characteristics in books which stimulate reader interest. Such work is sometimes treated as reading for interpretation, sometimes as reading for appreciation. Too often, it is not dealt with adequately. There seems to be growing emphasis on a skill-development program based on material which deemphasizes meaning. The crucial role of literature becomes clear if there is to be a counterbalance of attention to the higher comprehension abilities.

The Theory of Humor

If humor is to be considered as a basis for study, it is necessary to consider it in some structural arrangement. One of the most scholarly classifications of humor stimuli was published by Stephen Leacock.[4] His theory of humor is built on a superstructure which includes humor derived from words, ideas, situations, and characters. Each of the elements of humor suggested in the classification is clearly related to episodes in literature which cause laughter.

According to Leacock, the humor attributed to characters may arise from sympathetic appreciation of a predicament, or it may be based upon the misfortune of others. Such character humor is common in children's books. Laughter at a predicament is well defined in the "doughnut scene" from McCloskey's *Homer Price,* and laughter at the misfortune of others is evident in Lawson's *Mr. Revere and I.* Some character humor might be designated as an avenue of release from tension or as a vicarious way of showing dislike for enemies, as is evident in the laughter of one character at the expense of another. Leacock points to the humor in "exultation — the sense of personal triumph over one's adversary or sense of delight at seeing something demolished or knocked out of shape".[4] The burglar scene from *Pippi Longstocking* is a fine example of the laughter generated by release from tension. Pippi, alone in the world, is apprehended by two burglars while she is happily counting her gold. The reader, knowing that Pippi is a supergirl, feels some measure of confidence in her ability to take care of herself. Children will chuckle at small parts of the episode, but the real laughter comes when Pippi is really in trouble and quickly dispenses with the burglars by putting them, quite literally, on a shelf.

Another unit of the Leacock classification, the use of words as humor stimuli, has been the subject of many investigations. Freud considered adult humor to be mostly play on words, puns, and absurdities.[2] Other types of humor of words include repetition of words and alliteration, bad spelling and typographical errors, misuse of big words, faulty sentence structure, proper names altered to amusingly similar words, and satirical presentation.[4] There are some fairly obvious examples of humor of words in well-known children's books. The works of Kipling and Seuss abound with alliteration. Bad spelling is found in *Dorp Dead, Tom Sawyer,* and *Pippi Longstocking,* as well as many other books. One of the most recent characters to misuse big words is Jamie in Konigsburg's *From the Mixed-Up Files of Mrs. Basil E. Frankweiler.* A fine example of an altered name is the scene from *Mr. Popper's Penguins* in which Mr. Popper tries in vain to communicate with the people at the license bureau. As the confusion grows, Mr. Popper's name undergoes a number of changes, much to the delight of young readers. The humor of words is evident, at quite a different level, in the satirical presentations affected by the animal characters in Lawson's *Mr. Revere and I* and *Ben and Me.*

In addition to the humor of characterization and humor of words, Leacock identified the humor found in situations. He described such humor as "discomfiture, horseplay, incongruity, and confusion".[4] Sidis, in an analysis of humor, points out the laughter directed at a person or action that is ridiculed. He suggests also that humor frequently arises from surprise at the unexpected and deviation from the customary.[8] These elements of humor appear in books for people of all ages. The person familiar with a child's reactions to stories will recognize the surprise element as a favorite of most readers. Laughter as a form of ridicule is at once sophisticated and childish. Such humor often seems to serve as an outlet for inner feelings of insecurity. It is possible that an analysis of children's reactions to such situations might indicate the importance of laughter as a type of therapy. Consider, for example, the laughter stimuli in stories such as *A Pocketful of Cricket, Roosevelt Grady,* and *Pippi Longstocking.* The outstanding element may be surprise, but much of the laughter generated by surprise is actually laughter stemming from a release from tension.

There are many selections from children's literature pertinent to the category of humor labeled "situation humor." One passage which is an almost classic example of discomfiture and horseplay, both represented in the same episode, is from Farley Mowat's *Owls in the Family.* The reference is to the description of the "tailsqueeze game" in which Wol, the owl, patiently stalks the sleeping dog, Mutt, and sneaks up close enough to screech and squeeze Mutt's tail with his big claws. Mutt awakens, only to find Wol staring innocently at him from the top of a tree.

The scene from *Homer Price* in which the Super-Duper emerges, hurt and nearly weeping, from his wrecked auto is certainly a form of incongruity. So is the description given, in *Owls in the Family,* of Wol climbing a tree instead of flying to the top. As for the humor of confusion, one of the clearest and most enjoyable examples is the memorable bus scene in *Henry Huggins.*

Research on Humor in Literature

A look at book titles listed as favorites by children in grades three through six leaves little doubt as to the importance of humor. A third grade teacher studying the reading interests of children in her class reported that all of her third graders were able to find humor in books which she read to them, but many children did not find humor in books they read to themselves.[1] It is likely that both reading difficulty and group dynamics influenced the responses. Some of the books read to the children and enthusiastically recommended as funny were *Homer Price, Mr. Popper's Penguins, Mary Poppins, Pippi Longstocking,* and *Ben and Me.*

Many of the same titles appeared on a list of best-liked books in a 1965 survey of the reading of fourth and sixth graders.[2] Among the books best liked by fourth grade girls were *Pippi Longstocking, Henry Huggins,* and *Mary Poppins.* Books listed by fourth grade boys included *Pippi Longstocking, Henry Huggins, Tom Sawyer,* and *The Cat in the Hat.* One of the favorite books of sixth grade girls was *Pippi Longstocking.* The sixth grade boys liked *Tom Sawyer, Homer Price,* and *Henry Huggins.*

It is interesting to note the responses to books that are heavily loaded with humor. It is evident that *Pippi Longstocking* appeals to a wide age range and that *Tom Sawyer,* which appeared on best liked lists more than twenty years ago[10], is still well liked. In fact, as early as 1924, the companion book, *Huckleberry Finn,* appeared on a list of books best liked by boys.[11]

Although the appeal of a humorous book has been suggested by many contacts with children's reading, there have been few attempts to make in-depth studies of the specific characteristics which make books humorous to children. It is necessary, of course, to delineate the kinds of humor likely to be represented in books and to concentrate attention on those likely to be of interest to children.

One study, done with fifth graders, represented an attempt to learn what children found humorous about the books they read.[5] The writings of Stephen Leacock and others provided a basic structure of humor which included laughter at characters, surprising happenings, impossibility, play on words, and the ridiculous or incongruous situation. Some of the selections used in the study were from books appearing on the lists of books best liked by third, fourth, and sixth graders. The fifth graders read excerpts from *Pippi Longstocking, Charlotte's Web, Owls in the Family, The Cricket in Times Square,* and *Henry Huggins.* They judged each selection as "funny" or "not funny" and indicated the funniest sections of the excerpts.

All of the selections were enjoyed by a fairly sizable percentage of children questioned. It is not surprising to find that *Henry Huggins* received a great number of positive responses. Some of the answers to the question: What did you think was funny about the story, were: (1) when Henry and his dog got on the bus; (2) when the lady dropped her bag of apples; (3) when the fat man said, "Well, I'll be doggoned!"; and, (4) when Ribs started for the front of the bus and everything fell and the hose wrapped around the passengers.

The aspect of the story most often chosen as humorous was the description of Ribs moving toward the front of the bus while the hose wrapped around the passengers. Apparently in the excerpt it was the picture of a totally ridiculous situation that most amused the readers.

One of the selections taken from *Pippi Longstocking* was the scene in which two policemen visit Pippi, intending to take her to a children's home. Children said the selection was funny because (1) Pippi lived alone and didn't have anyone to take care of her; (2) she wanted to bring monkeys into the children's home; (3) Pippi told the policeman that she was a tiny little auntie who lived on the third floor at the other end of town; (4) Pippi was teasing the policemen; and (5) she said "pluttifikation." References to the last statement and other clever uses of words were the sources of humor mentioned most frequently.

A second selection taken from *Pippi Longstocking* was the burglar scene which ends with Pippi as the victor over two thoroughly cowed burglars. Children said the episode was funny: (1) because the burglars thought Mr. Nilsson was a man, not a monkey; (2) because Pippi could lift those two men; (3) because the burglars' names were funny; (4) when Pippi took the suitcase back from the burglars; and (5) when the burglars jumped down from the wardrobe and threw themselves on Pippi. The element of humor identified by the largest number of children was the surprise when the burglars mistook the sleeping Mr. Nilsson for a man rather than a monkey.

Several different elements of humor (amusing characters, surprising events, impossible happenings, play on words, and totally ridiculous situations) were evident in each of the excerpts used in the study. In each story, however, one element dominated the reactions of readers. And yet, despite that dominance, there were responses made by individuals to the other kinds of humor represented. It was evident that not all children liked the same selections and, just as important, that not all children liked the same element of humor in a given selection. Although space limits the discussion here, it might be noted that there were indications of some differences in the responses of sex, intelligence, and socioeconomic groups. Further research might well give information about the reactions of children from more carefully defined subgroups.

Analysis of the theoretical framework of humor and of the humor found in literature gives evidence of a multidimensional effect. The dimension, which is fairly easy to study, deals with the various elements of humor represented in literature for children. Another suggested dimension involves the level of sophistication of humor present in a story, the contrast between slapstick and whimsy or of broad humor and subtlety. A type of humor, such as laughter at a character, may be represented at a simple level in one story and at a more sophisticated level in another. Some work has been done with analysis of humor of adults and children. A study done in England found that children's jokes made more use of excessive exaggeration than did adults' jokes. There was also a greater amount of slapstick humor evident in children's humor than in that of adults.[9]

The selections chosen for discussion here represent a fairly straightforward type of humor. More subtle varieties of humor were used in some of the other selections, although no attempt was made to analyze responses of children to selections representing various levels of sophistication.

The bus scene in *Henry Huggins* is, essentially, broad humor. Henry succeeds in getting on the bus with Ribsy, only to have him escape from the paper bag and cause chaos among the passengers. There is a certain amount of tension building up in the scene, accompanying the question of whether Henry will succeed in fooling the bus driver this time and will reach home successfully with the dog. Ribsy's escape brings the whole thing into the open, thus releasing the reader from the fear of Ribsy's discovery. The reader has a chance to laugh at one of the many amusing people. Descriptions are vivid and to the point. Katharine Kappas,[3] in her excellent article on children's responses to humor, suggests that the humor in *Henry* and *Ribsy,* results from accidental, rather than intentional, troublemaking. She notes, also, that the whole essence of the books is well suited to the background and interests of children who will read it.

A somewhat different treatment of humor is found in Lawson's *Mr. Revere and I,* another story which generates a good deal of laughter at characters. Lawson's story uses words of greater abstraction and less straightforward description. Much of the humor is generated by use of Scheherezade's interpretation of characters and situations in the light of her own experiences and observations. It is also interesting to consider the humor in books like *The Wind in the Willows* and *Winnie-the-Pooh* which have appeal to a wide age range. Apparently different levels of interpretation are put into operation at early and later ages, providing interest to young as well as more sophisticated readers.

Humor as a Factor in Selection of Materials

One of the important and obvious keys to successful reading guidance involves knowing the characteristics of books which are likely to appeal to certain age groups or to individual personalities. A youngster may be very interested in books which are characterized by the humorous use of words, puns, or play on words. When he finishes one book of this type, it is likely that he will ask for another. Similarly, another child who is captivated by a book with a strongly humorous character is likely to request more books like the one just completed.

The task of filling book requests is monumental. A computerized system would be useful and is, in fact, being used in numerous situations. However, the typical elementary school book collection, whether housed in the classroom or in the library, has yet to be placed under the care of a computer. Reading guidance still requires that the book to be recommended be known by the adult who serves as a reading resource person. Acquaintance with the child's interests and with his reading ability is another important, if not essential, factor in reading guidance.

It is quite possible that some of the burden for book selection can be shifted from the teacher or librarian to the child. Indeed, a good many teachers now utilize self-selection of reading materials. Suppose, for example, that a chart is kept near the library corner. On the chart is the bold heading BOOKS TO LAUGH AT. The chart is divided into two columns, one headed "animal characters" and the other titled "human characters." Whenever a child finishes a book which he definitely classifies as "humorous," he enters the title in the corresponding column. The cumulative list, then, serves as a source of suggested reading material for others in the class. If another child wants a book with humorous animal characters, he can browse through books listed in that column.

The proposed chart might be developed on a more sophisticated level, to include column headings such as "humorous characters," "funny words," or "unexpected incidents." An important addition to the chart would be the page listings of favorite passages for each book. In this way, a would-be reader has a guide to his examination of the book. The child recommending the book benefits, also, because he is called upon to evaluate and read critically for striking passages.

Consider some of the books that come to mind as excellent examples of humorous literature. Are there elements of humor which are strikingly apparent? Do the books appeal to some children but not to others? What passages of the books would you designate as favorites?

From the Mixed-Up Files of Mrs. Basil E. Frankweiler, the 1968 Newbery Medal winner, is a book which contains some wonderfully humorous episodes. One sixth grade teacher read the book to her group and asked for reactions. Responses suggested a high level of interest and a fair amount of agreement as to the most amusing parts of the book. A great many children were captivated by the way Claudia planned diligently for the trip and by her clever scheme for the escape. A number of children expressed interest in the frequency with which Claudia corrected Jamie's grammar. Responses of these sixth graders indicated that the two episodes in the story which they thought most amusing were the ritual of hiding in the toilets during after-hours check and the bathing in the fountain. Laughter at the unusual and unexpected is strongly evident.

The Joseph Jacobs setting of *Tom Tit Tot* presents words in some new forms and generally elicits a good deal of laughter at words and at characters. There are a number of scenes in *Henry Reed, Inc.* which provide ample opportunity for laughter at confusion and also at words. Agony, the dog, and Siegfried, the cat, whose names match their noises, are in the middle of much of the confusion. These few suggestions will certainly call to mind other fine books or parts of books which have recognizable elements of humor.

Summary

The sixth grader referred to earlier, who read omnivorously but disliked the task of oral reading, was extremely intelligent about books. He knew many books and knew them well. Not all of the books he mentioned as favorites and/or humorous had appeared on lists of books taken from studies of children's reading habits. The preference of an individual is strongly evident. Yet the two books he found particularly amusing were well liked by large numbers of children in grades four through six. He was eager to discuss aspects of books which he felt were unusually appealing. And he made some very wise suggestions as to parts of books which might appeal to other sixth graders.

Youngsters who find little to interest them in books gradually cease reading anything except required material. The lack of interest may be closely related to inability to use reading skills adequately. However, it also seems likely that the child who rarely expresses enjoyment of books is not aware of what he does like to read. He needs acquaintance with specific elements of books, such as various types of humor, and a chance to do his own evaluation of reading material in terms of what currently appeals to him. If a sharpened focus on humor highlights enjoyment of reading, discussion of humor-producing elements in literature will likely stimulate greater interest in books.

References

1. Austinson, M. "A Study of the Types of Humor Children Enjoy in Their Literature." Unpublished master's paper, University of Minnesota, 1965.

2. Hurley, B. "What Children Find Humorous." *Childhood Education* 32 (May 1965):424–27.

3. Kappas, K. H. "A Developmental Analysis of Children's Response to Humor," in *A Critical Approach to Children's Literature,* edited by Sara Innis Fenwick. Chicago: University of Chicago Press, 1967.

4. Leacock, S. *Humor and Humanity.* London: Thornton Butterworth, 1937.

5. Monson, D. L. "Children's Responses to Humorous Situations in Literature." Unpublished doctoral dissertation, University of Minnesota, 1966.

6. *New Yorker.* January 13, 1968.

7. Peltola, B. J. "A Study of the Indicated Literary Choices and Measured Literary Knowledge of Fourth and Sixth Grade Boys and Girls." Unpublished doctoral dissertation, University of Minnesota, 1965.

8. Sidis, B. *Psychology of Laughter.* New York: D. Appleton and Co., 1913.

9. Williams, J. M. "An Experimental and Theoretical Study of Humor in Children." Unpublished master's thesis, University of London, 1945.

10. Witty, P. A.; Croomer, A.; and McBean, D. "Children's Choices of Favorite Books: A Study Conducted in Ten Elementary Schools." *Journal of Educational Psychology* 37 (May 1946):266-78.

11. Witty, P. A., and Lehman, H. C. "A Study of the Reading and Reading Interests of Gifted Children." *Journal of Genetic Psychology* 40 (1932):473-85.

Teachers tire of the reading authority who seems always to assail them
with, "Can't you do anything right?"
Yes, says Professor Iverson, teachers
can do things right, and they *are* doing things right—willingly and tire-
lessly every day.

The Role of the Teacher in Developing Lifetime Readers

WILLIAM J. IVERSON

I hope that most of you are elementary teachers. I hope so because I want to praise elementary teachers. And I would like
some of you to hear the praise firsthand.

You see I have become convinced that elementary teachers are
underappreciated. Leading the parade of underappreciators are
professors like me. We have retired to the comforts of the colleges
and universities. We no longer have to do the hard work of elementary teaching—if we ever did—and so we feel free to tell you

what you ought to do. But this time one professor is going to try to behave differently. At least once I want to refrain from pious exhortation. I want to celebrate the good things elementary teachers have been doing while pedagogues like me have been talking.

So let me begin. I begin with a solid affirmation. Elementary teachers now play their roles with admirable devotion in developing lifetime readers. Seventeen years ago the late Professor William S. Gray of the University of Chicago and I reviewed criticism of reading instruction. We worked long and hard at the review which was published in the *Elementary School Journal* and occupied the entire September 1952 issue. Seven years ago, James B. Conant, former President of Harvard, chaired a national conference called by the Carnegie Foundation to which twenty-eight persons interested in reading instruction were invited. As one of the group, I had another look at the quality of reading instruction. Our views were published in the pamphlet *Learning to Read,* issued by Educational Testing Service in 1962. Today Professor Ralph W. Tyler is directing a national assessment of learning in our schools. I do not know what it will show about reading. But my experience through all these appraisals has led me to believe that we need to underline the positive accomplishments of elementary teachers.

It has always been — it will always be — tempting to dwell on deficiencies. Of course they are there. I said I did not know what the current national assessment would reveal. But it would be naive not to expect uneven achievement in reading. There will certainly be parts of our land where lifetime readers are not being developed. What will we do when these predictable appraisals are revealed? Will we who live in the protected environs of higher education say, "Of course. We've been telling them for years what *they* ought to do?" I suspect many of us who are professors will indulge ourselves in just that kind of self-serving sanctimony. Before that happens, let me try to expiate some of my own past sins and perhaps even inoculate you who are elementary teachers against any forthcoming virulence.

The best way for me to do my penance, and I hope for you to protect yourselves against any future attack, is to emphasize what you as elementary teachers now do in developing lifetime readers. It seems to me that the roles which you play are many and the competence with which you act is considerable.

In the kindergarten you start, through the primary years and beyond you continue, to make real and personal and satisfying the aesthetic rewards of language. You tell stories and you read stories aloud. You show in your voice the sounds, the rhythms, the images, the appeals to emotion which is the language of literature.

You tell stories to make immediate the promise of reading. As children are laboring to perfect their skill in reading, you personify what the lasting pleasures are. You deliberately intrigue children with words: quiet words and noisy words, words which call the imagination and words which calm the spirit. You pattern the words in all the wonderful ways in which an English sentence can mold idea and feeling. You gradually extend the number and qualities of incidents in a plot. You add dimension to characters. You build substance in setting. You lead the children to see the ideas behind stories. You realize that a story well told is as rewarding to teller, as song to singer, as picture to painter.

You read aloud with equal zest. You read as if life held no greater pleasure. You make certain that children see at least one person who loves to read and rejoices in the opportunity to share that satisfaction. You know there is no more powerful incentive to want to read than the obvious, real, uninhibited pleasure in reading personified by a well-loved person.

You make certain that the stories you read offer substance for childhood. You want to build growth on solid food which takes some chewing. Pablum we have enough of already. You know that solidly nutrient stories come from varied sources. The old tales — folk and fairy and fable — out of the oral tradition of many peoples — are part of your fare. You read the myths and legends and hero stories which infuse literature around the world. You lend the impact of the lives of real personages, great and small. You read with natural affection the singing lines of poetry. Of course, whatever you choose, you guard against what William Jenkins has called an "attic mentality" which treasures only the old and dusty. You know literature is not substantive because it is aged. Literature is substantive because it is ageless.

You see to it that the classroom itself makes manifest the rewards of reading. You arrange so that the room can be littered with books. You make available an array: serious writing and humorous writing, writing of fantasy and writing of realism, writing of lands and times far away, writing of the here and now. You have long known that accessibility is a key factor in encouraging lifetime reading.

You do not forget yourself in keeping alive the joys of reading. In your own life, books are as present as food and drink. You know you can only retain a sense of the long-term reading vistas for children by keeping alive the prospects in yourself. You know that it is not only children who need to be reminded that the work is worth the while.

Now what is the panorama in literature which you wish to keep fresh for children? You want children to see the potentialities in all the various forms which literature can take. You know that this kind of vision requires solid teaching. A child can't enjoy what he can't read. So you labor long to invest him with the early skills in word recognition and in sentence patterns. But you notice that increasingly these reading skills are being mastered early by the majority of children. So wisely you turn early from the skills of language to the content which language bears. You do not make the mistake of assuming that enjoyment of literature just grows. You teach for it.

Nor do you make the mistake of assuming that the material for skill building can also be used for developing lifetime interest in literature. As I said earlier the ends of skill building and literature teaching are different. The materials must also be different. In developing lifetime interest in literature you know you must have stories, poems, biographies, essays read as they were intended. When any of these forms are adapted to serve as exercise material for skill building they no longer serve as literature. You do not argue that skill building is not necessary. That would be nonsense. You simply affirm that when you are building lifetime interests in literature you are in another role — equally important and equally deserving of appropriate material.

When you are playing this important role, what do you do? First you make clear what the resources of each literary form are. Appreciation of literature derives from specific qualities within each form. You know there is nothing nebulus about it. The qualities of each literary form have been known for centuries. So you show what the qualities are — whether it is a story, a poem, a play, a biography, or an essay.

You find that appreciating these qualities is not difficult once they are known to the children. You know that you can begin effectively in the first grade. You encourage individual creative responses. So long as the reader is true to the spirit of the writing, you help him see in his imagination, hear, taste, touch—whatever the appeal—in a way that is uniquely his own. You know that each child makes his own responses out of his own being, his own living, indeed his own reading.

As I said earlier, you encourage children to take a different attitude toward words as they read literature. In skill building you want a child to know *what* a word means. In literature you are more interested in *how* a word means.

You help children see the way in which a story is built, or a poem, or a play, or a biography, or an essay. You are not afraid to use the literary terms. In a story you talk naturally about plot, character, setting, theme. You know that words like climax, conflict, and suspense scare no one. Indeed, the specific literary terms add security because they make discussion clearer and better focused.

You keep a sense of priorities as you teach for lifetime interest in literature. In a story you realize that a child must first know what is happening before he can enjoy a plot. He must know who the characters are before he can identify with them. He must know where the story develops before he can transport his imagination there. He must think about what the idea behind the story is before he lends his approval or disapproval.

You have learned through painful experience that it is tempting to try to leap into the appreciations you want before the prior understandings are won. So you check before you move to teaching awareness of the artistry of the writer. When you are there, what awareness do you seek? In a story you look at plot. How did one event lead to another? You look at characters. How did the author make them appear alive and believable? You look at setting. How did the place make a solid footing for the story? You look at theme. How was the idea behind the story gradually revealed?

Of course you move into this kind of teaching sensibly. You do not cross-examine. You do not try to make a career of one story. You are selective in what you try to teach. You do not try to develop awareness of everything the craft of the writer might have fashioned. In short, you are economical, watching carefully to see when you are developing the lifetime appreciation of the children and when you are exploiting your own interests.

You are particularly sensitive to invite the children's own creative additions to what the writer has only suggested. You know that in all art forms — literature, music, painting — each individual diverges in his responses. It is not the same as in scientific or mathematical communication where the responses are expected to converge. If you show a child a map of the Mississippi River, the communication is quite explicit. If you show a child a painting of that same body of water, the communication is only suggested.

So as you show children how a writer builds a story, you are equally interested in how each child responds to the writer's suggestions. You do not expect each child to have the same responses. And so long as a child is not violating the spirit of the writing, you welcome his individual creative additions. For he *is* adding himself — seeing, hearing, smelling, tasting, touching — in a way unique to him. No one has lived precisely his life. He joins the writer and together they make new artistry.

When children have realized the most from a story — realized what the author said and how he said it — realized in their own persons how it all appeared — then you are ready to encourage them to make judgements. Why did the story succeed as well as it did? Why was the plot constructed as it was? Why did the characters behave as they did? Why was the setting placed where it was? Why did the theme develop as it did?

You have learned that the young do not always agree with their elders. You have learned to be humble. The books which are precious to you are not always dear at this very moment to those you teach. You know that you do not foster lifetime interests in literature by insisting that now and now only is the time for a given piece of writing. You realize that you can not hand anyone a satisfaction he does not feel.

So, though you may wince a bit, you accept diversity in judgement. You find that your willingness to teach for a common understanding of what the qualities of literature are helps make the bases of divergence clearer. You are not talking ambiguously about appreciation. Your children know the simple vocabulary of literary discussion. They can point with lucidity to the reasons why they chose to respond as they did. You do not attempt to coerce agreement but you do welcome references to those qualities on which divergence is based.

Now what about the other literary forms? Let's take biographies first. You have found that the persuasions of biography have much in common with the appeals of the story. Literary biography is written out of an artistic integrity which the biographer imagines for his subject. The incidents, the thoughts, the feelings described are chosen to be reported in accord with this aesthetic concept. You know that such biography is not an objective report. It is an emotional commitment to an image. There are, of course, currents and counter currents in a good biography. A unifying concept out of which a portrait is made does not rule out conflict and suspense just as unity does not eliminate these qualities in a story. Indeed a good biographer, constrained as he is by outcomes already fixed, still strives to lend a sense of both the day-to-day and the long-term uncertainties in the life of his subject.

Your students turn to biography to make both present and past seem to be living chronicles. You find they can apply essentially the same guides in assessment as they did in fiction. Of course they want to know *what* the man did. They are intrigued by *how* the life is conceived. They lend their own creative additions to the biographer's suggestions. They make their own judgements about *why* the man was sketched as he was.

Since there are now often a number of biographies written about the same man, you encourage boys and girls to judge differences in the several approaches. Thanks to your efforts, biography is fast becoming one of the more effective agents in recruiting lifetime readers.

The essay for children is also a rising literary form. Many of the books about the natural world are not purely reports of objective information. Many are personal responses to the wonder and beauty of nature. You find that children follow a writer like A. G. Milotte writing about a hippopotamus as avidly as they would a story. Or when Henry B. Kane writes about a meadow, you see that children are fascinated with the teeming action concealed within that green world. These essays draw all the color and excitement of good fiction.

And what about drama? You do not expect—and you do not find—much independent reading of drama. A play is meant to be played. So it is almost perforce a group activity. But many of you have found that creative dramatics lends support in developing reading interests. In this extemporaneous playing out of a story, or a biography, or a narrative essay, or a poem, you find many advantages. You find it permits full exploration of language under the stimulus of what has been read. You see that it develops incentive to improvise as the reader commits himself through his speech to an image of what he has read. You recognize it reveals sensitivity to situations in choosing diction and tonal vestments in language. You watch it permit emotional release, lending a sense of the power of the language which might have only been partially felt in silent reading. In brief, you sense that this kind of drama develops the creative additions essential to genuine involvement in literature. The mere fact that minimal settings and costumes are employed in creative dramatics requires inventing language to convey the reader's own responses to the writer.

I have saved until last that literary form which has caused you the greatest difficulty. That is, of course, poetry. Here I hope you will forgive the professor for saying that your successes have been modest. But then the successes have been even more modest at later levels of education. What success you have achieved in the elementary schools—and I do not mean to indicate the success has been inconsequential—modest, yes—inconsequential, no— has been due, first, to your early beginnings. You have shown that a child, who early hears and tastes on his own tongue the excitement of poetry, may indeed resist all the culture pressures and retain his affection for poetry. The solid charm of nursery rhymes still pervades many kindergartens and primary grades. Beyond these years, your efforts with poetry have been more oppressed.

Now why is your success with poetry as much as it is? First of all, poetry is beleaguered by a very hostile cultural stereotype. In our adult culture, poetry is little prized. It is especially little valued by men. Of course this hostility is not without its effects on children—and I'm afraid the effects are particularly negative on boys.

Now what have you done to counteract this hostility? You have watched the choice of poems. You have had to sacrifice some "footsteps quiet and slow at a tranquil pace under veils of white lace." You have had to indulge in some quickened beats of jungle drums. It is true that the girls sometimes have tired of this unabashed catering to male tastes. But on balance, I think most of you have discovered, that the girls, God bless them, have gone along.

But even given virile content, you have learned that the peculiar demands of the literary form in poetry make acceptance difficult. Poems are arranged on a page in a different way. The spatial arrangement is dictated by rhythm and, when it is present, by rhyme. The placement is also employed, especially in modern poetry, to fasten the attention on the separate pieces of statement. For example, look at these lines from William Carlos Williams:

> It is difficult
> to get news from poems
> yet men die miserably every day
> for lack
> of what is found there.

You know that children have to learn what purposes these spatial arrangements serve.

You realize, too, that the fundamental syntactical device in English of word order is often disarranged by spatial arrangement in poetry. Unusual ordering of words greatly increases difficulty in reading.

You see that poetry is very terse. The child cannot gradually slip into understanding. He must be prepared to use the same text for much rereading. Rarely does poetry yield its full impact on first reading.

You recognize that poetic diction is strange. It is the poet's effort to force the child to respond creatively. The poet wants to surprise his reader into new insights by his choice of words.

You observe that poets, of all literary artists, speak mostly by suggestion. This figurative language is also intended to evoke novel views of experience.

Now how have you coped with these difficulties of the poetic form? You have endowed poetry with your own genuine affection. You have read it and recited it naturally and easily. You have not employed any artificial lubricants. You know those who ooze from syllable to syllable kill interest in poetry forever. You have seized upon strategic moments. You know you can't move into poetry with the children fresh and fractured from recess. You use a modulating time with quiet talk, sometimes, when the logistics aren't too difficult, even with a little music. Whatever you do, you try to keep it all as normal and as unaffected and as attractive as you are on your best days.

Occasionally, you may even drag in an itinerant male, a father who likes poetry and reads it with virility, any male who cares —a pilot, a sports figure, a scientist, a businessman. It seems crass. But you do sense the necessity of surrounding poetry with some male aura, lent by men who are masculine and occupying positions boys value. You feel it is a pity to have to react with such obvious stratagems. But you know that it is a small price to pay for the lasting rewards which those who are caught young will gain from poetry.

So I have ended my celebration of you who are elementary teachers—you who have done so much to develop lifetime readers —you who exemplify every day the kind of devotion to books about which another academic spoke over 300 years ago:

Books are life's best business: Vocation to them hath more
emolument coming in, than all the other busy terms of life.
They are fee-less Counsellors, no delaying Patrons, of easy
access and kind Expedition, never sending away any Client or
Petitioner . . . Count thy books in the Inventory Jewels, wherein
a variety is the most excusable Prodigality, and right use . . .
the best Husbandry. They are for company, the best Friends; in
doubts, Counsellors; in Dumps, Comforters: Times Prospective,
the Home Traveller's Ship, or Horse the Mind's best Ordinary,
Nature's Garden, and Seed-plot of Immortality.

Zootomia, 1654

study questions

1. Doris Young cites the importance of objectives for literature study. Are such objectives feasible? Suppose that, preparing to present *Island of the Blue Dolphins,* you cite this objective: "My pupils will enjoy the book and gain insight into what it means to be courageous, independent, and resourceful." Must the objective be restated in order to be evaluated? If so, restate it. Explain, then, how evaluation might take place. What would be the *value* of such evaluation?

2. Toward the conclusion of her article, Young challenges teachers and librarians to evaluate responses to literature. How? Which of the many techniques for measuring response mentioned by Young could be adopted or adapted by school personnel? What additional techniques can you suggest?

3. One researcher expressed a cynical view: "You'll find that, as potency of response rises, literary quality falls. Children will jump up and down and whistle for Nancy Drew or the Hardy Boys. For *The Wind in the Willows* they won't twitch an eyelash." Is this an accurate observation? Is it borne out by data cited by Young? What information and advice from the present chapter—e.g. from Nancy Larrick's suggestions—can be brought to bear on this matter?

4. Cameron strongly disapproves of readers who "simply purr quietly while the author strokes them." Could such an assailment apply also to television watchers? What might be done to alter the receiver's passive stance to media? What procedures, for example, might be used in a school to begin such an effort? How early—for what beginning age level—might such a program be instituted?

5. How strong is the literature-must-be-pleasant tradition with which Larrick's "Baby Dolls Are Gone" seems to disagree? The article appeared in 1967. What has been the direction of children's literature since that time? Are baby dolls still gone? What are some titles Larrick might add to the list if she were to revise the article in light of today's trends?

6. What facets of motivation are implicit in the articles by Monson and Iverson? Which of the authors read thus far in this volume would probably place intrinsic motivation highest on the list of factors conducive to reading? Lowest? Which would probably make no necessary distinction between intrinsic and extrinsic motivation? What is your personal opinion?

7. Perhaps the overriding "message" of Iverson and Monson is that educators must read and relish books for children. List twelve (or twelve dozen) books you would like to read next in order to broaden and deepen your awareness of literature for children. Then instead of stopping there, go read them!

SEVEN

reading and the disadvantaged child

objectives

As a result of reading these articles and answering the questions at the end of the chapter you should be able to:

▨ identify factors that must be assessed in determining reading-instruction strategies appropriate for the disadvantaged

▨ present opposing points of view regarding the problems of providing reading instruction for the disadvantaged, including the rationales undergirding these opposing views

rationale

Although the disadvantaged do not really comprise a homogeneous group, the rubric has enabled us to identify some conditions that forestall equal educational opportunity and, specifically, opportunity and success in learning to read. In this chapter our authors examine some of these conditions. They speculate on procedures for alleviating the resultant reading problems. In a sense, the chapter is open-ended, for the authorities do not entirely agree, and most quite forthrightly confess some degree of quandary.

introduction

"The first interesting fact about sociological research on reading is that there has been so little of it," wrote Philip H. Ennis in 1964.[1] Evidence then and now points to the social-level factor as the single strongest indicator of success or failure in learning to read. That reading authorities were late in accepting and acting upon such evidence is puzzling. It may be, as Ennis supposed, that reading researchers are oriented toward "individual-level" variables rather than "social-level" variables. If so, the bias is not so surprising after all. Its roots lie deep in American culture.

Our social awareness has always been tinged with the Horatio Alger concept. It is the individual who matters, not his (initial) social status. Apropos of education, we have assumed that the individual can learn to read if he just *wants* to. We have further assumed that the motive is inborn and simply requires an act of will to be put into motion. We have been slow to realize that this belief can cruelly hinder educational opportunity.

Motive, in fact, is not innate. Like other factors involved in reading, it is substantially dependent upon environmental conditions. The entire gamut of factors conducive to reading becomes a matter of social responsibility: the opportunity to be educated entails adjustment of social conditions so that learning is made possible and even probable. Without this, social class loses its spirit of social mobility and becomes social caste.

Prince or pauper, the child does not choose the social class into which he is born. If his culture revolves upon "survival of the fittest" rather than "fitting the greatest number to survive," his chances for success in learning to read are predetermined. But if the culture makes provision for fostering his education, some balance point may be reached so that he can succeed.

This struggle to attain a balance point in educational opportunity has led us to designate various groups of learners in our
society as disadvantaged. The term is ambiguous and misleading
but probably no more so than any other term we might select.
We are probably forced at present to deal in overgeneralization
by the very nature of the social-level concept as opposed, say, to
the more specific concept of individual characteristics. To some,
disadvantaged connotes *deprived*—children whose environment
blocks wholesome development, as in George Mendoza's allegory
of a seed trying to sprout under a fallen leaf.[2] To others, disadvantaged connotes *culturally different*—children whose environment diverges from the predominant culture so that they are not
stunted, just different.

Those who would minister to the disadvantaged as deprived
would attempt to compensate for allegedly underdeveloped language and perception. They would "improve" habits of attention
and correct deficiencies attributed to malnutrition. Katrina de
Hirsch among many others recommends an intensive program of
"intervention" to correct conditions of the deprived.[3]

The "culturally different" theorists contend that reading instruction must become more flexible. It must adapt itself to the
needs and interests of disadvantaged groups. But in this view,
the disadvantaged component is not the subculture group at all:
it is the instructional design itself. Various instructional adjustments have been attempted along these lines, often with fine
results: the language-experience approach, utilizing pupils' language as a base for content, vocabulary, and syntax; materials
written expressly to engage subculture interest and understanding; inclusion in the instructional staff of parents and other paraprofessionals drawn from the subculture.

The two schools of thought, separate or merged, have made a
difference. In fact, it is rare to learn of a reading-for-the-disad-
vantaged program that *utterly* fails—at least, not on the criteria
established by its believers. *Ultimate* failure is a different matter.
We seem to have a host of promising programs producing promising effects against a rising sea of failure. It is a situation that
confounds the pragmatist: the operations are successful but the
patient still seems to be dying.

Everyone seems to have a solution and most publishers have
a whole bagful. If the selections in this volume do no more than
counsel more careful judgment in regard to linking factors to

materials and procedures, especially in work with the disadvantaged, they will have contributed something useful to the problem. Judgment, now that so many aspects of the problem have been explored, seems most needed. As preparation for the articles that comprise this chapter, we close with a few matters of judgment relevant to reading instruction for the disadvantaged.

First, we must point out that the disadvantaged do not comprise a homogeneous group. Any attempt to define the disadvantaged entails troublesome assumptions about homogeneity. It is one thing to say that lower socioeconomic strata present more reading problems than higher strata. It is another to assume that, since there appear to be equivalent social conditions, the reading problems are equivalent. In fact, there may be deprived groups and there may be culturally different groups – and the help needed by the two may be so varied as to forbid generalization from one group to the other. If this is so, then we are mistaken in the very basis of asking, "What do we do to teach reading to the disadvantaged child?" We may need to return somewhere to the "individual" factors and work from there, whether or not these factors seem to predominate in a particular social level. Those familiar with Francie's successful pursuit of reading amid squalor in *A Tree Grows in Brooklyn*[4] or the book-propelled determination of Dozie in *Behind the Magic Line*[5] know that much to do with reading lies outside the social-level context – or any other generalized context, for that matter.

Second, and quite related to the first, there are potentially a great many variables that may serve to identify target individuals for special reading aid. Race, family income, location, health, and prior learning record are outward signs. But what of the inward signs that conceivably we might now assess? What of the strength of the model for reading possessed by the child? What of his willingness to take risks, incumbent in most attempts at learning to read? What of his autonomy? his sense of fate-control? his "true grit"? When these and other factors are lacking, the successful reading program must make adjustments. And no social group is free of these problems: there is, after all, deprivation of the privileged existent in our society, accompanying the problem of the underprivileged.

Third, we are not dealing with a problem that was born yesterday – we should not be surprised that it has not been solved today.

There may be a strange unforeseen bonus in the arduous working out of its solution. We once assumed that we knew how to teach reading to the majority. We believed we knew why the majority should want to read, and what they should want to read. We thought we knew their values and aspirations. That was a long time ago, as long ago as 1964. Now, forced to reexamine our values and the part that reading plays in them, we have a good chance to evolve something better—not for the disadvantaged alone but for everyone.

Notes

1. Phillip H. Ennis. "Recent Sociological Contributions to Reading Research." *The Reading Teacher* 17, no. 8 (May 1964):577–82.

2. George Mendoza. *Starfish Trilogy.* Funk and Wagnalls, 1969.

3. Katrina de Hirsch. "Preschool Intervention." In *Reading Forum: A Collection of Reference Papers Concerned with Reading Disability,* edited by Eloise O. Calkins. Bethesda, Md.: National Institute of Neurological Diseases and Stroke, Public Health Service, 1971, pp. 71–107.

4. Smith, Betty, *A Tree Grows in Brooklyn.* New York: Harper & Row, 1947.

5. Erwin, Betty K., *Behind the Magic Line.* Boston, Mass.: Little, Brown and Company, 1969.

> You have known someone like this,
> but perhaps you did not know he
> was "disadvantaged." He is your—

Cipher in the Snow

JEAN E. MIZER

It started with tragedy on a biting cold February morning. I was driving behind the Milford Corners bus as I did most snowy mornings on my way to school. It veered and stopped short at the hotel, which it had no business doing, and I was annoyed as I had to come to an unexpected stop. A boy lurched out of the bus, reeled, stumbled, and collapsed on the snowbank at the curb. The bus driver and I reached him at the same moment. His thin, hollow face was white even against the snow.

"He's dead," the driver whispered.

I didn't register for a minute. I glanced quickly at the scared young faces staring down at us from the school bus. "A doctor! Quick! I'll phone from the hotel . . . ."

"No use. I tell you he's dead." The driver looked down at the boy's still form. "He never even said he felt bad," he muttered, "just tapped me on the shoulder and said, real quiet, 'I'm sorry. I have to get off at the hotel.' That's all. Polite and apologizing like."

At school, the giggling, shuffling morning noise quieted as the news went down the halls. I passed a huddle of girls. "Who was it? Who dropped dead on the way to school?" I heard one of them half-whisper.

"Don't know his name; some kid from Milford Corners," was the reply.

It was like that in the faculty room and the principal's office. "I'd appreciate your going out to tell the parents," the principal told me. "They haven't a phone and, anyway, somebody from school should go there in person. I'll cover your classes."

"Why me?" I asked. "Wouldn't it be better if you did it?"

"I didn't know the boy," the principal admitted levelly. "And in last year's sophomore personalities column I note that you were listed as his favorite teacher."

I drove through the snow and cold down the bad canyon road to the Evans' place and thought about the boy, Cliff Evans. His favorite teacher! I thought. He hasn't spoken two words to me in two years! I could see him in my mind's eye all right, sitting back there in the last seat in my afternoon literature class. He came in the room by himself and left by himself. "Cliff Evans," I muttered to myself, "a boy who never talked." I thought a minute. "A boy who never smiled. I never saw him smile once."

The big ranch kitchen was clean and warm. I blurted out my news somehow. Mrs. Evans reached blindly toward a chair. "He never said anything about bein' ailing."

His stepfather snorted. "He ain't said nothin' about anything since I moved in here."

Mrs. Evans pushed a pan to the back of the stove and began to untie her apron. "Now hold on," her husband snapped. "I got to have breakfast before I go to town. Nothin' we can do now anyway. If Cliff hadn't been so dumb, he'd have told us he didn't feel good."

After school I sat in the office and stared bleakly at the records spread out before me. I was to close the file and write the obituary for the school paper. The almost bare sheets mocked the effort. Cliff Evans, white, never legally adopted by stepfather, five young half brothers and sisters. These meager strands of information and the list of D grades were all the records had to offer.

Cliff Evans had silently come in the school door in the mornings and gone out the school door in the evenings, and that was all. He had never belonged to a club. He had never played on a team. He had never held an office. As far as I could tell, he had never done one happy, noisy kid thing. He had never been anybody at all.

How do you go about making a boy into a zero? The grade-school records showed me. The first and second grade teachers' annotations read "sweet, shy child"; "timid but eager." Then the third grade note had opened the attack. Some teacher had written in a good firm hand, "Cliff won't talk. Uncooperative. Slow learner." The other academic sheep had followed with "dull"; "slow-witted"; "low I. Q." They became correct. The boy's I. Q. score in the ninth grade was listed at 83. But his I. Q. in the third grade had been 106. The score didn't go under 100 until the seventh grade. Even shy, timid, sweet children have resilience. It takes time to break them.

I stomped to the typewriter and wrote a savage report pointing out what education had done to Cliff Evans. I slapped a copy on the principal's desk and another in the sad, dog-eared file. I banged the typewriter and slammed the file and crashed the door shut, but I didn't feel much better. A little boy kept walking after me — a little boy with a peaked, pale face; a skinny body in faded jeans; and big eyes that had looked and searched for a long time and then had become veiled.

I could guess how many times he'd been chosen last to play sides in a game, how many whispered child conversations had excluded him, how many times he hadn't been asked. I could see and hear the faces and voices that said over and over, "You're dumb. You're a nothing, Cliff Evans."

A child is a believing creature. Cliff undoubtedly believed them. Suddenly it seemed clear to me: When finally there was nothing left at all for Cliff Evans, he collapsed on a snowbank and went away. The doctor might list "heart failure" as the cause of death, but that wouldn't change my mind.

We couldn't find ten students in the school who had known Cliff well enough to attend the funeral as his friends. So the student body officers and a committee from the junior class went as a group to the church, being politely sad. I attended the services with them, and sat through it with a lump of cold lead in my chest and a big resolve growing through me.

I've never forgotten Cliff Evans nor that resolve. He has been my challenge year after year, class after class. I look up and down the rows carefully each September at the unfamiliar faces. I look for veiled eyes or bodies scrouged into a seat in an alien world. "Look, kids," I say silently, "I may not do anything else for you this year, but not one of you is going to come out of here a nobody. I'll work or fight to the bitter end doing battle with society and the school board, but I won't have one of you going out of here thinking himself into a zero."

Most of the time—not always, but most of the time—I've succeeded.

The specifics of failure, some characteristics of many disadvantaged children, some hopes and procedures for improvement . . . .

Are the Reading Goals for the Disadvantaged Attainable?

J. ALLEN FIGUREL

The ultimate reading goal for the disadvantaged reader is no different from that of other boys and girls. In his address, entitled "Target for the 70s: The Right to Read," to State Boards of Education, Commissioner Allen of USOE stated it so succinctly: competency in reading for every student. The short-term and day-by-day reading goals for disadvantaged boys and girls will have to be somewhat different if the ultimate goal is to be reached by the time they leave school. The approaches, practices, techniques, and sequential learning tasks have to be adjusted to the particular needs of disadvantaged students. The extent to which these adjustments are made will determine the degree of success that will be achieved in developing competent readers.

With the advent of the Great Cities Projects in the early 1960s
and with the enactment of the Elementary and Secondary Education Act in 1965, thousands of programs and projects have been
instituted to improve the education of the poor and disadvantaged. These have run the gamut from prekindergarten through
high school grades. Billions of dollars have been poured into these
programs. Needless to say, many programs have been concerned
with the improvement of reading. Yet the results, with a few
possible exceptions such as Head Start (funded by OEO), have
been definitely disappointing.

Reading Retardation Is Greater in Large Cities

Large cities, with higher concentrations of disadvantaged boys
and girls in ghetto and marginal areas, have a high degree of
reading retardation in their schools and consequently receive
much criticism about reading-test results. To help disadvantaged
children do better in reading, Detroit schools developed a series
of readers which depict black, oriental, and white children. The
new readers were developed for the primary grades. The content
style of the readers is very similar to that found in basal readers,
although efforts were made to include plot in some of the stories
to arouse more interest in reading. Reports of some teachers indicate that Detroit readers are very popular with all children.
The influence that they may have on reading achievement in
upper grades and high school has yet to be ascertained. One
thing is certain, children of Detroit, like those in all large cities,
still read quite below their capacity levels. Recently the superintendent of Chicago schools revealed that he was displeased
with the reading and I. Q. scores reported for all Chicago children.
He said that whereas beginning children are at national norms,
other students lose from 13 to 26 points by the time they are in
the twelfth grade. He stated further that the results of the citywide testing are worse today than they were three years ago.
Criticisms of reading in New York City and in Los Angeles
schools have been widely reported in the news media and do not
need further explanation here. Test scores for disadvantaged
children in all large-city schools indicate there is "progressive
retardation" taking place. The longer a child remains in school
the less progress he makes in relation to his capacity for learning
to read. In the first grade, he may be retarded six months. By the

time he is in the sixth grade, the retardation may be one, two, or even three years. In high school, the retardation may increase to four or more years. Of course, the degree of retardation varies from student to student and is based on both intrinsic and extrinsic causes. How can this retardation be stopped? Research has been of little help, for most studies have dealt with assaying and listing deficits and limitations of the language of the disadvantaged. Very few studies have dealt with learning methodology. And this is what teachers of the disadvantaged need and want. Answers must be found quickly, for sociologists say that by 1975 two out of three children in schools can be classified as disadvantaged. What a challenge for American schools!

The teacher is the focal point in any school activity. Her attitude and feelings are reflected in everything she does when children are around. Disadvantaged children sense this very quickly, especially if they think they are being personally rejected. Their efforts at learning tasks are in proportion to their feelings toward the teacher. They like teachers that show an empathetic attitude toward them and they will work very hard in trying to please a teacher that has this attitude. On the other hand, they will do their darndest to upset a teacher who they think rejects them, and in this they can be very rebellious. Effective reading teachers bring out the best in their students and this can only be done if there is positive interaction taking place between her and her students. This helps to set a positive atmosphere for learning in the classroom. The schoolroom climate enables the teacher to plan her work without interruptions. In planning reading lessons for disadvantaged children, teachers should keep in mind the unique needs of each child. Lessons should be organized around these needs. Disadvantaged children like short lessons. Their span of attention may be short. They are immediately interested in seeing how successful they have been. This idea encompasses the closure technique that psychologists talk about in relation to motivation. Disadvantaged children like concrete concepts better than the abstract. Reading material should reflect these concepts. Background information may be lacking in some children. When such information is required before an answer can be given, the teacher should furnish it. If a child asks for some aid, he should not be sent to some reference book to find it, but rather the teacher should give the assistance asked for. Above all, teachers should be approachable at all times.

What possible causes could there be that keep teachers from functioning effectively in inner-city schools? One can only surmise some of the causes since research studies in this area have often shown contradictory or confusing causations. Is it that teachers of ghetto schools are less prepared and have had less experience? There might be some truth to this allegation when one realizes that candidates for positions in many large-city schools take examinations for employment eligibility. The ratings on these tests determine their place on eligibility lists. The teachers with the highest rank on placement lists have first choices in selecting schools in which to teach, and to no one's surprise, they select white schools located in what is termed the outer city. In most cities the demand for teachers is often greater than the supply. Usually, many vacancies still exist after all who passed the test are placed. To fill the leftover vacancies, substitute teachers are placed in regular positions, which for the most part are found in inner-city schools. As a result children who need the best teachers often find themselves with the least prepared, and often uncertified teachers. And the heavy turnover in substitute positions seems to cause the situation to deteriorate further. Efforts to overcome such practices are being made in some cities but seniority and other uncontrollable factors have limited the movement of good teachers to disadvantaged schools. The use of paraprofessionals and modern materials has brought some relief to such schools, but these efforts so far have done little to improve the learning climate.

Even the good teachers who are found in disadvantaged schools sometimes seem to get poor results in teaching reading. A large number of middle-class teachers who teach in ghetto schools spend too much time in trying to make over disadvantaged children into children with middle-class mores. They feel strongly that the poor children have been denied so many middle-class niceties that it is their duty to bring to them the things which, in their opinion, will bring about the change. The time spent on such enrichment could very well be added to reading activities.

Language Capacity, Language Acquisition, and Reading

The language of disadvantaged children has been evaluated extensively in terms of its cultural and social variations rather than in its native or biological aspects. Statistically significant differences in the language development of disadvantaged, as compared with that of middle-class children, have been reported generally. In these studies language development is taken as a demonstration that it is contingent on specific language training. And this is partly true, but it is equally important, if not more so, to make a distinction between what children do in language acquisition and what they are capable of doing. The capacity for language development is the factor which is usually forgotten or not known by teachers. It is the basic factor that should be considered rather than keeping in mind the deficits which environment has brought about. The biological aspects of language are more basic than the sociological. In a carefully conducted research study on language, Lenneberg,* a neurobiologist, listed some basic concepts about language which should be considered by every reading teacher of the disadvantaged. These concepts may well serve to change the teacher's attitude on language and may serve to give her a beginning positive attitude toward the disadvantaged child's language acquisition, which is a basis for learning to read. According to Lenneberg, language has six characteristics: 1) it is a form of behavior in all cultures of the world, 2) in all cultures its onset is age correlated, 3) there is only one acquisition strategy—it is the same for all babies in the world, 4) it is based intrinsically upon the same formal operating characteristics whatever its outward form, 5) throughout man's recorded history these operating characteristics have been constant, and 6) it is a form of behavior that may be impaired specifically by circumscribed brain lesions which may leave other mental or motor skills relatively unaffected. He further stated that children begin to speak no sooner and no later than when they reach a given stage of physical maturation. Language development correlates more closely with motor coordination than with chronological age. It is interesting to note that on almost all counts language begins when such maturation indices have attained at least 65 percent of their mature values, and inversely language acquisition becomes more difficult when the physical maturation of the brain is complete. These observations will be of positive value especially to kindergarten and primary school teachers who can include in their activities coordination exercises. And

*Eric H. Lenneberg. "On Explaining Language," *Science.* 164 (May 1969): 635–44.

in assessing the degree of development of the capacity for language all teachers should use a few broad and developmental stages rather than to make an inventory of vocabulary, syntax, and the like. We learn from Lenneberg's study that disadvantaged children have capacity for language equal to that of children from middle-class homes. Let teachers begin with capacity rather than with acquisition of language analyses.

There is a difference between language capacity and language acquisition. One acquires the language he hears in relation to his capacity for language learning. Are disadvantaged children able to acquire language with the same rapidity as other children? One needs only to listen to a group of disadvantaged youngsters at play to learn that they are very talkative and learn language from each other very rapidly. In many classrooms, the teacher's greatest difficulty is to keep her pupils quietly at work. Disadvantaged children seem to want to babble all the time and find it harder to keep quiet than children who come from middle-class homes.

The language of disadvantaged children reflects all the deficits and limitations of environment. In most cases language patterns have been imported from the South and the patterns reflect the dialect of the South. It is a dialect of the English language and is not to be termed bad English as some teachers are prone to do. The dialect of the disadvantaged, in addition to differences in tonal effect, consists in the use of short and to-the-point sentences; verb irregularities; omissions, particularly at the end of sentences; repetitious vocabulary, and certain other irregularities. Nevertheless, it is English and can be understood by people who speak other dialects.

If a disadvantaged child has innate capacity for language and has shown that he can acquire language very rapidly, why is it so difficult for him to learn to read since reading is a facet of language? One would suspect that reading requires the knowledge of standard English patterns, which are not very well known by the disadvantaged. Ways must be found to have the disadvantaged acquire standard English patterns at an optimum time of language development. Two-, three-, and four-year-olds are now going to nursery schools for this purpose. But there are thousands of children who are already in school and ways must be found to help them soon for they, too, have a "Right to Read." Everyone is concerned about reading now: teachers, parents, employers, and the general public can't understand why schools turn out such poor readers. We have such beautiful buildings, educated teachers, and a wealth of materials including technological aids and in some instances, paraprofessionals.

When a disadvantaged child enters school he is all excited about the wonders that are contained in those large and beautiful buildings. Even an old building looks wonderful to him when he compares it with his tenement apartment. Upon entering the classroom he finds that he is in a different world. He can't seem to understand the teacher because she talks too fast. The teacher's language sounds alien and the child can't understand her. Incidentally, to most people who do not understand a foreign language, the speaker seems to speak very rapidly when in reality, to one who understands the language, the speed is very natural. The same impression is made on a disadvantaged child who first hears the standard English of the teacher. He finds it hard to communicate with the teacher. At first he may try to make sense of what the teacher is saying. He soon discovers that his answers are wrong and are not acceptable. He discovers very soon that it is much easier to say nothing and not be bothered by the teacher. A sense of frustration sets in and he soon begins to believe that he is not very bright. Thus begins the long line of failures and destruction of his self-image. When he gets into a reading situation, he finds that it, too, is strange. He tries hard to memorize words or letters, but since they mean very little to him he soon forgets them. The teacher may tell the words or sounds to him over and over again, but he still finds it hard to memorize them. As years roll by, he may learn to read a little, but he fails many times and he is always in the lowest group. Finally he reaches the end of the compulsory school age and quits school to become another dropout and possibly a street bum. How different this boy could have been had teachers understood his needs from the start.

Some Promising Practices

Some experiments have been conducted in certain schools to try to overcome some of the deficits and limitations that disadvantaged children have in learning to read. Some of these look promising. Consensus, however, has not been reached on ways to teach reading to the disadvantaged effectively. Ingenious teachers will find many ways of making disadvantaged children competent readers.

Linguists have been saying for a number of years that children should begin reading the language patterns they understand and use. The language-experience approach lends itself to this recommendation very well. Language-experience charts can be prepared by the teacher from children's own experiences or stories and used for reading. With the help of paraprofessionals, individual stories can be dictated by the children, written on personal sheets, and then used as reading materials. If the teacher is effective, she soon begins to make slight corrections when she does the manuscript work. Since the concepts will not be new, the children will find the reading material easy to read in spite of the changes. The procedure has endless possibilities. It permits the teacher to change the language patterns gradually until the child finds himself reading standard English without realizing the transition which has taken place. The difficult part of the procedure is to get the teacher to accept a pattern which in her own estimation is not good English. By making the first reading easy the teacher is building the child's self-image and giving him a feeling of being a successful reader. In fact, a child can even feel that he is an author by compiling all of his experience stories into a booklet with an appropriate cover and cover design.

Another practice which seems to have some promise is to delay formal reading until the child develops language sophistication in standard English. In this procedure the child spends most of his time in the early primary grades in oral English. Repeated practice sessions are held throughout the day. Objects are introduced. Children, for example, may pass a cup to each other saying, "This is a cup." The constant repetition eventually catches on and when it does a new object is introduced. More difficult language patterns are introduced as progress is made. Attention to informal speaking habits are noted and corrected later on. Language labs, tape recorders, record players, the Language Master, and other devices can contribute much to this procedure. Where this practice has been tried, it has been criticized by the parents who want their children to read when they enter school. Teachers are reminded that they are not trying to change a child's permanent dialect but rather that they are teaching a language pattern needed in school now and in his place of employment later on.

Some teachers still believe strongly that all children, the advantaged and the disadvantaged, should start with the basal reading program and continue with it from year to year so that the sequential reading skills may be learned in an orderly manner. Laboriously they work with the children from the reading-readiness books, through the preprimers, the primers, first readers, and on through the sixth readers. Since the three-group plan of organization is standard in such practice, disadvantaged children invariably find themselves in the lowest reading groups. In first grade they are almost always found in the reading-readiness group. Since progress in reading under this plan is slow for the disadvantaged all through the primary grades they always find themselves in the lowest reading groups. The slow groups may take one or two years longer to complete the designated readers. As children in these groups grow older they find themselves forced to read stories intended for younger children and thus become less and less interested in reading. If grouping is continued into the upper grades the problem becomes even more acute. Imagine a fifth grader becoming interested in material found in a second reader. The three-group plan in integrated schools causes another severe problem for disadvantaged children. Many of the retarded children in reading are black. Very often the slowest group is made up of all black children since they are the ones that have made the least progress in reading. This situation causes segregation. The resulting groups of children learn little from one another since they all have language deficits and limitations. Imagine the frustration of black children who find themselves in groupings which are segregated. Schools should guard against creating segregation through ability grouping which casts black children into slow groups.

If the teacher must use the grouping plan, she should organize her work so that the slow groups get more reading periods, perhaps two or even three a day. The purpose of the added periods is to help the slow readers catch up with others who need less time for reading. Some teachers will respond by asking how they can teach the science and the social studies if they spend so much time on reading. To such teachers one can say that the function of the elementary school is to teach the learning skills and of all the skills, reading is the most important. If a child has been taught to read effectively he will have plenty of time to catch up on the facts in junior and senior high school. But pity the boy or girl who goes to high school with deficient reading skills.

Space does not permit a discussion of how to adjust the intermediate reading goals with practices in teaching through the use of contemporary mediums and methods such as i.t.a., Unifon, Open Court, Phonetic Keys to Reading, the Phonovisual, Words in Color, the DMS, and the Rebus. If a teacher is thoroughly sold on a method, she should study its basic principles to see if they can meet the specific learning needs of disadvantaged children. If a teacher finds that something in the method does not work well with these children she should discard it or find ways of adjusting it so that it will. At times a combination of the best of two methods may be the answer.

Summary

It can be said that although the ultimate reading goal for the disadvantaged is no different from that of other children, the short-term goal needed to achieve the ultimate goal may be quite different, particularly in terms of approaches and methodology. The disadvantaged have equal capacity for language development. They also have equal ability in the acquisition of language. What language patterns they have acquired have certain deficits and limitations in relation to standard English. They have shown that they can overcome these deficits in doing their schoolwork. They need enlightened and empathetic teachers to aid them to acquire new language patterns needed for success and competency in reading. Can we do this for all children in the 1970s? The challenge has been given to us.

> Sing praise to diversity and plurality in American culture! But why, when the school bell rings, do these same qualities become "a pain in the neck"?

The View from the Margin

EDWARD MORENO

Introduction

I feel very honored appearing before you, for I recognize that it is a distinction those who organized this conference, and you, have bestowed upon me. In full candor, I must admit that there are basic differences that separate us, such as ethnicity and orientation, cultural milieus and specialization. But two important things also unite us; despite our varied origins, we consider ourselves good Americans, and all of us desire a better education for our children and the children of our communities.

What Is the Margin?

Let us begin by reaffirming the reality that the Anglo-American is the majority in the land, but that this picture changes very radically in some communities. Perhaps because most Anglo-Americans are conscious of the first part of this reality and choose to ignore the second equally important part, they tend to consider other cultures unintelligible or alien, with no proper place in American life, even when such cultures are truly native to American soil, or were there before the Anglo culture pushed them to the side. Thus, while a few very perceptive social scientists recognize the existence of the Mexican-American and his culture as part of the present-day reality of America, for the rest, our lot is called "culturally deprived," our adjustment to, and functioning in the general culture is a question of assimilation, or nonassimilation, or marginalism. Or to put it into the general cliché, what the melting pot cannot melt is "hard core," maladjusted, peripheral. America is the "unum," the "pluribus" must be erased. There must be one culture, one way of thinking, one single language. Even the indivisibility of our political nation must be expressed as physical and intellectual monochromism, a perfect theory, but a reality incompatible with the way America truly is. In this land of ours, almost all the languages of the Earth are spoken daily; as a people, we can claim ascendants or relatives in almost all corners of the world; and no racial stock, no cultural strain can claim monopoly to being a true, loyal, good American.

Wide and Narrow Margins

We pride ourselves in our ability to tolerate dissent, to criticize ourselves, and to search for better ways of mutual understanding. With the physical and economic means at our disposal, we travel to foreign lands for pleasure or business of all kinds. We fall in love with señoritas and geishas, get excited with toros and pagodas, learn quaint or exotic customs, come to appreciate foods and fads. We drink gallons of imported alcohols, drive a Volkswagen if we are commoners, a Mercedes or Jaguar if sophisticates or professors of education, dress our women in Chinese silks, photograph our kids with Japanese cameras. We dance to the Liverpool sound, and embellish our gaming nights with dancers imported from Montmartre or from Baia. We feed a famished India, ally our progress with our neighbors' poverty, and fill with our gold the coffers of the most covetous Frenchman we have ever known. We make our presence felt in Saigon, Canberra, Moscow, or Peking. And, despite all our external internationalism, our all-embracing ecumenism, we are provincial and parochial to the point of almost total intolerance of the expression of cultural manifestations dissimilar to ours in our midst.

To the Other Side

From my Anglo teachers I have learned an important thought, that to study any subject in depth, to really understand it, I must pay attention not only to the main text, but to all references and marginal notes. Let me give you back your own recommendation; in studying the ways to improve the education and opportunities for my people, the Mexican-American people and their children, *read beyond the printed page.*

Let us discuss what the orthodox reference does not do, and examine, even if partially, the reverse of the question. Few, if any, references available are written by Mexican-Americans, and even those that are cannot avoid circularity, that is quoting and requoting the Anglo point of view. There are works of Mexican and Latin American writers available, but even when somewhat applicable to the people of those origins in our midst, most of those works are unknown to you, or are written in the "alien" tongue.

So come with me to the very edge of the eight-point Roman bold, give a broad spiritual jump, and take a trip with me to what you call "the margin." This is the AGE OF THE TRIP, and the trip with me will be less dangerous and costly than the psychedelic, but perhaps more effective in amplifying perception and expanding consciousness.

Who Is Marginal

Despite what James B. Conant, Martin Mayer, and Vice-Admiral Rickover may say to the contrary, we know we have one of the best systems of education in the world. We educate teachers better and longer than most other nations to keep it that way. We teach them objectivity and methods of research. We try to make them expert in the art of never jumping to conclusions; well, at least not much ahead of the principal. We force upon them volumes of social science, and psychology, so that they can meet the needs of the child. For some fortunate ones we even have invented the "sabbatical leave," to let them go abroad, see the world, and return with a more liberal perception.

Then, one day, we give them an assignment in Boyle Heights, La Puente, or Pacoima, among children of Mexican descent, who are bilingual, have parents who, for their communication, prefer that tongue-twisting Spanish . . . and all our objectivity, preparation, internationalism, and liberal perception go out the window with that simple assignment. Our very nature claims that such a situation is intolerable . . . How those parents are doing a disservice to their own kids . . . and "If they like Spanish so much, why don't they leave the country, and go to where only Spanish is spoken . . ." With a mixture of chauvinism and evangelistic hypocrisy, and thundering against inconsiderate aliens, we set ourselves to change their reality to our own image and semblance. Quaintness then loses all its exotic attraction, and "one nation" means no cultural pluralities. Their "other-ness" is to our "we-ness" a pain in the neck. . . The margin, man, the unadapted, hard-core, resistant, unmelting, culturally deprived margin. Anathema!

Perhaps it is a question of perception. The Mexican and Latin American in our country are today a reality of some seven million people. A dynamic, measurable, tangible reality, bigger than the ideal ratio per class we face at Lincoln High, or Riggin Elementary in East Los Angeles. Seven million people; more people than in any of the Central American Republics, or some of the South American countries, or several of the new African states put together. Seven million people with a real live language, real live desires and aspirations, real presence in the life of the nation; as American as the rest of us; not separatist as the French *Canadien,* not oriented towards White Power, or Black Power, or Mexican Chili Powder, . . power, I mean, but loyal, good Americans, as the ratio of Medals of Honor per capita and the number of fallen in battle show with largesse.

True, we have our differences of opinion from conceiving Paradise as a boarding house for American tourists in Puerto Vallarta, to believing that total acceptance of, and total submission to, the Anglo culture is going to bring the individual total acceptance by, and total admission to, the Anglo culture. But this great mass, whose cultural tenets were already a reality in America at the time the tide of Manifest Destiny swept towards the West, has a right to remain as another one of our life influences. Not subordinate, not unequal, inferior, or destructible, but side by side with the Anglo culture, in full harmony with it, in perfect adjustment and adaptation, interwoven, yet apparent. That was the covenant, and that is the righted guarantee. And it is consonant with our insistent clamor for individual freedoms and rights and the main text of the book of our national existence.

Margin or Cultural Thread

We admit that there are various orders, or genres, of us Mexican-Americans, Hispanos, Latins, what-have-you. But almost all of us are in agreement that, despite our differences of thought, the ability to master the English language is a demand from reality we cannot ignore, and that although one is not a necessary consequence of the other, a better mastery may better our chances of success. There is no conflict with the feeling of many Latin parents that, at present, they can teach better Spanish to their children than our schools can; nor is there any quarrel with the belief that some of our children may never need to speak Spanish in their lives. Our main contentions are, as I see them: (1) with the orthodox methods used in teaching children from bilingual, bicultural families; (2) with the emphasis on imposing myths and orthodoxies on the curricula, at the expense of the real needs of the child; (3) with the concept that the bicultural person is marginal, unhappy, incompletely adjusted, and maladapted; (4) with the idea that the educator, being the only expert, has little or nothing to learn from the Mexican-American parent and his culture; and (5) with the concept that the Americanization process is the formal, academic process that ends with the last bell of the last period of the day in the case of the child, or with the granting of the high school diploma in the case of the adult.

Teaching the Marginal Child

Undoubtedly, one of the greatest needs of the child in some of our barrios is to communicate better in English. But when, for 18 years or more, I have observed that the schools have advanced very little in this field of teaching the child to communicate, I must conclude that there must be something wrong in the system. Even including some of the compensatory programs, the same methods have produced failure after failure, year after year. Isn't it time to take a good look at the system, and stop blaming the child alone?

Out of 1019 pupils in the Harrison Street School, at least 957 have Spanish surnames. In a class of 25 to 32 pupils of this type, and with one Anglo-American teacher, where do you place the margin? Who must begin making allowances? With what experiences must you begin building that proficiency you consider desirable? Have we ever stopped to consider that in such a situation, the annoying reality is that the real marginal person, the true minority, is the teacher, and not the pupils?

Specialized programs such as the Tenaya School project in Merced, the NES program of Belmont High in Los Angeles, and the hush-hush Malabar Reading Project in East Los Angeles, have confirmed my suspicions that more daring and nonorthodox methods are needed to teach English to our children. These are methods in which the communication resources a child brings to school, even if these resources are that confusing mixture of Spanish and English we irreverently call "Chicanglish," are fully considered and used. These are methods in which origin, cultural background, language, and parental influences are totally accepted as "necessary," and are even recognized and encouraged. These are methods in which the conversion to English is effected gradually, without drastic demands of total abjuration of loyalty to one's own culture, nor the adoption of a false role, nor the suffering of undue anxiety and opprobrious confusion.

And, before anyone mentions the "Hawthorne effect," that defense many of us use when we try to cover our own indolence, jealousies, or impotence to formulate and carry to success new experiments, let us learn all we can about the projects mentioned, and let us see them in operation. With pleasant surprise we will notice the change in affect, perception, and participation attained, for instance, in the Spanish-for-Spanish-speaking group at Belmont High; or the community pride developed by Malabar and its Reading Project; or the degree of cohesiveness and enthusiasm noted at the Tenaya School; or how similar methods can operate in another dissimilar culture, such as the Japanese, as proven by the success of the Maryknoll Mission School. Then, those accustomed to the mutism, reticence, shyness, and withdrawal of the bilingual school body, will perceive a dynamic, vocal, aggressive, articulate, participating, and accomplishing student, who has acquired a new pride in playing the role of what he really is. The difference might lead us to speculate that perhaps a little more of that which produces the "Hawthorne effect," is what is needed to teach the bilingual, bicultural child.

When We Impose Our Orthodoxies

When someone tries to impose his orthodoxy on children of another cultural orientation, scenes like this develop. Margarita, a child of Mexican-American extraction on her first day, in second grade, is asked to introduce herself to the class. Already under undue anxiety, for, in her culture, modesty is a prime virtue, she blurts: "I am Margarita . . ." The rhythmic cadenzas of Darío's poem still dance in her ears,

> "Éste era un rey que tenía
> un palacio de diamantes . . .
> Un trono de malaquita,
> un gran manto de tissú, . . .
> y una linda princesita,
> tan bonita, Margarita,
> tan bonita como tú."

Then, the cold lash of reality across the face. In precise, and perfectly rounded syllables, the teacher retorts, "Yes, but you know now that we are in an Amer-i-can school. So your name is *really* Margaret . . . Right, children?"

American has now all the exclusivist connotations of the zealot's gospel. But the stoning of the sinner cannot be yet fully enjoyed, nor justified by her conscience, without the full assent of the captive audience. So, Margarita, who for all the seven years of her life has been Margarita, must now be a different child, or herself, but under false pretenses. For Mrs. All-Understanding-and-Accepting requires, for total acceptance, that one become ashamed of what one really is and that, after public abjuration, one pretend to be what one really is not. An isolated incident? Oh, no! This is a daily occurrence in many of our schools.

Can you now imagine the case of a child from very traditional parents, who was named in honor of the saint of the day, Petronila, or Pancracia. Can you imagine the day of the rechristening . . .

the teasing thereafter in the play yard . . . the unbearable psychic pain . . . Would you believe "Peternelle," or "Punkcraze" . . ?

Dealing with the psychiatric patient, and from the lips of master therapists, I learned the meaning of the concept *depersonalization,* the state in which a person loses the feeling of his own reality, which is characteristic, I was told, of a serious personality deterioration. So the price of adjustment we are exacting from the child in our classes is the very symptom the psychiatrist is trying to cure in his patient in the clinic. We are asking our children to escape from their own identity, culture, and reality, and adopt a false role. No wonder the healthy personality rebels against blind compliance. No wonder those who submit sometimes show such a shallow affect and disloyalty to Anglo and Latin cultures alike, and so tenaciously cling to that strange world of their own fabrication, that of being a nonbeing.

Unhappy Who . . . ?

Someone in the literature began the rumor that what is generally called the "marginal man" is an unhappy being, not fully Anglo, nor fully Latin; with problems of one side and from the other. I do not think of George Santayana as marginal par excellence, or of Salvador de Madariaga, or the hundred others who have attained intellectual, economic, and social success, as unhappy or maladapted despite maintaining their own identity. On the contrary; with the tendency our abundant civilization has to satiate, and cause ennui, isn't it fortunate he who can ascend, as well as rise, fall as well as descend, who can add depth and profoundness to his expression; who can titillate his palate, tired of roast beef and hamburgers, with paella, and who tired of roast turkey can sink in the ardent sea of mole oaxaqueno, "black as sin and hot as hell, and as both so tempting . . ." who can delight his full senses with the velvety emerald of guacamole, and can find some new pleasures with the pungent tastes of the guava and the quince compote . . . ?

Leave the manacles of the Liverpool sound and the Nashville twang for the intolerant monocultural who prefers his state of grace. I have, in addition to that, the mariachis that Herb Alpert appropriated for his unrivalled success, the amorous tempo of my beloved bolero that fascinated George Gershwin, and the picturesque impressionism of Granados and Albéniz which so impressed Leonard Bernstein. Why should I live in an impenetrable one-room castle? I want for my expression the primitive beauty of the Walt Whitman verse, or the refined elegance of Ruben Darío. For my conceptions of democracy I want the expressions of Lincoln and the maxims of Juárez. I wish to drink, taste, and enjoy the same fountains that delighted Washington Irving, John Steinbeck, and Ernest Hemingway, among many . . . Look, ma . . . no chains!

Reading the Marginal Notes

The emphasis on the total abandonment of the maternal language and culture that many educators express as necessary to succeed in school leaves me baffled for its inconsistency. In order to be able to pick it up again at high school, I must, at the elementary level, forget my language. What will later be a requirement, I am now required to forget. To better understand a world in which my country has an undeniable preeminence, and in order to understand my country and its formation, I must abandon my present participation in, and understanding of, one of the cultures of my own country. To free myself from provincialism, I must adopt parochialism. We, who believe that we must give our children the richest, amplest, most complete, and varied, and expensive, and practical education, must place our children from so-called minorities in an emotional concentration camp where we must feed them the monocultural inflexible line? This, when we learned as V. G. Childe said that "Human minds are not . . . mass-produced machines into which uniform experience has only to be fed for them to turn out uniform thoughts"?

But We Are the Experts

But we are the experts. The teacher is supposed to know all the liturgy and incantations which produce "good Americans." And these unsophisticated parents, what can they really offer?

These parents which many educators consider so poor, unreliable, culturally disadvantaged, dull and unsophisticated, are a very interesting lot, if we take at least the trouble to know a little bit more about them.

Poor? Despite their lack of education, their average income is over $5700 per year. Unreliable? Their credit rating is excellent, in general; their savings amount to quite a lot at Pan-american Bank, their own bank, and at Eastland, Atlantic, Home, Monarch and other savings associations. Illiterate? They support two local dailies, seven other daily editions of Mexican papers, more than one hundred weekly and monthly magazines of all topics. From one of their specialized bookstores alone, they buy more than 1200 volumes per month, from eighty-nine cent paperbacks to fifty-nine dollar deluxe editions. At La Casa del Mexicano, they have for their perusal too, more than five thousand volumes of all topics.

Disinterested? They listen to two full-time radio stations and a variety of other programs, watch two television stations, have more than seventy-two clubs, and support a movie house showing Spanish-language films in almost everyone of their neighborhoods.

Culturally disadvantaged? These dull nonsophisticates prodded the Mexican government into exhibiting in Los Angeles the Masterworks of Mexican Arts, the most fabulous exposition the local museum has ever seen. They also persisted, until the Native Arts and Crafts Exposition of Mexico came here, where it was a tremendous success despite Northridge, and the miserable locale where it was presented; and their support of the Ballet Folklorico de Mexico has allowed the troupe to visit this city three times already.

Why then, do the same teachers who rave and rant about cold cultural artifacts, or marvel at the dazzling dances, consider as dull the individuals to whom such rich manifestations of culture really belong?

When we blame the Mexican-American for being uncommunicative and rustic, couldn't we just search a little within ourselves to see if perhaps our superior attitude has helped alienate them? With this question in mind one of our local schools decided to be revolutionary. When the parents did not come to the school, the teachers went to the parents' homes; when the program for the school year was planned, the school asked the parents to help it set curricula, and to make to the original plan the necessary changes, and then they began implementing them. And it went beyond the cold formalities of the "Open School Day," and established the "Open School Year." Harmony and communication improved to such a point that last Christmas, in the supposedly wild and dangerous neighborhood, the teachers, on their own time went Christmas caroling, receiving only the warmest and friendliest welcome ever. Ask Malabar who has taught what to whom in this unique experiment. The answer is worth at least six additional credits in Human Relations.

Understanding the Comparisons

Americanization should not be the process that ends with the last bell of the last period of the day, and the granting of the high school diploma. Forced by the realities observed in some of our barrios, some of us have tried to develop the concept of "schools that work." This is a school which never closes, but acts as a real community center, teaching and learning; where, when the children have gone home, the other aspect of total service to the community can begin. This school not only teaches formal curricula, but it is also the place where all the community needs are traded for services. It is the school that has become a repository for the cultural manifestations of the locale, that helps develop local talent in all orders of life, that operates cultural fairs and even acts as town forum. With such a school, with such a penetration into the community, can you imagine the savings just in the reduction of vandalism against it? Can you imagine parents giving you a hand as volunteers with your groups, your clerical details, your beautification projects? Can you imagine the school helping the individual in consumer programs, better understanding of the American system of government, serving as clinic, acting as a museum, theatre, and so forth, a true part of the community?

Let Us Erase the Margin

I am encouraged by the results we are beginning to observe even in a scanty way, and by the interest of the governments at all levels, by State Teachers Associations, the NEA, and other professional associations in compensatory programs. But there is much yet to be accomplished, especially in the revision of textbooks and programs, which have failed to give the Mexican-American the feeling that he and his culture are a real part of America past and present. And although change is difficult to come by, it is already occurring. We need only to speed it. The

Malabar Reading Project, with its first objective investigation and new methodologies, is a great hope for the elementary level. So is the Tenaya Intermediate School project for the junior level.

For high school, let's now experiment, for instance, with an ungraded plan of 23-minute units instead of the sacrosanct 48-minute unit, a program in which there is regrouping according to the ability of the student and the results of his entrance tests. In this program, and wherever possible, all academic requirements are conducted in Spanish. Spanish-for-Spanish-speaking is conducted as in the experimental plan of Belmont High, but with at least one daily period devoted to comparative language structure. We now have a large block for English as a second language. Let's also include now the traditional "buddy system" of the army, and allow those with greater proficiency in English help teach the less proficient student. It is an idea.

We have all kinds of clubs. How about beginning a new one, right at the elementary level? At first we are the Cabrillos interested in California as it has really been; then we move to the intermediate level, a Columbus Club, for a comparative study of cultures; and finally we expand to the Panamerican Club in high school for deeper studies in all areas about Latin America. In all three levels we will require participation in cultural manifestations of folkloric, interpretive, pictorial, or musical art. It's another idea.

We want quality education; and inventiveness, creativeness, resourcefulness, and community involvement are the only ways to get it. Texts, materials, aids, and resources we do not now possess can be obtained or created. We are creating some of them right now.

Business and industry have discovered the necessity of handling our people as another one of their vertical markets. But with them, it is perhaps imperative for survival. Well, in their case the success and rewards have been plentiful. How long does education have to wait for its success?

The problem is not so big. Bring yourselves to full acceptance and understanding of us; we will bring ourselves and our children to full development and complete accomplishment as you define it. Give us your instant of positive recognition, we'll give you our lifetime of total involvement.

Epilogue

We are celebrating this year the Centennial of Ruben Darío, the prince of poets of Spanish literature. I'd like to close with one of his most famouse epigrams. If you cannot translate it yourselves, have it translated. It is full of insight. It reads:

> Ve un zorzal a un pavo real
> que se espanta y gallardea;
> le mira la pata fea
> y exclama: "¡Horrible Animal!"
> sin ver la pluma oriental
> el pájaro papanatas.
> Gentes que llaman sensatas
> son otros tantos zorzales
> que si encuentran pavos reales
> sólo les miran las patas.

Happy insight, ladies and gentlemen.

References

Childe, V. G. *Social Worlds of Knowledge.* Hobhouse Memorial Lectures 1941–1950, London, Oxford U. Press, 1952.

Darío, Ruben, *Poesias Completas,* Madrid: Aguilar, S. A. de Ediciones, 1954.

Preceding selections have dwelt on problems of the disadvantaged, together with general solutions. Here is a description of a program that works! What are its successful components?

Success for Disadvantaged Children

MARTHA FROELICH,
FLORENCE KAIDEN BLITZER,
JUDITH W. GREENBERG

Introduction

The question of what constitutes a good beginning reading program is of particular concern to those who work in disadvantaged areas. The beginning reading program described in this article has been successful for several years (1962 to date) in developing reading competence among disadvantaged children at the John H. Finley School located in a low-income area of New York City.

The report discusses the philosophy and goals of the Finley program, some of the materials and procedures through which it is implemented, and the results of evaluation measures.

A sense of personal involvement and the need to experience success are deemed particularly important for children of a deprived socioeconomic background. The cornerstone of the Finley program is a careful system of individual pacing of instruction designed to allow each child to be involved according to his developing ability and to build a positive image of himself as a successful learner. The program emphasizes the development of independence in reading and study skills and of a sense of responsibility for learning. The involvement of parents is an integral part of the program so that the child feels he has support from the home.

The salient features of the program stated here briefly are elaborated in the sections that follow. There is intensive emphasis on oral language development based on daily classroom activities, involving each child individually. Initial reading activities are introduced and reading skills are developed through carefully structured and controlled work charts and experience stories which have immediate personal meaning for the children. Children are tested regularly and are supplied with books appropriate to their level of reading ability. The school maintains a large selection of trade books and readers classified according to a sequence of difficulty levels developed in this school. Horizontal reinforcement (reading of many books at any one level) is provided to the extent that each child needs this before moving to a higher level. Independence in reading and study skills is encouraged: a) by seeing that the child gets books that he can read silently with comprehension and enjoyment; b) by providing worksheets for specific books with questions to be answered; and, c) by having the child take responsibility for record keeping that dramatizes his reading progress and stimulates him to further effort. Reading homework is a serious part of the program, starting as soon as the child receives his first experience story on the first day of school. Parent involvement is encouraged through having parents check the child's reading at home and by providing conferences and demonstrations for parents at school. Extensive evaluation is built into the program to provide the detailed knowledge of each child's current status which is needed for careful pacing. Teachers' ratings and records of progress, graded word-list tests at frequent intervals, and standardized tests are used.

The program does not rely upon any single theory or method of beginning reading instruction—linguistic, language experience, sight, phonic-word, basal, or individualized; the approach is pragmatic and eclectic. However, the close and continuous evaluation of each child's reading progress and the pacing of materials and activities to develop each child's pattern of reading growth and language development necessitate training, supervision, and cooperation of the teaching staff. The program is concerned with ways of changing teachers' attitudes and classroom procedures with respect to the so-called "slow learners" and "discipline problems" in order to build a classroom climate that fosters success.

It should be pointed out that the philosophy and approach of the Finley program need not be limited to the instruction of children from disadvantaged areas. In fact, the program was developed in a middle-class school, although it has been applied most extensively in a depressed urban setting and meets the particular challenges that such a situation contains. The neighborhood in northwest Harlem where the Finley school is located is typical of city tenement areas. The school includes six grades with 1100 students of whom approximately 89 percent are Negro and 10 percent Puerto Rican.

For analysis, different facets of the program are discussed separately in this report. The program operates most intensively in the first grade, but the principles of pacing, sequence, and evaluation are applied throughout the primary grades and into the upper grades as well.

Reading Materials and Procedures

At the beginning of first grade, "reading" is introduced through the use of workcharts and experience stories. The workcharts focus on beginning reading skills and are used from the first day of school. Several types of workcharts appear in each classroom and serve as a means of recording the planning and organization of the daily activities of the class. There are charts for recording attendance, duties of helpers, special news, weather, calendar, pledge to the flag, and the assignments in the work-play period. The charts are designed with slots into which children insert prepared strips with the appropriate responses—their names, a word or phrase, or a numeral or picture. Thus word, phrase, sentence, and later paragraph comprehension, word-attack skills, and work-study skills are introduced through the reading of workcharts under the direction of the teacher or a pupil helper.

The experience stories, elicited from the children by the teacher, also provide a vehicle for teaching beginning reading skills. The stories are highly personal, repeat children's names, and focus on the immediate and familiar. The story is recorded on the chalkboard by the teacher. The vocabulary of the stories is controlled and is gradually extended as activities are engaged in which broaden the children's experiential background and concepts. Each child maintains his own "experience story reader" by pasting hectographed copies of the stories in a hard-covered notebook. Pictures enliven the text and serve as reading clues. Later in the year, as handwriting skills develop, the copying of the story affords directed practice in penmanship.

Changes in the workcharts and experience stories reflect progress of the children in reading. Increasingly complex vocabulary and language tasks are used in the workcharts; a prescribed sequence of structured, meaningful language patterns, first oral and then written, is followed. In addition to providing successful reading experiences, the materials are designed to extend concepts, promote growth in oral language, and interrelate learnings in all the curriculum areas.

Language games and differentiated techniques are planned for the children who make slower progress. Constant use is made of the chalkboard and of individual slates for the development of oral and written language and for practice in word-perception skills. The decision to introduce trade and textbooks is made for each child individually, based on detailed observations by his teacher and the director. The workcharts and experience stories are used as a frame of reference to help the child recognize and recall familiar sight words when he meets them in the unfamiliar context of the printed book.

The introduction of book reading in grade one, as well as the number and level of difficulty of books read, is tailored to each child's progress. A variety of trade and textbooks is used, following a sequence developed in the school. A classification of approximately three-hundred different titles, ranging from the first preprimer through second-reader level and higher has been prepared and is constantly refined. The designated levels do not always follow publishers' recommendations but are based on experience in using the books with the children in the Finley School. For example, *Laugh with Larry,* in the preprimer-three category of the Detroit integrated series, is read with ease in the Finley preprimer-one sequence. On the other hand, in the Bank Street integrated series, *In the City* is classified as a first preprimer and *People Read* as a second preprimer. Both books are read in the Finley preprimer-two sequence. Also many other titles are available in class libraries for individual reading or use with small groups.

Children are not hurried from one level of difficulty to another. Some need slow pacing and exposure to many books at one level; others may be paced more rapidly. For example, at preprimer-one level, thirteen texts are available. One child may not need to spend any time with books at this level; another child may take a few days; still another may remain at this level for as long as a year.

Silent reading is encouraged from the start by having each child read a book he can handle independently. Faster-moving children act as "buddies" to help slower classmates with specific word-recognition problems. Teachers meet with small groups or individuals who need further development of reading skills and reinforcement through additional reading of workcharts and experience stories, while the others engage in silent independent reading and other language experiences.

In the second grade, children are grouped on the basis of their progress in reading. From this point, the pacing is done by classes rather than for individuals, using the same principles of fitting the level of books to reading ability of the child and providing horizontal reinforcement. It should be stressed, however, that class organization lines are fluid and that children are frequently shifted during the year as their reading performance warrants.

To document the pacing of reading instruction, the records of the number and levels of books read by the second-grade classes in 1964–1965 and 1965–1966 were examined and are summarized in table 1. The books read included readers, social studies and science texts, and trade books classified at varying levels of difficulty.

It can be seen that in each class the children read many books during a school year, a striking contrast to situations in which several basal readers constitute the reading fare for the year. Moreover, the difficulty level of these books was differentiated according to the reading ability of the class. Thus, while a low-achieving class may have read many preprimers and primers, a more advanced class would have omitted these levels and read more books at the higher levels.

It should also be noted that the record for 1965–1966 shows progress over 1964–1965 in that the second grade classes read

TABLE 1

NUMBER OF BOOKS READ AT EACH LEVEL OF DIFFICULTY BY GRADE TWO CLASSES OF DIFFERING ACHIEVEMENT IN ACADEMIC YEARS ENDING JUNE 1965 AND JUNE 1966

Difficulty Level — Finley Program	Number of Books Read by the Children in Each Class*									
	2-1†		2-2		2-3		2-4		2-5	
	'65	'66	'65	'66	'65	'66	'65	'66	'65	'66
Preprimer 1	13	—	5	—	—	—	—	—	—	—
Preprimer 2	9	—	9	—	8	—	—	—	—	—
Preprimer 3	16	16	16	10	17	6	3	_	—	—
Primer	4	7	7	7	7	7	4	4	—	—
Trade Book–List A	7	11	10	11	8	11	8	11	—	—
First Reader	—	6	5	6	6	6	5	6	3	4
Trade Book–List B	—	14	4	15	18	19	23	22	20	25
Social Studies (First Reader)	1	3	1	2	3	3	2	2	4	3
Science (First Reader)	2	4	2	4	1	2	2	6	4	6
Second Reader	—	1	1	6	5	2	9	12	12	12
Social Studies (Second Reader)	—	—	—	3	—	3	1	8	12	12
Science (Second Reader)	—	—	—	—	1	—	—	7	—	14
Total Number	52	62	60	64	74	59	57	78	55	76

*Each of these books was available in class sets with a copy distributed to each child in the class.

†2-1 is the class with the lowest reading ability; 2-5 is the highest.

more books than in the previous year, an average of sixty-eight books in 1965–1966 and sixty books in 1964–1965. There are, of course, variations from class to class attributable to differences in experience of teachers with the program. Further, the increase in books read was seen chiefly at the higher levels of difficulty, indicating that the program in both first and second grades has become increasingly effective. It will be seen in table 2 that this progress is also reflected in standardized test results.

At the beginning of the year, teachers in each grade hold planning conferences with the director to implement the total program. Classroom demonstrations are given to show specific techniques and emphases. Group and individual teacher conferences follow the demonstrations, so that an immediate opportunity is afforded to discuss techniques and to provide for questioning and appraisal of the principles involved.

Worksheets and Records

In keeping with the program's emphasis upon early development of independence in learning and of good work habits and study skills, special worksheets which test comprehension have been devised by the director of the program and are introduced with the beginning of book reading. At first, only multiple-choice or "yes-no" responses, involving circling the answer, are called for. As the child learns to write, more challenging responses are elicited. Correction sheets are provided. The teacher or the director studies the child's responses and, in a group or individual meeting with the child, ascertains the cause of any difficulty. Individual conferences are held several times a week with all children to check on word recognition of the vocabulary of their silent-reading homework assignments. Children are taught self-study techniques for recall of the isolated words in the vocabulary list. The vocabulary check always follows the reading of the text, with the children encouraged to refer back to the context when they do not recall a word in the list.

Class and individual record-keeping forms, as well as individual folders of each child's work, are considered essential in this program. The record forms have been designed to provide the primary grade teachers with a perpetual inventory of each child's progress and to facilitate articulation from grade to grade. These same forms help the director of the program form ability groups for team-teaching sessions, for instruction in specific reading skills, for the sharing and enjoyment of a particular book or story, as well as for the individual pacing of books. From the very start, the child learns the importance of records by participating in and recording workchart activities.

Homework and Parent Involvement

Communication with the home is maintained through the children's daily home assignments and through letters, conferences, and interviews. Specified reading homework is assigned to each child in accordance with his reading level so that he is able to do his reading homework independently. The parent is encouraged to help by: (1) seeing that the child has a quiet place where he can read silently to himself; (2) seeing that the child checks the words in the vocabulary at the end of the book and then repeats them to the parent; and (3) signing the child's reading-homework slip each day. A form is enclosed in each book the child takes home, indicating pages to be read, words to check, and a place for the parent's signature. Subsequent letters keep the parent informed of the child's progress and suggest additional supportive home activities such as a trip to story hour in the neighborhood library. Library visits are considered important, and 100 percent membership in the public library is achieved by most classes.

Class and individual instructional conferences are held with the parents to show them specifically how they can help and to explain the differences in children's reading performance. The need for approbation and support of the child, whether the child's initial response to reading be quick or slow, is stressed. Demonstrations of "home-study" practices are given to parents and to older siblings. No child is left to struggle alone. An attempt is made to maintain close home-school contacts even during school vacations.

In order to ascertain the extent to which parents were cooperating in supervising homework, an examination was made of letters and slips which children were asked to have signed at home for assignments. It should be noted that for the individually paced children in grade one, this entailed specific homework adapted to each child's level in the particular book he was then reading. The first graders also had review assignments in their "experience story" notebooks and *Weekly Readers*.

In the first grade classes, heterogeneously grouped, 85 percent of the parents signed the letter and 76 percent signed the silent-reading record which involved a signature for each day's assignment slip. In grade two, 91 percent of the parents signed the letter and 89 percent signed the reading-assignment record. The parent response in grade two did not vary systematically with the ability level of the class. The above percentages indicate that most of the parents complied with the school request. (Thus, though it is often stated that parents in lower socioeconomic areas are apathetic in response to school overtures, Finley parents have been cooperative and involved.)

Methods of Evaluation

Evaluation of each child's growth in language, in reading, and in social behavior begins on the first day of school. A Beginning Reading Class Profile, devised by the director, assesses the pupil's ability on a four-point scale. Highest on the scale are those children who contribute sentences to be recorded in the experience stories and on workcharts, who recall sentences after an interval, and who recognize words instantly. Lowest on the scale are those who have difficulty repeating sentences and who are unable to match words. The scale also provides space for notations, such as "parent does not regularly sign homework." Problems (behavior, foreign language, excessive lateness or absence) are also noted so that appropriate measures for improvement may be taken by the school nurse, teacher, parent, director, guidance counselor, or principal.

The child's standing on the Beginning Reading Profile scale is the first formal record of his reading growth. In addition, the Finley adaptation of the *Harris Sample Graded Word List* (1961) is administered once a month to each child in grade one and every six weeks to each child in grade two to evaluate growth in word recognition. The school has prefaced the test with a list of words at the experiential level based on the workcharts used daily. The child's scores on his worksheets are a continuing evaluative measure.

The *New York Tests of Growth in Reading* (1947, 1948) have been given at the end of each year in grades one and two. In 1966, the children in grade two were also given the *Metropolitan Achievement Test* (1966) as part of a citywide testing program instituted by the Board of Education. These standardized tests, however, are not the only criteria used for placing a child or appraising his ability. The judgment of the teacher and of the director, based on observation of the child's daily performance, analysis of his standing on the class profile, his results on the Harris Test, and conferences with the parent, is also used in pacing instruction.

The standardized tests do provide a formal measure of the progress of the children in the reading program and enable comparisons to be made with established norms. Table 2 presents grade-equivalent quartile scores on the *New York Tests of Growth in Reading, A* and *B,* for grades one and two from 1963 to 1966. It should be noted that before the present program was initiated fewer than half of the children in grade one were judged able to participate in the testing. From the first year of this program (1962–1963), all children have been tested in grade one as in other grades.

TABLE 2

RESULTS OF NEW YORK TESTS OF GROWTH IN READING GIVEN
AT END OF GRADES 1 AND 2 (1963–1966)

| | Grade Equivalent Quartiles | | | |
	Q_1	Median	Q_3	Range
Grade 1–Test A (ceiling 3.5) (Time of Testing: 1.9)				
1963 (N = 154)	1.9	2.2	2.6	(0.0–3.5)
1964 (N = 154)	1.9	2.3	2.7	(0.0–3.5)
1965 (N = 144)	1.9	2.1	2.6	(0.0–3.5)
1966 (N = 166)	2.1	2.4	2.7	(0.0–3.5)
Grade 2–Test A (ceiling 3.5) (Time of Testing: 2.7)				
1963 (N = 148)	2.3	2.8	3.3	(0.0–3.5)
1964 (N = 143)	2.8	3.1	3.4	(1.7–3.5)
1965 (N = 146)	2.7	3.2	3.4	(1.9–3.5)
1966 (N = 125)	2.9	3.3	3.5	(2.3–3.5)
Grade 2–Test B (ceiling 4.2) (Time of Testing: 2.9) 1963 (Not given)				
1964 (N = 136)	2.6	3.2	3.7	(0.0–4.2)
1965 (N = 141)	2.3	3.1	3.7	(0.0–4.2)
1966 (N = 121)	2.8	3.7	3.9	(0.0–4.2)

Results on test A have been fairly consistent in grade one since the introduction of the program with some indications of progress as the program has become increasingly well established. Median grade-equivalent scores have been somewhat higher than the norms for the end of first year, ranging from 2.1 to 2.4. The third, or top, quartile scores of 2.6 or 2.7 show that 25 percent of the children have been achieving, by the end of the first year, above the norm for the middle of second grade. The grade-equivalent score marking the first, or lowest, quartile each year was just about at the norm for the end of grade one with some rise noted for the year 1966.

Children in grade two were also given the *New York Tests of Growth in Reading Test A* each year. The median scores showed continuous improvement and have surpassed the norms for the end of the second grade. The performance of children at the lowest end of the range has been brought up, and the current first quartile scores approximate the norm median level. Since many children achieved the ceiling score on test A (3.5), the entire grade was given the more difficult *New York Tests of Growth in Reading Test B*. Here the higher achievers had an opportunity to demonstrate their superior reading ability, resulting in a grade equivalent of 3.9 at the third quartile for the most recent year and 3.7 in the previous years. In 1966, the median score for test B (3.7) also exceeded the ceiling for test A.

Table 3 presents the grade-equivalent quartiles for the two subtests of the *Metropolitan Achievement Test* given to children in grade two in May, 1966. This test does not provide for one overall score as the New York Tests do, but it can be seen that the median score was at grade level for reading (2.8) and somewhat higher for word knowledge (3.1). Again the upper group of children, with the higher ceiling afforded on this test, performed well enough to achieve a third quartile score which is equivalent to a year or more above grade level. There is some indication that the slower readers may find the format of this test more difficult than the New York Tests.

In interpreting the reported test results, it should be borne in mind that these were achieved despite the fact that the school is subject to typical problems of high teacher and pupil mobility found in disadvantaged urban areas. Also, most children start out with a relatively meager background for learning. For example, the median score of the first grade, tested in the fall of 1965 on the *New York State Readiness Tests* (1965) fell at the twenty-sixth percentile, with the first quartile at the thirteenth percentile and the third quartile at the forty-seventh percentile of the normative population. Despite the low distribution of readiness scores, when the same children were tested at the end of grade one in 1966, over three-fourths of them scored above grade level. (See table 2.)

TABLE 3

RESULTS OF METROPOLITAN ACHIEVEMENT TEST, UPPER
PRIMARY READING TEST, FORM C END OF GRADE 2, 1966*
(N = 122)

Subtest	Grade Equivalent Quartiles			
	Q_1	Median	Q_3	Range
Word Knowledge (ceiling 6.0)	2.4	3.1	4.1	(1.8–6.0)
Reading (ceiling 8.5)	2.3	2.8	3.8	(1.8–5.5)
*Time of testing: 2.8				

It is, of course, necessary to exercise caution in making comparisons from one test to another, even within the same battery, and to keep in mind the variability and limitations of formal test scores. In summary, however, it seems clear that the results of the standardized tests have been encouraging, comparing favorably with published norms rather than falling below them as is so often observed in depressed areas.

Conclusion

The preceding account of beginning reading at Finley School has attempted to describe some of the facets of the program. One would anticipate that the diverse approaches to instruction; the emphasis on oral language development; the great variation allowed for in both levels and rates of learning; the interrelationship of reading with other curriculum areas and classroom activities; the encouragement of individual responsibility; the frequent evaluations; and intensive pupil, teacher, and parent involvement should all contribute to greater progress for each child. Experience with the program thus far indicates that the goals are being realized.

References

Durost, W. N. (ed.); Bixler, H. H.; Hildreth, G. H.; Lund, K. W.; and Wrightstone, J. W. *Metropolitan achievement tests.* New York: Harcourt, Brace & World, 1966.

Harris, A. J. *The development of reading ability.* New York: McKay, 1961.

Hildreth, G. H.; Griffiths, N. L.; and McGauvran, M. E. *New York State readiness tests.* New York: Harcourt, Brace & World, 1965.

New York City Board of Education. *New York tests of growth in reading: test B and test A.* New York: New York City Board of Educational Research, 1947, 1948.

A therapeutic technique known as bibliotherapy has received sporadic but enthusiastic attention for many years. Now its use and application are thoughtfully recommended to improve personal, ethnic identification of the disadvantaged.

Bibliotherapy in the Development of Minority Group Self-Concept

EUNICE S. NEWTON

Within the past few years special projects and services have proliferated which are designed to increase the academic attainment of students who progress ineffectively in conventional American educational programs. Despite differences in the materials and activities of these innovative programs, and in spite of the fact that the target populations range from preschool to the college years, almost without exception their proponents subscribe to belief in the vital role that a positive concept of self plays in the development of a fully functioning personality.[1] A positive concept of self, it is argued, is essential to the learner's personal, social, and intellectual growth and development. Bibliotherapy is frequently utilized in these compensatory programs as one of the vehicles through which personal and ethnic identification may be effected as a means of enhancing concepts of self.

An examination of the educational activities of some of the current programs for inadequately functioning students will reveal that, while bibliotherapy is presented as a standard feature to be utilized in the development of self-concept, rarely if ever is there given the rationale of its use or specific suggestions for practical classroom application of bibliotherapeutic procedures. In this paper, therefore, an attempt will be made to (1) review significant psychological theory relevant to the development of self-concept through identification, (2) present a rationale for the use of bibliotherapy in this process, and (3) suggest some possible bibliotherapeutic procedures to be utilized specifically by teachers of so-called minority groups—Negro, Puerto Rican, Appalachian white, American Indian, Mexican and, most recently, Cuban.

Theories on the Acquisition of Self-Concept

The composite portrait of the child who does not benefit from conventional educational programs has been drawn within recent years with increasing accuracy by Clark, Goldberg, Davis, Deutsch, and others.[2] The relevant literature attests to the fact that the so-called minority-group child learns of his assigned inferior status at an early age and, as a result, experiences deep feelings of humiliation and rejection. Consequently, even prior to his ability to verbalize his feelings, the minority-group child may become confused about his personal worth because of the lack of social support for positive self-esteem. Under certain conditions usually found in depressed areas in our country today—physical and economic deterioration, family transiency and instability—the child may develop conflicts with regard to his feelings about himself and about the group with which he is identified. The end product of these conflicts, doubts, and confusions frequently is self-hatred, a defeatist attitude, and a lowering of personal ambition.

Personality theorists[3] emphasize that from early childhood the individual's concept of self is an important factor in guiding both his immediate behavior and the later development of his personality. The child acts consistently in terms of the kind of person he believes himself to be—bright or stupid, attractive or unattractive, capable or inadequate in meeting the challenges of life. The concept of self is thus his personality viewed from within, and into it are integrated the sum total of the child's experiences.

The development of a concept of self appears to evolve through a sequence of experiences similar in nature to those in the development of attitudes—emotional interaction of the learner with an adult or peer model. The learning of attitudes and the development of concept of self, therefore, may be explained by the same general process which we believe functions in other types of learning. It is generally accepted today that the learner confronts a situation, identifies goals, makes a provisional try, and finds his expectations confirmed or denied. In his choice of beliefs (whether about himself or others), he is guided to certain provisional tries, beliefs, by the example of other people—that is, the learner imitates certain models. He "tries on" roles successively and adopts those with which he feels comfortable—roles which meet his needs and already developed attitudes.

The child's first identification is normally with his parents (or parent substitutes) within the immediate family circle. The parents are termed the "primary identifying figures" and the child's initial interaction is believed to establish with them his basic style in subsequent coping behavior with others. Whether the child's personality will be basically *adient, abient,* or *ambient* may be a result of his early emotional interaction with his primary identifying figures.[4]

Adults outside of the home may be identifying figures, too. Teachers, recreation leaders, and close relatives with whom the child frequently intermingles, as well as his intimate and constant playmates, all may be categorized as "secondary identifying figures." In a hierarchy of prepotency, these secondary identifying figures influence the development of the child's concept of self almost as much as the primary figures. In fact, as the early and middle childhood years wane, the role of the secondary identifying figures customarily increases in importance, and for many children quickly exceeds that of the primary ones.

As reading, television, and community contact broaden his knowledge of people, usually by the time the child is eight years old his choices of identifying figures increase markedly. It is possible for him to establish strong identification with fictional characters, historical personages, or famous athletes. In some instances, these "tertiary identifying figures" exert critical control of and make vital contribution to the molding of the child's self-concept at this stage of his development.

Identification is a complex way of perceiving another person — partly rational and partly emotional. At this time, psychological theory cannot adequately identify the totality of the process whereby a child selects his chief models. Sometimes the child himself does not know whose example he follows. It is believed that in some instances a veritable human *pasticcio* has been constructed by the child from which he emulates salient traits. It is vitally important that the teacher of minority-group children understand the development of self-concept, for the self-concept in the fully functioning personality dictates the outcome of the teaching-learning interplay.

The Role of Bibliotherapy in Developing Concept of Self

Bibliotherapy is based on the belief that a person is affected by what he reads. This belief is as old as literate society and has been remarked upon in some of the literature of antiquity.[5] While bibliotherapy is formally defined as "the use of selected reading materials as therapeutic adjuvants in medicine and psychiatry," for teachers and other educators bibliotherapy is simply the directed reading of books to aid in modifying the attitudes and behavior of children and youth. The effect of reading upon the young has been studied widely and has been, also, the subject of provocative speculation and heated debate.

While direct personal influence of the child's primary and secondary identifying figures is paramount in the formation of self-concept, it has been long appreciated that models in literature may make a positive contribution. The fact that a literary figure may arouse such close empathy that significant influences upon the reader result is of ancient acceptance. In classical times, the library was often called "the healing place of the soul,"[6] and the curriculum of both past and present educational institutions has included the study of literature as a valuable source of vicarious interaction in the human experience. The possibility of the learner following examples of successful living and avoiding the errors others have made is widely endorsed by educators as reasonable expectations of directed reading.

It is accepted by theorists in the field of bibliotherapy that books may be the sources of significant models only to the extent that the learner's psycho-social needs are being met.[7] It has been suggested that "wish fulfillment" may be the determining module in identifying with a literary character or notable personage. The child's wishes, dreams, or desires may be gratified through "putting himself in the model's shoes" where he may find the role satisfying and fulfilling to his needs. Stated another way, in the evolvement of literary identifying figures, there is an inextricably interdependent relationship between the nature of the reader and the nature of the reading material. For the educator, in its highest level of conception, bibliotherapy is guided reading which takes the learner beyond literal comprehension to discovery through identification of new and personal values. At this level of reading comprehension the learner approaches Rogers'[8] conceptualization of "pervasive learning" — learning that affects the individual's present and future behavior, his attitudes, and his personality. This is the kind of learning in which there is a change in self in the direction of self-enhancement.

Bibliotherapeutic Methods for Teachers of Minority-Group Learners

Teachers of minority-group children and youth may introduce them to the world of books in the expectation that a sense of self-discovery may result from discovering the common elements in human experience. A dual role is required of these teachers: they must be cartographers of the map of the world of books as well as skillful guides able to lead their students through the peaks, valley, plains, and rivers of the accumulated record of the culture of man.

In earlier sections of this paper, the theoretical bases were established for the processes whereby concepts of self are developed and for the role of bibliotherapy in self-identification. At this point, guidelines for teachers of minority-group children and youth will be presented which may be used in guided reading for the development of self-concept. While the principal materials, presented in the ensuing part of the paper will be limited specifically to the Afro-American minority, the guidelines have broad applicability to Puerto Rican, American Indian, Mexican, Appalachian White, and Cuban groups.

Directed Reading of Afro-American Content

Within recent years as an adjunct to the Afro-American's new vigorous thrusts for comprehensive inclusion in the American way of life, there has been published a body of biographical and autobiographical literature about distinguished personalities of African antecendents who have made signal contributions to America. In addition to the foregoing, several historical works and historical fiction have appeared which purport to present the story of the Afro-American in America, both past and present. These literary efforts which have appeared in hitherto unprecedented volume are of a wide range in format, age appeal, and standards; but for the most part, they represent sincere efforts to fill in a long-neglected area in American history.

Unlike the teacher of a few decades ago, the teacher of Afro-American children today finds no dearth of works of fiction and non-fiction which abound in easily identifiable racial and ethnic characters, plots, settings, and themes. The volume and diversity of this recent literature, however, poses a critical problem concerning its most profitable use in today's schools. In addition to the customary problems of book selection with works of varying literary standards, there is a new problem complicating book selection caused by ambiguous and paradoxical educational objectives currently besetting the Afro-American community. The teacher of Afro-American children is called upon today to decide *which* models in literature possessing *which* societal values shall the students be encouraged to emulate in the realization of *which* educational goals for living in *which* world—integrated or separated.

Within the framework of his school's objectives, the teacher of Afro-American children must plan and execute his bibliotherapy program through (1) selecting and utilizing appropriate guidelines for matching children and books, (2) establishing criteria for book selection, and (3) developing guided reading activities which insure maximum literary identification.

1. *Guidelines for Matching Learners and Books:* From research in human growth and development, learning theory, and children's interests, the teacher of minority-group children and youth may secure significant information about the characteristics and needs of the young at different ages and stages of development. It should be noted that the findings of these researches transcend racial and ethnic vagaries and as such, have broad applicability. A few generalizations with pertinent bibliotherapeutic implications from these fields of study will be presented at this point. Through understandings such as the following the teacher may secure increased competence in bringing together the right book and the right child.

a) From child-development theory is garnered the pivotal premise concerning the uniqueness of the individual. Inherent in this principle is the fact that since one's biological heritage cannot be replicated, each person's life has its own story, and its own particular themes and continuity. Thus one's experiences and aspirations help mold the individuality of one's present and future behavior. Closely allied with this primary concept are theories of the dynamic unity of the human organism, the sequential unfolding and development of phylogenetic characteristics from conception to maturity, the universality of human needs, and the important role of the environment in shaping the quality and quantity of intellectual development. Theories of the multidimensional and multi-determined nature of behavior, also, have special merit for the teacher of minority-group children. *It may be implied from the foregoing that the literary needs of children would be infinitely diverse and highly specialized, and that the environmental opportunities and the child's needs at different ages and stages of development should be continually considered in guided reading activities.*

b) From learning theory the teacher of minority groups may find the following generalizations helpful. Learning may be conceived of as problem-solving behavior resulting from goal-seeking motives. The degree of relevance of the learning activity to the student's life style and the magnitude of the personal involvement and interaction with the environment will all contribute to the success of the learning. Approval, recognition, and reward—especially from an identifying figure whom the learner holds in high regard—will similarly enhance learning. *It may be implied from the foregoing that guided reading should be an integral part of the in-school and out-of-school life of the child, and that book selection should utilize the student's goals, preferences and interests as primary motivational and orientational forces.*

c) Finally, from researches of children's interests, the teacher of minority-group children may find the following guides of help in matching books and children: Interests are determined by a multiplicity of factors—physiological structure and needs, culture-based sex roles, experiences, and level of psycho-socio development. Interests are learned and are needs satisfying. To a great extent, interests depend upon the child's environmental opportunities for experiencing and learning. The child who feels adequate for the task at hand because of cumulative success is able to explore new areas of living— whether through real or vicarious activities. *It may be implied from the foregoing that directed reading which satisfied psychosocio needs should be capitalized upon and used to extend the child's interests.*

2. *Criteria for Book Selection:* For the teacher who wishes to assist students in the selection of books which are expected to supply Afro-American identifying figures and situations, a thorough knowledge of this field of literature is required. Knowing the individual needs, interests, and abilities of children and knowing the world of books are the two sides of the coin of effective book selection. Since there is no shortage of tools to assist in the selection of books, the possibility of eliminating unwise choices can today be minimized.

The criteria in general acceptance today for evaluating books transcend racial and ethnic themes and characterization.[9] The essentials of effective writing upon which books are judged include (a) the nature of the plot, (b) the quality of content, (c) the theme, (d) the characterization, and (e) the style. While surveying the book or a qualified resumé, the teacher should read with the following in mind: Does the book tell a good story, or in the case of nonfiction, are the factual sources reliable? Is the content worth the presentation? Is there meaning or significance behind the story? Are the characters credible, viable, consistent in their portrayal? Is the style appropriate to the plot, subject, theme, and characters? In addition to the preceding criteria, the format of the book should be evaluated, for it has been found that illustrations, typography, and even the quality of the paper as well as the jacket design can all attract or repel a potential reader.

Without the help which the teacher may secure from specialized book-selection aids, it would be almost impossible for him to cover the current field of Afro-American literature. The catalogs, book lists, and periodicals that follow are a few of the distinguished publications in this field.

Adventuring with Books. National Council of Teachers of English. Champaign, Illinois, 1968. This is a carefully selected list of old favorites and books of recent publication which are classified and annotated.

Books About Negro Life for Children. Augusta Baker. New York: New York Public Library, 1967. Selected titles which are submitted to stringent criteria as to themes, language, and format. The entries are briefly annotated and classified as to age groupings.

Children's Catalog. Marion L. McConnel and Dorothy H. West. New York: H. W. Wilson Company, 11th ed., 1966. Classified list giving titles, author, publisher, date, price, approximate grade level, and brief synopsis.

Council on Interracial Books for Children, Inc. 9 E. 40th Street, New York 10016. A list of "recommended" books of fiction and nonfiction that present fairly and constructively the pluralistic society in America — as to color, economic level, religion, urban and nonurban.

The Horn Book. The Horn Book, Inc. Boston: Published six times yearly. It includes current reviews of books for children and youth classified by subject and age level. Reproductions of many illustrations from the newest books are incorporated as well as articles about authors and illustrators.

The International Library of Negro Life and History. New York: Publishers Company under the auspices of the Association for the Study of Negro Life and History, 1967. Five comprehensive volumes which treat the history of the Negro in medicine, music and art, the theatre, the Civil War, and historical biography.

The Negro in Schoolroom Literature. Minnie W. Koblitz, ed. New York: Center for Urban Education, 33 W. 42nd Street, 1967. A comprehensive bibliography of over 350 books about the Negro-

American heritage. Listings include full bibliographic information, grade levels, critical annotations for kindergarten through sixth grade.

We Build Together. 3rd Rev., Charlemae Rollings, ed. Champaign, Illinois: National Council of Teachers of English, 1967. A reader's guide to Negro life and literature for elementary and high school use. This new edition contains perceptive and complete annotations of books about the Negro in various avenues and levels of life in America.

3. *An Approach for Directed Reading Activities:* At its highest level of conception, the reading process is a virtual dialogue between the reader and the author which involves subtle interaction with the mood, tone, and plot of the story. In order for children and youth to secure the most from literature, it has been long-established that they must learn the skills of interpreting what is read even as they must master the learning-to-read skills. It has been assumed, and research has substantiated it, that the greater the degree of reader comprehension, the greater are the chances for meaningful identification.

For a number of years teachers have used a variety of activities in an attempt to get students personally and deeply involved in comprehending literature. Book reports, book reviews, teacher-directed discussions, and book fairs and displays have been used most frequently to stimulate interest in and understanding of recreatory and therapeutic reading. To a lesser extent have been used the graphic arts, music, the dance, and informal drama. It is the position of this paper that in this age of profuse auditory and simultaneous visual-auditory communication, it would be wise to incorporate these modes of expression as the dominant part of literary interpretation.

The image of the minority-group child portrays him as generally favoring concrete, stimulus-bound learning situations and possessing perceptual styles uncomplementary to isolated, abstract visual stimuli. In addition, this child is reported as responding most effectively to learning situations in which the goals are easily recognizable and readily attainable.[10] For these reasons it would seem profitable to have the directed reading activities for the minority-group child utilize such promising instructional innovations as:

a) Peer-directed reading discussions — Encourage students to "do their own thing" when communicating their feelings, views, and understandings of the author's theme, mood, perspective. Let the students select the classmate whose "style" would probably be best for interpreting or sharing a particular book.

b) Relating popular music and dances to literary works — Why not allow students to find popular "soul" records for classroom presentation which reflect their views of a character's traits, predicament, or role? Why not encourage the creation of or display of current dances which in the student's view are expressive of critical moments of a story?

c) Open-ended book reviewing — Students should not necessarily have to agree with an established view as to the motives of a character. As long as a student can present a rationale for his view which is defensible from some aspect of reality, the class should be able to accept it.

d) Informal dramatics and role playing — Singly or in small groups students may participate in charades, pantomimes, or a form of the TV game, "Password," in order to get their classmates to guess the names of characters in stories read by the entire group. Students may review a story up to the climax and then act out the most exciting part. The tape recorder may be used by individual students or small groups to record unstructured reactions to stories for sharing with classmates or other classes.

e) Graphic arts to interpret literary reactions — In the spirit of the current vogue of free expression in tempera, oils, clay, wood, et al., there is no reason why students should not be encouraged to use these media for literary interpretation. The author's mood, theme, or central plot could all be expressed as well as specific characters' dominant traits in nonrealistic reactions. Unhampered oral explanations of the choice of certain colors to express one's view of a literary episode or tone should prove a fertile source of catharsislike therapy.

A Final Word

In America today, with a sense of urgency perhaps never before witnessed in any literate society, we are striving to ensure the maximum development of all the children of all of the people.

We are consciously attempting to bring into fruitful participation in our culture the able-bodied and able-minded from all segments of our society. Functional literacy is essential for even marginal participation in our way of life, and the higher-level skills of comprehending beyond literal meanings are now required of the citizen who aspires to a place in our world in the upper socioeconomic strata.

It is the thesis of this paper that despite the philosophy of Marshall McLuhan, understanding the printed word will be pivotal to full participation in our culture during the lifetime of those alive today. Especially for the minority-group child is it important that literacy be developed commensurate with his potential. It is submitted herein that bibliotherapy may be an effective medium through which the dual goals of the development of a positive self-concept and increased literary involvement and interpretation are realized.

Notes

1. Edmund W. Gordon and Doxey A. Wilkerson. *Compensatory Education for the Disadvantaged, Programs and Practices: Pre-School Through College.* New York: College Entrance Examination Board, 1966.

2. A. Harry Passow, ed. *Education in Depressed Areas.* New York: Bureau of Publications, T.C. Columbia University, 1963.

3. "Psychological Aspects of Education in Depressed Areas," *Education in Depressed Areas,* Part II. New York: Bureau of Publications, T.C. Columbia University, 1963. William C. Kvaraceus, et al. *Negro Self-concept: Implications for School and Citizenship.* New York: McGraw-Hill, 1965.

4. Lee J. Cronbach. *Educational Psychology.* 2nd ed. New York: Harcourt, Brace & World, 1963.

5. William K. Beatty. "An Historical Review of Bibliotherapy." *Library Trends* 11 (October 1962):107–17.

6. International Reading Association Bibliography #16. *Bibliotherapy: An Annotated Bibliography.* Newark, Delaware, IRA, 1968.

7. American Council on Education. *Reading Ladders for Human Relations.* 4th ed. Washington, D.C.: The Council, 1963.

8. Carl Rogers. *Client-Centered Therapy.* Boston: Houghton-Mifflin Company, 1951.

9. Charlotte S. Huck and Doris Y. Kuhn. *Children's Literature in the Elementary School.* 2nd ed. Holt, Rinehart & Winston, 1968.

10. Martin Deutsch. "The Disadvantaged Child and the Learning Process." *Education in Depressed Areas.* New York: Bureau of Publications, T.C. Columbia University, 1963.

Change the name, the faces, and the town — but you still may not have a "multi-ethnic" story. The author indicates pits of hypocrisy in the well-intentioned children's literature and textbook fields.

The Dawning of the Age of Aquarius for Multi-Ethnic Children's Literature

DAVID K. GAST

For the past nine years I've been interested in the depiction of nonwhite, minority Americans in teaching materials and especially in children's literature. I feel like an old-timer in this field because my study (begun in 1961, finished in 1965, and reported as "Minority Americans in Children's Literature," in *Elementary English,* January, 1967) was started before the events in Watts and Detroit and the rise of minority power politics. These events turned both public and academic communities to a serious and active consideration of inequalities in our society, including inequities in the schools and in teaching materials. But really, I'm not an old-timer, because the study of the portrayal of minorities in teaching materials has been periodically investigated for the past thirty-five years. Any decent review of the literature in this field would reveal the names of pioneer scholars including: Davis-Dubois, Rollins, Baker, Taba, the ACE Committee on the Study of Intergroup Relations in Teaching Materials, Tannenbaum, and Marcus. Though it's a sad commentary that, despite the findings and suggestions which were made over the years to bring about a culturally fair portrayal of minority Americans, no great interest was shown on the part of a smug and complacent dominant public, the publishers and, sadly enough, educators themselves until our cultural sore spots festered into violence, civil conflict, assassinations, and the politics of confrontation. It was the social action that spoke louder than academic words which really brought about the clamor to integrate school textbooks and to do something about the all-white world of children's literature.

A few short years ago the bandwagon started rolling and in the recent past we've witnessed some very constructive changes. Along with these changes we've observed a great deal of retrospective breast-beating and cries of mea culpa on the part of guilt-ridden middle-class whites. At the same time, academic hacks have enjoyed a journalistic field day gleefully rediscovering previously noted inequities in teaching materials. One segment of society viewed any attempt to portray a multi-ethnic society, and contributions of minorities to American life as a Communist plot. And for their part, the militants have sounded ominous warnings that the pedagogical change we see is too slow, too piecemeal, a cop-out concession to the racist establishment which will be corrected only by a massive change in myth—a pantheon of new gods.

Well, it hasn't been easy or at all times gratifying to be a constructive part of this social and educational revolution. But it has been exciting. And as the old vaudeville master of ceremonies used to say, "You ain't seen nothing yet, folks!" There's more to come because we have inextricably moved into a new age—the dawning of the Age of Aquarius for multi-ethnic teaching materials and children's literature.

I'd like to make a few observations on the present state and possible future of multi-ethnic children's literature, hoping, of course, that my comments might serve to elicit discussion. Let me start out by disclaiming any great expertise in the field of children's literature. My training has been in the social, scientific, and philosophic foundations of education. With this background I made my now reasonably well-known study in children's literature. Of course, I got hooked on it. So you're listening to a fellow who divides his academic interests between philosophy of education and children's literature, at first thought an unseemly combination, but in reality a rather delightful one. My comments are random rather than organized.

First, let me say that we educators and scholars find ourselves all too often on the trailing edge of innovation in education and society. Quite often we know what needs to be done but we are seldom innovators, partly because we see our role as objective interpreters of what passes for reality, partly because we fear taking a stand, partly because we have little direct influence, and partly because we might lose our heads and our academic respectability in going for a "cause." The real innovators can mainly be found in the creative arts. Surely the search for tomorrow is taking form in the heads and hearts of those who risk their respectability by disavowing belief in a deterministic world dominated by old myths.

Our problem with children's literature and teaching materials (and with all other areas of education as well) is that of keeping the human spirit and potential in stride with our free-wheeling technology and the social implications this technology has. Because, as we ought to know, technology is a two-edged sword. Among other things, technology has made us aware of poverty in a consumer-product-oriented America and our ability to do something about it if we decide to. So we have increasing educational concern in our day for the social imperative voiced about 200 years ago by Immanuel Kant: "Man is to be treated as an end, not a means."

You are probably in agreement with this last sentiment or you would not be concerned that educational literature should reflect a viable past, present, and future for minority Americans. And I surely believe most of you are interested in dispelling old myths about minorities.

Children's literature is a conservative media in a traditionally conservative social institution. But as a number of scholars have shown, children's fictional literature has been a more flexible, up-to-date vehicle for mirroring social reality than the media of textbooks. This will probably continue to be the case for some time even though some publishers are giving up "mint julep" editions of their various lines of textbooks. So we have hope. But we also have some problems. How do we presently view minorities in children's literature? How will we view them in the future?

Let's take a look at some past, present, and possible future approaches to the treatment of minorities in the literature. The categories that I enumerate here are not mutually exclusive. I've been somewhat facetious in labeling them but I think you'll recognize them.

The Invisible-Man Approach. Perhaps the worst treatment of minorities is no treatment at all. A number of studies have indicated that our literature is guilty of sins of omission. The minority American is the man who just doesn't enter into the picture when we reflect upon our society.

The Noble-Savage Approach. Since Rousseau, Western man has had a fondness for the ideal of the noble savage, the simple natural man who lives a rugged and virile life close to nature without the bonds of complex social restrictions. Of course this is a hopelessly romantic view that overlooks actual hardships and implies a separatist existence with little interest on the part of the minority portrayed as desiring integration or holding dominant American values. American Indians and Mexican-Americans have typically been portrayed in this way. It's interesting to note that many liberal middle-class whites now view Negroes in this light, somewhat jealous of the alleged black freedom of physical expression.

The White Man's Burden Approach. A familiar approach in older texts and children's literature is the explicit or implicit idea that the minorities portrayed are dependent upon white benefactors. This view is inherent in darky-on-the-old-plantation settings. It is also the message when history books talk of immigrants as being social problems. Recent literature has largely moved away from this kind of patronizing.

The Minstrel-Show Approach. Largely limited to children's books about Negroes, this approach portrayed the Negro as a happy-go-lucky, tattered "coon." Low comedy was achieved through situational farces and stereotyped dialect. Inez Hogan's

Nicodemus books were typical of this category and were printed up until 1945. We no longer tolerate such books.

The Queer-Customs Approach. Literature in this category is usually a well-meaning attempt to illustrate the unique cultural traditions and beliefs, generally of American Indians, Spanish-Americans, or Chinese-Americans. Most books about Indians fall into this category as well as books like Leo Politi's *Pedro, The Angel of Olvera Street,* and *Moy Moy.* At worst, such books stereotype minority Americans in regard to dress, occupation, and life style. At best, children should not be fed a steady diet of these books. A related and disturbing fact is that many teachers assume that books dealing with life in the land of national origin will provide sound generalizations for understanding a minority American. I'm thinking particularly of reading about life in Mexico in order to understand a bi-cultural person, the Mexican-American.

The Multi-Ethnic Dick-and-Jane Approach. This is a new approach and in many ways a viable one. In primary and easy reading books children are portrayed in multi-ethnic settings in school. They are all getting along well with one another. This approach illustrates an ideal but is subject to the same kind of criticism leveled at Textbook Town—too aseptic, too goody-goody, and artificial.

The Reversed-Stereotype Approach. We are still trying to overcome occupational and life-style stereotypes that have dominated the literature for many years. One surefire but questionable way to do it is the stereotype switch. We've seen this in the media of television and in some books. For example, showing all blacks as middle-class professionals is likely to cause problems of reader identification among ghetto children. One must say however that such books are in the American tradition of encouraging middle-class values and virtues.

The Tell-It-Like-It-Is Approach. This category is perhaps the most popular genre in children's literature today. Few punches are pulled. Ghetto and tenement living is shown. Discrimination, racial conflict, family hardships are all dealt with in a realistic fashion usually devoid of moralizing. Dorothy Sterling's *Mary Jane* was one of the first books about Negroes with this approach. Clyde Robert Bulla's *Indian Hill* shows the problems of Indians trying to make a life for themselves in the city.

The Remanufactured-Past Approach. Although we have a

great distance to go in honoring the historical contributions of various minorities to American arts, letters, and science, some pitfalls are apparent. We must avoid the hastily contrived out-of-context appendix to history. And we must also avoid giving the false notion that minority American inventors, professionals, and artists were as numerous and prolific as their white counterparts. Let's face it, social conditions didn't always foster minority contributions. History has been interpreted, rewritten, and fictionalized as long as man has been on earth. It's a natural part of man's tendency to seek mythic support for his beliefs. The question is how scholarly and objective do we wish to be.

I am sure that you can think of other categories, especially possible categories of future depictions. And that brings me to another consideration. What are the present and future taboos in children's literature dealing with minority Americans and multi-ethnic portrayals? An advertisement of Houghton Mifflin Company Children's Book Department claims, "So far as we know there is no taboo against fantasy, against discussion of unpopular politics, sex, booze, integration, mischief, and mayhem . . ." But surely there are taboos dictated by present attitudes and tastes, sales appeal, reading level, maturity level of reader. What are the taboos? At what grade levels and in what ways can social problems and conflict situations be introduced? Or should conflict situations be the only thematic vehicle for bringing about intergroup understanding?

Some of our recent tell-it-like-it-is books are hard-hitting accounts of social realism including topics of: black power, poverty, fierce racial pride, integration, inner-city living, and family disorganization. When are we going to approach interracial dating and marriage, mixed marriages, Oriental war brides and Eurasian children? I've just taken note of a new book by John Neufield entitled *Edgar Allan* about a white family who adopts a Negro boy. To what extent are these areas taboos?

In closing I'd like to say that children's literature can be an effective means of transmitting values and attitudes about minorities and their relationship with white Americans. You all realize its tremendous potential in what we might call "culture therapy" and also bibliotherapy.

We should not forget that children's literature has a mythic quality and function. Otfried Müller has told us that myth is a narrative that unites the real with the ideal. We have cultural ideals and we have manifest cultural reality. We need to unite the two. And it seems to me that this is part of the reason for producing and using children's literature. Any culture in which reality and ideal are greatly separated is a culture which suffers from what Durkheim called *anomie,* with the resultant alienation of individuals and social groups. We'd hope that literature could help prevent cultural disintegration by reflecting a rapprochement of the ideal and the manifest culture in acceptable mythic form.

Yet, there are some cautions. Back in 1908 Georges Sorel suggested that myth was the most effective political and ideological weapon known to man. Ernst Cassirer reiterated this view in 1945 when he said that myth is "a thing of crucial importance. It has changed the whole form of our social life."

So for those of us interested in the minority Americans in children's literature — teachers, scholars, authors, publishers, librarians — the basic questions remain philosophical: What ideals do we wish to promote? How far beyond the present social status quo do we go in depicting the future reality our children will be living with? How can we help promote the good life and the good society for all citizens? In short, ladies and gentlemen, it is the dawning of the Age of Aquarius for multi-ethnic portrayals in children's literature. We've all got a lot to live. So — where are we going? How will we get there? And how will we know we've arrived?

NOTE: Dr. Gast's current investigation in the depiction of Minority Americans is made possible by San Diego State College Foundation Research Grant #263007.

study questions

1. What would you say is the message of *Cipher in the Snow?* What is its pertinence to the field of reading? What, if any, is the *procedural dimension* of this message?

2. "Disadvantaged children seem to want to babble all the time and find it harder to keep quiet than other children," writes Figurel. Supposing this to be true at least for *some* groups of disadvantaged children, how would you explain the behavior on the basis of Lenneberg's findings? Which of Figurel's recommendations are compatible with this behavior and your explanation of it? What procedures found in other selections in this chapter seem especially promising in regard to what we now know about the language factor?

3. What is included in the "Hawthorne effect"? Research usually attempts to discount this effect from its results, since tı ansfer to new situations seems impossible to plan. Moreno, among others represented in this book, expresses a different opinion. What is it? What might be its significance in programs for teaching reading to the disadvantaged?

4. Which of the selections in this chapter contend that minority groups represent a culturally different but not a culturally deprived segment of the population? How do the authors of these selections suggest that reading procedures adapt to the differences?

5. What factors in reading are specifically attended to in the beginning reading strategy designed by Froelich, et al? Can you think of other factors that might be involved in the success attributed to the program? Which of the procedures described might be of help to other groups—for instance, those identified by Figurel and by Moreno.

6. What guidelines for preparation or selection of reading materials are implicit in Newton's discussion of bibliotherapy? In what other ways do the selections in this chapter suggest enhancement of self-esteem as a component of reading instruction?

7. Compare Gast's *Dawning of the Age of Aquarius* . . . with Larrick's *Baby Dolls are Gone* (Chapter 6). Do the two authors agree on criteria for literature about ethnic groups? Do they seem to you to introduce a change from categories derided by Gast? Which of these recent works merit use with disadvantaged pupils? What criteria does Gast imply for their evaluation?

8. The introduction to this chapter appears to identify social level as a determiner of disadvantaged groups. Articles in the chapter suggest other variables such as race, family instability, and inappropriate schools. Having read the entire chapter, how would define the disadvantaged? What do you see as the major values and/or weaknesses of the term and the concept it designates?

EIGHT

evaluation in reading

objectives

As a result of reading these articles and answering the questions at the end of the chapter you should be able to:

▨ explain the essential aspects of educational evaluation

▨ specify uses and limitations of norm-referenced and criterion-referenced test interpretation

▨ explain the concept of accountability and its possible uses in reading teaching

rationale

"There is nothing permanent except change," wrote Heraclitus in the fifth century B.C. And nowhere is change more evident than in the area of evaluation, simply because people are asking with increasing frequency and intensity whether schools are accomplishing what they ought to be, or even what they claim. This chapter provides an understanding of educational evaluation and its uses and limitations in improving reading programs.

introduction

Evaluation is judging the value of an object or process by comparing it with some criteria. Its meaning can best be explained with an example where a judgment about value must be made, as in a beauty contest. While the poet may well be correct in saying that "beauty is in the eye of the beholder," the nature of beauty contests demands the selection of a winner. The task of evaluating the beauty contestants is accomplished by comparing each against the criteria of feminine pulchritude.

Objects	Criterion	Evaluation
(Beauty contestants) 1. Jane 2. Margaret	A definition of what constitutes feminine beauty.	1. Jane is a very pretty girl. 2. Margaret is not as pretty as Jane.

The job is simple enough as long as the criteria of feminine beauty have been clearly stated and accepted by all judges, and Jane and Margaret are not identical twins.

Educational evaluation is but a step away and has the same built-in room for dispute — more, really; most things evaluated in education are less tangible than feminine beauty. A relatively simple task for educational evaluation might be the selection of a plan for a new elementary school. Again, the job of evaluation is simple enough as long as the criteria of what facilities are contained in the ideal school have been clearly defined and

Objects	Criterion	Evaluation
(Plans for two schools) 1. Round School 2. Square School	A definition of what facilities the ideal school should contain	1. Round School is very attractive 2. Square School has more facilities

accepted, and the two school plans have some obvious differences. The selection will never be made cooperatively if the group has not already agreed on how much space in the classrooms should be devoted to chalkboards or bulletin boards, and whether each classroom should have a bathroom.

A more complex task for educational evaluation might be an assessment of the reading-skill progress children make over the period of a year.

Progress	Criterion	Evaluation
(Reading-skill improvement over the past year) 1. Mary 2. John	A definition of reading skills operationalized into an achievement test. The children received scores on two tests, one given a year ago and one given this year: Mary 5.4–6.4 John 5.7–8.1	1. Very good. Mary made a full year of progress. 2. John made even more progress. Wonderful.

The job of assessing the children's reading-skill progress over the last year is not overly difficult as long as everyone involved in the evaluation agrees on the definition of reading skills and accepts the achievement test as a satisfactory measure of those skills.

By now you are probably coming to realize that the most crucial part of evaluation is the *criteria*. Unless the criteria have been clearly defined and accepted, judgment cannot occur. All that can occur with weak criteria is the giving of unsupported opinion. "I like the Round School plans because they appeal to me." "I think Jane is prettier because she's my kind of girl."

Criteria used in evaluation have two parts: (1) a definition that describes a desirable attribute or behavior, and (2) an instrument that operationalizes the definition in such a way that the defined behavior can be observed. One criterion used in judging the beauty contest might be described as a well-proportioned face.

Criterion	
Definition	Instrument
The definition would state that the contestant should have a well-proportioned face.	The instrument would consist of a checklist to be used in assigning a score for each of the features considered indicative of well-proportioned faces.

In order to be of any use in judging the beauty contest, the beauty judging instrument must be clear enough that the judges could look at five different faces and agree on the score each face should receive.

The major problem in educational evaluation is in selecting instruments that are suitable for definitions. In education the definitions are generally stated as objectives. The problem of matching objectives (definitions) and instruments becomes increasingly difficult as the objectives become more complex. If reading is defined as a relatively simple matter of pronouncing printed words correctly with little or no regard to their meaning, the selection of a suitable instrument is not difficult. The instrument could consist of having a child read aloud and scoring the percentage of words correctly pronounced. A child who correctly pronounces 95 percent of the words in a selection can be judged as being a better reader than a child who correctly pronounces only 91 percent of the words in the same selection. On the other hand, if reading is broadly defined to include thinking and feeling, the designing of a suitable instrument becomes more difficult. The oral reading instrument would certainly not be suitable for measuring thinking and feeling.

Many of the conclusions reached in current educational evaluations are very questionable because the evaluators confuse objectives and instruments and sometimes ignore objectives altogether. These evaluators adopt an existing instrument as the criteria of reading progress without ever trying to match the instrument with previously identified objectives. When asked what reading objectives they are trying to evaluate, they give the thoroughly unsatisfactory answer, "The test measures whatever reading skills are measured by the test." The practice of ignoring objectives in selecting an instrument because it is handy makes about as much sense as using a scale to weigh the beauty contestants as the sole evaluative instrument just because it is available. If one were going to be logical about judging a beauty contest he would want first to define the characteristics of feminine beauty, and then develop instruments to use in identifying these features when they occur.

In educational evaluation, the state of the art is such that suitable instruments, and sometimes even objectives, cannot be identified until a program has been in operation for some time. For example, in chapter 5 (Organizing for Instruction: Personnel) a study was reported (Greenleigh Associates, Inc.) where adult illiterates achieved higher scores on an achievement test when taught by high school graduates than when taught by certificated teachers. High school tutor John Smith followed the prescribed program closely, and really got his students ready for the test, and they won. But after a closer examination of the program and its graduates we find that certificated teacher Miss Stars not only did not follow the prescribed program very closely, but her students seem imbued with a desire to visit the library. Surprise! We had no idea that the deviations that Miss Stars made from the prescribed program would lead to that effect. Upon reflection, we decide that visiting the library is a very satisfactory way of observing an objective that we could only vaguely define as: "The student should *want* to read." Until educational evaluation becomes much more sophisticated than it is at present, we must temper our evaluations of children's reading progress with a good deal of skepticism. We do not as yet know how to measure, or even define, many of the more desirable outcomes in reading.

The problem of matching objectives and instruments is more involved than just finding test instruments suitable for complex objectives such as thinking and feeling in reading. The match is also dependent on the purpose for which the evaluation was made in the first place. Educational evaluation can be conducted for two purposes, assessment and instruction.

The purpose of doing an assessment evaluation is to judge whether a learner made satisfactory progress. The example given earlier of evaluating the reading-skill progress of Mary and John was a use of assessment evaluation. Assessment generally leads to an assignment of accountability. Someone is held accountable for the child's reading-skill progress. In the past children were held accountable for individual success in the classroom. They received a grade as a symbol of their degree of progress. More recently we have been prone to consider the child a product of his environment, and thus hold both the child and parent accountable. Sometimes materials have been held accountable. But now the concept of accountability has taken a new turn, in the direction of the teacher. In the evolving notion of accountability the teacher is held responsible for the child's progress. Teachers in some schools are even paid according to the amount of reading-skill progress their students achieve; a kind of reverse grading system. The articles reprinted in this chapter describe some of the uses and limitations of assessment evaluation and the resulting assignment of accountability.

The purpose of doing an instructional evaluation is to identify the specific instruction appropriate for each learner. In its ideal form, tests are tied to instruction so that the conclusion reached as a result of the evaluation is that the child does or does not need a certain item of instruction. If a child takes the tests for objectives 1 through 4, and fails to perform adequately on the test for objective 3, the conclusion reached on the evaluation is that the child needs the instructional item for objective 3. The instructional item is a single reading-skill

Objectives	Tests (T)	Instructional Items (II)
1	T_1	II_1
2	T_2	II_2
3	T_3	II_3
4	T_4	II_4

lesson. No one is held accountable for the child's performance. The question of accountability is not even relevant. The purpose of the evaluation is simply to identify the specific instruction the child needs.

An indication of the relatively primitive level at which we operate in the development of evaluation can be seen in the general weakness of instruments suitable for instructional evaluation. Standardized achievement tests, although most commonly used for instructional evaluation, are not very useful. They give a score that appears to be very precise, but one which is not readily translatable into specific instructional items. For example, what specific instruction is indicated by these reading-achievement test scores?

Students	Grade Placement Score	Percentile Score
Mary	3.5	64
John	3.1	45

The only interpretations possible from these scores are that Mary reads better than John, Mary reads better than 64 percent of the children with whom she is being compared, and John reads better than 45 percent of the children in the comparison group. About the only instructional conclusion the teacher might make is that both children could be placed in a third-grade basal reader. The test is not sufficiently precise to identify which lessons in the third-grade basal reader each child needs. Both will start at the beginning, even though Mary appears to be somewhere ahead of John. The teacher not using basal readers is given even less instructional guidance by the test.

Improvements in instructional evaluation will come as more appropriate instruments are developed and as teachers become more diagnostically orientated in their teaching of reading. The text *Competency in Teaching Reading* develops a teacher's competency in designing and using instruments for instructional evaluation.

The articles in this chapter provide background on educational evaluation, instruments of measurement, and accountability in reading teaching.

The conceptualization of educational evaluation has changed over the last quarter of a century, and Ralph Tyler is the one man most to praise, or blame, for that change. An indication of his influence can be seen in the fact that the Eight-Year Study, which he mentions here, is often used by current advocates of "free schools" to justify their position that as much, or more, learning will occur when high school students are allowed complete freedom in selecting instructional activities as occurs when they are required to follow the traditional high school curriculum. The study was completed in 1941.

What is Evaluation?

RALPH W. TYLER

Over the past quarter of a century the term "evaluation" has been used with increasing frequency, until today it is the most common word used in referring to educational appraisal. Also, during those twenty-five years, there has developed an increasingly articulated conception of the nature of educational evaluation and the procedure involved. In reviewing this history of evaluation, I find four distinguishable phases.

Educational Values and Objectives

The selection of the term "evaluation" has largely arisen from dissatisfaction with the direction that the so-called scientific movement in education had taken. The products of learning were being "measured" by tests which reflected the content of teaching materials but which were not built on a systematic analysis of the educational values to which good schools were dedicated. For example, reading tests of that time were constructed on detailed analyses of vocabulary and of the percentages of pupils answering questions correctly, but without systematic examination of the major educational values sought in the teaching of reading. As a result, most test items required only simple comprehension of reading passages or an unanalyzed mixture of pupil responses. Experienced teachers were sure that a number of values in addition to "plain sense comprehension" of reading passages could be and often were achieved in the teaching of reading. Interpretation of reading materials, for example, was much more than straightforward comprehension. Lifelong reading interests and sensitive responses to poetry are two illustrations of values which loom large in a reading program. These were minimally reflected in educational appraisals of that time.

Out of this background, the term "evaluation" meant a procedure for appraising the educational values actually developing in an educational program. The first step in working out a plan of evaluation in the Eight-Year Study, begun in 1933, was to identify the values which teachers were attempting to reach; that is, we sought early in the study to find out what educational objectives were aimed at in order to plan appraisals to find out how far they were being attained.

To say that evaluation should begin with the educational objectives is simple enough, but to obtain a list of objectives clearly enough defined to guide the construction of means of appraisal is not easy. Many teachers have not stated their objectives; in fact, some which they consider most important may not have been explicitly formulated in their own minds. Hence, the listing of objectives requires a good deal of thought and discussion guided by such questions as, What are we trying to help students acquire in and through our reading program? What abilities, skills, knowledge, attitudes, interests, habits, and the like do students need to get the most out of reading? Which of these can we develop through our reading program? Why are we using these materials or these procedures in reading? Do they suggest certain results or objectives that we are or ought to be aiming at? These are simply different ways of reminding ourselves of possible objectives, but often several different questions are needed to stimulate teachers and students of education to reflect upon their own experiences and purposes.

A second problem in getting objectives useful in guiding evaluation is the difficulty of defining objectives clearly. The purposes or objectives of education are to help the student acquire ways of behaving, that is, ways of thinking, feeling, and acting, which he has not previously followed. Thus a child may develop a mode of attacking unfamiliar words which he has not previously used, or a pupil may acquire an interest in reading science periodicals which he had not previously had, or a college student may develop a way of interpreting and responding to poetry which is new to him. These are a few random illustrations of the varied kinds of behavior which teachers may seek to develop in and through reading. If an evaluation is to be made, we need to know what kinds of student behavior we are looking for; hence our objectives need to be defined in terms of student behavior. When we talk about comprehension as a reading objective, what kind of behavior is involved and with what kind of reading materials? Such a definition provides a set of specifications for an appraisal of reading comprehension.

We discovered in the early days of evaluation that skills and abilities were easier to define than such objectives as interests and appreciations. Working over the years with teachers, we have found some fairly common agreements in defining some of these less tangible objectives. Interest in reading, for example, is often defined in terms of the following behavior: "The student likes to read. He gets satisfaction in reading. When he has free time, he often chooses voluntarily to spend time in reading." Usually teachers are concerned not only that students become interested in reading, but that they become interested in reading many types of books and magazines and that the content of the reading they choose voluntarily shows increased complexity and maturity as time goes on. Such definitions of objectives in terms of behavior make it possible to plan appraisals based on the important educational objectives. This was a first significant phase of the development of evaluation.

The Nature of
Educational Tests

Since the purpose of educational appraisal is to find out how far each of the important educational objectives is actually being realized, means for describing or measuring actual student behavior are essential. Without real evidence of what students are learning, we tend to rely heavily on our own preconceptions, and our temperaments, optimistic, skeptical, or pessimistic as they may be, will largely color our conclusions.

However, twenty-five years ago the prevailing conception of educational tests was a paper-and-pencil device, usually consisting of true-false or multiple-choice items. These devices could provide evidence of the amount of information the student could recall and could indicate, too, his facility in manipulating mathematical expressions and his ability to comprehend reading passages. But they were not relevant to some other important objectives. They did not provide evidence of habits, attitudes, interests, and appreciations. Few exercises required depth of understanding or of interpretation. As we sought to develop means for evaluation, it became clear that we must broaden the concept of an educational test. We now think of an educational test as a series of situations which call forth from the student the kind of behavior defined in the objective and permit a record to be made of the student's actual behavior. A test of reading interpretation should consist of a series of situations in which the student is stimulated to read and to interpret what he is reading and in which a record can be made of the student's interpretations. A test of reading interests should consist of a series of situations in which the student is free to choose activities and a record can be made of the extent to which he freely chooses to read.

This conception of an educational test makes possible the use of a variety of testing devices; not only can paper-and-pencil exercises be used, but also such procedures as observation, interview, questionnaire, samples of products made, and records obtained in other connections may serve as evaluation devices. To appraise habits, observation may be employed or, under certain circumstances, questionnaires may be useful. To appraise appreciation of literature, interviews focused on the student's responses to his reading and his feelings and judgments are sometimes helpful. Records of book circulation in the library may sometimes provide evidence of reading habits and interests. Hence, although the realization that comprehensive educational evaluation requires evidence about several important objectives made the task seem more difficult, the further recognition that a variety of appraisal methods could be used encouraged us in the work.

The accepted criteria by which to judge measuring devices — validity, objectivity, and reliability — were not abandoned in the development of evaluation, but they were redefined in terms appropriate for the broader conception of educational measurement. Validity, the requirement that a measuring device actually measures that which it purports to measure, is still the most important criterion. However, in terms of evaluation this means that the testing device should actually obtain a sample of the kind of behavior stated in the objective with reference to the content implied by the objective, or the device must be shown to appraise behavior that is highly correlated with the behavior stated in the objective. Furthermore, the content of the test should be appropriate to the objective; that is, the reading passages used and the new words involved should be appropriate to the definition of the objective aimed at with this pupil. This conception of validity is central to evaluation and is quite different from coefficients of validity derived from internal homogeneity of items.

Objectivity is also an essential criterion of a satisfactory evaluation device. All appraisal involves human judgments: the kind of behavior to be appraised, the units of measure to be used and their definition, those involved in the comparison of the pupil's reactions with the measuring standards, and those required in the interpretation of the measures. In this sense, subjectivity can never be eliminated in appraisal. But, as in physical measurements, purely individual idiosyncrasies in judgments can be greatly reduced, and the appraisal made by one set of judges can be very similar to the appraisal made by another set. This increase in objectivity is made possible by agreeing on objectives, by clearly defining the objectives, by constructing devices that more clearly and adequately give records of the kind of behavior thus defined, by agreeing on the units of measurement or the categories of description to be used, by training judges in the use of the devices, by employing methods for analyzing responses which are consistent with the objectives, and by checking interpretations through further empirical studies.

Reliability is also an important criterion for an evaluation device. An evaluation instrument is unreliable when the results obtained from it vary markedly from those obtained from similar devices. Unreliability arises from the fact that any appraisal can include only a sample of a student's behavior. A vocabulary test could not include all the words a pupil might know. A comprehension test could not include all the reading passages a student might be able to read. A test of habits could not cover every minute of the student's life. Hence, conclusions are drawn from a sample of situations in which the student reacts. To assure a reliable test, samples of behavior should be included which involve the known variations likely to influence the student's reactions; that is, the test should include a representative sample of situations which evoke the desired behavior. Furthermore, to assure a reliable test, the size of the sample, the number of exercises, or the time intervals involved should be large enough to cover variations attributable to unknown or chance factors; that is, the sample should be adequate. The usual coefficient of reliability is an estimate of the adequacy of the sample, but it does not provide an estimate of its representativeness. Representativeness can be assured only through the selection of situations or test exercises.

Evaluating Characteristics of Learners

As we begin to appraise student learning in the Eight-Year Study and to observe the varied effects of different procedures, materials, teaching personalities, and the like, it became clear to us that the educational effects in many cases appeared to be related to a number of the students' characteristics. A free reading program in the ninth grade which showed great influence on the quality of reading interests in one school seemed to have much less effect on the quality of interests in another school. Yet the appraisal of mental ability revealed no appreciable differences in the distribution of these scores. Similar findings in important areas led us to recognize the need for evaluating a number of student characteristics if we were to understand and report the values of various kinds of educational experience. Instructional procedures, materials, and principles of curriculum organization were often effective for students with certain characteristics and not for others. Hence, the conception of evaluation developed to include the evaluation of the learners' characteristics as well as the outcomes of the learning. Among the significant characteristics, in addition to age, sex, and mental test score, were social class, educational and occupational goals, cultural level of the home, parents' attitude toward importance of education, interests, types of motivation, social acceptance by peers, physical growth, and work experience.

Probably the number of characteristics relevant to planning a comprehensive reading program is greater than for any other school subject. Hence, it is necessary in developing a plan for evaluating reading to select those characteristics of students which are likely to have most influence in determining the kinds of reading programs to provide. Without an evaluation of the learners' characteristics, important information is not available on which to plan educational programs and with which to interpret the results.

Assessing the Conditions of Learning

When the Eight-Year Study began, it was commonly assumed that curricular plans, teaching methods, and instructional materials were in themselves clearly defined factors which could be assessed in terms of their effectiveness in producing desired learning in the students. Educational experiments had been conducted comparing the "laboratory method" of science instruction with the "lecture demonstration method," comparing "large-class instruction" with "reading method" of language instruction with the "grammar-translation method," and so on. Often several investigations of the same "methods" yielded quite different results. In the Eight-Year Study several schools explored such innovations as "pupil-teacher planning" and the "core curriculum." As we observed the developments in different schools of what was thought to be the same innovation, and as we talked with teachers about them, we began to realize that a phrase like "pupil-teacher planning" takes on concrete meaning in terms of the way in which such an innovation is conceived, developed, and actually carried on by the teacher. We sometimes found as much variability in results obtained among classes purportedly using the same "method" as we found among several different "methods."

It is clear that educational evaluation should include an assessment of the conditions of learning if the results of appraising what the students are learning are to be understood. This assessment will usually include descriptions of some conditions of learning and also more precise appraisals, depending on the ease of assessing the particular condition. What conditions of learning should be assessed depends to some extent on which ones appear to be critical for the educational program under study. Generally, a description or appraisal of the following conditions of learning will give a very useful picture of the teaching methods, materials, organization, and the like.

1. Student motivation
2. Recognition by the student of the need to learn new behavior
3. Guidance in developing new behavior
4. Availability of appropriate materials to practice the kind of behavior to be learned
5. Time for effective learning
6. Satisfaction obtained by the student from the desired behavior
7. Provision for sequential practice with learning experiences provided from day to day
8. Student standards of performance which for them are high but attainable
9. Valid and practical means for the student to judge his performance

Conditions for learning, such as the foregoing, provide a more useful way of describing teaching procedures than a description in terms of the proportion of lecture, discussion, small-group activity, and the like. It is possible for creative teachers to get results by a variety of procedures. But, whatever methods they use or however they stimulate reactions, their effectiveness can be more clearly understood by examining the teaching in terms of the extent to which the conditions of learning are provided.

What Is Evaluation?

In the light of the history of the past quarter of a century, evaluation is seen as a growing conception. Used as a term to cover the process of appraising the results of learning, it has developed into a process involving educational objectives, educational tests and measurements, the appraisal of the learner's characteristics, and the assessment of learning conditions. I believe that the conception will continue to grow as we identify other important areas which must be described or assessed if we are to understand education more fully, and more wisely guide the learning of our students.

Test to many people, is a four letter word. It is related to grading, to further confirming the negative view a student already has about himself. But grading is not the only, or even the most important, reason for testing. Prescott describes a type of test interpretation that is totally unrelated to grading.

Criterion-Referenced Test Interpretation in Reading

GEORGE A. PRESCOTT

An increasing interest is being shown in what is referred to as criterion-referenced testing or, perhaps more accurately, criterion-referenced interpretation of test scores. This interest has been stimulated by such developments as the controversial National Assessment of Educational Progress, by the expanded use of programmed instruction and computer-assisted instruction techniques, and by an increasing preoccupation with educational accountability and performance contracting. The purpose of this discussion is to point out what the author believes are uses and limitations of this method of test-score interpretation.

Nature of Norm-Referenced Interpretation

The problem of accurate and meaningful interpretation of test performance is as old as testing itself. The particular frame of reference for interpreting the performance of a pupil depends upon the particular question to which one is seeking answers. For example, if the question is, "Is Mary reading as well as she should?" one might logically look at her score on a reading test in relation to some estimate of her potential to read. If, on the other hand, the question is, "How much has Mary improved in reading this year?" a comparison of her end-of-year and beginning-of-year status in reading would be in order. "What are Mary's particular weaknesses or deficiencies in reading?" and "Is Mary reading well enough to warrant promotion to the next higher level?" are other questions one might ask. In any event, one typically asks several questions and, for each question, a different kind of information is needed or different interpretations of the same information are indicated. In most instances, however, the frame of reference for interpreting the test performance of an individual is the "typical" performance of some defined group. In other words, the reference is a "norm."

Interpretation of performance on standardized tests by comparing an individual's score with a norm based upon the performance of many other individuals of the same age, grade, or level of training has been standard procedure since the beginning of standardized testing. It involves comparing the score of an individual with the distribution of scores made by a representative sample of other individuals in some way like the person tested. Thus norms can be by age or grade; separate for boys and girls; or, if desired, for state, area, or local groups as well as national. The choices are limitless, the selection depending upon the particular needs of the test user. For most standardized achievement tests, a variety of *types* of norms are available. For example, grade equivalents, percentile ranks, and stanines are commonly provided.

Occasionally, even norms for *each item* in a test are provided. For example, item difficulty values, in terms of the percent of various groups of pupils answering each item correctly, are provided for Forms *F, G,* and *H* of the *Metropolitan Achievement Tests,* 1970 Revision. Typically, these are the percent of a norm group answering an item correctly. Thus, if 72 percent of the grade five norm group answer a particular item correctly, the "norm" for that item is said to be 72 percent, or to have a Difficulty Index of .72.

Nature of Criterion-Referenced Interpretation

In criterion-referenced — or content-referenced — test interpretation, no attempt is made to compare the performance of an individual with that of others. Rather, one seeks to evaluate performance in terms of whether an individual has achieved or has failed to achieve specific instructional objectives. It seeks to answer the question, "What specific skills, knowledges, and understandings has a pupil acquired?" Can he, for example, spell the word *believe?* Can he use the word *dormant* in a meaningful sentence? Can he suggest an appropriate title for a story? In its most elemental form, the response of each pupil to each test item is evaluated as correct or incorrect; the skill or ability, or whatever, measured by a test item has either been mastered or it has not. The criterion is 100 percent mastery.

Test results may be reported in several ways. On a ten-word vocabulary test, for example, one might identify the particular words that each pupil knows or the particular pupils who know each word. In the first instance, one might report that Michael knows the meanings of the words *stifle, random, origin,* and *expose.* In the latter instance, one might report that Michael, Florence, Dorothy, and Robert know the meaning of the word *stifle.*

The same kind of report can be made for clusters or groups of test items. This can be illustrated clearly in the case of a spelling test covering specific rules or generalizations in which four of the words to be spelled involve adding suffixes to words ending in *e.* Michael may have spelled all four words correctly; Florence and Dorothy, three; and Robert, only one. Clearly, Michael has passed the criterion test of mastery of such words. If one were

willing to agree that three out of four words spelled correctly
were evidence of mastery, Florence and Dorothy would be added
to the list. This is the gist of criterion-referenced test interpretation. It attempts to reveal whether a pupil has achieved some
specific objective or can perform some specific task.

For all practical purposes, criterion-referencing is precisely
what is done in programmed instruction. A pupil studies some
particular segment of a text on some subject—usually a highly
structured one—after which he is asked a question. If he does not
know the answer to the question, he is referred back to the text
to review the subject and/or is referred to some supplementary
source of information to clarify his understanding. Thus fortified,
he returns to the question. If his answer is correct this time, he
proceeds to the next unit of content.

Computer-assisted instruction works on much the same principle. The student at the keyboard of the console answers the
question the computer prints out for him. If his answer is incorrect, he is directed to go back to study some more and cannot proceed until he is able to produce the correct answer. In both instances, a pupil proceeds step by step through an instructional
unit. He proceeds to the next step only after he has exhibited
mastery of a particular skill or bit of information.

Proponents of criterion-referenced interpretation see this mode
of interpretation as being particularly useful (1) in evaluating
the effectiveness of a teacher's instruction and (2) in making decisions concerning appropriate instructional programs for individuals. Norm-referenced interpretation is found wanting by
some because, it is claimed, comparing a pupil's performance
with that of some norm group does not tell one very much about
a pupil's actual mastery of important objectives.

Criterion-referenced interpretation is also appealing to some
because it avoids the necessity of making "invidious" comparisons
among pupils. A pupil either meets the standard or he doesn't;
an answer is either correct or it isn't.

It should be pointed out, however, that criterion-referenced
interpretation does *not* escape the need for a base of reference.
Consider a question requiring a pupil to punctuate this sentence:

Can my friend Susan go with us to meet the plane

Would this be an appropriate question to ask a pupil in kindergarten? First grade? Third grade? The answer to this question

can come only through a knowledge of the in-school and out-of-school experiences of the pupil. Obviously, such a question is inappropriate for a typical five-year-old kindergarten pupil. But how about a pupil at the end of the third grade? It probably *is* reasonable to expect a correct response if the pupil has been exposed to all the needed instruction and has at least average mental ability. In short, criterion-referenced interpretation is *not* free from a norm-reference prerequisite; the judgment that the question is appropriate at third grade implies the judgment that the "norm" (typical response) should be a correct response.

Assumptions Underlying the Criterion-Referenced Approach

Several important and interrelated assumptions appear to be implicit in the criterion-referenced approach to test interpretation.

First: Mastery is a Reasonable Criterion

A well-known saying goes, "Whatever is worth doing at all is worth doing well." In terms of this discussion, it might be paraphrased thus: "Whatever is worth teaching at all is worth teaching to the point of mastery." Here is a basic weakness of criterion-referenced test interpretation—one that severely limits its applicability—because it is not universally true. In fact, it does not happen in practice nor can it, to any real extent, until each pupil has an individually prescribed curriculum. What a pupil learns to the point of mastery is conditioned by a whole host of psychological and environmental factors, important among which are: (1) the pupil's level of mental ability, (2) the relevance of the content to be learned, and (3) the effectiveness of instruction.

A requirement of 100 percent mastery of any skill can be justified *only* if the skill is demonstrably prerequisite to learning at a later stage. This is extremely difficult to demonstrate except, perhaps, in the case of the simplest skills. Assume, for the moment, that punctuation is introduced in the following order: period, question mark, comma, semicolon, colon. Is it necessary to require mastery of periods and question marks before proceeding to commas, or to demonstrate mastery of commas before proceeding to semicolons? Furthermore, is it necessary to exhibit mastery of *all* situations requiring comma punctuation before proceeding to semicolons?

To accept less than 100 percent mastery, some lesser standard must be established. 90 percent? 75 percent? If 75 percent, for instance, on how large a sample of all possible questions? It would appear that the only logical approach would be to study what the *population* does; and the moment population is considered, one has moved from a criterion-referenced to a norm-referenced interpretation of test performance.

It is easy to assume that a pupil has mastered an item once he has given the correct answer to a particular question. This may not be true, of course, and it is much less likely to be true if the questions are of the multiple-choice or similar objective type where there is an element of guessing involved.

Actually, use of the multiple-choice item (or its variants) is questionable when the criterion-referenced approach is paramount since it sets up a "loaded" situation to which the pupil responds. The alternatives are chosen as "distractors" because, in the mind of the test-item writer, these actually are the possible choices an individual might make in his ignorance. The multiple-choice aspect of the test item functions only when the pupil has partial information on which he may make a correct choice by considering and rejecting the choices one by one. If he makes a guess because he has no information, the item measures nothing, even though his guess is correct.

It should be noted that if distractors are carefully devised, an analysis of the *errors* made is more significant than an analysis of the items answered correctly. This is especially true if the distractors have been so chosen as to indicate difficulties of a particular nature.

Second: Each Item in a Test Has
Inherent Worth

Test items measure certain desirable knowledges and skills which are representative of the whole body of knowledge or skill in a particular area. In other words, an individual item is but a sample of all possible questions that could be asked. Thus a word in a spelling test is not considered to be of great relevance in and of itself, but only as representative of a class of words; that is, the spelling of any word is of little consequence except as it represents a group of words of a certain type or level of difficulty.

Third: A Definite Hierarchy of
Skills and Knowledge Exists in
Any Skill or Content Area

Perhaps the most fundamental assumption implicit in criterion-referenced interpretation is that there exists a generally agreed upon hierarchy of skills or knowledges in the field in which one wants to test. Basically, the criterion-referenced approach is of little value unless the assumption is made that mastery of one skill or bit of knowledge is essential for mastering another skill or bit of knowledge of a somewhat similar character at a *higher level of difficulty or complexity.*

In reading there is, as yet, no clearly established hierarchy; there is not even general agreement as to the best method of teaching reading to beginners. Some advocate that the pupil be taught to recognize a complete word as a unit, while others recommend that he be taught to sense the sounds of the separate letters or letter combinations. Still others recommend some combination of these two quite different approaches. A hierarchy in reading, therefore, is a construct dependent upon the acceptance of a basic philosophy concerning the teaching of reading which dictates the order in which skills are introduced. It is similar to choosing a particular route to an agreed-upon destination (objective), which is one of several alternate routes.

In teaching reading, it is difficult, then, to set up specific goals in hierarchical form after one gets beyond the very beginning stages if at all. It may be desirable to teach a pupil a minimum vocabulary comprising such important words as *and, but, house, cat, dog, walk,* and so on, but once a basic list of words is taught—the composition of which is difficult to establish—the base widens rapidly, and the total English language becomes the subject of instruction. The many thousands of words in the English language make preposterous the idea of teaching all of them in school. Furthermore, a pupil's vocabulary results far more from self-motivation and self-teaching than from formal instruction. No two pupils have the same vocabulary. One's vocabulary is additive indefinitely but, without the reinforcement of regular use, meanings are soon forgotten. Some words that are relevant to one are nonfunctional to another. Thus one pupil may master *dossier* because he likes detective stories, while another would never master it because he has no use for it. Consequently, there can be no such thing as a *third grade vocabulary* or a *sixth grade vocabulary* because the parameters of difficulty are so complex.

A dozen series of reading textbooks could be developed, each using a different vocabulary; and each author might be able to advance sound arguments that his particular approach utilized only essential and useful words. Hence, one certainly cannot consider the development of vocabulary as having any hierarchical characteristic in the teaching of reading. There are just too many important words to permit ordering them in any *correct* sequence for learning.

Perhaps one can look at this another way. Formulas used to estimate reading difficulty of material include such factors as length of sentence, complexity of sentence, number of prepositional and adverbial phrases, and so forth, along with difficulty level of the words. This is not very helpful, however, in determining sequence of instructional steps. A pupil may learn a simple and frequently used word easily, but he may also learn to use a complex and rarely used word if it happens to have particular meaning for him. Much of the so-called difficulty of many words lies simply in the fact that there are few occasions to use them, not because they are intrinsically difficult.

Need For New Tests

There is some disagreement concerning whether a different type of test is required if scores are to be interpreted with reference to a criterion as contrasted with interpretation by norms. The writer believes that, in general, the same type of test may be used although, as has been noted above, free-response items appear to be more suitable for criterion-referenced interpretation.

In both instances, test items flow directly from the instructional materials. No attempt is made to prejudge what the instruction *should* be, the test author limiting himself, contentwise, to what teachers have used by way of textbook and other instructional materials. In the typical standardized test (hence, norm-referenced), it is true, test items of a very high level of mastery, i.e., very easy items, are eliminated since they are not important from a measurement point of view. This does not gainsay the fact that the standardized test comprises items, all of which have instructional significance even though the test cannot cover the entire field of instruction one-hundred percent because of the elimination of nonfunctioning items. Thus, scores on any good standardized achievement test can be interpreted with reference to a criterion by locating the grade level within the local system where a particular skill or knowledge is presumably taught (or mastered) and by studying the actual level of mastery of the items pupil by pupil, and for the defined group. Such individual item statistics may indicate either that a particular skill or knowledge is misplaced in the instructional program or that instruction ought to continue in a subsequent grade because that particular skill or knowledge has not been mastered.

The Criterion-Referenced Approach in Individualized Instruction

It has already been intimated that criterion-referenced interpretation has greatest significance or meaning when associated with a program of individualized instruction. What better way to individualize instruction than to start out with a carefully executed analysis of what pupils know by administering a fairly comprehensive standardized test early in the fall. One need not be overly concerned with the total score. Of much greater importance is the item-analysis information for a class or grade within a school. Item-analysis data from the national population is interesting and does provide a rough guide as to what may be expected in the case of a particular item; however, the nature and extent of the instruction locally is far more important, especially when one is dealing with a specific skill or knowledge.

Computers are now able to provide the test user with printouts showing the pupils' names on one axis and the items, identified by number, on another axis. For every pupil the printout indicates whether he has passed, failed, or omitted the item in question. Thus an examination of one column (if the items are arranged horizontally across the page) will reveal the names of the pupils answering each item correctly. Following across the page on any line will show, for a given pupil, the specific items passed, failed, or omitted. This technique provides the opportunity for the teacher to apply the criterion-referenced principle. The teacher — and the teacher alone — is able to say for a particular pupil or class that a particular skill or knowledge should have been mastered since the sequence of instruction is not the same for all pupils or classes, especially if individualization of instruction is really the instructional policy.

Summary

Most test authors probably would agree that criterion-referenced interpretation of test performance can provide information helpful in the guidance of pupil learning and in the evaluation of instruction. It should not, however, be thought of as a replacement for norm-referenced interpretation. The latter still provides essential information concerning a pupil's performance on a body of material carefully selected to be representative of what is being taught nationally within a given subject-matter field and at a particular grade level.

> **Lessinger maintains that we have eroded our own claim to professionalism and dissipated that confidence the public once reposed in us because we have resisted the one test of professionalism that a skeptical public would accept: proof of results. Moreover, we are now failing with one child in four, a greater failure ratio than we would be willing to accept from automobile manufacturers.**

Robbing Dr. Peter to "Pay Paul": Accounting for Our Stewardship of Public Education

LEON M. LESSINGER

It is hardly news any more to report that our society is undergoing continued and upsetting crises. Things we used to count solid are now found to be soft, almost all our major problems seem insurmountable, and we are finding that our cherished material and technological civilization may not be *the* answer to man's quest for a better and more humane society.

Professor Peter's principle, explaining why things always go wrong, is too impressive. I'd like to "rob" Dr. Peter to suggest some constructive ways to "pay Paul"—to steer a course for accountability to our citizenry for better results, improved service, and answerable decisions. While my remarks will center upon public education—particularly the public schools—I believe that they are generalizable to other significant areas of public and private enterprise.

You will recall that, according to Dr. Peter, ". . . in a hierarchy every employee tends to rise to his level of incompetence." Since public education and most of our major enterprises are hierarchically or bureaucratically organized, this means that given sufficient time every post in these enterprises will be served by an employee who is incompetent to carry out his duties.

While our first inclination is to be somewhat amused by this insight, sober reflection soon erases the humor and forces either a feeling of anger, anxiety, or just plain hopelessness. Dr. Peter effectively destroys examples of seeming exceptions and is rather convincing that his principle is ubiquitous.

I believe I have an antidote to the Peter Principle, and I believe further that it grows out of Professor Peter's own insights.

In his book, *The Peter Principle,** he shares this important insight: ". . . An employee's competence is assessed, not by disinterested observers like you and me, but by the employer or —more likely nowadays—by other employees on higher ranks in the same hierarchy. In their eyes, leadership potential is insubordination, and insubordination is incompetence."

What Dr. Peter is showing us, I believe, is that bureaucracy tends to be self-regulating, cut off from the control and assessment of those outside it and therefore not accountable to the client or citizen for whom the organization or institution was established. I have the counter-principle to Peter; it is the Principle of Public Stewardship through Accountability. It states: *Independent, continuous and publicly reported outside review of promised results of a bureaucracy promotes competence and re-*

*Peter, Laurence J., & Hull, R. *The Peter Principle.* New York: William Morrow, 1969, 179 pp.

sponsiveness in that bureaucracy. Let us illustrate and explore this principle in public education, while remembering that it may have wider applications.

Fifty years ago, even twenty-five years ago, if a youngster was failing in school, he could drop out and still get some kind of job. Education—particularly higher education, but including secondary as well—was still a frill, frosting on the cake. It was pleasant to be able to quote Shakespeare and to manipulate the Binomial Theorem—but as long as you could read, write, and figure, you could make a living. Employment requirements were inching up after World War I. But first the Depression and then World War II concealed any deficiencies in the schools that might have been revealed through the inability of uneducated Americans to get jobs. The Depression hid such deficiencies behind a breakdown in our economy, and the war created a market for manpower of every description regardless of its quality.

The result was that public education had nothing but satisfied customers, because the dissatisfied ones tended to leave without complaining. The children of the affluent could seek educational improvement in private schools or in other communities, and the children of the poor could ignore educational failure by seeking employment. Public education had a captive market and no competition; it was a benign monopoly, and its occasional critics were dismissed as cranks.

We all know the factors that forced public education out of its protected environment, so I shall cut short this exposition by simply naming them: more demanding job requirements, stemming from the increased intellectual and technological complexity of modern employment; a new militance among ethnic minorities, proceeding from the tension between extraordinary affluence among some Americans and continuing poverty for others; a new perception of social injustice rising from a communications explosion that brought the squalor of Harlem into the living rooms of Scarsdale, and the comfort of the suburbs onto the TV sets of the ghetto; and the raw courage of some Americans who read the Constitution as if it really meant what it said.

One factor in the abrupt transition from educational tranquility to educational trauma seems to have gone generally unnoticed and hence deserves special mention: What I would call a fatigue with, and a rejection of, *expertise.* To a greater degree than in any preceding age, we have seen in our time a disenchantment among the general population with the elite who supposedly lead the masses. Our society has discovered that Ph.D.s and presidents, bankers and brain surgeons, politicians and parents are quite as capable as the young or the ignorant of making fools of themselves.

This idea itself is nothing new. You can find ridicule of the learned in Chaucer, criticism of attorneys in Hamlet, and gleeful parodies of the conventional wisdom of politics, business, and religion in Sinclair Lewis. Today, however, the commoners have gone beyond suspecting that the nobility doesn't know as much as it claims; they have converted their doubts into widespread criticism and action.

In family life, we see this disenchantment as a revolt by many young people against their parents' views, as a rejection of the age-old claim of maturity to superior knowledge. In business, we see it as a rejection by many college graduates of commerce, as dull and uninspiring, when compared to the opportunities for service, offered by such organizations as the Peace Corps and VISTA. In domestic affairs, particularly education, we see it as a demand by poor people for a voice in shaping government programs that affect them. Across the spectrum of our national concerns, we have a new cry for "participatory democracy" and a deep sense that the people at the top don't always know what's good for the people lower down. And these people are learning how to communicate their demands to the power structure and to those at the top.

In elementary and secondary education, of course, we have a rash of such demands for participation in the decision-making process: teacher power, student power, black power, parent power, and flower power. Instead of dealing with only one another, the school boards and administrators now have to deal with a half-dozen constituencies which, until recently, had remained silent. These power blocs, each with specific interests that sometimes coincide but often conflict, constitute a new electorate in education. They constitute a new politics of education.

Fundamental to all politics — new or old — is communication.

It is interesting to consider the ability of administrators and the educational establishment to communicate effectively with this new electorate. The whole tradition and mythology of public education have converged to leave us with virtually no ability at all. No reference book that I have consulted indicates who first said, "Let us keep politics out of education, and education out of politics."

Perhaps in some paradise of the future, politics and sustained communication with these various competing groups will play no part in education. As long as we have public schools, however, and as long as public funds support the education of our young, politics — the voters' response to the broad world beyond the school — will affect, if not absolutely dictate, school policy and practice. The domestic and international circumstances that gave rise to the National Defense Education Act of ten years ago, to all the federal aid bills passed since then, and to Title IV and VI of the Civil Rights Act, are adequate proof that broad social developments reach into the schools. The current demands by the urban school systems for more state aid and the hundreds of bond issues offered local voters every year simply reinforce the point that education is in politics up to its neck and needs effective communication as never before.

It is obvious that each member of the education hierarchy has a personal stake in understanding this new electorate and in having that diverse group understand him. It may not be quite as obvious why ability to handle these new realities of power is important to education and other bureaucracies as well.

Certainly we cannot reject out of hand the demand from our new electorate for a voice in making decisions that affect their lives. Nor, I think, do we want to do so.

The real problem, it seems to me, is the danger that professional decision making will be entirely abandoned and education regarded as a populist free-for-all in which every man has equal say. The perhaps nasty, but nonetheless solid, truth is that every man should *not* have equal say. And lest this sound like humbug, or a rationale for reaction, let me clarify what I mean by drawing an analogy from medical practice.

If an injured person brought into an emergency ward needs immediate attention but has to lie there for several hours before he gets it, we would all say that this is sheer incompetence on the part of the medical staff. In demanding improvement, we would feel well within the layman's proper sphere of criticism. We are not invading the physician's professional domain, but simply claiming that an institution should meet the human needs it was established to serve. We are simply asserting lay wisdom to the specialist.

Yet democracy can go only so far. We respect the skill of the surgeon, and the years of education and experience he has invested in the refinement of his ability. We do not say, "Look here, I'm as American as you are, and this is a democratic country; give me the scalpel and let me take out that appendix."

The point is that there is a gradation of responsibility in any profession, ranging from those areas at one end of the scale in which every man has equal say, to the other end at which only the professional has any legitimate say at all. This may sound undemocratic, but knowledge is undemocratic: We cannot change the square root of three by taking a vote on it. A patient complains about symptoms and may even aid the doctor's diagnosis; he does not, however, prescribe the cure.

In the same way, the new educational electorate is entirely within its rights in complaining about school deficiencies. It can help make a diagnosis by specifying the symptoms and suggesting possible causes of the trouble. But it is the professional educator's job to translate demands for educational improvement into a program for educational improvement — for the ability to do so constitutes the very core of his claim to being a professional.

Yet educators are poorly prepared to argue the just claims of professionalism, for we have resisted the one and only ultimate test of professional competence: *proof of results*. If a man goes to medical school for twenty years, but winds up killing half of his patients, his peers lose no time drumming him out of the profession. If an attorney loses as many cases as he wins, he will soon have none but the most ignorant or impecunious of clients. Neither specialized training nor experience by itself validates his claim to special wisdom. Professionalism, in other words, goes hand in hand with *accountability*, with clear-cut proof of performance. And in education we have time and again refused to produce that proof.

Our public elementary and secondary schools enroll 44 million students, employ 1.9 million teachers, and spend more than $30 billion in tax funds annually. We have all kinds of measurements of where the money goes: We can pin down per-capita expenditures in any school district in the country, state how much any of them spent for construction and service on its debt, and enumerate pupil-teacher ratios until the sun goes down.

But all this seems to add up to learning more and more about less and less that is really relevant to the education of our children.

We have virtually no measurement of the results that our enterprise yields. We do not know, for example, what it costs on the average to increase a youngster's reading ability by one year; all we know is what it costs to keep him *seated* for one year. All the indices we have measure our skill as *financial* managers; not a single one evaluates our effectiveness as *educational* managers. It would make much more sense if we moved from a "per-pupil cost" to a "learning-unit cost" — to focusing on the level of learning, not on the maintenance of children in school. The definition of effective teaching may well be measured in terms of how well the students learn.

We have made few such moves to measure our results, however. And our dereliction is made all the more embarrassing because ample proof of our failures has come out despite our reticence. Today, about one of every four American children drops out of school somewhere between fifth grade and high school graduation. In 1965, one of every four 18-year-old males failed the mental test for induction into the armed services. And hundreds of thousands of parents, particularly of minority children, reacting to this information, have decided that their children are *not* stupid — that either some educators are incompetent, or that methods they are using are inadequate.

Why did these measurements of our failures have to come from *outside* the school system, rather than from within it? Why haven't we been alert to the symptoms of our failures, so that we could learn to cure them? Our schools are somehow failing one youngster in four, and we have not acted to arrest the social and economic fatalities which every school dropout represents. It is no wonder, then, that critics such as Paul Goodman and Edgar Friedenberg feel that many dropouts are better off on the street than in the classroom. And it is no wonder that some parents — I think of those who took over P.S. 201 in Harlem, for example — feel that rank amateurs can do no worse a job of running a school than the self-styled pros. In refusing to give our clients proof of performance while they gathered their own proof of our flops, we have set the stage for the raucous and bitter confrontation of power blocs which characterize American education today.

Moreover, we have eroded our own claim to professionalism; we have dissipated that confidence which the public once reposed in its educators; and we have, finally, almost completely erased those distinctions between the specialist's knowledge and the layman's concern that demarcate anarchy from order. The most important result of this melancholy process is not that educators are threatened, and deserve to *be* threatened. It is that many aspects of the educational endeavor *do* require a professional's knowledge.

If we are to meet the new demands for change, we must join accountability to public education. And by "accountability" I mean much more than such simple indices as numbers of drop-outs and the results of reading tests. We must go far beyond such general outlines of general results and find out what specific factors *produce* specific educational results. We must find out what specific educational results can be achieved with different groups of children for investment of different amounts of financial resources.

Like all the organizations Dr. Peter researched, we in education have been traditionally concerned with quantitative *input:* the amount of financial and human resources that have gone into buildings, into teacher salaries, into textbooks, and so forth. Listing expenditures by such categories is a legitimate way of showing the public where its money went.

But it is totally irrelevant to show the public what is *received* for its investment in education; it is not a legitimate way of demonstrating qualitative output, or what I call "proof of performance." The distinction is easy to make as soon as we ask what result the public expects for its investment.

Does the public expect that, as a result of having spent X millions of dollars, it will have Y number of teachers? Does it expect to own a given number of textbooks, of test tubes and analytical balances, of trombones and world globes? Obviously not. What it expects from its investment is educated children, able to meet their own needs and society's needs to the full measure of their potential.

In his Education Message in 1970, President Nixon stated, "From these considerations we derive another new concept: *accountability.* School administrators and school teachers alike are responsible for their performance, and it is in their interest as well as in the interests of their pupils that they be held accountable."

This is a most radical departure from present-day practice. It attempts to put us in a position to tell the public and ourselves what we accomplished by the expenditure of a given amount of funds. It permits us to judge our system of instruction by the results we produce. There is hope that it will lead to cost-benefit data and insights.

The symbol of our educational system has been the bell-shaped curve. The philosophy of the bell-shaped curve is that a given number of any group of children are failures or rejects on our academic scale. This philosophy permits us to cover up our inadequacies as educators by blaming our failures on the type of raw material with which we have to work. Why should we have human rejects in our school system? Why should we regard each class of students with the theory that some of them will excel, that most of them will be about average, and that some few will not make it? We should have a policy of "Zero Rejects" in the basic competencies of American citizenship, while encouraging wide and deep diversity among those who would extend knowledge and become our champions and specialists.

Secondly, the public expects greater relevance in what we teach. The children who ask "Why do we have to learn this?" have a point. We ought to be able to give them a better answer than that "It's always been required."

The third issue is human dignity. The public has a right to ask that we deal effectively not only with individual differences of children, but also with their individual similarities. All children have certain needs and wants in common: They need a favorable self-image; they want to be understood; they want to be accepted; they need a sense of human dignity.

In principle, the American educational commitment has been that every child should have an adequate education. This commitment has been stated in terms of resources such as teachers, books, space, and equipment. When a child has failed to learn, school personnel have assigned him a label—"slow," or "unmotivated," or "retarded." To move toward accountability, our schools must assume a revised commitment—that *every child shall learn.* Such a commitment includes the willingness to change a system which does not work and find one which does; to seek causes of failure in the system and its personnel instead of focusing solely on students; in short, to hold ourselves as professionals accountable for results in terms of student learning rather than solely in the use of resources.

Perhaps it is time now to draw some conclusions from our exploration of education, and return to our anti–Peter principle.

Devoted and intelligent men and women are working in bureaucratic organizations all over our country. They have a good deal of which they can be proud. Yet even as we honor their accomplishments we know that the problems we face now and in the future will not yield to the ideas and programs which represent business as usual.

Progress and reform are clearly in order. *Progress* is a nice word, but *change,* its instigator, is not. For change destroys comfort, implies criticism of what *is,* and provokes feelings of fear. Change means that someone's professional feathers will be ruffled, that pet programs might die, and sacred cows be placed out to pasture.

Perhaps the most fitting way to rob Peter to pay Paul is provided by the desperate action of a mayor of a drought-stricken Mexican town. Robert Silverberg, in the book *The Challenge of Climate: Man and His Environment,* quotes the ultimatum issued by the mayor to the clergy to hold them accountable for results: "If within the peremptory period of eight days from the date of this decree rain does not fall abundantly, no one will go to mass or say prayers . . . if the drought continues eight days more, the churches and chapels shall be burned, missals, rosaries, and other objects of devotion will be destroyed . . . If, finally, in a third period of eight days it shall not rain, all the priests, friars, nuns, and saints, male and female, will be beheaded."

Fortunately for the clergy, Divine Providence responded to this no-nonsense approach by sending torrential downpours within four days.

The crises in delivery on promises are not quite that bad! But the moral is clear: Results are what count, not promises or lamentations. Dr. Peter, take heed!

"O.K. So I am willing, nay eager, to
be held accountable for my teaching.
But how do I do it?" Wildavsky provides some answers.

A Program of Accountability for Elementary Schools

AARON WILDAVSKY

The request for accountability in the sense of holding the school
responsible for the achievement of children in critical areas is a
good one. Consumers of governmental services are entitled to
know what they are getting. Truth in packaging applies just as
much to government as to private industry. Indeed, the field of
education may be on the verge of making a contribution to the
general evaluation of governmental programs. The ability of
ordinary citizens to appraise whether they are getting what they
want is of critical importance in a system of democratic government. Yet no one today knows what citizens will do with this
kind of information. In view of the inevitable tendency to oversimplify, it is desirable to add to public understanding through
an assessment of what accountability means and what it will
and will not do. The best way to get these ideas across is to set
up procedures for accountability that embody them.

A student's ability to read is critical for later achievement.
His ability in mathematics is indispensable for a whole range of

occupations. Achievement in these two areas must be evaluated in terms of standardized tests. It is true that such a test does not by any means measure all that a teacher does or attest to all of his impact. No such test can be devised. Nor is it necessary to do so. To say that what a teacher does is so exotic that it cannot be measured is simply to say that he ought to do what he pleases, and that is not tenable. All the impalpable qualities of "growth" mean nothing if students cannot hold jobs as clerks in drugstores because they cannot make change correctly or cannot be messengers because they cannot read street signs. Before a student can do other things he must be able to read, and it is sufficient to say that he must develop in this direction as well as in others. The deprived child needs this skill more than other children.

It may be said that the standardized tests are culturally biased, but I think this is beside the point. Few doubt that if one took an article about the life of the Yoruba tribe in Africa or the city-state of Benin, equally remote from the experience of all students, those students who read well would be able to answer questions about the material and those who read poorly would have difficulty. The same would be true of a book directly concerned with the black man's experience in America. To say that one must wait until tests without cultural bias are developed is simply to say there will be no accountability. I should add that there is a great deal of difference between tests designed to help parents hold schools responsible and tests that work to exclude people from opportunity for higher education and better jobs.

At this point I would like to add a word of caution about the problem of cheating on tests. As the pressure grows to improve student performance on standardized tests, teachers will be tempted to cheat. It is one thing for teachers to prepare students by giving them exercises similar to ones on the test; it is another for teachers to feed their students the exact words and phrases that will be used on the test. That practice should be discouraged. I find here an analogy with the New York State regents' examinations I used to take when I was a high school student in that state. One learned a great deal by going over previous examinations, and that was not considered a form of cheating. Rather than relying merely on negative sanctions, I would suggest providing a lengthy series of sample "previous" examinations, so that teachers will feel quite free to use them.

All standardized testing should be turned over to an extra-school organization — a state agency or a private business that will administer the tests and see that they are fairly conducted. Tests should not be brought into the schools until the morning of the testing day, and observers from the testing organization should be present. One drawback of this proposal is its expense, but if there is to be confidence in accountability, there must be assurance that the test scores mean what they say.

Teachers I know have told me that they fear spending most of their time gearing students to pass certain examinations. My reaction is: What is wrong with that, if the examinations are good indicators of what we wish students to learn? Learning a limited vocabulary by rote may be useless. If we wish to increase cognitive ability by enabling students to read material with understanding within a certain time, however, a test that measures that skill is a good idea. The ideal situation is one in which a student's ability to do well on this exam means that he can also pick up any other similar body of material and understand it well.

I am aware that reading ability may be affected by many things. Reading may be a function of the personality. It may be a result of motivation; children may not read because they see no reason to do so. It may be a function of certain high-level cognitive processes that are imperfectly understood. And so on. Let us say, then, that reading is a very complex matter, a product of many circumstances, most of which are badly understood and some of which may not be known at all. So what? Who said that one must know the causes before propounding the cure? The history of medicine has taught us that many diseases may be cured before their etiology is perfectly known. For present purposes it is sufficient that students be enabled to read a certain level of material with a certain degree of comprehension, whether or not the teacher or the researcher fully understands the processes by which this is done. No doubt more basic research should be conducted in reading. Surely, few would suggest waiting twenty years before we begin our efforts to improve performance through accountability.

There may be quick ways of getting at motivation to read by developing measures based on the amount of reading done by students. All the discussion of developing motivation would be beside the point unless the motivated student read more (or perhaps even a greater variety) of literature than his fellows. I would not wait until such a measure was perfected, however, before beginning a simpler use of accountability.

There are important conceptual difficulties with a program of accountability. Presumably we are after something like the economic concept of "value added." We want to know what impact exposure to a particular teacher or school has had on a child's reading or mathematical ability, compared to what it would have been in other circumstances. This requires some base-line knowledge of where a child would be expected to be, given his previous rates of achievement and those of other students similarly situated. Since reading and cognitive ability are not simple matters, the requisite talents may be developed in more than one class. How much of a student's progress (or lack of it) is due to his reading teacher versus other teachers would be exceedingly difficult to determine. How much is due to school versus home environment is a tricky question. Parceling out a single cause from many is never simple. I believe that rough-and-ready answers can be found to these dilemmas if the problem of causation is approached in a practical spirit.

To hold someone accountable is to assess how well he is performing. A program of accountability requires standardized tests on the one hand and significant norms on the other. Yet it is not easy to decide what these norms should be. The first that suggests itself is a national standard for reading or mathematics by grade. If this standard, however, is much higher than present performance, it will appear unrealistic to teachers and students alike. They may despair at ever achieving it and therefore not make the required effort. Should an accountability group be performing above the national standard, they would have no way to measure their progress. Another way to handle the problem of setting the norm is to make it a subject for bargaining between local school boards, parent groups, teachers, and principals. This approach would have the advantage of allowing participation in setting norms and might have the effect of committing the participants more strongly to their achievement. Unfortunately, however, the negotiations may simply reveal who is more powerful or determined or aggressive. The result may be terribly low norms in some places and unfairly high ones in others. It would become impossible to determine either how a city as a whole was doing or how the various subgroups were faring. The level of conflict would surely rise without much hope of corresponding benefit.

A third alternative would be to divide all elementary pupils in a city into five or six groups based on the mean score by grade on the standardized tests. Students would be tested each September, and the focus would be on the rate of change during the year. Each school would then be rated on the basis of its ability to secure more rapid changes by grade in the mean scores of its students. Immediately we are faced with a major dilemma. One of the purposes of modern reform in education is to escape from the syndrome of helping those most who need it least. If the students who perform better initially are also the students who are capable of showing the greatest rate of change, teachers and principals will find it most efficient to concentrate attention on these students in order to improve total performance. We will be back again to the adage "To him that hath shall be given." One way of surmounting this difficulty is to require not only the mean but the median scores, so that schools are rewarded for securing improvement in the largest number of students as well as for the total rate of improvement. Another way of dealing with the problem is to use tests that have a "top" to them so that those who score the highest have difficulty in improving by a large percentage. Whatever the formula used, the principle is clear: The school gets rewarded more for improvements among those students who start out at the lower levels of performance than it does for the students who start out at the higher levels. The rational man will, therefore, exert his effort to bring forward those who need it most.

My preference is for a fourth alternative in which different norms would be set for different groups of students. It should be possible to compare groups of students with similar backgrounds. Groups can be defined largely in terms of previous opportunity. I would suggest working up a *short* list of the principal extra-school variables that appear, in terms of current knowledge, to be relevant to student performance, such as socioeconomic level, rate of movement from one neighborhood and one school to another, and so on. It would then be possible to place each elementary school in one of five or six groups. Each group of schools could be rank-ordered according to student performance on standardized tests, with the results given three weeks after school starts and again sometime around the first week in June, so that progress during the school year could be measured. (The early tests are necessary because many students lose a lot of learning over the summer.) The norms against which progress is measured would not be the same for the entire city, but would differ for each of the five or six accountability groups.

The five top schools within each subgroup could be taken together and their current achievement and average growth used as the normative standard. In this way participants in each school's activity would know that the norm set for them had in fact been achieved by students in situations comparable to their own. Norms would be reasonably objective and realistic. Selection of these norms, however, is critically dependent on factual information about the degree of homogeneity within elementary schools. If the differences in achievement between schools are greater than the differences within schools, this proposal is feasible; if the heterogeneity within schools is great, however, it will be difficult to make sense out of the performance of the school as a whole, and it will be necessary to deal with different classes of students throughout the entire system.

Determination of the level of accountability within the school system is also a difficult problem. Should it be a single teacher, a school, a district, or the entire school system? In a sense, all levels must be accountable and the efforts of all must be appraised. Determination of the center of accountability, however, cannot be avoided because if all are in some vague sense accountable, it will be difficult to hold anyone responsible. Making a large geographical district or the entire system accountable will prove too imprecise. Nor will holding individual teachers directly accountable work. The problem of causality—how much does that teacher's effort contribute to the total result?—will prove insuperable. Teachers may also prove unable to cope with the pressures that come directly at them.

I recommend focusing accountability on the principal of the school because he is the one with the essential power in the system. My understanding is that the district superintendent, although nominally responsible for what the teacher does, usually gives him wide latitude. Local boards may change the situation, but it is too early to tell. The principal, therefore, is the one who is capable of limiting and usually does limit the teacher's discretion. The principal, moreover, could be assumed to have a longer-term commitment to the school system. If his work can be improved, or if he is replaced by others whose work is better, that is bound to have a profound impact throughout the system.

If principals are to be held accountable, however, they must receive training in teaching. I do not believe that the concept of the principal as the master teacher is accurate today in view of the mechanisms of recruitment that obtain. For the moment it would be sufficient for principals to hire qualified people to assist them. Principals should also be given adequate administrative help or at least each one must have the same kind of help. In some school districts the amount of administrative help per pupil varies considerably from school to school. Either administrative help per pupil must be equalized or principals with a relative lack of administrative help must not be required to do as well. If accountability is to get support it must be as fair as we know how to make it.

However good a system of accountability is worked out, it will always have defects. Some teachers will find that their students are especially difficult to teach; others will find that their students make more rapid progress than they had thought. Some teacher may be especially gifted in dealing with children with special reading difficulties, while others do better with different kinds of students. If accountability is placed on the teacher it will be difficult to take account of their differing capabilities. By placing accountability on the principal, however, he will be able to take these special circumstances into account and not require the same level of performance from all his teachers regardless of the difficulty of their assignments. The requirement he must face is that the school as a whole show reasonable progress. While the principal is, in effect, charged with maximizing a kind of educational production, he may set different goals for his teachers in order to make the best showing for the school as a whole. In a different context a number of teachers could perform the same function by forming accountability groups with a school.

In order to envisage the problems encountered by making schools accountable through their principals, let us imagine that such a system were adopted. Everyone would presumably know which schools were performing better and worse than others. There would naturally be a tendency for parents to send their children to the schools shown to be performing better for children like their own. One way of handling this problem would be to prohibit movement from one school to another based on this criterion. Otherwise the normative basis of the school would change rapidly because those parents and students most interested in improving performance would go to the better schools. The result would be a reallocation of students, leaving certain schools worse off than they were before. A long-run solution, after accountability has been in force for a number of years, would be to treat the phenomenon as part of a market system and give the better school additional resources to accommodate new pupils. Here accountability would merge with some of the proposals for giving parents vouchers allowing them to send children where they hope to get a better education. In the short run, however, it would be better to restrict movement and to place emphasis on improving the performance of schools that show the least progress in meeting the norms.

Realism compels us to recognize that there is more than one way to improve the performance of children: There are ways we would like, and there are ways we would hate. One of the easiest ways to improve school performance, for example, is to remove those children who are most troublesome and whose scores on achievement tests are likely to be the lowest. It would be sad to see accountability used to justify defining children as behavioral problems or as victims of mental disturbance just so they would be eliminated from the school population. Schools should be allowed only a very small proportion of transfers on these grounds; otherwise they will be in the same position as a football team that finally achieves a winning schedule by choosing only the weakest opponents. A trigger mechanism could be used so than any transfers on these grounds above a certain minimum would result in an investigation.

The problem of sanctions for failure to perform is an integral part of a system of accountability. If those who do badly are allowed to continue, the system will not work. If those who do well are not rewarded, there will be no incentive for them to continue. My preference is to accentuate the positive. Teachers and principals who show the greatest progress should receive recognition, promotion, and freedom. By "freedom" I mean that those who show excellent progress should be given the right to innovate in teaching methods and with the curriculum. Rather than attempt to control their behavior through prescription of detailed curricula, we should let them devise their own with broad limits. As a contribution to this effort, the superintendent of schools should make available a diverse number of curricula for various grades and of methods for teaching various subjects among which teachers might choose but to which they would not be limited if they performed well. One can choose to direct teachers by inputs—standard curricula and teaching methods—or by outputs—norms of achievement—but not by both. If the output norms are met, the inputs should be left to the teachers.

Before sanctions are applied, principals and teachers should be given supervisory help. Their administrative superiors should work with them to improve performance. Additional personnel and financial resources should be provided. The imposition of negative sanctions should be downgraded but cannot be entirely avoided. For the most part, teachers will simply have less freedom. Should a teacher or principal reveal consistently poor performance, it should be possible to transfer him, or ultimately, remove him from the system. Agreement should be sought with the teachers' union on procedures to be followed in this eventuality so that abuse will be minimized. If the union will not agree, then accountability is not possible.

In order to reduce anxieties and to take cognizance of the difficulties of the enterprise, the procedure for accountability should be reviewed every two years. The groups that serve as the normative schools should be revised according to their performance.

No plan for accountability can succeed unless all the major participants in the educational process—parents, teachers, students, principals, superintendents, and board members—see something in it for themselves. It is worthwhile, therefore, to explore the advantages and disadvantages of this plan as the various participants might see it.

The hard part for teachers would be the fact of being judged on a rather narrow level of performance according to strict standards that may not be entirely valid. If they consistently fail to move their students toward the norm, teachers would be subject to sanctions. Under current conditions, however, teachers suffer psychological punishment due to a feeling of failure. Their ability to show progress, indeed even to know the direction toward which they and their students should be moving, may provide tremendous relief. Standards of accountability may also give teachers a mechanism for guarding against arbitrary action by principals. If a teacher can show that his students have made excellent progress toward the norm, or have even achieved it, he has prima facie evidence of competence. He should thus be entitled to a reward in the form of permission to work under less supervision with greater leeway to introduce his own ideas.

The initial reaction of principals to the idea of accountability may well be negative. It will be hard for them to see themselves as responsible for behavior of students and teachers which they find difficult to control. As the most visible manifestation of the school authorities, principals are easy to blame and to pillory in public. Fear and defensiveness by principals would be understandable. Yet first thoughts are bound to give way to deeper considerations. Principals are already being held responsible according to vague standards and under rules that guarantee dissatisfaction. National norms are held up as appropriate by some and are condemned by others. Principals may come to believe they will be better off if they have a hand in shaping reasonable norms. If they are held to account by their administrative superiors and by parents they will also gain additional leverage in regard to recalcitrant teachers. If performance is poor, a principal can move to change teacher behavior with more than the ordinary amount of justification. He can also show his administrative superiors that he is doing a good job in a more convincing way than before. Accountability has its defects, but the norms it enforces on the principal are superior to "keeping out of trouble" or "pleasing the boss" or others one can think of.

Parents may be expected to give initial endorsement to a program of accountability. They should feel that at least they have a mechanism for appraising the performance of their children and the school in which they are taught. (Accountability not only means that the school is responsible to the parents, however, but that the parents are responsible for the school. They need to help teachers whose children fail to make adequate progress.) It is often difficult for parents to gauge the legitimacy of complaints made by their children or school critics; knowledge of whether their children are making progress with regard to the norms of accountability should help them decide where reality lies. When parents are asked to mobilize themselves concerning school policy, they may decide whether to become involved by consulting public information on school achievement.

Accountability, defined in terms of achievement in reading and math, will not satisfy those parental and neighborhood groups that are looking to schools to inculcate their cultural and/or political values. To them, accountability may be a barrier to control of schools, because it (in their view) falsely suggests to parents that schools are doing well. There is no escaping the fact that accountability is not a neutral device—it encapsulates a view of the educational function in which basic cognitive and mathematical skills are primary. Cultural, artistic, or political values would still receive expression (it could hardly be otherwise), but they would not be dominant.

The job of the superintendent of schools has become increasingly frustrating. He is placed at the very center of every controversy. At times he appears utterly surrounded by swirling clouds of controversy. Yet when all is said and done, he is too far from teaching and learning to know whether his efforts are worthwhile. Often he must feel that all he does is stay alive while the purposes for which he originally became an educator become increasingly remote. For such a man a program of accountability must have great meaning. It is his opportunity to affect education directly. It is his opportunity to participate in an innovation that could make his tenure in office worthwhile. The drawback is that progress, if it can be achieved at all, may be painfully slow. No one can be certain that the statement of educational goals will lead to their achievement. The factors that guide improvement in reading and mathematics for large populations may not be known to anyone. The special problems faced by deprived children may not respond to available techniques. While various schools and teachers may meet with notable success, average rates of growth may not change at all, or may even decline for reasons no one knows. Yet the superintendent may be regarded as a failure because a particular norm of accountability has been specified, when he might have escaped under the nebulous criteria which would otherwise exist. Still, he is unlikely to escape unscathed, and norms of accountability are as good a measure of progress as he is likely to get.

The board of education can find accountability of great use in defining problem areas and in questioning the superintendent about them. The board can choose to hold the superintendent responsible for systematic performance or it can investigate problems according to the geographic area, grade, or level at which they occur. The board's greatest role, if it is so willing, will be to monitor the system of accountability and suggest revisions of it to the interested parties. It should take the lead in suggesting changes in the norms by which measurement is accomplished, the incentives and sanctions employed, and the tests used.

Very young children are unlikely to question these arrangements. As they get older, students may well be the people most difficult to satisfy on the question of accountability. They may feel that *no* system of norms gives them sufficient freedom. They may dislike the idea that a single set of norms appears to define them when they know that each individual is much more than that. They may fear that they will be stigmatized if greater publicity is given to test results. They may not even want their parents to know how well or how badly they are doing. Part of the difficulty may be overcome by holding individual and class scores confidential except to parents. Another part will be dealt with by giving students special liberties in taking courses if they perform at an acceptable level. Ultimately, however, they must be persuaded that accountability is a useful mechanism for improving the performance of school children in general and that it is therefore of special benefit to those whose performance is now at a low level. Some students, like some teachers and principals, will have to accept sacrifices for the common good. It will not be easy.

If a student makes one month of
progress, you are paid nothing. If
he makes five months of progress,
you are paid $19.00. But if he makes
twelve months of progress, you are
paid $30.00. That is performance
contracting. Reynolds, too, has some
qualms about carrying accountability that far.

Performance Contracting
. . . Proceed with Caution

JERRY D. REYNOLDS

Performance contracting is another promise for education to
guarantee more return (output) for the time and dollars (input)
invested in instruction . . . a yet unproven innovation in which
private corporations and teachers will be paid according to their
ability, as assessed by pre- and post-standardized tests, to improve specified skills of a given group of students. Thus far, the

several programs in operation have been geared to improving reading and mathematical skills of students who are performing substantially below grade level.

Because of the qualified success of the program operated this past year at Texarkana, Arkansas, under a Title VIII grant from the Office of Education, the Office of Economic Opportunity (OEO) has decided to expand the program to eighteen school districts, with six firms working with over 15,000 children in a five-million-dollar, one-year experiment. Government officials and the six firms involved are optimistic about the revolutionary changes that could evolve from these experiments. Many educators and reading specialists are more cautious: educational contractors, incentives, and learning machines do not assure the realization of the goal, as articulated by former U.S. Commissioner of Education James E. Allen, Jr., "that by the end of the 1970s . . . no one shall be leaving our schools without the skill and the desire necessary to read to the full limits of his capability."

The purpose of this writer is neither to support nor to find fault with the performance-contracting/accountability concept. He would rather share his experience in which one Iowa school district has tried to help some of its students improve their reading performance by selecting those aspects of this program which were considered desirable and could be adapted effectively to the local school system.

In an effort to determine early last spring whether the Keokuk Community School District should seriously consider such a venture, we applied for and received Title I funding to evaluate the performance-contracting concept such as that found in the Texarkana, Arkansas, schools and to launch a pilot summer-reading project that incorporated some of the desirable features found in our evaluation of the Texarkana program.

Five of us flew to Texarkana in May, where we spent several days observing the project in operation, visiting with supervisory and teaching personnel, and studying the materials and machines used in the reading instruction. Our group was representative of different perspectives—Janet Hayes, a seventh-grade reading teacher; Mary Olson, a fourth-grade teacher; Velma Anderson, an active PTA worker who recently launched a Paperback Read-In program in several of our elementary schools; Bruce Meeks, a junior high principal; and, me. Although we had some serious reservations about certain parts of their experiment, we decided that many aspects of the program could be adapted to our pilot summer-reading project in Keokuk. Based upon the results of our project, we could then decide whether to incorporate particular approaches to reading within our regular school program in the future.

The Texarkana project is a Dropout Prevention Program: help the child to succeed and, thus, to stay in school by improving his math and reading skills. The gains made by the students from October to May were impressive, particularly in light of several factors. The program did not begin until well after the opening of school in the fall. The target group of about 360 students had poor attendance records, were achieving at least two years or more below grade level as measured by the *Iowa Tests of Basic Skills*, and were diagnosed as potential dropouts. In its first year the project was understaffed—six teachers (instructional managers) and six paraprofessionals; the project director for Dorsett, the company selected from a group of ten companies to operate, staff, and equip the Rapid Learning Centers on a guaranteed performance basis; the project director for the school system, Martin Filogamo, a former elementary school principal; one qualified reading teacher; and twenty local teachers who served as consultants to help in making the transition when the program is fully implemented within the entire system. Students were admitted to the program if their I. Q. was 75 or higher (the average I. Q. score was approximately 84 for the entire group).

In spite of these factors that would tend to limit performance, after sixty hours of instruction in reading, the students had grown, on the average, 2.2 grade levels; and after a comparable number of hours of study in math skills, the group had progressed 1.4 grade levels. Eighty hours is about one semester of the school year. Typically in the past the dropout rate for these students was about 12 percent, but under this program the rate dropped to 1 percent. Although two-thirds of the students were counselled into this program and the other one-third were volunteers, there was a waiting list in March of several hundred students who wanted to enter the program when space was available.

The "contingency management concept," commonly known as incentives, is another feature of the Texarkana program. Extrinsic motivation is not new by any means, but giving students green stamps, transistor radios, "free" time to listen to records and to read paperbacks and magazines for their achievement based on periodic tests is another factor that produces motivation. What happens when the motivation of the candy is removed was best answered by Project Director Filogamo: "When all of it is said and done, the kid is still basically motivated by a desire to improve . . . personal achievement is the true incentive." This explains why the tangible incentives fall off in their appeal soon after the student begins to experience the success of his own efforts.

With more funds being poured into the one-year experiment in eighteen school districts, OEO will have to refine its assessment procedures to separate the actual or permanent factors accounting for the achievement from those Hawthorne effects that often produce immediate gains but which for various reasons are not sustained over a period of time. In the original letter of intent, the Dorsett Company and the school agreed to the clause specifying that the target students would be retested at a time six months following completion of the program. However, later this important clause was dropped because of the many problems in administering it. The effect of this clause would have determined the degree of retention of skills supposedly acquired through the program. Final payment of the contract would have been predicated, in part, upon this clause. What is achieved immediately upon completion of an intensive program like this one may be far different from what is actually *retained* six months or longer beyond the completion date.

How some of these techniques could be adapted to our summer project was our first concern when we returned to Keokuk. We decided to employ one of our own reading teachers to handle the instruction because we believe that diagnosis should be an ongoing part of such a program, with a qualified reading diagnostician to handle these duties. At Texarkana, however, none of the six project teachers had any formal training in reading other than several weeks of inservice study at the beginning of the project. Qualified diagnosis with follow-through remedial or corrective work was practically nonexistent in their program. By selecting one of our experienced and qualified reading teachers who has a master's degree in reading, we would have a qualified reading instructor who could provide competent and ongoing diagnosis for the students. Janet Hayes, a reading teacher in our junior high school and also a member of the group that visited Texarkana, was selected as the key teacher for the project.

It was decided that the target group would be comprised of sixty students who had just completed the sixth or seventh grade, who have an I.Q. of 90 or higher, and who were reading one or more years below their grade level as determined by the *Iowa Tests of Basic Skills,* the *Stanford Reading Test,* or the *Diagnostic Reading Test.* Having no pattern to follow for writing a performance contract, we had to develop an agreement that would fit our purposes.

Since our summer-school program lasts for six weeks, the contract specified that the teacher would instruct each of the sixty students a maximum of thirty days (comparable to six weeks of instruction during the regular school year) and a minimum of twenty-two class hours in a reading-improvement program, and that the total number of instruction hours of the entire project not exceed 180 hours. These specifications were to help us later in assessing the correlation between achievement and hours of instruction.

Most of our students had taken the *Iowa Tests of Basic Skills* each year and it had been used as one of the basic instruments for the selection of students for this program. Therefore, another instrument was selected as the pre- and posttest to determine the degree of growth for each student during the instructional period. The *Nelson Reading Test* was chosen because of its reliability and its broad norming sample by percentiles and grade-level scores.

The following table was developed to determine the amount of pay based upon each student's total gain in reading, with the stipulation that no payment be made for any student making less than two months of growth. Since this was an experimental program, it was agreed that the teacher be guaranteed a salary of $600. She could earn, however, a maximum of $1,500 if the test scores reflected a high degree of growth. Normally a teacher working a comparable number of hours in our summer program would earn from $750 to $900. Thus, the project teacher could earn $150 less and up to $600 more than she would normally earn under the traditional program. As it turned out, she earned several hundred dollars more under this contract than she would have under our regular summer-school contract.

Total Gain Per Student	Amount Paid Per Student
0–1 month	no pay
2 months	$12.00
3 months	$15.00
4 months	$17.00
5 months	$19.00
6 months	$21.00
7 months	$23.00
8 months	$25.00
9 months	$27.00
10 months	$28.00
11 months	$29.00
12 months	$30.00

For gains of more than twelve months, one dollar was added to the $30 for each additional month of growth.

The teacher was also permitted to hire aides to assist in the nonteaching duties of the project; the aides were paid by the school district, the total cost not exceeding $300. The instructor also developed a modified performance contract for the aide, a recent high school graduate. She received a basic hourly rate plus 10 percent of what the teacher earned above $600.

A relatively small amount of money — $75 — was allocated to the student-incentive concept that was built into the project. These incentives included paperbacks and candy given to students as rewards for their achievement on such items as comprehension checks, attendance, weekly progress, and vocabulary growth. At the end of the course, ten students were paid $1–$10 for the best gains in reading.

A large amount of the Title funds was also allocated for the purchase of instructional materials which would then be available for use by the school district upon completion of the project.

One can see that no attempt was made to incorporate all aspects of the Texarkana program to insure performance or accountability. We did, however, include performance contracting with both teacher and aide, and we provided tangible incentives for students to work up to their full potential. The major thrust of the program was individualizing the instruction which permitted students to learn at their own rate. For example, upon arriving at the lab each day, the student picked up his own file folder which contained his progress sheets and outlined his assignment for that fifty-minute period. This assignment was based upon a periodic diagnosis of his progress and deficiencies. Although we had no contract with an outside corporation and we used no teaching machines, we did have a wide diversity of materials and activities: shadowscopes, programmed materials, skill builders, controlled readers and pacers, *SRA Labs, Springboards, Phonics Rummy* and other reading games, current magazines, and hundreds of paperbacks. Students who missed class because of vacations or illness were able to make up those days since the program was tailored to each child rather than to the entire group. Conducting this type of project in the summer proved to be tough competition with the host of camps, swimming and music lessons, and general summer vacation plans. That the attendance held up well could be attributed to the individualized approach, the variety of materials, the incentive concept, and the enthusiastic attitude of the teacher and the aide. The factor of performance for all concerned provided the needed motivation to make the project succeed.

Some of the results of the program:

- During the six-week period, gains in total reading scores as determined by the *Nelson Reading Test* ranged from 0 to 30 months. The average gains for the sixty students were seven months in vocabulary, seven months in comprehension, and seven months for the total score. Whether these gains are sustained will be determined by testing the students during the school year.
- At the beginning of the program, Test *A* showed that thirteen students were at or above grade level on total score and forty-seven were below grade level. On Test *B*, thirty-four students scored at or above grade level and twenty-six scored below grade level.
- Through the open lab, which allowed students to make up absences or to extend their study by working beyond the end of their class, about forty students took advantage of the opportunity to work more than an hour on some days.
- The results of a questionnaire administered to the students at the end of the course revealed that twenty-seven students felt they had made much progress in reading, twenty-seven indicated some progress, and one saw no progress.
- Students also indicated they liked the incentive concept: forty-four favored it, seven said it made no difference, and

three did not like the idea of incentives ("bribes" as one student labelled them).

•The results of the questionnaire also showed that many students change their attitude toward reading during the course. Ten who had a negative attitude at the beginning of the course developed a positive attitude. Twenty-two who had been neutral in their feelings became positive. Two who had been negative now had no particular feeling toward reading. Three who were neutral at the first developed a negative attitude by the end.

Overall, the program was considered fairly successful and the average class gains were good. Since it ran for only six weeks and there was no control group to ascertain the effects of the incentive concept, the results of this program cannot be reliably compared with those of other programs. What the staff has learned, however, through this experiment should provide a more reliable basis for determining whether our schools should consider implementing aspects of this concept within the regular school program or limiting its application to our summer-school remedial reading program. In either case, such a program could be improved in several ways—reducing class size, screening students more carefully for selection, tightening the controls on attendance, diversifying the techniques and materials in the teaching of reading, allowing more time for thorough diagnosis, and altering the performance contract to provide greater incentives for the instructor and aide.

Some of these same factors are recommended by authorities in the teaching of reading as a means to improve any reading program. Regardless of the variety of methods, materials, and approaches employed in the teaching of reading, much of the research has generally shown that the single most important factor contributing to the success of a reading program is the *teacher*—the trained and experienced teacher who is open to new designs in reading instruction and who is willing to implement these approaches in his reading lab.

Does a school need a private industry, with its managers, machines, and software, to come in and handle the program defined by the specifications of the contract between them and the local school? Or should the school use its own professional teaching personnel in more effective ways by giving them not only more opportunities to experiment with new methods and materials but greater pay incentives with built-in accountability features that protect the taxpayer, the teacher, and the child? After all, even though education is becoming computerized and occasionally imitates the jargon of corporate management, educators and taxpayers must remember that schools are working with human resources—students—and that the standards of performance for them should not be patterned after those of DuPont or General Motors. It is for this reason that although the concept of performance contracting/accountability may have promise in revolutionizing American education, the entire venture must be approached with caution. One of the challenges that has faced American education for years—helping every child "to read to the full limits of his capability"—can be met if we are careful to temper our high degree of commitment with a commensurate degree of caution and deliberation.

study questions

1. Tyler defines an educational test as ". . . a series of situations which call forth from the student the kind of behavior defined in the objective and permit a record to be made of the student's actual behavior . . . the testing device should actually obtain a sample of the kind of behavior stated in the objective. . . ." Does Tyler's notion of an education test apply to criterion-referenced test interpretation only, to norm-referenced test interpretation only, or to both kinds of test interpretation? Explain your answer.

2. In what ways is our concept of a test instrument like or different from Tyler's concept of an education test?

3. We identified instruction and assessment as the two purposes for conducting educational evaluation. Prescott identifies two types of test interpretation, norm referenced and criterion referenced. Are these different names for the same two essential processes, or are we and Prescott talking about entirely different processes? Explain your answer.

4. Do you agree with Lessinger when he claims that professionalism "goes hand in hand with accountability, with clear-cut proof of performance?" Why?

5. Wildavsky takes a very pragmatic position about evaluating reading teaching when he maintains that our present test instruments can be used for evaluation even though researchers do not as yet fully understand the process by which a person reads. In an analogy to medical practice, he states, "The history of medicine has taught us that many diseases may be cured before their etiology is perfectly known." Do you agree or disagree? On what basis?

6. Which of the two purposes for educational evaluation, assessment or instruction, is most appropriate for reading programs when performance contracting is being used? Explain your answer.

7. Why does Reynolds think performance contracting should be approached with caution?

8. What are some ways that schools might adapt the notion of accountability to improving their reading programs?

acknowledgments

continued from iv

Neil Postman, "The Politics of Reading," *Harvard Educational Review* 40 (May 1970):244–252. Copyright © 1970 by President and Fellows of Harvard College. Reprinted with permission of the publisher.

"Treatment of Nonreading in a Culturally Deprived Juvenile Delinquent: An Application of Reinforcement Principles" by Arthur W. Staats and William H. Butterfield. From *Child Development* vol. 36, 1965. (Revision by the authors.) © 1965 by the Society for Child Development, Inc. Reprinted with permission of Arthur W. Staats and the publisher.

"Sources of Knowledge for Theories of Reading" by Marion D. Jenkinson. From *Journal of Reading Behavior* 1 (Winter 1969):11–29. National Reading Conference, Inc. and College of Education of the University of Georgia. Reprinted with permission of Marion Jenkinson and the publisher.

How We Think by John Dewey. Reprinted by permission of the publisher, from J. Dewey, *How We Think*. (Lexington, Mass.: D. C. Heath and Company, 1933).

Art of Controversy by G. Schopenhauer. Oxford University Press, 1932. Reprinted with permission of the publisher.

"Ontological Relativity" by W. V. Quine. *The Journal of Philosophy* 65 (April 1968). Reprinted with permission of *The Journal of Philosophy,* Columbia University.

Mind: An Essay of Human Feeling 1, by S. K. Langer. The Johns Hopkins Press, 1967. Reprinted with permission of the publisher.

"Reading: Psychological and Linguistic Bases," by Emmett Albert Betts. From the April, 1966, issue of EDUCATION. Copyright, 1966 by The Bobbs-Merrill Company, Inc., Indianapolis, Indiana. Reprinted with permission of the publisher.

Language by Leonard Bloomfield. © 1933, Holt, Rinehart & Winston, Inc. Reprinted with permission of the publisher.

"Linguistic Insights into the Reading Process" by Ronald Wardhaugh. Reprinted by permission from *Language Learning* XVIII Nos. 3 and 4, (December 1968) pages 235–52.

"Why a Linguistic Society?" by Leonard Bloomfield. *Language* 1 (1925) Linguistic Society of America. Reprinted with permission of the publisher.

Linguistics and Reading by Charles C. Fries. © 1963 Holt, Rinehart & Winston. Reprinted with permission of the publisher.

LEARNING TO READ: THE GREAT DEBATE by Jeanne Chall. Copyright © 1967 by McGraw-Hill, Inc. Used with permission of McGraw-Hill Book Company.

"The Cooperative Research Program in First Grade Reading Instruction" by G. L. Bond and Robert Dykstra. *Reading Research Quarterly* 2 (Summer 1967) International Reading Association. Reprinted with permission of Robert Dykstra.

"Guidelines for Teaching Comprehension" by Helen J. Caskey. From *The Reading Teacher* (April 1970):649–54. Reprinted with permission of Helen J. Caskey and the International Reading Association.

"The Responses of Good and Poor Readers When Asked to Read for Different Purposes" by Helen K. Smith. *Reading Research Quarterly,* 1967. International Reading Association. Reprinted with permission of Helen K. Smith.

"Research in Comprehension in Reading" by Frederick B. Davis. *Reading Research Quarterly* 1968. International Reading Association. Reprinted with permission of Frederick B. Davis.

"Some Experimental Evidence on Teaching for Creative Understanding" by Martin V. Covington. *The Reading Teacher* 20 (1967). Reprinted with permission of Martin V. Covington.

"Devices to Improve Speed of Reading" by Miles A. Tinker. From *The Reading Teacher* (April 1967) 605–609. Reprinted with permission of Miles A. Tinker and the International Reading Association.

From Toward Better Reading by George D. Spache. Garrard Publishing Co., Champaign, Illinois. Reprinted with permission of the publisher.

"Remedial Reading at the College and Adult Levels," by G. T. Buswell, *Supplementary Educational Monograph* no. 50 (1939). Copyright 1939 by the University of Chicago. All rights reserved. Published November 1939. Reprinted with permission of the publisher.

"Basals Are Not for Reading" by Fred Busch. From *Teachers College Record* 72 (September 1970):23–30. Reprinted with permission of Fred Busch and *Teachers College Record.*

"Identity and the Life Cycle" by Eric H. Erikson. *Psychological Issues,* vol. I. Published by International Universities Press 1959. Reprinted with permission of the author.

"The Informal Reading Inventory: How to Construct It, How to Read It" by Frazier R. Cheyney. Reprinted from the February, 1970, issue of Grade Teacher magazine with permission of the publisher. This article is copyrighted. © 1970 by CCM Professional Magazines, Inc. All rights reserved.

"Paperback Books and Reading Attitudes" by Lawrence F. Lowery and William Grafft. From *The Reading Teacher* (April 1968):618–23. Reprinted with permission of Lawrence F. Lowery and the International Reading Association.

"AV in the Total Reading Program" by Gloria F. Nicolich and Domenick Canepa. From *Audiovisual Instruction* 12 (September 1967):699–702. National Education Association. Reprinted with permission of the publisher.

"Sign and Significance: The Jabberwock Rides Again" by Jeannette Veatch. From *Claremont Reading Conference Thirty-third Yearbook* (1969):100–111. Reprinted with permission from Claremont Reading Conference, Claremont University Center.

The *Arizona Republic,* February 2, 1969. Reprinted with permission of the publisher.

New Yorker, January 13, 1968. Courtesy New Yorker Magazine, Inc.

"The Role of the Teacher in Developing Lifetime Readers" by William J. Iverson. From *Development of Lifetime Reading Habits,* International Reading Association (1966) 5–13. Reprinted with permission of William J. Iverson and the International Reading Association.

"Asphodel, That Greeny Flower" (5 lines only) William Carlos Williams, PICTURES FROM BRUGHEL AND OTHER POEMS. Copyright 1954 by William Carlos Williams. Reprinted by permission of New Directions Publishing Corporation. British rights by permission of Laurence P. Pollinger, Ltd.

"Cipher in the Snow" by Jean E. Mizer. From *NEA Journal,* (November 1964): 8–10. Reprinted with permission of National Education Association of the United States and Jean E. Mizer.

"Are the Reading Goals for the Disadvantaged Attainable?" by J. Allen Figurel. From *Reading Goals for the Disadvantaged* (1970):1–10. International Reading Association. Reprinted with permission of J. Allen Figurel and the International Reading Association.

"On Explaining Language" by E. H. Lenneberg. *Science* 164 (May 9, 1969): 635–43. Copyright 1969 by the American Association for the Advancement of Science. Reprinted by permission of Eric H. Lenneberg and the publisher.

"The View from the Margin" by Edward Moreno. From *Claremont Reading Conference Thirty-first Yearbook,* 1967. Claremont University Center. Reprinted with permission by Claremont Reading Conference.

"Success for Disadvantaged Children" by Martha Froelich, Florence K. Blitzer, and Judith W. Greenberg. From *The Reading Teacher* 21 (October 1967):24–33. Reprinted with permission of Martha Froelich, Florence K. Blitzer, Judith W. Greenberg and the International Reading Association.

"Bibliotherapy in the Development of Minority Group Self-Concept" by Eunice S. Newton. From *The Journal of Negro Education* 38 (Summer 1969):257–65. The Howard University Press. Reprinted with permission of the publisher.

"The Dawning of the Age of Aquarius for Multi-Ethnic Children's Literature" by David K. Gast. From *Elementary English* 47 (May 1970):661–65. Copyright © 1970 by the National Council of Teachers of English. Reprinted by permission of the publisher and David K. Gast.

Advertisement of Houghton Mifflin Company Children's Book Department. Reprinted with permission of Houghton Mifflin Company.

"What Is Evaluation?" by Ralph W. Tyler. From *Evaluation in Reading,* H. M. Robinson, editor. Originally published in *Supplementary Educational Monograph* no. 88 (December 1958):4–9. © 1958 by *The University of Chicago. Published* 1958. *Composed and printed by* The University of Chicago Press, *Chicago, Illinois,* U.S.A. Reprinted with permission of the author and the University of Chicago Press.

"Criterion-Referenced Test Interpretation in Reading" by George A. Prescott. From *The Reading Teacher* 24 (January 1971):347–54. Reprinted with permission of George A. Prescott and the International Reading Association.

"Robbing Dr. Peter to 'Pay Paul': Accounting for Our Stewardship of Public Education" by Leon M. Lessinger. From *Educational Technology* 11 (January 1971):11–14. Educational Technology Publication. Reprinted with permission of the publisher.

Laurence J. Peter and Raymond Hull, THE PETER PRINCIPLE. Copyright ©

About the Authors

Sam Leaton Sebesta is Professor of Elementary Education at the University of Washington, Seattle. A graduate of the University of Kansas, he received his M.A. from Northwestern University, and an Ed.D. from Stanford. He is a frequent contributor to educational journals and has coauthored texts in both reading and literature programs. His teaching experience includes elementary as well as college classes. Dr. Sebesta is also a consultant on children's films. He is currently a member of the editorial board of the International Reading Association.

Carl J. Wallen is Associate Professor of Curriculum and Instruction at the University of Oregon. A graduate of the University of California at Santa Barbara, he received an M.A. from San Francisco State College and an Ed.D. from Stanford University. He taught in the elementary grades before going on to college teaching. He is a frequent speaker at education conferences and has been actively involved with a variety of language arts research projects. Much of his previously published material consists of journal articles. In addition to coauthoring *The First R,* he is the author of *Competency in Teaching Reading* (SRA 1972) and *Word Attack Skills in Reading* (Charles Merrill 1969).

The First R: Readings on Teaching Reading and *Competency in Teaching Reading* provide parallel approaches to the teaching of reading. *The First R* supplies background information and a consideration of current issues in education as they relate to reading. *Competency,* a work text, prepares the student to apply the basic principles of designing and conducting tests and lessons relating to recognition and comprehension skills. It trains the future teacher to determine exactly what skills a certain child has and then how to teach only for those skills he lacks.

The text of this book was
set in 9 point Century Schoolbook.
This versatile type was designed
in 1890 by L. B. Benton for
the American Typefounders
and has been a standard face for
American printers ever since.
Display heads were set in R and K Caps
and Headline Open.

Composition was done by
Typographic Sales, Inc., St. Louis, Missouri.

Printing and binding were done by
Webcrafters, Inc., Madison, Wisconsin.

Project Editor	**Toni Marshall**
Designer	**Barbara Ravizza**
Sponsoring Editor	**Karl Schmidt**

2345/54321